The Origin

of the

Roman Catholic Church

in Korea

REV. HAM SUK-HYUN STUDIES IN ASIAN CHRISTIANITY

Series Editor: Heerak Christian Kim (Jesus College, Cambridge)

Number 2

*The Origin of the Roman Catholic Church in Korea:
An Examination of Popular and Governmental
Responses to Catholic Missions
in the Late Chosôn Dynasty*
(Jai-Keun Choi)

The Origin of the Roman Catholic Church in Korea:

*An Examination of Popular and Governmental
Responses to Catholic Missions
in the Late Chosôn Dynasty*

Jai-Keun Choi

The Hermit Kingdom Press
Cheltenham ♦ Seoul ♦ Bangalore ♦ Cebu

The Origin of the Roman Catholic Church in Korea:
An Examination of Popular and Governmental Responses
to Catholic Missions in the Late Chosôn Dynasty

Copyright © 2006 by Jai-Keun Choi

All rights reserved.
No part of this work may be reproduced or transmitted in any form or by any means, electronic or mechanical, including photocopying and recording, or by any information storage (INCLUDING COMPUTER AND WEB) or retrieval system without permission from the publisher.

For information address:

The Hermit Kingdom Press
12325 Imperial Highway, Suite 156
Norwalk, California 90650
United States of America

* * * * *

Hermit Kingdom
12 South Bridge, Suite 370
Edinburgh, EH1 1DD
Scotland

ISBN: 1-59689-063-0 (Hardcover)
ISBN: 1-59689-064-9 (Paperback)

Library of Congress Cataloging-in-Publication Data

Choi, Jai-Keun.
 The origin of the Roman Catholic Church in Korea: an examination of popular and governmental responses to Catholic missions in the late Choson dynasty / Jai-Keun Choi.
   p. cm. -- (Rev. Ham Suk-Hyun studies in Asian Christianity)
 Includes bibliographical references.
 ISBN 1-59689-063-0 (hardcover : alk. paper) -- ISBN 1-59689-064-9 (pbk. : alk. paper)
 1. Catholic Church--Korea--History--19th century. 2. Korea--Church history--19th century. I. Title. II. Series.
 BX1670.5.C525 2006
 282'.519--dc22
                                                            2006017632

*Dedicated to Elder Yung-soo Won
and Rev. Manwoo A. Kim*

Table of Contents

Introduction 1

Chapter I. The Founding of the Catholic Church 9

1. Background of the Period
2. Contact with Western Learning
3. Study of Western Learning as Science
4. Acceptance of Catholicism and the Founding of the Catholic Church

Chapter II. Catholic Converts in Chosŏn Korea: their efforts to practice and transmit their faith 36

1. Pseudo Ecclesiastical Hierarchy
2. Efforts to Invite a Priest
3. Provisions of Catechisms
4. Doctrinal Educations

Chapter III. The Growing and the Persecutions of the Early Period 62

1. Growing of the Church
2. Catholic Incident during the Chŏngjo Reign
3. The Sinyu Persecution (1801)

Chapter IV. Rebuilding of the Chosŏn Catholic Church and Establishment of Korean Vicariate Apostolic 142

1. Formation of Kyouch'on
2. Introduction of Priests
3. Establishment of Korean Vicariate Apostolic
4. Doctrinal Training in Practice
5. Korean Catholic Church in the 1860's

Contents

Chapter V. The Persecutions of the Later Period 169

1. The Persecutions of the 1830's and the 1840's
2. The Pyŏngin Persecution of 1866

Chapter VI. The Causes of the Persecutions 220

1. Ideological Causes
2. Sociological Causes
3. Political Causes

Chapter VII. Comparison of the 1801 and the 1866 Persecutions 275

1. Comparisons of the Two Persecutions
2. Prohibition Policy of the Government
3. Reflections

Conclusion 324

Appendix: The Proliferation of Church Influence Through Hereditary Ties 336

Family Tree of Early Catholic Converts 364

Select Glossary 371

Bibliography 376

Acknowledgement

This book represents the publication of my Ph.D. thesis at Harvard University. Many people have helped me complete the Ph.D. dissertation, directly and indirectly. I would first like to express my deep appreciation to my mentor at Harvard, Professor Edward W. Wagner, who first drew my attention to the topic researched for this book. Professor Wagner opened my eyes to take a renewed look at religions in Korean history, and then he patiently guided and helped me through his comments and suggestions for many long years. It is a pleasure to express my enormous gratitude to him. I would also like to thank Professor Milan Heijtmanek for his suggestions, encouragement, and friendship. Dr. Kathleen McCarthy read an earlier draft and made valuable comments and corrections. I deeply appreciate her invaluable help.

Twenty years have passed since I left Korea for the University of Toronto on a my intellectual quest in the West that came to its completion at Harvard University. Over the years, the following people supported me financially and morally. Without their help, I could not have completed my study: the late Dr. Wôn Yông-su and his family, Dr. Lee Kûn-sam, Dr. Hong Chi-mo, Dr. Lee Chae-hwan, Mr. Cho Kwan-yôn, Mr. Han Su-yôl, and Rev. Manwoo A. Kim. I express my deep gratitude to them.

Finally, I am very grateful to my wife, Seungja who understood me and my intellectual journey, encouraged me and helped me in many ways. She is a scholar in her own right, having completed her Ph.D. in linguistics at Yale University and having taught Korean for many years at Yale. I thank my daughter, Eileen and my son, Ken for their patience, love, and constant encouragement as their dad spent many hours throughout their youth in search of knowledge and truth. Their selfless support made this intellectual contribution to the study of Korean history

Aknowledgement

possible. In a real sense, Seungja, Eileen, and Ken are equal participants in this research contributing to the better understanding of the Korean people and our history. Anyone feeling indebted to me for my research in Korean history also owes a debt of gratitude to Seungja, Eileen, and Ken, because without them this book would not have come into fruition. I would also like to thank my parents. My parents in Hadong, Korea prayed everyday for me to complete this research project. They embody the spirit of the Christian martyrs described in this book as their son went off into a foreign land for over 20 years to make an academic contribution to the study of Korean Christianity and leave a record of the enduring sacrifice of the Korean people for the sake of the Christian faith. They shared in my mission and patiently denied themselves of my filial duty that is required of Korean sons in the Korean society.

The Origin of the Roman Catholic Church in Korea

INTRODUCTION

Over their long history Koreans have at times shown a marked receptiveness to new ideologies and religious faiths introduced from beyond their borders, principally through its contact with China. Buddhism and Confucianism, were adopted and adapted, and up until the latter part of the Koryŏ dynasty (918-1392) coexited in relative harmony. But after the advent of the Chosŏn dynasty in 1392, as Neo-Confucianism increasingly informed philosophical attitudes and social mores, tolerance of other systems of belief waned.

When Catholicism, then called Sŏhak (Western Learning), was introduced to Korea in the latter part of the eighteenth century, it represented a new value system which the governing elite came to perceive as dangerous and threatening, and in the end they responded with a century of persecutions: from 1785, the year after the baptism of the first Catholic, Yi Sŭng-hun, until 1866, approximately ten thousand converts were executed.[1]

The first study of Korean Catholicism was Charles Dallet's *Historie de l'Eglise de Coreé*, published in Paris in

---

[1] The first persecution occurred in 1785. It was followed by the Sinhae Persecution in 1791, the Ŭlmyo Incident in 1795, the Sinyu Persecution in 1801, the Ŭlhae Persecution in 1815, the Chŏnghae Persecution in 1827, the Kihae Persecution in 1839, the Pyŏngo Persecution in 1846, the Kyŏngsin Persecution in 1860, and lastly by the Pyŏngin Persecution in 1866.

1874. While the general historical accuracy of his account is recognized by scholars today, his sympathy with the goals of the missionaries led him to emphasize the dramatic aspects of persecution and martyrdom to the exclusion of other factors. And indeed much of the previous research on Korean Catholicism has followed this approach and focused on the ardor of believers who embraced death rather than renounce their faith.

The first book written by a Korean on Catholicism in Korea was Yi Nŭng-hwa's *Chosŏn kidokkyosa kŭp oegyosa* 'The Church history and Diplomatic history of Korea' published by Kidokkyo Ch'angmunsa in 1928. The heyday of research and publication by Koreans, however, started in 1945 and many articles and books were published around the bi-centennial anniversary of the Christian Church in Korea in 1984.

Japanese historians have largely tried to claim that traditional Chosŏn society was incapable of self-developing on its own into a modern society, emphasizing the factionalism which was involved in the oppositions to Western Learning and persecution of Christian believers. [2] Furthermore, by attempting to prove that Catholicism in Chosŏn dynasty was an extension of the history of Christianity in Japan, some Japanese scholars claimed that Christianity was introduced into Korea through Japan.[3]

Seeing the introduction of Catholicism into Korea

---

[2] Oda Shogō, "Richō no hōtō ryakujo shite tenshūkyō haku gai ni oyobu (A brief discussion of factional strife in the Chosŏn dynasty as it pertained to the Persecution of Catholicism)," *Seikyū gakusō* I. (1930).
Ishii Hisao, "Rigaku sijo shugi Richo he no tenshukyō no chōsen (The Challenge of Catholicism to the Confucian dominated Chosŏn dynasty)," *Rekishigaku kenkyū*, vol.12, no. 8. (1942) and others.

[3] Yamaguchi Masayuki. "Yasokai senkyōshi no nyūsen keikaku (The Jesuit missions' plan to enter Korea)," *Seikyū gakusō* 3. (1931) and others.

Introduction

as an encounter between East and West, some researchers[4] have tried to analyze the process of acceptance of Catholicism into Korean society by examining the similarities of traditional Confucianism and Catholicism from the perspective of ideological and cultural interaction. Yu Hong-nyŏl, and Ch'oe Sŏg-u, among other researchers, analyzed the expansion of the Catholic Church and the persecution of Catholicism by the government from a religious history perspective.

On the other hand, some scholars have approached the issue from the socio-intellectual perspective,[5] and have tried to explore the crumbling social structure of late Chosŏn society by looking at the characteristics of the Catholic community. Through statistical analyses of the social status of its believers, they presented a view of Catholicism as a social movement. Cho Kwang, who is among this group, viewed Catholicism as a movement for social reform, particularly, and against the constraints of a feudal system.[6]

Novels depicting the Catholic believers and their persecutions in the late Chosŏn dynasty such as Han Mu-suk's *Mannam* (Encounter),[7] Yi In-hwa's *Yŏngwŏnhan chekuk* (The Everlasting Empire),[8] Pak An-sik's *Sohyŏn seja* (The Crown Prince Sohyŏn),[9] and Yi Yŏn-ch'ŏl's

---

[4] Ch'oe Sŏg-u, Kŭm Chang-t'ae, Hong I-sŏp, Kim Ok-hŭi, Yi Wŏn-sun, and Yu Hong-nyŏl

[5] Cho Kwang, Choi Yong-gyu, Kim Han-gyu, and Ko Hŭng-sik.

[6] Cho Kwang, "Sinyu pakhae ŭi sŏngkyŏk (The Characteristics of Sinyu Persecution)," *Minjok munhwa yŏngu*. 13. Seoul: Koryŏ taehakkyo, Minjok munhwa yŏnguso. 1978.

[7] Han Moo-sook (Han Mu-suk), *Encounter*. (Berkeley & L.A.: University of California Press, 1992). *Encounter* is a translated version of *Mannam*. published in Seoul by Chŏngŭmsa, 1986.

[8] Yi In-hwa, *Yŏngwŏnhan chekuk*. (Seoul:Segyesa, 1993).

[9] Pak An-sik, *Sohyŏn seja*. I & II. (Seoul: Ch'angjak kwa pip'yŏngsa, 1996).

Paegyo ilgi (A diary of Apostasy)[10] have become bestsellers in recent years.

The history of Catholicism in the late Chosŏn dynasty is traditionally divided into three periods: the period of acceptance of Catholicism from the beginning of the 16th century until 1784, the period of persecution from 1785 to 1886, and the period of religious freedom since 1886.

The purpose of this book is to examine the persecutions which occurred form 1785 to 1886 from a political, ideological and sociological perspective, particularly the first great nationwide persecution of 1801 and the last persecution of 1866, with an emphasis on how Catholicism spread, and developed both institutionally and doctrinally. The underlying assumption is that the outward power of the church as an institution which was linked to church organizations in the outside world, and the inner power of the believers' faith in the doctrine and catechism of Catholicism enabled church in the late Chosŏn dynasty to overcome the persecution. [11]

In Chapter I, I explore the history of Catholicism in Korea: when, where, how and by what classes of Chosŏn society was Catholicism introduced and spread? Generally, a new religion is introduced into a society through the devoted and strenuous efforts of proselytizing missionaries. The case of Catholicism in Korea was strikingly different, for it was accepted through the active efforts of the Korean people themselves, and not through foreign missionaries.[12] Chosŏn intellectuals prompted by their own curiosity, studied books on Catholicism which had been translated

---

[10] Yi Yŏn-ch'ŏl, *Paegyo ilgi*. (Seoul: Hanttŭt, 1994)).

[11] Primary sources include *Chosŏn wangjo sillok, Ch'uan kŭp kukan (Introgation and trial records) Sahak chingŭi* and other, and the churches' documents. Secondary sources are studies based largely on these primary sources.

[12] It is also true in the case of the Protestantism, which was accepted one century later into Korea.

Introduction

into Chinese. More than a century after they began to study, scholars associated with the School of Practical Learning (*Silhak*) organized a church. This indicates that there was a longing for something new within the society.

Chapter II examines how the Chosŏn Catholic community was formed, how the Catholic faith spread, and how it developed institutionally. What was the structure of the early Korean Church which consisted of only lay people without priests? How did they provide leadership for the new Christian community? Through what process did they invite a priest? How did they learn the doctrine of the new religion? How did the doctrine evolve and spread? These are questions of interest, because the early Korean church is unique in that it was an autonomous one which had no connection to the West.

Chapter III examines the formation and proliferation of the Catholic Church in Korea through hereditary ties, and extending to the first persecution, the Sinyu Persecution in 1801. Government officials, having watched in alarm as the popularity of the Catholic faith increased, found reason to act when they learned of the refusal of a rural scholar-convert, Yun Chi-ch'ung, to perform obligatory rites before the shrine of his ancestors; this was a precipitating factor in the Sinyu Persecution of 1801. From this point condemnation of Catholicism as unethical and anti-Confucian were consistent elements in the government's characterization of it.

Factional politics, an important fact of political life in Korea from the end of the sixteenth century, at first inhibited the persecution of Catholicism. During the reign of Chŏngjo (1776-1800), under the Chief State Councillor Ch'ae Che-gong, the Southerners (*Namin*), a group more hospitable to Western learning, wielded considerable political power. But this changed with Chŏngjo's death and the accession of Sunjo (1800-1834) at the age of eleven, since the regent ruling in his stead now came from a faction hostile to Catholicism, that of Queen Dowager Kim. This group had regarded the proselytizing activities of a Chinese priest, Chou Wen-mo, who had entered Korea secretly in

1795 and eluded capture despite a warrant issued for his arrest, as a threat to national security. When he voluntarily gave himself up in 1800, his presence became another factor leading the next year to the Sinyu Persecution. A letter written on silk by Hwang Sa-yŏng reporting the details of the persecution to the bishop in Beijing, intercepted by the authorities, provided further confirmation for those who feared foreign influence at work.

In Chapter IV, while the Catholic community had been decimated in 1801, survivors gathered together and continued to live in hiding, eventually forming clandestine organization called *Kyouch'on* 'Village of Believers', which then appealed to Beijing and the Vatican in Rome asking for priests to be sent. On their behalf the Chosŏn Diocese was formally established, and missionaries form the Paris Foreign Mission society illegally entered Korea. Thus the underground Church began to grow, provoking official persecutions in 1839 and 1846.

Chapter V examines the domestic political tensions of the three next decades (the 1850's - 1870's) which became entangled in international diplomatic intrigue, as Russia, France, and America vied for trading rights in Korea. Catholic believers advocated an alliance with France in the hope of gaining religious freedom, thereby fueling the fears of those who viewed Catholicism as the intrusion of foreign influence and confirming their isolationist tendencies. The docking of a French ship at Kanghwa Island and the sinking of the American ship, the General Sherman, on the Taedong River exacerbated those fears and were precipitating factors in the Pyŏngin Persecution of 1866.

In Chapter VI, I will also discuss the ideological dimension of the history of Catholicism's reception in Korea: similarities and differences between Christianity and Confucianism in terms of the views of God, the eternality of soul, and the view of heaven and hell are explored. I believe that through this comparison, the reasons for the persecution can be more clearly identified, because the ideological basis of the conflict between Confucianism and Christianity lies in the differences between the doctrines of the two religions. I also examine the *Ch'ŏksa sasang* 'reject heterodoxical doctrine' of Confucianism, *Ch'ŏkpullon* 'anti-Buddhism arguments' in the early Chosŏn, and *Ch'ŏksa sasang* against Christianity in the late Chosŏn dynasty comparatively.

Why and how the isssue of ancestor worship became so important a factor in the persecutions is also explored. In addition, the question will be posed as to how the Christian concept that men and women are equal affected Confucian ethics and social structure. Further, the Catholic believers' relations and activities with foreigners will be examined in detail, because their association with the foreign powers made the Chosŏn government highly suspicious about the believers and hence provided justification for persecutions.

In the Chapter VII, the 1801 Persecution and the 1866 Persecution are analyzed from a sociological perspective and compared in terms of the social classes of the believers, the ratio of male to female believers, place of residence, and their vocations. Through these comparisons the growth of the Church and changes in its membership will be revealed.

The views of Catholicism and the policies towards it held by the Korean monarchy from Chŏngjo (r. 1776-1800) through the Taewŏngun, regent for Kojong (r. 1869-1907) are examined. What kind of laws did they apply to the believers in carrying out the persecutions? Was there any change as time went on in the policies on Catholicism? Precisely what was a *Ch'ŏksa yunŭm* (Edict proscribing Catholicism), which was issued four times, will also be discussed.

Finally, despite the banning of Catholic books and the brutal persecutions of Catholicism on the part of the government, why was Catholicism not uprooted? What aspects of the Catholicism, especially, made the believers devoted to the new religion to the degree that they embraced death to maintain their faith? In short, two aspects, the institutional development of the Church and its doctrinal development will be explored.

Chosŏn society was organized primarily as a network of kinship relations, geographical ties and academic lineages. By examining the genealogies of several prominent *Namin Silhak* scholars who converted to Catholicism in the appendix — including Yi Sŭng-hun, Chong Yag-yong, and Kwŏn Ch'ŏl-sin — I will illustrate how traditional marriage connections influenced the spread of Catholicism.

CHAPTER I

The Founding of the Catholic Church

1. Background of the Period

Religious and Ideological Background

When Catholicism was first accepted into the Chosŏn dynasty at the end of the 18th century, the culture of Korea had been shaped by the internalization of Confucian ideologies. Following the founding of the Chosŏn dynasty at the end of 14th century (1392), the rulers had adopted Chu Hsi's Neo-Confucian doctrine from Sung China as their political and ethical foundation. The main role of Confucianism was to protect the interests of the *yangban* bureaucrats. As a result, Confucianism served not so much as a religion but as an ideology that maintained the existing order rooted in land holding and slavery. It was, thus, a ruling philosophy that formed the very foundation of the politics and culture of the Chosŏn dynasty.

Neo-Confucianism placed great emphasis on moral duties of individuals and consequently, attached most importance to *li*, a patterning that dictates the nature of normative daily activities and behavior. Within households, practices such as the four ceremonies of coming-of-age, marriage, funeral and ancestor worship were promptly observed. The family was in itself an ethical structure that centered around paternalism, which placed priority on filial piety. Neo-Confucianism extended beyond the family structure of the Chosŏn dynasty to serve as the ultimate frame of reference that was infused and internalized within Chosŏn society and politics. As a national religion and a code of conduct for ordinary every day activities, its influence surpassed that of Buddhism, Taoism and Shamanism, not only at the level of intellectualism and scholarship, but also at the level of the daily lives of individuals. Its foundation rooted in highly theorized Neo-Confucianism, the ruling class enforced upon the commoners only the system of Confucian thought while oppressing and rejecting all other non-Confucian ideological systems.

Entering the latter half of the Chosŏn dynasty, the Confucianism of the Ch'eng-chu School gradually lost the freshness of an ideology based on empirical principles. Instead the focus of discussion came to be centered on a code of conduct that dictated a strict observance of the ceremonies of coming of age, marriage, funeral, and ancestor worship, and dress codes according to individuals' social rank. Development of these debates on ritual practices became entangled with party politics, to the extent that the political leaders made them a critical aspect of their political strife. The literati class immersed itself in the debates regarding *Sadan chilchŏngnon* (The Theory of Four Beginnings and Seven Sentiments) centered on the Neo-Confucian Chinese Classics, as a result, impeding the advancement of various studies including history, medicine, literature, law and natural science.[13] Meanwhile, the movement to bring back the Old Classics had been thriving in mainland China, and its spirit spilled over to the Korean peninsula, heightening the sentiment against the formalized Neo-Confucianism.

---

[13] Kim Yong-dŏk, "Chosŏn hugi sahoe wa sasang" (Society and thought of Late Chosŏn). *Han'guk chŏngsin munhwasa taegye 5*. (Seoul: Han'guk chŏngsin munhwa ŏn'guso, 1992), p.26.

Social and Political Background

The traditional society of the Chosŏn dynasty was a ridged class, broadly divided into four classes: *yangban* (officials of the two orders, military and civil), *chungin* (middle people), *yangin* or *sangin* (free born or commoner) and *ch'ŏnmin* (low born). The *yangban* class dominated the ruling class of Chosŏn society, since by definition its members constituted the core group from which the upper officialdom, both civil and military, was taken. The *chungin* class consisted of various types of professionals such as military cadre members, translators, doctors, and accountants. *Sangmin* were those devoted to agriculture, commerce and manufacturing, whereas the *ch'ŏnmin* class comprised, entertainers, shamans and butchers, but primarily of slaves.

The ruling class *yangban* stressed to the ruled the importance of faithful service to society and Confucian moral ethics. Even within the homogeneous group of literati, they exercised discrimination by distinguishing themselves according to birth status, geographical affiliation, and lineage. They further praised filial piety and obedience as the ultimate ethical concepts. However, during the periods preceding and following the Japanese and Manchu invasions, deep-rooted changes began to develop within the sociopolitical order. Eventually, then, new doctrines emerged to contest for favor in the minds of the intellectual class. The situation thus became ripe for the appearance and acceptance of new doctrinal beliefs, and the new thought, called *Silhak* (Practical Learning), before long began to take over intellectual leadership from the outworn Neo-Confucianism. And, indeed, from the second half of the 18th century, general trends in thought focused on the phenomenon of the collapse of Neo-Confucianism.

Neo-Confucianism, on the other hand, suffered from various misfortunes, such as the division of society as a result of several purges of scholars, factional strife, and the chaos and destruction left by the invasions of the Japanese and the Mongols. As a result, Neo-Confucianism came to reverse its ideological role in history. Thus emerged a historical inclination that pursued and advocated reality instead of emptiness, actual proof instead of abstraction, and utility instead of concepts. It was in such an environment that the movement for *Silhak* gained momentum. As topics such as political systems, industrial policies, introduction of new technologies, and studies of Korean Classics increasingly drew interest, by the end of the reigns of Yŏngjo and Chŏngjo(1800) *Silhak* had gained recognition as a distinct scholarship.

Imbued with a new sense of respect for their own culture, *Silhak* scholars attempted to move beyond the usual practice of viewing the world as centered around China. To do so, they strove to re-discover the traditions and the values of their own culture.[14]

At the same time, the *Silhak* scholars also sought eagerly to satisfy their curiosity about Western Learning. Among the *Silhak* scholars, the School of Northern Learning (*Pukhakp'a*) advocated importation of the new science and technology described in books on Catholicism which had been translated into Chinese, and further urged Industrial development. It was amidst such social changes that Western thought, culture, and religion could be introduced, transmitted and accepted into Chosŏn society.

Factional disputes were a significant feature of Chosŏn political life from at least 1575, when a dispute between two officials over who was to occupy the pivotal post of head of the Ministry of Personnel split the officialdom into two main groups of their supporters, Easterners and Westerners. Approximately 15 years later, another dispute involving designating King Sŏnjo's heir produced a further division among the ranks of Easterners into Northerners and Southerners. The Southerners lost out so consistently in the unceasing struggle for political power that many turned exclusively to pursuing their academic interests in seclusion. Among them was Sŏngho Yi Ik (1681-1763), considered to be one of the greatest *Silhak* scholars. Yi Ik sought to

---

[14] *Han'guksa*, vol.14 (Seoul: Kuksa p'yŏnch'an wiwŏnhoe, 1975), pp.8-9.

gather and systematize a wide range of Western books through extensive reading and careful examination of those materials.

Yi Ik's view came to regard the Catholic God and the Confucian *Shangti* (Sovereign on High) as one and the same, but criticized the Catholic concept of heaven and hell. He acknowledged the practical benefit of Western Learning while rejecting the spiritual dimensions of Catholicism. Reflecting his ambivalent view, his disciples divided themselves into two groups, one with a tendency to reject heterodoxy as embodied in Western Learning and another with an attitude of acceptance. Disciples with strong Neo-Confucian backgrounds who criticized Catholicism at the theoretical level such as: An Chŏng-bok (1712-1791), Sin Hu-dam (1702-1761), Yun Tong-kyu (1695-1771) and Yi Hŏn-kyŏng (1719-1791),[15] are considered to be from the "school of the right." They were those who denounced Western Learning, holding that although Western Learning made available useful information in the areas of science and technology, its elements present in religious and ethical teachings posed a considerable danger.

On the "left side" of Sŏngho were those who advocated the acceptance of Western Learning. Prominent figures were Yi Pyŏk (1754-1786), Yi Ka-hwan (1742-1801), Kwŏn Il-sin (1751-1792), Kwŏn Ch'ŏl-sin (1736-1801), Chŏng Yak-chŏn (1758-1816), and Chŏng Yag-yong (1762-1836). This "left" group pursued a new interpretation of the Confucian classics and scrutinized Neo-Confucianism with a skeptical and critical attitude. In addition, their advocacy of an immediate embrace of Western ideas and technical knowledge became an integral part of their scholarship.[16]

Besides these two groups proposing either complete

---

[15] Yi Wŏn-sun, *Chosŏn sŏhaksa yŏn'gu*, (Seoul: Ilchisa, 1986), pp.184-235.

[16] Yi Wu-sŏng, *Han'guk ui yŏksasang*, (Seoul: Ch'angjak kwa pip'yŏngsa, 1982), pp.104-105.

rejection or complete acceptance, there was another circle of scholars whose selective views represented a middle ground. They rejected the religious and ethical elements of Western Learning while advocating an understanding and acceptance of the positive elements of Western science. Key members of this group were Hong Tae-yong (1731-1783), Pak Chi-wŏn (1737-1805), Pak Che-ga (1750-1815), and Yi Tŏng-mu (1741-1793).[17]

Background of Catholicism outside Korea

The major geographical discovery of the new world and its routes at the turn of the 16th century had a considerable impact on Christianity by bringing an awakening of interest in missionary work and prompting the organization of two new societies, one by Ignatius Loyola (1495-1556) and the other by Francis Xavier (1506-1552), who established The Society of Jesus in 1543 in Paris (which was approved by Pope Paul III on September 27, 1540). The Society of Jesus in particular set as its objective to recover in Asia the influence of Catholicism that had deteriorated in Europe.[18]

Amidst the competition between Spain and Portugal in their discovery of the new world, Pope Alexander VI allocated to the two countries the areas for missionary purposes by dividing them over the ocean, Korea, China and Japan to Portugal, and South America and the Philippines to Spain. Japan was the first country in the Far East to be visited; in 1549 Francis Xavier and his Jesuit companions landed. They spread Christian gospel to the *daimyo*, the castle lords, warriors and commoners, and their efforts were notable to the extent that this period was referred to as the "Christian Century" in the missionary

---

[17] Yi Wŏn-sun, *op.cit.* p.243.

[18] John W. O'Malley, *The First Jesuits*, (Cambridge & London: Harvard University Press, 1993), p.23.

interdiction of 1639 Tokugawa.[19]

The Jesuit Matteo Ricci arrived in Beijing in 1601 and received official permission from the Ming Emperor Shen-tsung to conduct missionary work in China. Seeking a method that could effectively transmit Catholic teachings to a traditionally Confucian society, he devised an approach he called "Supplementing Confucianism." It was an attempt to avoid the conflict that might arise between the two world views each bent on explaining Catholic teachings in terms of their similarities to Confucian ideologies. Along with this accommodating approach, Matteo Ricci learned the Chinese language and the classics. He further sought to capture the attention of the social elites and the intellectuals of China by introducing up to date maps and inventions. Such efforts came to be recognized even by the royal palace.

After the Ch'ing established their dynasty, Jesuit missionary activity continued. During the first year of K'ang-hsi (1662), the number of Catholics reached nearly 150,000.[20] During Yung-cheng's reign (1722-1735), missionaries were prohibited from entering China and Catholicism was banned. However, there were Westerners working in the royal court as well as open harbors through which missionaries could freely enter China.

As part of their proselytizing work Catholic missionaries translated into Chinese, edited, wrote and published various writings on Western religion, ethics, geography, astronomy, history, science and technology. These works are referred to as the "Chinese translations of Western books."[21] Approximately five hundred of these translations were published between the reign of Shen-tsung of the Ming dynasty (1601), when the Catholic missionary

---

[19] George Elison, *Deus Destroyed*, (Cambridge & London: Harvard University Press, 1988), p.1. cf. C.R. Boxer, *The Christian Century in Japan, 1549-1650*, (Berkeley, 1951)

[20] *Ibid.*, p.81.

[21] Yi Wŏn-sun, *Chosŏn sŏhaksa yŏn'gu* (A Study of the history of Western Learning in Chosŏn), (Seoul: Ilchisa, 1986), p.81.

activities were reinitiated, and the reign of Kao-tsung of the Ch'ing dynasty, when the persecution of Catholics intensified and the Jesuits were purged (1759).[22]

2. Contact with Western Learning

Contact with Catholicism through the Japanese Invasion

In the vanguard of the Japanese troops that invaded Korea in the Hideyoshi invasion of 1592 was a daimyo named Konishi Yukinaga.[23] As the invasion became prolonged, his troops retreated to Ungch'ŏn in southern Kyŏngsang province where they had established a stronghold. In order to improve the morale of his officers, Konishi requested that a chaplain from The Society of Jesus in Japan be dispatched to the camp, and a Spanish born priest, Gregorio de Cespedez, and a Japanese friar, Foucan Eion were sent.[24] The two priests visited each Japanese military base in Ungch'ŏn and conducted various Catholic religious rituals such as baptism and confession.[25] Although they were the earliest Catholic missionaries to have entered Korea, there is no record of any other

---

[22] *Ibid.*, p.61.

[23] Yu Hong-nyŏl, *Han'guk ch'ŏnju kyohoesa, (sang),* (Seoul: Kat'ollik ch'ulp'ansa ,1975),p.26.

[24] Charles Dallet, *Histoire de L'Englise de Corea toure I & II.* (Paris: Victor Palme, 1874). Translated into Korean by Ch'oe Sŏg-u, An Ung-yŏl, *Hankuk ch'ŏnju kyohoesa,* (sang), (Waegwan: Pundo ch'ulp'ansa, 1979), pp.280-281.

[25] At this time, there was a claim that some children of Chosŏn were baptized, but there is no record that attests to this neither claim nor evidence of their continuing religious pursuit. 'Juan Ruiz de Medina, *The Catholic Church in Korea*, (Seoul: The Royal Asiatic Society," 1991).

missionary activity they engaged in or evidence that any churches were built; perhaps their activities were limited to the Japanese military base and that they were unable to remain at great length. Meanwhile, some among the prisoners of war who had been taken to Japan converted to Catholicism, though their exact numbers are not known. A few prisoners returned to Korea.

Contact with China

Less than 30 years after the Japanese invasion, the invasion by the Jurchen (later referred to as Ch'ing) occurred in 1627 and 1637. This invasion is known as the Manchu invasion. The Ch'ing, having won in this war, requested war supplies and even manpower from Korea to sustain its war with Ming China. In addition, Ch'ing took as hostages Crown Prince Sohyŏn and Prince Pongnim of Korea. In 1644, Ch'ing captured the capital of the Ming dynasty, Beijing, which they made their own capital. At that time, Crown Prince Sohyŏn and Prince Pongnim were also transferred from Shenyang to Beijing.

During his stay in Beijing, Crown Prince Sohyŏn befriended Adam Schall von Bell, a priest from The Society of Jesus, who was at the time the Chief of the Astronomical Observatory of the Ch'ing dynasty. Crown Prince Sohyŏn took interest in the Western science promoted by the Catholic priests, and Schall, in turn, took interest in Crown Prince Sohyŏn, a hostage from Korea, for his missionary purposes. Their relationship, however, did not last long, for Crown Prince Sohyŏn returned to Korea only a few months later. Prior to his departure, Crown Prince Sohyŏn sent gifts to Adam Schall, who in a return courtesy sent books on Catholicism and on calendrical calculation, Western scientific tools, Catholic doctrines and a Catholic holy image. The Crown Prince politely returned the holy image for fear of an inadvertent blasphemy.[26] The Crown Prince requested a missionary to accompany him on his return trip,

---

[26]Yu Hong-nyŏl, *Han'guk ch'ŏnju kyohoesa*, (sang), p.45.

but there was none available for such a mission.27 Instead, Prince Sohyŏn returned to Korea with five eunuchs and a court lady, who had been bestowed upon him by the emperor of the Ch'ing dynasty.28 He left Beijing on November 26th 1644, and arrived in Seoul on February 11th 1645.

Twenty days after his return to Korea, Crown Prince Sohyŏn "returned to the Ministry of Finance 400 *pil* of silk and 19 *nyang* of gold"29 among the items that he brought back from China. This action was an indication of a serious happening surrounding the Crown Prince. He fell ill from malaria in April, and after several futile attempts to cure the illness, the Crown Prince died within seventy days after returning from Beijing.30 Subsequently, the eunuchs and the court lady who had accompanied the Crown Prince were sent back to China. This thwarted Adam Schall's intention to transmit Catholicism to Korea. The gifts that the Crown Prince had brought with him were either burnt or thrown into water in accordance with a shaman's claim that the death of the Crown Prince had been caused by angry divine spirits and that their anger would not otherwise cease in the future.31

Introduction of Western Books by the Envoy to Yen-ching/Beijing.
Envoys who frequently traveled to China were the first ones to come in contact with Western Learning and the first

---

27 *Ibid*, pp.45-46.
28 *Chosŏn wangjo sillok*, Injo 23rd year 2nd month Sinmi.
29 *Chosŏn wangjo sillok*, Injo 23rd year 3rd month Imjin.
30 *Ibid.*, Injo 23rd year.4th month.Muin.
31 *Chosŏn wangjo sillok*, Injo 23rd year.7th month.Sinmi.

to introduce it to Chosŏn society.³² Although the envoys' function was diplomatic, they provided as well a pipeline for economic and cultural influence,³³ and it was the only available 'window' through which Korea came into contact with the outside. It is not surprising, then, that even the government of the Chosŏn dynasty recognized the cultural significance of the envoys to Beijing.³⁴

The Catholic churches in Beijing, having acquired a reputation as worthy of attention, became stops on the itinerary of Korean envoys, and places where they gained knowledge of Western culture and institutions. The priests of The Society of Jesus eagerly provided the Korean envoys with requested materials, particularly translations of Western works. Approximately 167 envoys of various purposes were dispatched during the 147 years, up to 1783, the year of Yi Sŭng-hun's visit to Beijing.³⁵

The items brought back by the Korean envoys ranged greatly in their variety: Catholic doctrinal books translated into Chinese, books on astronomy, geography and mathematics, world maps, sundials, telescopes, and musical instruments. Some of the prominent figures who first acquired and imported these Western materials were Yi Su-gwang, Yi Kwang-jŏng, Hŏ Kyun, and Chŏng Tu-wŏn. Yi Su-kwang, who is considered to be the father of *Silhak* scholars, traveled to Beijing three times during the years 1590, 1597 and 1611, as an emissary to Beijing. He selected some 348 items of written materials on various

---

³² From the establishment of the Chosŏn dynasty, *sadae* envoys were sent to Beijing on an annual basis and during the special holidays as a customary practice under the *sadae* foreign policy of 'serving the great' towards Ming and Ch'ing China.

³³ Yi Wŏn-sun, *op.cit.* p.24.

³⁴ *Chosŏn wnagjo sillok,*, Chungjong 11th year 9th month. Imin, Musin.

³⁵ Chŏn Hae-jong, *Hanjung kwankyesa* (History of Korea and China relations), (Seoul: Ilchogak, 1970), pp.72-73, except 1662-1665.

places and periods, which he collected and studied, and compiled an encyclopedic work, the *Chibong yusŏl* (Topical Discourses of Chibong) according to topical categories. It was in *Chibong yusŏl* that Matteo Ricci's *"Tien chu shih i"* (The True Meaning of the Lord of Heaven) was first introduced.[36] In addition, it recorded Yi Kwang-jŏng's trip to Beijing in 1603 (Sŏnjo year 37) during which he had acquired a *k'un yu wan kuo ch'uant'u* (Map of the World) created by Matteo Ricci.[37] By indicating the existence of other nations besides China and suggesting how advanced scientific technology was in the West, this world map enlightened yet shocked Koreans whose outlook had all along been centered on China.

In 1610, under King Kwanghaegun, Hŏ Kyun is said to have visited Beijing as a member of a diplomatic entourage to Ming China, where he acquired a prayer book called "Twelve Prayers."[38] On this account, some scholars such as Pak Chi-wŏn and Yi Kyu-gyŏng considered Hŏ Kyun to be Korea's first Catholic. In 1631, the 9th year of Injo, another Korean envoy to China, Chŏng Tu-wŏn (1561-1634) was traveling to China by sea, and in Shantung met Johannes Rodriquez, from whom he learned about Catholicism and received as gifts various objects such as a musket, telescope, alarm clock, world maps, and guns.[39] Unlike the envoys discussed above, Chŏng was the very first envoy to bring back with him these Western materials.

In the 46th year of Sukchong (1720), Yi I-myŏng (pen name: Sonam) became acquainted with Fr. Joseph Saurez

---

[36] Yi Su-kwang, *Chibong yusŏl*, kwŏn 2.

[37] *Ibid*, kwŏn 3.

[38] Yi Nŭng-hwa, *Chosŏn kidokkyo kŭp oekyosa* (A history of Christianity and foreign relations in Korea), (Seoul: Han'gukhak yŏn'guso, 1977 Reprinted), pp.23-24, 27-29.

[39] *Kukcho pogam*, (Chosŏn dynasty chronicles), 35: 17-18. Michael Cooper, *Rodriques the Interpreter*, (Tokyo: Weatherhill, 1974), pp.347-50. Yi Ik, *Sŏngho sasŏl*, 4: Yuk Yak-han. *Chosŏn wangjo sillok*, Injo. 9th year.7th month. Kyemi.

and Fr. Ignatius Kögles during his visit to China. He had conversations on the topic of Catholicism and learned from them about astronomy, geography, and the Roman calendar. He also brought back with him several Chinese translations of Western books, and continued to exchange correspondence upon his return to Korea.[40]

From 1603, when Yi Kwang-jŏng brought a map of the world back to Korea, to 1783, when Yi Sŭng-hun was baptized in Beijing, the number of Western books imported to Korea by the envoys and emissaries were counted to be thirty seven.[41]

As previously mentioned, representative Western books introduced in Korea were *T'ien chu shih I* (The true meaning of the Lord of Heaven) by Matteo Ricci and *Chi ke* (Seven overcomings) by Didace de Pantoja. Others are *Chen tao tzu cheng* (The true way is self evident) by Emericus de Chavagnac, *Sheng shih chiu jao* (The teachings of the church in everyday language) by Joseph de Mailla, *Ling yen li shao* (On the soul), by Francis Sambiasi and *Chih fang waichi* (On world geography) by Julius Aleni.

3. Acceptance of Catholicism and the Founding of the Catholic Church

---

[40] Yi I-myŏng, *Sojaejip* (Collected works of Yi I-myŏng), 19. After reading C. Clavius' *Epitomic Arithmatical Practice*, translated by Matteo Ricci, Yi I-myŏng concluded that the teachings of Catholicism was similar to those of Confucianism.

[41] Pae Hyŏn-suk, "Chosŏn e chŏllae doen ch'ŏnjugyo sŏjŏk" (Bibliographical Characteristics of Catholic books introduced to Korea), *Han'guk kyohoesa nonmunjip*, I.(1984), p.6. From 1784 to 1795, 13 types of Western books were introduced. From 1795, when Fr. Chou Wen-mo entered Korea, to 1837, when Fr. Liu Fang-chi was active in his missionary work, 24 types are known to have been introduced.

Study of Western Learning as Science

Scholarly interest in and curiosity about Western Learning began with three books by Matteo Ricci: *T'ien chu shih i* (The True Meaning of the Lord of Heaven), *Chiao yu lun* (The Treatise on Friendship) and *Chie jen shih p'ien* (Ten Discourses of a Stranger). In them Ricci argued that the concept of 'Sovereign on High' (*shang ti*) mentioned in the Confucian classics was precisely the God of Catholicism. He excluded Buddhism and Taoism as religious cults because of their stress on 'nothingness.' He further concluded that the atheistic theory of *T'ai chi li chi* (the supreme principle and material force) of Neo-Confucianism during the Sung dynasty was a distortion by later Confucians of earlier Confucian teaching. He cast his discussion as a dialogue between Chinese and Western scholars, and attempted to identify similarities between Catholicism and Confucianism within the context of the Chinese classics and to actively incorporate Catholicism into Confucianism. Buddhism and Taoism, on the other hand, were consistently criticized.

The meeting at Chuŏsa

Along with the emergence of individual Catholic converts, a critical meeting that prepared the foundation for a new religious public organization took shape in a collective structure. According to a written record, the very first meetings on the Western Learning were the conferences at the Chuŏ temple and at the Ch'ŏnjinam hermitage ("The meetings at Chuŏsa") in 1779.[42] These conferences were held by the scholars of the Chosŏn Confucian society at secluded temples or country houses for the purpose of studying common academic topics. Young scholars residing in the capital or in the countryside attended these conferences, and they included Kim Wŏn-song, Kwŏn Sang-hak, Yi Ch'ŏng-ŏk, Chŏng Yak-chŏng, Chŏng Yak-chŏn, Kwŏn Ch'ŏl-sin, and Yi Pyŏk. These were from the Kŭngi School, who had acquired a passion for "Sŏhak" (The Western Learning) from Sŏngho Yi Ik.

---

[42] Chŏng Yag-yong, Nogam myochimyŏng.

They organized the conference with much admired Kwŏn Ch'ŏl-sin as the central figure.

In the writings of Chŏng Yag-yong there is no mention of studying the Catholic doctrine at these conferences. This may have been due to his intentional avoiding of the topic, having declared apostasy, and being wary of others opinions. The purpose of the conferences was to study and refine their scholarship of Chu-tzu and Chung-tzu and to accumulate wisdom and for self-cultivation.[43] This also may have been in order to intentionally avoid any potential controversy. Dallet sees the conferences as "studying the most important subjects of the heaven, of this world and of man's nature. In order to acquire a complete understanding of these meanings, the scholars devoted themselves to investigating the books written in Chinese by the Western missionaries on the topics of philosophy, mathematics and religion."[44] The nature of the meeting was to discuss the fundamental issues in human life, focusing on their ethical aspects, and to survey the theories of the sages through conferences on Confucianism. It can be understood that such meetings eventually led to the study of the Western books translated into Chinese.[45]

Subsequently, the conferences at the Ch'ŏnjinam and Chuŏsa were essentially meetings organized by like-minded thinkers holding academic lectures and discussions on the subject of the Catholic faith.[46] Because the attendees of these meetings had not been baptized, the organization could not be considered as the beginning of the public organization of a so called "church."

The conference was an opportunity to hold a

---

[43] Chŏng Yag-yong, Ch'anam myochimyŏng.

[44] Dallet, *op.cit.*, (I), p.301.

[45] Yi Wŏn-sun, "Ch'ŏnjinam Ch'uŏsa kanghakhoe nonbyŏn." p.715.

[46] *Dr. Kim Ch'ŏl-ho hwagapkinyŏm sahaknonsul.* (Seoul: Chisik sanŏpsa, 1983), p.719.

preliminary organizational meeting that demonstrated an aspect of the acceptance process of a foreign culture by the progressive intellectuals of the Chosŏn society. It was, further, an opportunity to initiate acceptance of a new system of thought that included a new religion and a new ethics. In other words, this was an occasion at which point Catholicism became a religious subject rather than an academic subject of interest.[47]

Before Catholicism was accepted into the Korean society as a religious movement, it had been introduced and evaluated by the leading intellectuals for over a century. During the thirty years following Yi Ik, Catholicism was subjected to various academic discursive investigations and ideological excursions that examined its pros and cons, and with the aid of the autonomous pioneering spirit of the *Silhak* intellectuals, the ground on which Catholicism was to be accepted as a Western religion was laid in the latter part of the Chosŏn dynasty.

Founding of an Autonomous Church in Chosŏn

Although the founder of the Catholic Church in Chosŏn is considered to be Yi Sŭng-hun, he was greatly influenced by Yi Pyŏk(1754-1786).[48] As a Namin and as a member of the *Sinsŏp'a* of the *Sip'a*, he was well versed in the Chinese Classics, and his excellence in scholarship is reported to have impressed Chŏng Yag-yong and

---

[47] Choe Wan-gi, "Pakhaegi Han'guk ch'ŏnjukyohoe wa p'yŏngsindo undong." *Han'guk ch'ŏnjukyohoe changsŏl 2baekchunyŏn kinyŏm han'guk kyoheosa nonmunjip II*, (Seoul: Han'guk kyohoesa yŏn'guso, 1985), p.236.

[48] Yi Pyŏk was a member of an elite Kyŏngju Yi lineage, and a descendant of Yi Chŏng-hyŏng, who was a meritorious retainer during the Japanese Invasion as well as a Neo-Confucian scholar.

Chŏngjo.[49]

Yi Pyŏk studied books on Catholicism and attended the meeting at Chuŏsa and Ch'ŏnjinam, and his interest in it grew.[50] In 1783, when Yi Pyŏk learned that his friend Yi Sŭng-hun was to accompany his father Yi Tong-uk as envoys to Beijing, he asked him to visit a Catholic church there, meet with a Western scholar, and bring back books on Western Learning, suggesting to Yi Sŭng-hun that he ask to be baptized as well, to impress his earnestness upon the scholar. He also asked his friend to bring back a varied selection of Western curiosities.

When Yi Sŭng-hun arrived in Yenching, he met French missionaries at the North Church, and after listening to their Catholic teachings and studying the books they had given him, he decided to become a member of the Catholic Church, and with his father's approval, he requested to be baptized. Accordingly, Priest Louis de Grammont baptized Yi Sŭng-hun and bestowed the baptismal name Peter on him, its significance being that Yi Sŭng-hun would become a foundation as firm as a rock for the Chosŏn Catholic church.[51] At that time, he was 27 years old, and it was towards the end of January in 1784.

In the third month of 1784, Yi Sŭng-hun returned to Korea, bringing back with him the gifts received from the

---

[49] Hong I-sŏp, *Ch'ŏng Yag-yong ŭi chŏngch'i kyŏngje sasang yŏn'gu*, (Seoul: Han'guk yŏn'gu tosŏgwan, 1959), p.234. Chŏng Yag-yong, *Chungyong kangŭi*, Supplementary Vol.I.

[50] C. Dallet (tr.), *op.cit.*, (I), p.302. In 1777, under the guidance of Kwŏn Ch'ŏl-sin, there was a meeting of Confucian scholars at Chuŏsa Buddhist temple. Since then, they met also Chŏnjinam. During these meetings they discussed Confucian classics and on the newly introduced Western Learning books translated in Chinese.

[51] L. Pagés, *Histoire de la Religion Chréienne*, t.1, (Paris, 1869), p.122. The baptism of Yi Sŭng-hun did not mark the beginning of the Chosŏn Catholic church, for there were Chosŏn people who had been already baptized in Japan as war prisoners during the Japanese Invasion

missionaries, including a number of books on Catholicism,[52] such as "The True Meaning of the Lord of Heaven," and many other items, including geometry books, binoculars, holy images, and holy cross rosaries. Together with Yi Pyŏk, Yi Sŭng-hun thoroughly studied these books and propagated the teachings of the new religion among their friends and relatives, thus building a foundation on which a church could be established.

While, at the same time, his older sister provided a familial tie through her marriage to Chŏng Yag-yong's older brother, Chŏng Yak-hyŏn,[53] Yi Pyŏk carried out scholarly exchanges with Tasan as well as maintaining an intimate friendship with him.[54] With this relationship in place, in 1784, Yi Pyŏk introduced Tasan and Chŏng Yak-chon to Catholicism on a boat trip back from visiting the Chŏng clan family in Kwangju, Kyŏnggido, on the anniversary of his older sister's death.[55]

Later in the same year 1784, Yi Pyŏk approached a Kwŏn lineage family residing in Yangkŭn, Kyŏnggido, which at that time was illustrious in its scholarship and reputation and who were also known as great scholars among the Namin. This was motivated by Yi Pyŏk's belief that the Kwŏn family's high prestige and popularity could substantially aid in the propagation of Catholicism. He spread the doctrine of Catholicism and led the meetings as a leader. Among the five Kwŏn brothers, the second one, Kwŏn Il-sin, immediately joined as a member of the Catholic church, whereas Kwŏn Ch'ŏl-sin, being the oldest among them, became a Catholic only after some period of

---

[52]*Chosŏn wangjo sillok.* Sunjo First Year. 2: Sinmi. Hwang Sa-yŏng paeksŏ 43rd-44th line.

[53]Kyŏngju Yi clan geneology.

[54]Chŏng Yag-yong, "Chach'an myojimyŏng." *Yŏjudang chŏnsŏ*, Che 1 chip 16 kwŏn (hereafter 1:16).

[55] Chŏng Yak-yong, Sŏn chungssi (Chŏng Yak-chŏn) myoji myŏng) *op.cit.*, 1:15.

hesitation, for he feared damage to his reputation.[56]

Yi Pyŏk also converted Yi Ka-hwan, a leading Confucian scholar of his time, who had actually visited Yi Pyŏk in order to convince him to abandon Catholicism. As it turned out, it was Yi Ka-hwan who was persuaded by Yi Pyŏk to convert to Catholicism.[57]

Having successfully converted a *chungin*, Kim Pŏm-u,[58] Yi Pyŏk crossed the boundaries of the social classes and attempted an even more aggressive propagation of Catholicism among the *chungin*. Afterwards, a number of translators, such as Ch'oe Ch'ang-hyŏn, Ch'oe In-gil, Chi Hwang and Kim Chong-gyo, became members of the church.[59] Ch'oe Ch'ang-hyŏn (1754-1801), as a Chinese translator, played a role with Yi Pyŏk and Chŏng Yak-chong in establishing the Church and he was also actively involved in the invitation of a priest. Later, he translated the doctrinal books in Chinese into Korean. Ch'oe In-gil (1764-1795), a *chungin* and translator, was baptized by Yi Pyŏk, having first attended a meeting at the house of Kim Pŏm-u in 1785, and had Father Chou Wen-mo stay at his house, which later cost him his life. Chi Hwang (1753-1801) went to Beijing in 1793 to invite a priest and later was arrested and died a martyr. Kim Chong-kyo (1753-

---

[56]Chŏng Yag-yong, "Chŏnghŏn myojimyŏng," (The epitaph of Yi Ka-hwan), *op.cit.* 1:15.

[57]Hwang Sa-yŏng Paeksŏ 48th-49th lines. However he refused to be baptized to the end, for the reason that he wished to be baptized directly by a priest in China. In the epitaph of Yi Ka-hwan, Chŏng Yag-yong recorded that it was in 1784 that his friend Yi Pyŏk propagated Catholic teaching for the first time. (Chŏng Yag-yong, "Chŏnghŏn myojimyŏng,"*op.cit. 1:15.p.315.)*

[58]Kim Pŏm-u (1751-1786), a Chinese translator, was baptized by Yi Sŭng-hun at the house of Yi Pyŏk. In 1785, he was arrested, exiled to Tanyang, and died a martyr there. His younger brothers, I-u and Hyŏn-u also died martyrs.

[59] Ch'oe Sŏg-u, *Han'guk ch'ŏnju kyohoeŭi yŏksa*, (Seoul: Han'guk kyohoesa yŏn'guso, 1982), p.22.

1801), a descendant of a medical doctor (*ŭigwan*), was converted in 1784, baptized by Chou Wen-mo and died a martyr in 1801. Although Yi Pyŏk had not yet been baptized himself, because it was due to his own strong will that he came to understand the doctrine and confess his faith, he was able to introduce the new religion to his acquaintances with a firm conviction. In 1784, the year of Yi Sŭng-hun's return from Beijing upon being baptized by Father Grammont, Yi Pyŏk requested his friend to baptize him. Following the baptism of Yi Pyŏk, Yi Sŭng-hun baptized several other individuals including, Chŏng Yak-chŏn, Chŏng Yag-yong, Kwŏn Il-sin, Ch'oe Ch'ang-hyŏn, and Kim Pŏm-u.[60] In a letter to the Holy See, Bishop Antonelli, on October 6th, 1790, Bishop Gouvea of the Beijing diocese reported that several people were baptized by Yi Sŭng-hun and thus the Chosŏn Church was formed.[61]

A Japanese scholar, Yamaguchi Masayuki, opposes the generally accepted view that the Chosŏn Catholic church was unique in that it was established in the absence of missionaries' efforts. On one hand, he acknowledges the development of the academic investigation of Catholicism into a religious pursuit through the efforts of scholars such as Yi Sŭng-hun. On the other hand, however, he diminishes the significance of such a development by claiming that it was simply one form of cultural exchange that emerged naturally as a result of the subordinate relationship of cultures between Korea and China.[62]

A French church historian, Adrien Launay, objects to Yamaguchi's claim, arguing that the origin of the Korean Church represents a unique and special example, illustrating the potential of the wisdom of mankind under the guidance of divine wisdom. He believes that the phenomenon is a

---

[60] *Ibid.*, p.25.

[61] *de Gouvea's Letter in Mannam kwa midŭm ŭi kilmok esŏ*, (Seoul: Han'guk kyohoesa yŏn'guso, 1988), p.133.

[62] Yamaguchi Masayuki, *Chōsen seikyōshi*, (A history of Korean Catholic church), (Tokyo: Yuzankaku, 1967), pp.172-175.

fruit of neither the missionaries' enthusiastic efforts nor the influence of churches in Japan, China or Vietnam.[63]

On May 9th, 1925, Mgr. de Guebriant stated before Pope Pius XI that the origin of the Korean Catholic Church is a unique example in modern missionary history. Without any direct evangelistic efforts, the universal faith was explicated through those books obtained by the Korean scholars with their own will as well as through the actions of divine grace.[64] This position is supported by the majority of Korean church historians.

Under the circumstance, the acceptance of Catholicism into Korea was indeed a fruit of the spontaneous efforts by the Koreans, not of the Western missionaries' activities.[65] This was a unique phenomenon in Christian mission history. Korea's acceptance and absorption of the new religion took place partially due to the internal demands of late Chosŏn society and partially as a form of an autonomous process of acculturation.

Place of Worship of the Early Catholic Church

In the earlier stages of the Chosŏn Catholic church, however, erecting a church building was not feasible, and thus the church members rotated in holding gatherings at their houses. The very first worship by the followers of the new belief took place in 1784 (8th Year of Chŏngjo) at Yi Pyŏk's house near Sup'yogyo in Seoul,[66] and was held on Sunday. "On the Lord's day, they put up a

---

[63] Adrien Lanunay, *Martyrs Francais et Coreéns, 1838-1846.* (Paris, 1925), p.9.

[64] *Ibid.,*

[65] This phenomenon of an autonomous seeking of the truth recurred a century later during Korea's acceptance of Protestantism, which also came about through the efforts of those Koreans who sought after the truth, not through the activities of Western missionaries.

[66] Chŏng Yag-yong, *op.cit.*, 1:15.

silk curtain and sat on their knees in front of the Lord's image, where they read Catholic books and pondered on the grace of the Lord."[67]

In the spring of year ¬lsa (1785), when the regular worship meeting held at Kim Pŏm-u's house was discovered by the Board of Punishments, the Board reported that "their faces were powdered and they wore a blue towel on their heads. Yi Pyŏk's way of preaching and edification were stricter than the mannerisms between our Confucians teachers and students."[68] From such a report, it can be assumed that they performed the Catholic rituals in accordance with Yi Sŭng-hun's account and description of the mass in Beijing. However, the extent to which the original Catholic rituals had been followed was not possible to measure, since the majority of the members were laypeople and there was not even a church building nor a Catholic tradition. Following the worship gathering at Kim Pŏm-u's house, the proscription order rendered gatherings themselves illegal, and the church members had no choice but to meet in secret as it had in Rome during the initial period of Christianity.

In 1795, ten years after the founding of the Chosŏn Catholic church, the Ch'ing Chinese Priest Chou Wen-mo entered Korea and revived the missionary activities and the performance of the rituals of the new religion. He began the ministry at his residence, which was at the house of a Chinese language officer, Ch'oe In-gil. Six months later, the arrest of Priest Chou Wen-mo was ordered, which forced him to relocate to the house of the head of the Catholic women's club, Kang Wan-suk, and her stepson, Hong P'il-chu. Here, the Catholic Church members gathered in absolute secrecy. Yun Chŏm-hye, who was under the "personal care" of Kang Wan-suk, stated that

---

[67] *Sinyu sahak choein Yi Ka-hwan tŭng ch'uan* (Trial record of the heretic offenders Yi Ka-hwan and others in Sinyu (1801) year), Chia-ching 6th year 2nd month 11th day.

[68] Yi Man-ch'ae (ed.), *Pyŏgwip'yŏn*, (Seoul: Yŏlhwadang, Reprinted 1971), p.105.

services were held six to seven times, or sometimes ten times a month, and on the days of a feast, male and female fellow believers from various places gathered at her house.[69]

They also gathered at the house of Kim I-u, the younger brother of the *chungin*, Kim Pŏm-u, who provided the place of worship in the earlier stage of the church. In his house, there were instruments necessary for the feast and holy images,[70] and from this it appears that the two brothers, Kim I-u and a third brother Hyŏn-u participated frequently in the religious activities. However, there is not much written on the nature of their activities.[71] The church members performed a mass every seven days at the house of Hwang Sa-yŏng,[72] "the foremost among the male church members," [73] "the most notable among the *yangban*."[74]

Chŏng Kwang-su (~1801) who, like Hwang Sa-yŏng, also belonged among "the foremost of the male church members" and "the most notable among the *yangban*,"[75] provided a separate worship place. As he left Yŏju for Seoul in Kimi year (1799), he borrowed 40 *liang* from Hong Si-ho, 20 *liang* from his wife's sister, Yun Chŏm-hye, and gathered 100 *liang* from fellow church members. With the money collected, he acquired a house in Pyŏk-tong, Seoul and built a cloister on an empty lot, which he designated as the place of worship. Church members gathered there, some even lodging, to learn and study the

---

[69] *Sahak chingŭi*, (A Warning against Catholicism), (Seoul: Pulham munhwasa, Reprinted 1977), p.109.

[70] *Ibid.*, p.82.

[71] *Ibid.*, pp.82-84.

[72] *Ibid.*, p.276.

[73] *Ibid.*, p.344.

[74] *Ibid.*, p.98.

[75] *Ibid.*, p.98 & p.344.

new religion, and performed masses under the supervision of a priest.[76]

Besides the above figures, there were several *chungin,* such as Ch'oe P'il-che, Ch'oe P'il-gong, Son Kyŏng-yun, Son Kyŏng-mu, and Son In-wŏn, who opened pharmacies where they communicated with other church members. The arrest of Ch'oe P'il-che during a mass at a pharmacy indicates that the pharmacies were often used as places of worship.[77] Son Man-ho's house can also be considered as a place of worship, evidenced by the record that seven to eight widows gathered there to study Catholic books.[78] Because it was during the time in which no church building could be built, it can be said that the places where a priest visited were used as the places of worship. Besides the places mentioned above, other church members such as Ch'oe Ch'ang-hyŏn and Chŏng Yak-chong, Yu Hang-gŏm of Chŏnju, Yi Chung-bae of Yŏju and Yi Ki-yŏn of Ch'ungju provided places for the church members to gather together to hold services and study doctrines.[79]

Starting many days preceding the mass, the church members gathered at the place of worship, to clean and to put up a tent or a curtain. They hung a portrait of Jesus or a painting of suffering and lit candles, by the light of which the priest read out aloud verses from the Bible, and the attendees repeatedly recited prayers and verses until the mass came to an end. During all this time, female members worshipped from outside the building, peering through the windows.[80]

The members of the early Catholic Church in Korea as often elsewhere, centered their religious lives on the masses. To these Catholics who carried out their religious activities

---

[76] *Ibid.,* pp.117-118.

[77] *Ibid.,* pp.74-76.

[78] *Ibid.,* p.370.

[79] Hwang Sa-yŏng paeksŏ 8th-9th line.

[80] *Sahak chingŭi,* pp.370-372.

within the underground church, the masses served as the fountainhead of a new power. Opportunities to attend a mass with only one priest present were rare and thus, using mass prayer scripts, books for the cultivation of individual faith, and biographies of saints, the church members prayed, meditated, and read doctrines.

Regional Dissemination

Relationships based on geographical ties were strong among the *Namin* scholars, so that they also aided the spread of Catholicism throughout the local regions, such as Seoul, Kyŏnggido Machae, where Chŏng Yag-yong lived, Yangkŭn and Yŏju where Kwŏn lived, Chŏllado Chŏnju where Yu Hang-gŏm and the Kwan-gŏm brothers were active, and Naep'o Ch'ungch'ŏngdo where Yi Chon-ch'ang was active. The Yŏngnam region lagged slightly behind in the process.

Catholicism spread throughout the country to the extent that an official record states that already by 1788, there was no place from Seoul to the countryside where Catholicism had not reached.[81] In 1791, in a long letter to Ch'ae Che-gong, Hong Nak-an wrote, "Between Kyŏnggido and Chŏllado, there was no place that remained safe."[82]

Yun Chi-ch'ung and Yu Hang-gŏm were the first ones to convert to Catholicism and worked to disseminate the religion in Chŏllado. The two were *yangban* by birth and were maternal cousins.[83] Yu Hang-gŏm, the richest man of Chŏnju, visited Kwŏn's residence in Yangkŭn upon hearing about Catholicism. Having received Kwŏn Il-sin's teachings he converted to Catholicism, and when he returned to his hometown, he persuaded many of his family members to join the Catholic Church, thereby making a significant contribution to the establishment of the church in

---

[81] *Ilsŏngnok*, Chŏnjo Musin year, 8th month 2nd day.

[82] Yi Man-ch'ae, *op.cit.*, pp.127-128.

[83] *Sahak Chingŭi*, Kwŏn II, p.228.

the Chŏllado region.

As for Ch'ungch'ŏngdo, having learned Catholicism and being baptized during his study at Kwŏn Il-sin's house in Kyŏnggido, Yi Chon-ch'ang returned to his hometown in Ch'ungch'ŏngdo where he spread Catholicism through converting his relatives and friends.[84] He came to conduct missions as the "Apostle of Naep'o," and as a member of the organized pseudo ecclesiastical hierarchy, he took charge of the missionary work.[85] The Catholic communal organization formed in the Ch'ungch'ŏngdo Naepo region was one in which *yangin* and *nongin* classes constituted the dominant people.[86] This is in contrast to the early proliferation of Western Learning which occurred with the *yangban* class as its focal point.

Hong Yu-han, who can be considered as the first Catholic in the Yŏngnam region, moved to a place called Kudŭlmi[87] at the foot of the Sobaeksan, in order to read the books on Catholicism and to practice himself the Catholic doctrines, although there is no record of any missionary work he might have engaged in there.

The very first individual who attempted to spread Catholicism in the Yŏngnam region was Hwang Sa-yŏng (1775-1801). In the 17th year of Chŏngjo (1793), he visited Yi Pok-un (1776-?) of a *hyangni* (local functionary) family in Sangju, and tried to convert him, but failed.[88]

---

[84] Charles Dallet, (trans. Ch'oe Sŏg-u& An Eŭng-yŏl), *op.cit.*,(sang), pp.312-313.

[85] *Ibid.*, p.324.

[86] Cho Kwang, *Chosŏn hugi ch'onju kyohoesa yŏngu* (A study on the history of the church in late Chosŏn dynasty), (Seoul: Koryo taehakyo, 1988), p.49.

[87] The present Kyŏngbuk Yŏngjugun Tansanmyŏn Kuwuli. Charles Dallet, (trans. Choi Sŏg-u& An Eŭng-yŏl), *op.cit.*,(sang) pp.296-297.

[88] Cha Ki-jin, "Chosŏn hugi ch'ŏnjugyo ŭi chibang chŏnp'a wa kŭ sŏngkyŏk," (Propagation of Catholicism in Yŏngnam area and

Even during the period of the Catholic Persecution surrounding the Rites incident of 1791, the Yŏngnam region "adhered well to the Confucian teachings and was yet to be polluted by heresy," and it is recorded that, therefore, Chŏngjo conferred posthumous posts on the descendants of Yi Ŏn-jŏk and Yi Hwang.[89] From this, it can be inferred that even by 1791, when the persecution progressively intensified, Catholicism had not proliferated in the Yŏngnam region.

In 1798, Hwang Il-kwang, who became a Catholic due to Yi Chae-ch'ang's proselytizing effort, moved to Yŏngnam with his brother in order to freely practice the Catholic doctrines.[90] The record indicates that following the prohibition order, many took refuge in Yŏngnam as the persecution of the Catholics became increasingly oppressive due to the controversy over ancestor worship, and as a consequence, Catholicism was spread in the region. In 1801, Hwang Sa-yŏng recorded in his *paeksŏ* that the Catholics were hiding in Kyŏngsangdo and Kangwŏndo, and also gave evidence that Catholicism was introduced through the Catholics in hiding before the Sinyu Persecution.[91]

---

its characteristics during the final period of the Chosŏn kingdom), *Kyohoesa yŏn'gu*, No.6, (1988), pp.204-205.

[89] *Chosŏn wangjo sillok*, Chŏnjo 15th year: 11th month ¬lmi day.

[90] Charles Dallet, *op.cit.*, (sang), p.473.

[91] Hwang Sa-yŏng paeksŏ, 94th line.

Chapter II

Catholic Converts in Chosŏn Korea: Their Efforts to Practice and Transmit and Their Faith

1. The Pseudo Ecclesiastical Hierarchy

The Catholic churches developed in Chosŏn Korea through the efforts of laity. After its founding, Yi Pyŏk, Yi Sŭng-hun and Kwŏn Il-sin assumed key roles in the activities of the church.[92] Yi Sŭng-hun and Kwŏn Il-sin, in particular, assumed a central role in renewing their church, following the Ŭlsa Board of Punishments Incident in the spring of 1785, when Kim Pŏm-u and his fellow worshippers were arrested for adopting a church system, electing leaders, and refining the organization. Their main purpose in reorganizing the church was to enhance the effectiveness of the propagation of the new religion and its gospel, to strengthen the faith among the existing converted Catholics, and to foster the overall development of the church. Such activities illustrate the shift from interest in Catholicism as an intellectual pursuit to engagement in a religious movement.

The Catholic Church in the Chosŏn dynasty

---

[92]C. Dallet, *op.cit.*, p.312.

differed substantially from the traditional European Catholic churches, in that those of the Chosŏn dynasty were autonomous in their operations and spontaneous in their origin. The Chosŏn church was dominated by the laity out of necessity since there were no priests, teachers of doctrines or missionaries. Yi Sŭng-hun was selected as the chief of the laypeople's organization, for he was familiar with the church institutions from his trip to Beijing and had acquired a general knowledge of the appropriate religious rituals.[93]

A council was formed as a part of this lay organization, and it centered around Yi Pyŏk, Kwŏn Il-sin and Yu Hang-gŏm.[94] The council was democratic in nature; the members of this council rotated in managing various affairs of the church, and important issues of the church were required to pass through the council.[95] However, the problems encountered by the church were not administrative, but rather those that surrounded the original duty and purpose of a church, i.e., provision of spirituality and performance of the seven sacraments. The performance of the seven sacraments, except for baptism, required an ordained priest in order for them to be valid.

During the spring of the tenth year of Chŏngjo (1786), the lay organization held a discussion regarding the methods of conducting confessions. They came to a decision that if A confesses to B and B confesses to C, then B may not confess to A nor may C confess to B.[96] Because the leaders' knowledge of the church institutional system at that time was inadequate, the hierarchical order that they

---

[93] Akagi Nihei, "Chōsen ni okeru tenshukyō o ryūnyū to tenrei mondai ni tsuite," (The Introduction of Catholicism into Korea and the Rites Controversy), *Shigaku zasshi*, p.130.

[94] Ch'oe Sŏg-u, *Han'guk ch'onju kyohoe ui yŏksa*, (Seoul: Han'guk kyohoesa yŏn'guso, 1982), p.25.

[95] *Ibid.*

[96] *Ibid.*, p.25.

created within their church was based solely on their own limited understanding and acceptance of the gospel. The result was what may be called a pseudo ecclesiastical hierarchy.

From the spring of 1786 to 1787, the lay organization decided to bestow upon Yi Sŭng-hun the authority to supervise the performance of masses and confirmations. He granted similar authority to ten of his colleagues and gave them the title of priest.[97] These included they were Kwŏn Il-sin and Hong Nak-min, *yangban* from Seoul, the *chungin*, Ch'oe Ch'ang-hyŏn, Yi Chon-ch'ang from Naep'o, Ch'ungch'ŏngdo, Yu Hang-gŏm from Chŏnju, Chŏllado, and others. These priests had the authority to conduct sacraments. Under their system, the Chosŏn Catholics referred to those who conducted baptism as priests and to those who taught the Catholic doctrines as godfathers. The ten priests charged with defy in the Pseudo Ecclesiastical Hierarchy sought active communications and relationships with each other and formed a small group to carry out the missionary work. However, they ended up being dispersed and loosely knit, and failed to develop the systematic structure that was necessary to encompass the entire Catholic church membership, which numbered over a thousand by this time.[98]

Within less than a year after Yi Sŭng-hun had been baptized and returned to Korea, Catholicism was being rapidly propagated throughout the country. Catholicism was disseminated within Seoul, and to Majae, Yanggŭn, and P'ochŏn of Kyŏnggido. Furthermore, through the efforts of these underground priests, Catholicism spread throughout the provinces. Yi Chon-ch'ang, for example, developed a public religious organization in Naep'o, Ch'ungch'ŏngdo,

---

[97] *Ibid.*, Ch'oe Sŏg-u, *Han'guksa 14*, (Seoul: Kuksa p'yŏn ch'an wiwŏnhoe, 1981), pp.109-111.

[98] Ch'oe Sang-ch'ŏn, "Chŏngjo jo ch'ŏnju kyohoe undong ŭi sŏngkyŏk." (The nature of the Catholic movement during Chŏngjo), *Ch'oe Sŏg-u sinbu hwagab kinyom nonchong.* pp.14-15.

and strove to propagate Catholicism throughout that area. Yu Hang-gŏm, who was taught by Kwŏn Il-sin of Chŏllado, devoted his wealth's, and fervor, and together with Yun Chi-ch'ung, sought to spread the gospel to regions in Chŏllado.[99]

Dissenting Opinion against the Pseudo Ecclesiastical Hierarchy

The fact that this lay organization was violating church doctrine by performing rites that could only be administered by a priest was pointed out by Yu Hang-gŏm, who subsequently wrote a letter to Yi Sŭng-hun requesting that it be disbanded. He further sent a messenger to the missionaries in Beijing urging them to specify an order of action.[100] Thereafter, even Yi Ka-hwan acknowledged the inappropriateness of the pseudo ecclesiastical hierarchy.[101]

Even after such objections had been expressed, the performances of the sacraments, however, did not come to an immediate halt. Although they were aware of the blasphemous nature of their institution, the members nevertheless felt they had had no alternative but to continue their practice until they received a formal order from the missionaries. This was because they feared that if they ceased to carry out the sacraments altogether, the road to salvation would no longer be available to them, and anxiety and fear would overwhelm their members. Meanwhile, Yu Hang-gŏm adamantly opposed Yi Sŭng-hun and his colleagues' support of the continuation of these practices, arguing "do not sin and do not fall under the temptations of fear. All sacrament performances should be stopped immediately, and we must send a letter to the missionaries

---

[99] Cho Kwang, *Chosŏn hugi ch'ŏnju kyohoesa yŏn'gu.* pp.32-50.

[100] *Ibid.*, p.15-18.

[101] *Sahak chingŭi*, pp.231-232.

in Beijing."[12] In order to resolve the problem, it was decided that an inquiry to a bishop in Beijing should be sent.

At the end of the 13th year of Chŏngjo (1789), Yun Yu-il, a student of Kwŏn Il-sin, was dispatched as a secret envoy disguised as a merchant, accompanying the winter solstice embassy to the Ch'ing court. Once in Beijing, he was led to Father Nicholas-Joseph of the Lazaristae Order in the North Church. Yun Yu-il delivered Yi Sŭng-hun's letter and informed the priest of the dilemma faced by the Chosŏn church. On his return trip, he carried with him a pastoral letter from the Bishop of Beijing. The expenses of the trip were paid for by Yu Hang-gŏm.[102]

In their reply, the missionaries of the North Church in Beijing, whose objective was to encourage the development of the Catholic church in Korea, did not criticize the lay organization's structure and its performances of sacraments, because they considered their behavior unenlightened but well intended. They merely ordered the Chosŏn church members to seek salvation through repenting and to devise a method to properly participate in the sacraments.

Upon Yun Yu-il's return to Korea in 1790, the Korean church members accepted the orders from the Beijing Bishop. They came to a clear understanding that a priest must be present in performing sacraments and further gained new knowledge on Catholic doctrines and organizations.

Such a pseudo ecclesiastical hierarchy was in fact a violation of the church law. However, given the situation at that time, it was an illustration of the autonomous and active characteristics of the church's establishment in Korea. These were distinctive features of Korean Catholicism.[103] Dallet viewed the institution in a positive light, suggesting

---

[102] *Sahak chingŭi*, p.229.

[103] C. Dallet, *op.cit.,* (sang), trans. pp.323-328. Yu Hong-nyŏl, *op.cit.* ,(I),p.93.

that it strengthened the faith of those in charge and that the number of churches increased dramatically due to their ardent missionary efforts.[104]

2. Efforts to Invite a Priest

Upon reading the pastoral letter brought back by Yun Yu-il, the Korean church members saw a need for a missionary in order to promote the propagation and deepening of their faith. They reselected Yun Yu-il as an emissary to Beijing Catholic church to petition for a missionary to be dispatched to Korea. In 1790, Yun Yu-il left Seoul for the second time as a member of the diplomatic entourage to Beijing.[105] The entourage was to celebrate the eightieth birthday of Emperor Ch'ien-lung. When he went to the North Church in Beijing and requested a missionary to be dispatched to Korea, the missionaries of the North Church sent him to the South Church, where Bishop Gouvea of the Beijing parish, who had the authority to dispatch a missionary, was residing at the South Church at that time.[106] Upon his meeting, Yun Yu-il inquired of Bishop Gouvea about the issue of ancestor worship, which was of great concern to the Korean Catholics. In contradiction to the Jesuit mission policy, Gouvea's response was a prohibition of the practice of ancestor worship. The reason for his absolute rejection of the practice derived from the fact that he was a priest of the Franciscan order who argued for the abolition of ancestor worship during the Rites Controversy. However, Yun Yu-il was successful in receiving a verbal promise for a missionary to be dispatched. At that time, the Jesuit order being disbanded, there was a

---

[104] C. Dallet, op.cit., (sang),pp.322-6.

[105] The chief delegate of the entourage was Hwang In-jŏm.

[106] Ch'oe Sŏg-u, "Pari oebang chŏngkyohoe ŭi Han' guk chinch'ul," Han'guk kyohoesa ŭi t'amgu, p.118.

serious shortage of missionaries, and an immediate dispatch of a missionary to Korea proved difficult. Nevertheless, Gouvea was interested in the propagation of Catholicism in Korea and thus actively promoted the dispatch of a missionary to Korea. Gouvea reported to the Papal Court that he decided to send a missionary to Korea because he did not want to desert the Korean Catholics by leaving them without a priest and did not want to forego a chance for missionary work in Korea.[107]

In 1790, Bishop Gouvea dispatched the first missionary to Korea, and the priest was a Macao born Chinese named Priest Oh (his Portugese name was Johan dos Remedios).[108] In February of 1791, he left for his new post in Korea. Upon his arrival at the border,[109] however, he failed to meet the fellow Korean church members including Yun Yu-il[110] and was unable to enter Korea, at which point he returned to Beijing.[111] At that time, the Korean church members were prevented from meeting Father O because the persecution of Catholic Churches in Korea had just begun.

Bishop Gouvea's order prohibiting ancestor worship gave rise to the Chinsan Incident of 1791, leading in turn to oppression and a persecution of the movement to invite priests, and as a result, this came to a temporary halt. However, following the year of oppression, the number of believers in Korea again increased, and as a new church

---

[107] *Kyohoesa yŏn'gu*. No.8, pp.81-203.

[108] C. Dallet, *op.cit.*,(chung), p.375. He was a member of the Macao parish and "though quite young, was diligent, genuine, and gentle in nature. He also possessed sufficient knowledge on ethics and theology and had received Western education." Gouvea sŏhan, *Kyohoesa yŏn'gu* 8, p.184.

[109] *Ibid.*, p.146.

[110] Kim Yŏ ch'uan, 4th month 2nd day.

[111] He passed away in 1793 and never had another chance to enter Korea.

group of leaders took shape, people wanting invitations of priests also increased in their number. Another attempt to invite missionaries was made in 1793 through the ultimate solstice embassy. The secret envoys were Chi Hwang (Saba) and John Po.[112] Chi Hwang was able to accompany the diplomatic entourage by disguising himself as a merchant.[113] Upon their arrival in the Beijing parish, they made a detailed report on the persecutions of the Sinhae year (1791). Then they sought to accomplish the most crucial purpose of their trip, which was to request dispatch of a priest to Korea.

In response to the Korean church members' continuous requests for a priest, Bishop Gouvea decided to dispatch a Chinese born priest, Chou Wen-mo (Jacques Vellozo, 1752-1801). Priest Remedius, who was originally designated to be sent to Korea, had died by then. Priest Chou was from Chiangnan in China. He was a churchgoer since his childhood and was a first year graduate of the Beijing parish seminary. He also had received holy orders from Bishop Gouvea.[114] The fact that he tried the civil service examinations demonstrated his substantial scholarship, which later must have considerably aided his pastoral work among the *yangban* class.

The reason behind dispatching Father Chou Wen-mo as the very first priest to Korea stems from Bishop Gouvea's enthusiasm for mission work, combined with a personal entreaty from the Pope and his pastoral consideration for the Korean church. He selected a Chinese born priest, recognizing the shortcomings of a European born priest and taking into consideration the situation of both the Beijing parish and the persecuted Korean church. Thus, similar to the autonomous founding of a church in

---

[112] Gouvea's letters, op.cit., p.192.

[113] *Ch'uan kŭp kukan,* 25. (Sahak choein Yi Ki-yang tŭng kukan, p.204.

[114] Cho Kwang, "Chu Mun-mo ŭi ipkuk kwa kŭ hwaltong," *Kyohoesa yŏn'gu,* 10, p..59.

Korea, the invitation of a priest was the result of ardent and continuous request by the Korean church members, not of the effort of the mission orgarnization, as was the case in China and Japan. The Korean church members' need for a priest derived from their heightened interest in the religion and their desire to participate in sacraments, as well as the desire to acquire an accurate understanding of the doctrine.

Chou Wen-mo's Arrival in Korea and his ministry

Priest Chou Wen-mo was designated to conduct missions in Chosŏn by the Beijing parish, and left Beijing in February of 1794, arriving at the border after 20 days of traveling on foot. Although he met Chosŏn fellow church members who came to greet him, he was not able to cross the border to enter Korea, because the ice on the surface of Amnok River had melted, rendering smuggling impossible.[115] The Chosŏn church members promised to reconvene in the 12th month of that year and waited for the freezing season to return. Meanwhile, Priest Chu spent the period making rounds to churches in Manchu areas and in the 12th month, he returned to the border, at which point he met two secret Chosŏn church envoys, Chi Hwang and Yun Yu-il, who had accompanied the Winter Solstice envoy to Beijing in 1784. Under their guidance, he smuggled himself into Ŭiju on the 12th month, 3rd day, 1794,[116] and then traveled to Seoul disguised as a horse handler, moving around only at night.[117]

The key figures in bringing Chou Wen-mo to Korea were Chi Hwang, a devoted Catholic from a family of palace pharmacists,[118] Ch'oe In-gil, another pharmacist, Yun Yu-il, a *yangban* who had frequented Beijing on several

---

[115] Yi Ki-yang tŭng ch'uan, *op.cit.*, 3:15.

[116] *Ibid.*, p.205.

[117] Yi Man-ch'ae, *op.cit.*, p.311.

[118] Charles Dallet, *op.cit.*,(sang), p.314.

occasions as a secret envoy in the past, Kang Wan-suk, who entirely funded the required expenses,[119] and Pak Yo-han, who accompanied Chi Hwang. Dallet conjectures that Pae Mattea who died a martyr in 1801 was another key figure in inviting Priest Chou.[120] Furthermore, it appears that the church leaders residing in Seoul at that time, such as Ch'oe Ch'ang-hyŏn, Ch'oe P'il-kong, Ch'oe In-ch'ŏl, and those residing in the countryside, such as Yi Chon-ch'ang, also participated in the effort as well.[121] Under the ministry of Father Chou Wen-mo from 1795 until 1800, the Chosŏn church came to form a unitary organization with a priest at its vertex. Chosŏn church members realized that the Seven Sacraments could not be performed without a priest and thus the activities of the church could not be executed.[122] And arising from such self-realization, their fervent desire to invite a priest from abroad and earnest effort to have a priest to head the pseudo ecclesiastical hierarchy ultimately gave them a priest for the very first time in Korea. This is a characteristic of the Chosŏn church members that illustrates their religious passion in founding, institutionalizing and organizing a church on their own.

Upon his arrival in Seoul, Chou Wen-mo stayed at Ch'oe In-gil's house, presumably because Ch'oe In-gil was a *chungin* translator who had a good command of Chinese, and thus the concern for communication was taken into consideration. At his house, a Catholic church decorated in an outlandish way was in place.[123]

---

[119] *Sahak chingŭi*, pp.363-364.
[120] Charles Dallet, *op.cit.*, p.613-614.
[121] *Sahak chingŭi*, p.152.
[122] *Ch'uan Kŭp kukan* (Trial for felony), (Seoul: Asea munhwasa,1983), p.539.
[123] Yi Man-ch'ae, *op.cit.*, p.221.

First Mass

The new communal organization conducted a mass under a priest for the first time on Easter Sunday, April 5th, 1795. The Chosŏn Catholic church, which had been built strictly from the Koreans' own acceptance of Christianity and their request for a priest, was finally beginning to take shape as a formal organization and to practice a religious life in the acceptable way. A record reveals the enthusiasm of the Chosŏn church members towards their first priest; "the believers paid respect to the priest as if he were a spirit from heaven who came down from the sky."[124] It is unnecessary to mention the extent to which the arrival of Priest Chou had given an indescribable amount of joy and comfort to the newly founded Chosŏn church.

The Founding of Myŏngdohoe (Society for Illumination of the Way)

Priest Chou devoted himself to learning the Korean language, and he conducted baptisms of the followers as well as re-baptizing those who had already been baptized before. In this way, he gathered together the church members who had scattered due to the Sinhae Persecution (1801) and began to pursue an organizational mode that tied everyone together under a priest. In order to provide the doctrines, he translated, wrote and taught books during the day, and from time to time, personally corrected the church members' flaws, strictly enforcing loyalty to all Catholic principles.

Father Chou Wen-mo placed the focus of his ministry on the establishment of the church's organizational structure and provision of Catholic doctrines. He visited the Catholics, and at night he conducted masses and sacraments through an association that he formed called *Myŏngdohoe*. He designated a president to whom he allocated various church tasks and made the association efficient, thereby strengthening it. *Myŏngdohoe* was the representative

---

[124]Gouvea's letter, *Kyohoesa yŏn'gu 8*, p.197.

organization in the early Catholic Church, its meaning being "a meeting that teaches the dogma," and was ultimately established for the Catholic missionary purpose of sowing the knowledge of its doctrine among the Catholic Church members and to have them teach others. [125]

As martyrs and apostates continued to increase due to the Catholic persecution, the number of Catholics was dramatically reduced, and re-structuring of the members' organization became another task of the association. [126] The association was also a materialization of actions taken in response to the needs of the church, in its now not so rigidly institutionalized and organized situation. This situation, of course, was mainly due to the post- persecution apostacy that resulted from the ancestor worship conflicts and changes at the church leadership level. Although *Myŏngdohoe* had its own rules, [127] there is no record of such. Hwang Sa-yŏng's confession during his interrogation says: "There was an organization called *Myŏngdohoe* within the church. Five to six people were selected, and this list was then reported to the priest, and they proceeded to learn the doctrines from the priest. Those who were diligent in maintaining good conduct in prayer, and in doctrinal study for about a year were permitted to join the *Myŏngdohoe* , and those who were otherwise were not granted membership."[128]

As mentioned above, the *Myŏngdohoe* organization began by gathering a small number of people, five to seven, and by reporting the list to Priest Chou. They gathered together, studying and holding discussion on the books, and those who wished to become members of the Western

---

[125] C. Dallet, *op.cit.*,(sang), p.391.

[126] Yi Wŏn-sun, "Chosŏn kyohoe ŭi ch'angsŏl kwa chŏngch'ak," *Kyohoesa yŏn'gu,* 10. p.218.

[127] *Sahak chingŭi,* kwŏn. 2.

[128] Sinyu Sahak choein, Hwang Sa-yŏng tŭng ch'uan, *Ch'uan kŭp kukan,* p.816.

Learning group were evaluated on their maturity and grasp of prayer, good conduct, and studies for a period of one year and then their membership eligibility would be decided.[129]

There were six places where the *Myŏngdohoe* met, and those were sometimes called the *Yukhoe* (Six Assemblies). They were the houses of Hong P'il-chu, Hong Ik-man, Kim Yŏ-hang, Hyŏn Kye-hŭm, Hwang Sa-yŏng and one other. The group in which Hwang Sa-yŏng participated was made up of six members, consisting of himself, Nam Song-no, Ch'oe T'ae-san, Son In-wŏn, Cho Sin-haeng, and Yi Chae-sin.[130]

It could be that Hwang Sa-yŏng's being unaware of other *Yukhoe* was partially due to an intentional effort to prevent the discovery of the organization, but it is also possible that the entire *Myŏngdohoe* organization operated under such absolute secrecy that even Hwang Sa-yŏng had no knowledge of other meeting places. Subsequently, it is possible that there were other secret groups in addition to those five mentioned by Hwang Sa-yŏng. It is not certain, but besides these groups, there were others referred to as Tongdang ("Same Group"), Hyŏldang ("Blood Group"), Sadang ("Death Group"), that appear to have been related to the *Myŏngdohoe*.[131]

Right after the incident of detection of the Catholics in 1785, the prohibition order on Catholicism rendered open and public performances of religious activities impossible. Because from the beginning of the acceptance of Catholicism, the church could only carry out their mission through a pseudo form of church, such association was necessary in order to deal with the persecution. In the views of the government, these secret meetings and underground organizations which could only posses the characteristics of a pseudo church, due to the national prohibition order, could only be understood as

---

[129] *Ibid.*

[130] *Ibid.*

[131] *Sahak chingŭi*, p.70, p.74, p.86.

either a genuine conspiracy or as an attempt to overthrow the political order then in power.

Among the members of the *Myŏngdohoe*, those figures that attracted attention were Chŏngjo's brother born of a concubine, Ŭnŏngun (In)'s wife Song-ssi and his daughter-in-law Sin-ssi. When his son, Sanggyegun(Tam) was exiled for treason, Ŭnŏngun was closed to Kanghwado in connection with the same incident, while his wife and his daughter-in-law were confined to the Yangje palace, which was then closed. It was a Catholic convert Kang Wan-suk who paid a visit to these politically abandoned individuals, and with Father Chou Wen-mo, worked to convert them and to have them receive sacraments, and eventually made them members of the *Myŏngdohoe*.

Father Chou appointed a lay leader of the church, *chungin* Ch'oe Ch'ang-hyŏn of Kwanch'ŏng, as the president of the Society (Ch'onghoejang).[132] This again is an illustration of the Catholic ideology and achievement of equality amidst the rigid social customs of the time. For each regional organization, Chou Wen-mo appointed a president to be in charge. Chŏng Yak-chong was appointed as a president,[133] and Kim Sŭng-jŏng appears to have been also so appointed.[134] Chŏng Pedro became the president of the Naep'o region.[135]

Kang Wan-suk and Yun Chŏm-hye became presidents of Chapters for female members. At that time, men and women were not allowed to sit together in the same place, and since two thirds of the believers were women,[136] a separate division for women believers was necessary. Because at that time social activities by women were essentially forbidden, the appointment of female

---

[132] Hwang Sa-yŏng Paeksŏ, 32nd line.

[133] Ibid, 42nd line, C. Dallet, (sang), p.391.

[134] C. Dallet, *Ibid.*, p.505.

[135] *Ibid.*, p.420.

[136] Hwang Sa-yŏng paeksŏ, 20th line.

presidents was a notable event.

The organization of the early church can be seen to comprise the lay group (Ch'oe Ch'ang-hyŏn), women's group (Kang Wan-suk), and *Myŏngdohoe* (Chŏng Yak-chong). This organization only included Seoul and its nearby regions, and was not a nation-wide organization.[137] It was a frame work in which the organic entity of the church amid the persecution was maintained and advanced.

In organizing such group, the priest must have recognized the limits to his ability to provide for the needs of the ministry of the Chosŏn church entirely on his own, because of the growing task of overseeing the increasing number of believers despite the accompanying suffering, and because of the geographically dispersed individuals in the Southern region.

The Myŏngdohoe was a frame in which the organic entity of the church amid the persecution was maintained and advanced. Because it was an organization invisible to the external world, it possessed the characteristics of a kind of clandestine group, a pseudo church. The fact that even Hwang Sa-yŏng, who was considered to be one of the most highly regarded leaders, did not have a clear grasp of the Myŏngdohoe entity is evidence of the clandestine nature of the organization. These groups formed in each region contributed significantly to the advancement of the Chosŏn Catholic church during the persecution era.[138]

As many fellow Catholics became members of the Myŏngdohoe, Hwang Sa-yŏng prayed diligently for its success in April of the year of 1800. Those who were not members of the Myŏngdohoe were so moved by his earnest effort that they assumed the mission to be their own personal duty, and during the fall and the winter of that year, the numbers of those becoming Catholics grew enormously.

---

[137] Ch'oe Sang-ch'ŏn, "Chŏngjojo ch'ŏnju kyohoe undong ŭi sŏngkyŏk," (The nature of the activities of the Catholic church in the reign of Chŏngjo), *Ch'oe Sŏg-u sinbu hwagap kinyŏm, Han'guk kyohoesa nonch'ŏng*, (Seoul, 1982), p.19.

[138] Cho Kwang, *op. cit.*, pp. 138-141.

Among the new church members, about two thirds were women and the remaining one third were uneducated *p'yŏngmin*, while those from *yangban* background who chose to believe and follow the new religion were very few in numbers, due to their fear of the dire consequences.[139]

Such a covert organization, which transcended social status rankings and, as a communal spiritual organization confessed Jesus Christ to be the savior of Chosŏn society, was dramatically different from the former dominant religions such as Buddhism and Confucianism, perhaps especially at the organizational level. For the Catholic church had formed a communal organization that distinctly focused on the laypeople, and the church members responded by adding their strength, thus aiding and encouraging each other during the persecution that was soon to follow.

Number of believers in 1801

At the time of the church founding in 1784, there were approximately 1,000 believers,[140] and ten years later in 1795, there were 4,000 followers even during the persecution.[141] Since Priest Chu Mun-mo's arrival in Korea and his ministry, the church grew to nearly 10,000 followers[142] by the time of the Sinyu Persecution.

Around 1800, Hwang Sa-yŏng wrote in his *Paeksŏ* that the number of followers did not exceed several thousand.[143] This can be seen as a decrease in the number of followers due to the persecution on several occasions, and it is perhaps more accurate to estimate a rough figure

---

[139] Hwang Sa-yŏng paeksŏ, 20th line.

[140] Gouvea's letter, 1790, *mannam kwa midŭm ŭi gilmok esŏ*, (Seoul: Han'guk kyohoesa yŏn'guso, 1989), p.133.

[141] C. Dallet, *op.cit.*, (sang), (trans Ch'oe & An), p.37.

[142] *Ibid.*, p.393.

[143] Hwang Sa-yŏng paeksŏ, 88th line.

between 2,000 and 10,000[144] since there was no formal investigation of the exact number and since an error in the estimation process must be taken into account.

In 1801, the total population of Korea was 7,513,792, in 1,757,913 households.[145] That year was seventeen years after the founding of the Chosŏn church, and the fact that the number of the followers reached approximately 10,000 even under the Catholicism prohibition order and subsequent persecution is a testimony to the radical increase in the number of the Catholic believers.

At that time, Catholic believers were scattered throughout the country with central areas ofconcentration in Seoul, Yangkŭn and Yŏju of Kyŏnggido, Ch'ŏngju and Naep'o of Ch'ungch'ŏngdo and Chŏnju of Chŏllado. Subsequently, if considered only within the population ratios of these regions, 10,000 followers and its consequent percentage are quite substantial. Furthermore, it testifies to the growth, not a shrinking, of the church members in such unfavorable circumstances starting from the *Ŭlsa chujo chŏkpal* incident in 1785, to the Chinsan incident in 1791, the subsequent prohibition order by the government and the Sinyu Persecution following the unsuccessful attempt to arrest Father Chou Wen-mo and others. This signifies the proliferation of a group of converts and regions, including *yangban*, *chungin*, farmers, laborers, *chŏnmin*, and the destitute.[146]

Upon witnessing such regional dissemination, transcending the boundaries of social class, the Chief State Councillor Kim Ch'i-in proposed a prohibition order and a countermeasure in 1787.[147]

---

[144]Cho Kwang, *op.cit.*, p.24.

[145]*Chosŏn wangjo sillok*, Sunjo the first year, (Sinyu year) 12th month Kyŏngo.

[146]C. Dallet, *op.cit.*, p.321.

[147]*Chosŏn wangjo sillok*, Chŏngjo,11th year, 8th month Ŭlyu.

The conditions shaped by the struggle of a rebellious force against a feudal order, the consequences of societal fluctuations in the later years of a dynasty already well past its prime,[148] participation by the leaders of the Catholic church organization, Catholic notions of equality and charity, and Korean translations of catechisms all played key roles in the rapid increase in the number of followers among the common people and country people.

3. Provision of Catechisms

Investigation and discussion of the Catholic teachings had begun in the late 1770's through key founding figures like Kwŏn Ch'ŏl-sin, Yi Pyŏk and Chŏng Yak-chŏn and the transmission and discussion of their new knowledge at the *Ch'ŏnjinam* and *Chuŏsa* meetings. The conference was an opportunity for a collective investigation regarding the issues of the Catholic faith, which so far had been investigated individually through studying books on Western Learning and had been understood through conversations among friends with similar interests.[149]

In 1784, the doctrinal materials brought by Yi Sŭnghun from Beijing[150] were delivered to Yi Pyŏk, who had a great interest in the Catholic dogma, and he came to achieve a general understanding of the new religion upon his careful study and investigation.[151] Questions regarding the doctrines of the new religion were resolved through seminars of small groups, and these seminars became one of the unique

---

[148]Han U-gŭn," Ch'ŏnjugyo ch'oki palchŏn kwa kŭ yŏnghyang. " *Han'guk ch'ŏnju kyohoesa nonmunhŏnjip*, p.118.

[149]Ch'oe Sŏg-u, "Chosŏn kyogu sŏlchŏng ŭi yŏksajŏk kyegi," *Kyohoesa yŏn'gu* 4, 1983, p.8.

[150]*Chosŏn wangjo sillok*, Chŏngjo, 8th year, 3rd month, Ŭlyu.

[151]Charles Dallet (trans.), *op.cit.*,(sang), p.307.

characteristics of this study group.[152]

However, after the Rites Controversy erupted in 1791, government scrutiny rendered such seminars impossible and the number of those who independently studied the doctrines through books and came to believe in Catholicism gradually increased.

Before Western Learning was accepted as a religion, study of Western Learning was mostly the subject of academic and investigative demand by intellectuals. However, upon the formation of an organization of followers, even the common people came to read the books on the Western Learning, and consequently, the availability of Catholic books dramatically enhanced. The Catholic materials ranged from a scroll of a mere few pages containing short verses from the Bible to a catechism in a complete set of several volumes. Their writing also ranged from those recorded in difficult Chinese characters to those in the Korean script. Kim Yŏm-i, the wife of *chungin* Chi Hwang, learned the dogma through reading the Catholic books at her husband's residence. Yun Un-hye, the cousin of Yun Yu-il, was the younger sister of Yun Chŏm-hye and the wife of Chŏng Kwang-su, and her sister-in-law was Chŏng Sun-mae, all learned the doctrine from her mother Sin Sosa. Discovered selling Catholic books and religious items,[153] she was arrested and executed, accused of cultural seduction.[154]

Kang Wang-suk, a female Catholic living in Ch'ungch'ŏngdo Naep'o region, came into contact with Catholicism also through books circulated in her region.[155] Im Tae-in, who was also residing alone in Nampo near the Naep'o region, read the books on the Western Learning written in the Korean language and subsequently joined the

---

[152] *Sahak chingŭi*, kwŏn 2.
[153] *Sahak chingŭi*, pp.93-111.
[154] *Sahak chingŭi*, pp.105-107.
[155] Hwang Sa-yŏng paeksŏ, 65th line.

Catholic Church.156 A *chungin* of Seoul, Chŏng In-hyŏk borrowed five books written in Korean from Ch'oe Ch'ang-hyŏn and joined the Catholic church after having had a full discussion with Ch'oe P'il-che.157 These above examples are only few of many, and in actuality, the force of the Catholic Church expanded through these catechisms, which became the single most important missionary tool.

The total number of the Chinese translations of the Western books published in Chosŏn during the Ming and Ching dynasty is known to be approximately 350. However, those that were actually descended total approximately 130 items.158 The transmitted Catholic books that have been identified were 64 items in total (132 in total including the anonymous works), including 37 during the investigative period of the Western Learning, 13 during the pseudo ecclesiastical hierarchy following the founding of the church, and 14 during the period of under the Chinese priest (68 anonymous works). In addition, 14 categories of books were translated into Korean and published.159

Sŏnggyo chŏlyo (The Essence of Holy Church), is a Western book translated into Chinese, published in 1705, and its author or the time at which it was transmitted to Chosŏn is unknown. But according to Yi Ki-kyŏng's *Pyŏkwip'yŏn*, this book appears to have entered Korea and been read before 1789. A Korean version of *Sŏnggyo chŏlyo* in 37 volumes has been handed down to this date. Its contents includes *Sŏnghogyŏng* (In the name of the Father, Son and the Holy Spirit), *Ch'ŏnjugyŏng* (The Lord's

---

156 "Sahak choein Yi Ka-hwan tŭng ch'uan," *Ch'uan kŭp kukan*, p.53.

157 *Sahak chingŭi*, p.77.

158 Yi Wŏn-sun, *Han'guk ch'ŏnju kyohoesa yŏn'gu*, (Seoul: Han'guk kyohoesa yŏn'guso, 1986), pp.19-20. Pae Hyŏn-suk, "Sip ch'ilp'al segi e chŏllae doen ch'ŏnjugyo sŏjŏk," *Kyohoesa yŏn'gu* 3, p.41.

159 *Ibid*, p.43. Pae Hyŏn-suk, "Chosŏn e chŏllae dŭen ch'ŏnjukyo sŏjok," *Han'guk Kyohoesa Nonmunjip, I*, (Seoul: 1984), p.12.

Prayer), *Sŏngmogyŏng* (Hail Mary), *Singyŏng* (The Creed), *Sipkye* (Ten Commandments),*Sŏnggyo sagyu* (Sin and Virtuous Conduct).

During his ministry in Chosŏn, Chou Wen-mo, the first and only priest in Chosŏn at the time, compiled several catechisms such as *Kohae yori, Kohae sŏngch'an, and Sŏngch'e mundap.*[160]

4. Doctrinal Education

Among the dissemination methods used by the early Chosŏn Catholic church, most of the church members of the *yangban* class practiced education that centered around their families, in particular on the teachings by mothers to their daughters within their own individual family in transmitting Catholicism. Yun Chŏm-hye and Yun Un-hye, for example, learned the Catholic doctrines from their mother.[161] In the case of Yi Sun-i, the husband of Yu Chung-ch'ŏl, he received teachings on the Catholic doctrines from his mother Kwŏn-ssi (Kwŏn Ch'ŏl-sin's younger sister), and eventually died a martyr.[162] Even after becoming a widow, Han Sin-ae, Cho Si-chong's wife, taught doctrines to her daughter Cho Hye-ŭi.[163] A court lady, Mun Yŏng-in's father was non-Christian, but her mother, being a devout believer in Catholicism, earnestly sought to persuade her each time she visited home from the palace, and she was eventually martyred.[164] As a virgin,

---

[160] Ch'oe Sŏg-u, "Sahak chingŭi rŭl t'onghaesŏ bon ch'ogi ch'ŏnju kyohoe," *Kyohoesa yŏn'gu,* 2, p.41.

[161] *Sahak chingŭi,* p.93, 111.

[162] C.Dallet, *op.cit.,* (sang), pp.334-335.

[163] *Sahak chingŭi,* p.98.

[164] C. Dallet, *op.cit.,* (sang), pp.502-504.

Pak Sŏng-jŏn received doctrinal education from her mother in July of 1800. Her sixth cousin, Chŏng Pun-i and Kang Wan-suk's slave girl, So-myŏng came together to meet her and offered assistance to her, upon which she came to strengthen her faith further and was banished to Yŏngil.[165]

Doctrinal Understanding of Early Catholic Converts

In order to estimate the extent to which the Chosŏn Catholics at that time understood the doctrine, the content of the catechisms that were circulating at that time must be analyzed and the proclamation status must be examined.

Due to the lack of a priest and many problems rising from the newly founded church and from its incompleteness, it was not possible for doctrinal education to occur uniformly among different individuals. Because much depended on the personal missionary work by those who first came to understand and believe, the level of understanding varied significantly from individual to individual.

The *yangban* read books such as Matteo Ricci's *The True Meaning of the Lord of Heaven*, and thus they recognized Catholicism from the perspective of it being supplementary to Confucianism. They read other Western books translated into Chinese such as *Chi ke* and *Chen tao tzu cheng*, mentioned above, and came to understand the Catholic doctrine through these books. There was a layman like Ko Kwang-sŏng, who had in his possession sixteen books and read them day and night.[166]

On the other hand, uneducated and ignorant church members were educated through the simplest doctrinal teaching, memorizing the Ten Commandments from the *Hymn in the Honor of God*. There were cases in which some could not memorize all ten and quit after having

---

[165] *Sahak chingŭi*, p.335.

[166] *Sahak chingŭi*, p.90.

learned only two or three commandments.¹⁶⁷ It is recorded in *Sahak chingŭi* that the church members at the time considered the Ten Commandments as the ethical standard and that approximately 31 members had memorized them, and this leads to the conclusion that the memorization of the Ten Commandments was especially stressed among the church members.¹⁶⁸

Yu Kwan-gŏm considered the Commandments extremely crucial, telling Yi U-chip that practicing the Ten Commandments was without a doubt a duty of theirs,¹⁶⁹ and refused to recognize the violators of the Commandments as fellow church members.¹⁷⁰ This is evidence to their belief that the Ten Commandments were the most important virtue in Catholicism.

In addition, they were required to memorize daily prayers such as *Chomanka* (Prayerbook) and *Samchongkyŏng*. The *yangban* Catholics such as Yu Kwan-gŏm gave *Chomanka* to another *yangban* Yi U-chip,¹⁷¹ and Han sosa gave it to Sin sosa.¹⁷² Furthermore, Hwang Sim taught *Samchongkyŏng* to Pang Sŏng-p'il. ¹⁷³ This illustrates the emphasis that was placed on the daily prayer among the Catholics of all social classes whether noble or poor.

Generally, early believers studied catechisms written in Chinese, and those either translated or written in Korean, such as *Chugyo yoji*, were widely read by the intellectuals or Korean-reading Catholics. In addition,

---

¹⁶⁷*Sahak chingŭi*, p.332.

¹⁶⁸*Ibid.*, pp.112, 161, 168, 191, 219, 242, 246, 255, 317, 320, 330, 331, 332, 341, 369, 374.

¹⁶⁹*Ibid.*, p.246.

¹⁷⁰*Ibid.*, p.161.

¹⁷¹*Ibid.*, p.246.

¹⁷²*Ibid.*, p.339.

¹⁷³*Ibid.*, p.331.

much was emphasized on instilling the Catholic doctrines through simple doctrinal teachings appropriate to the different educational levels of the believers.

Yangban scholars, such as Kwŏn Ch'ŏl-sin, understood Catholicism as a philosophical faith and stated the following at the Sinyu Persecution trials on the topic of universal validity of the faith: "When first encountering the scholarship of Catholicism, I heard that it was vain and could not be believed. Later on however, upon opening and reading the book, I discovered the theory of the God of Superintendence, the theory of the three kind's spirits of plants, animals and humans, and the four elements theory on fire, energy, water and land, and these were all very reasonable and truthful so that they could not be assumed to be false. After one reads the book, it is impossible to criticize and refute it."[174]

Chŏng Yak-chong firmly believed in the Catholic teachings as the most truthful, stating, "How could this soul of mine practice [Catholicism] if I had acknowledged it as an evil doctrine? I know [Catholicism] to be of an ultimately true way that is very fair and just, and thus from the very beginning, even after the previous year's proclamation of the prohibition order of Catholicism, I never thought twice to convert out of my Catholic faith. I will not have even a small amount of regret if I were to die and be sentenced ten thousand times."[175]

Wŏn Si-jang (1732-1793), under the baptismal name of Peter, was a *yangin* (free born) Catholic from Ch'ungch'ŏngdo Hongju who converted to Catholicism and persuaded his relatives to follow his example:

> "He began to explain the existence of God who created all things of the beginning and of the end, the concepts of the original sin, incarnation, the commandments of the Lord,

---

[174] *Sahak choein Yi Ka-hwan tŭng ch'uan*, p.31.
[175] *Ibid.*, p.49.

heaven and hell, and all others that he possessed the knowledge of. He also added, 'Well, it means all those who have good intentions will live forever. You all should consider my words as testament and follow me and believe in Catholicism.'"[176]

Defending against the criticisms by the government and the society that Catholicism was a religion without a father nor a king, he adamantly claimed that he genuinely regarded the Western religion as the truth and is not aware that it is without a father nor a king.[177]

In the confession to the government by an uneducated Yi To-ki, who could not read Chinese and had neither teacher nor student, he revealed his knowledge on the doctrine, claiming that the Lord is the creator of the universe and the superintendent of all things, and that he serves his parents well according to the Ten Commandments.[178] It can be inferred from such a confession that he understood the doctrine from reading Korean catechisms. Although it is possible that his knowledge had been gained through hearing from others, from the record in an official document that "even an ignorant country man can translate or reproduce in Korean,"[179] it can be reasonably concluded that his doctrinal knowledge was self-taught mostly through Korean catechisms.

Following the Sinyu Persecution, a great scholar, Yi Man-su, wrote *Tosa pan'gyomun* (Edict for the Punishment of Treachery), and its following comment on the behavior of the Catholic believers at the time reveals an aspect of the doctrinal study and missionary work: "[They] studied and discussed among themselves at a secret place deep into the

---

[176] C. Dallet, *op.cit.*, (snga), p.367,
[177] *Sahak choein Hwang Sa-yŏng tŭng ch'uan*, p.727.
[178] C. Dallet, *op.cit.*, (sang), p.402.
[179] *Chosŏn wangjo sillok*, Chŏngjo 15th year 11th month Kapsul.

night and during the day at times publicly gave speeches and instigated the masses in the open area of a city."[180]

Practice of one's faith

There were church members who led the lives of a friar such as Kim Chong-sŏn Thomas who lived as a pauper and gave away any decent clothes or shoes that came his way. [181] Peter Wŏn also demonstrated the exemplary conduct of a Christian, sharing his wealth with the poor and striving to adhere strictly to the Catholic guidelines.[182] Such practice marked a turning point in the Catholic mission, for it was Catholic doctrine put into practice, not merely studied and discussed. By sharing one's possessions, each church member demonstrated a new aspect of a Catholic religious communal organization and refined the framework as a communal group.

---

[180] *Chosŏn wangjo sillok*, Sunjo, the beginning year 12th month Kapja.
[181] C. Dallet, *op.cit.*,(sang) p.398.
[182] C. Dallet, op.cit.,(sang), p.367.

Jai-Keun Choi

CHAPTER III

The Growing and the Persecution of the Early Period

1. Growing of the Church

Proliferation of Church Influence through Hereditary Ties

The value system of Chosŏn society had been institutionalized by thoughts and actions that placed a foremost emphasis on human relationships among those of closely related bloodlines. Relationships based on geographical and school ties also formed the basis of mutual understanding among Korean men, and they reinforced and strengthened such ties by infusing them with social and political power.

The diffusion of Catholicism in Korea and the speed at which it was transmitted owe much to the routine dissemination that occurred among families and clans related by blood. The Catholic communal organization was even considered to be a religious group that resembled a kind of a secret society formed upon clan ties.[183] An

---

[183] Hwang Sŏn-myŏng, *Chosŏn chonggyo sahoesa yŏn'gu*, (A study of religious and social history in Chosŏn dynasty), p.307.

official record used the term "party of the blood" to describe the principle of its organization.[184] The Chosŏn family was essentially a large communal organization tied by blood with a paternal figure at the apex. Due to the significant role and influence of a father figure, familial and hereditary lines tended to be clear and distinct.

The role of marriage-based relationships in family units was much more significant and its contribution much more substantial to the proliferation of Catholicism than that of relationships based on blood ties. Catholicism was further disseminated through local geographical relationships of Seoul, Kyŏnggi, Chŏlla, and Ch'ungch'ŏng, and the early Catholicism was founded and expanded through school ties mainly based on the *Namin* Sŏngho school, that is close knit intellectual ties that by now had formed among the disciples of the "Southerner" scholar Yi Ik.

In the case of the *Namin,* since Kyŏngjong's reign (1720-1724), many of those who fell from political power and who had a keen interest in academic scholarship became *Silhak* scholars. When Western Learning was first introduced to Korea, they were the ones who expressed the most sincere interest and positive attitude towards its acceptance. Among them, there were Kiho Namin who were deeply interested in understanding a new field of knowledge.

Among those who centered on the politically disadvantaged *Namin,* most had established relationships through intricate networks of intermarriage. Likewise, *Sŏin* and *Pugin* also limited their correspondence, academic exchanges and marriage ties to those in the same party faction. This is a vital point which demonstrates the deep rootedness of the Korean Catholics kinship network, with its strong proclivity for factional exogamy. Such kinship ties can be said to have emerged in response to the existing clan ruling system.[185] In other words, practicing the

---

[184] *Sahak chingŭi. p.70.*

[185] Hwang Sŏn-myŏng, *op.cit.*, p.291.

Catholic belief, which centered on the intellectuals of the *Namin* Sinsŏp'a (Pro Western Faction), constituted a substitute kinship relationship that was reacting to the dominance of the existing clan ruling system. Therefore, essentially, the practice of Catholicism can be seen as a challenge or confrontation of a political nature between two clan lineages. Such a clash clearly would shake the existing political power structure.

According to *Sahak chingi* (A Warning against Heterodoxy)[186], Catholic converts among *Namin* appear to have had a greater abundance of close marriage relationships with their fellow *Namin* than had hitherto been realized. At this point it would be well to investigate these numerous marriage relationships in greater detail. A good place to begin with might be with a man named Yi Yun-ha, a descendant of Yi Su-kwang (1563-1628), a literati titan who introduced Western Learning for the very first time in Korea. More immediate figures would be Yi Sŭng-hun, who was the founding father of the Chosŏn Catholic church; Yi Ka-hwan, a nephew of the great *Silhak* scholar Sŏngho Yi Ik; Yu Hang-gŏm, who contributed significantly to the expansion of the faith in Chŏlla and to its sound financial foundation; Yun Chi-ch'ung, a descendant of Yun Sŏn-do who refused to carry out the custom of "ancestral worship" and so was the first one to die a martyr; Chŏng Yag-yong, one of the greatest scholars of the Chosŏn dynasty who narrowly escaped martyrdom; Hong Nag-min (1740-1801), who passed the higher civil service examination, and died a martyr as did his son and his grandson[187]; Kwŏn Ch'ŏl-sin, the greatest scholar of his generation; Yi Ki-yang (1744-1802), the seventh generation descendant of the great bureaucratic figure Yi Tŏk-hyŏng (1561-1613).

The most representative cases of overlapping

---

[186]The book was serendipitously found in the memorial hall of the martyrs in Yanghwachin in 1971 and reprinted by Han'guk kyohoesa yon'guso in 1977.

[187]Hong Nag-min died in 1801, his son Chae-yŏng in1839 and his grandsons, Pyŏng-ju and Yŏng-ju in 1840 and Pong-ju in1866.

marriage relationships are the following *Namin* families, already enumerated above: the Kwŏn family who lived in Yangkn Kyŏnggido, the Chŏng family of Kwangju Majae Kyŏnggido, the Yu Hang-gŏm family of Chŏnju Chŏllado, and the Yun Chi-ch'ung (1759-1791) family. Yun was a seventh generation descendant of Yun Sŏn-do (1587-1671, penname Kosan) who had an excellent reputation as a distinguished scholar, a poet and a statesman during the Chosŏn dynasty. He was also the great-grandson of Yun Tu-sŏ, who was the foremost painter of his generation.[188]

Despite the fact that Yun Sŏn-do had been accused as the leader of the *Namin* and was forced to live in harsh exile in places such as Kyŏngwŏn, Yŏngdŏk and Samsu, his renowned scholarship and his family members' successes in the civil service examinations nevertheless gave him the reputation as one of the most distinguished scholars of the dynasty. His great-grandson, Kongjae Yun Tu-sŏ, passed the *chinsa* examination in 1693, and he was so gifted in painting live creatures that he, along with *Hyŏnjae* (Sim Sa-chŏng) and *Kyŏmjae* (Chŏng Sŏn), could have been considered as the *Samjae* of Chosŏn.[189]

Yun Kongjae married a great-granddaughter of Yi Su-kwang, who was a sixth generation descendant of the Lord of Kyŏngnyŏnggun, one of the sons of T'aejong, Chosŏn's third king. His father-in-law Yun Tu-sŏ married the Royal Secretary Yi Tong-kyu, who was the second son of Sŏng-ku. Sŏng-ku was Yi Su-kwang's eldest son, and a former Chief State Councillor under Injo.[190] The two

---

[188] *Haenam Yun-ssi sebo* . From the fifth generation descendant Ku (1516), sixth Hong-jung (1546), seventh Yu-gi (1580), eighth Sŏn-do (1633) to In-mi (1663) all successfully passed the civil examination. *cf. Mansŏng taetongbo* (Grand genealogy of the ten thousand names) , vol. 1 pp.281bpp.

[189] An Hwi-chun, *Han'guk misulsa* (A History of Korean Painting), (Seoul: Ilchisa, 1984), p.213.

[190] For the very first time in Korea, Yi Su-kwang introduced "The True Meaning of the Lord of Heaven" by Matteo Ricci in his

families were both from the *Namin* background and thus seem to have married within the same faction.

Yun Tu-sŏ and his brothers Hng-sŏ and Chong-sŏ were the "three brothers *Chinsa*." The fourth son among the nine sons of Yun Tu-sŏ, Tŏk-yŏl, had a son Kyŏng who married a daughter of Kwŏn Ki-jing of the Andong Kwŏn clan and gave birth to Yun Chi-ch'ung, who died a martyr.[191]

The following is an investigation of the family relationships of Kwŏn Ki-jing, the father of Kwŏn Sang-yŏn, who was executed along with Yun Chi-ch'ung, the pivotal figure in the Rites Controversy of 1791. Kwŏn Ki-jing was also closely acquainted with Yu Hang-gŏm, who was a key contributor to the expansion of Catholicism in Chŏllado. His great-grandfather was Kwŏn Si, pen name T'an'ong, who had served as Hansŏng-bu Uyun (Vice Magistrate of Seoul).[192]

Having five daughters but no son, Kwŏn Ki-jing adopted his cousin Wi-jing's son, Se-hak. Ki-jing's brother, Sŏng-jing, also adopted a cousin Yŏ-jing's son. Among his five daughters, the eldest married Yun Kyŏng and gave birth to Yun Chi-ch'ung. His second daughter married Yu Tong-kn and gave birth to two sons, Hang-gŏm and Kwan-gŏm. Subsequently, Yun Chi-ch'ung and the two brothers, Hang-gŏm and Kwan-gŏm, who were earlier Catholic Church members, became cousins through maternal ties.[193]

Kwŏn Ki-jing's youngest daughter married Yun Chi-sang, who was a nephew of his eldest son-in-law Yun Kyŏng and also a son of Yun Kyŏng's cousin Yun T'aek. In the Kyuchanggak edition of the *Nambo*, the name Chi-sang

---

Chibong yusŏl. Afterwards, many Catholic figures emerged from among his descendants. *Haenam Yun-ssi sebo* (Imobo),vol.4, p.2a

[191] *Mansŏng taedongbo*, vol. 1, p.281b. *Nambo* (Owned by Yu Hong-nyŏl).vol.1, p.751.

[192] Andong Kwŏn-ssi Ch'amigongp'a.

[193] *Sahak chingi*, kwŏn II, Yu Hang-gŏm, p.228.

appears as Kyu-sang. In genealogy books and the *Nambo*, the two characters in the names *chi* and *kyu*, often appear interchanged.[194] Among the cousins of Yun Chi-ch'ung and Chi-hŏn, Kyu-ng, Kyu-baek, Kyu-han, Kyu-bŏm, and others were promoted as civil service officials, switched the two characters *chi* with *kyu*. This was probably because they felt ashamed to be cousins of the Catholic Yun Chi-ch'ung brothers and were afraid that the relationship might have a negative impact on their scholarly reputations. As described thus far, Kwŏn Ki-jing, therefore, had an extremely close relationship with the family of Yun Chi-ch'ung. Kwŏn Ki-jing's grandson, Kwŏn Sang-yŏn, a son of Se-ki, who died a martyr along with Yun Chi-ch'ung, had a son, Hyŏk. He did not have a son, and his daughter married Han Kwang-yŏl.[195]

Yun Chi-ch'ung's younger brother Yun Chi-hŏn married Hang-gŏm's cousin, Yu Chong-hang.[196] Therefore, Yun Chi-hŏn's marriage was one that already overlapped within the family of Yu Tong-kn because of the relationship with his father. It is generally understood that Yun Chi-ch'ung came to believe in the new religion as a member of the politically ostracized *Namin* faction, and was influenced by his father's family and his mother's family.

The descendants of Yun Chi-ch'ung's family suffered from the battle between Yun Sŏn-do and *Sŏin* (The Westerners). In the case of Yun Tu-sŏ, for example, despite his talent in academic scholarship, he led a life of misfortune, devoted entirely to the arts. It also appears that although Yun Chi-ch'ung himself did not become a *Chinsa*, his frustration at his faction's isolation drove him to abandon his dream early on of achieving success in the civil

---

[194]*Nambo* (Owned by Kyuchanggak), p.587.

[195]*Andong Kwŏn-ssi chokbo*, hwang (Kapinbo).

[196]In the*Nambo*, Chi-hŏn is recorded as Chng's son. However, according to the 1911 *Sinhanbo* edition of the genealogy, Chi-hŏn is Yun Kyŏng's adopted son.

service examination.[197]

In addition to the marriage ties described above, Yun Chi-ch'ung was able to cultivate interest in Catholicism through his family's close relationship with the family of Chŏng Yag-yong. His paternal aunt was the second wife of Chŏng Chae-wŏn, who had served as a *moksa* (Magistrate) in Chinju. Chŏng Chae-wŏn had Chŏng Yak-hyŏn with his first wife Uiryŏng Nam Ha-dŏk's daughter, and upon her death, he married the daughter of Yun Tŏk-yŏl. With his second wife, who was Yun Chi-ch'ung's aunt, Chŏng Chae-wŏn had Yak-chŏn, Yak-chong, Yag-yong and a daughter. Chŏng Chae-wŏn's son-in-law was Yi Sŭng-hun, one of the founders of the early Chosŏn Catholic church. Therefore, Yun Chi-ch'ung and Chŏng Yag-yong were cousins through his father's sister and Yun Chi-ch'ung and Yi Sŭng-hun were also relatives. Furthermore, Yi Pyŏk's elder sister was Chŏng Yak-chŏn's wife, and thus Yun Chi-ch'ung was also distantly related to Yi Pyŏk. Consequently, with such numerous familial ties, Yun Chi-ch'ung was able to come into contact with Catholicism earlier than others.

Another reason stems from the fact that both his father's and his mother's families had a keen interest in *Silhak*. Although the anti-Western faction launched a severe attack at the time of the Rites Controversy, his clan did not engage in a harsh rebuttal. This is perhaps an illustration of the ideological progressiveness on the part of the members of both families.

The Yu Hang-gŏm family

A man of national renown,[198] Yu Hang-gŏm of Chŏnju was a priest of the false ecclesiastical order of the early Chosŏn Catholic church and had contributed significantly to the dissemination of Catholicism in Chŏllado. Until now, his family origin had not been closely

---

[197] Chu Myŏng-jun, *op.cit.*, p.32.
[198] *Sahak chingi*, kwon 1, p.28.

investigated, and it was only recently that he was found to be from the Chinju Yu clan.[199] Yu Hang-gŏm's half brother, Kwan-gŏm, actively participated in church activities along with him. Their father was Yu Tong-kn; Hang-gŏm's mother was a daughter of Kwŏn Ki-jing, and Kwan-gŏm's mother was the daughter of Yu Ŏn-do.

One of his ancestors, Sŏjae Yu Sun-sŏn, had passed the *Sama* examination in 1546, the *Munkwa* (civil service examination) in the following year. In 1556, he even passed the *Chungsi* examination. At this time, he corresponded with Yun Sŏn-do's grandson, Yun ¬i-jing, and maintained a kinship relationship until the generation of Yun Chi-ch'ung and Yu Hang-gŏm.[200]

Yu Hang-gŏm's descendants had served successively in office. However, since Su-bang, Yu Hang-gŏm's ancestor of the fifth generation above him, had been successful in the civil service (1673), none of the others were successful in attaining a government post. After Yu Hang-gŏm's family moved to Chŏnju, only his elder brother Ik-kŏm and his cousin Kuk-kŏm passed the *Saengwŏnsi* examination, and the rest of the family enjoyed not a single examination success. The cause behind such a trend can be seen to be rooted in the fact that their family was *Namin*.[201]

Despite such a disadvantage, the two brothers, Yu Hang-gŏm and Kwan-gŏm did not abandon their past and continued with their challenge.[202] The reason for which they aspired to a position in the civil service was because "it soon became a primary determinant of social status and also provided a major means whereby economic wealth might be accumulated. In a society that recognized government service as the chief glory to which man might properly aspire, the successful examination candidate during the Yi

---

[199] Chu Myŏng-jun, *op.cit.*, pp.50-59.
[200] *Ibid.*, p.64.
[201] *Ibid.*, p.68.
[202] *Sahak chingi,* Vol.II. pp. 228-234.

occupied a truly unique position."[203]

Furthermore, just as marriage was considered to be critical among the *yangban* families, Yu hang-gŏm's family also put great importance on marriage ties from generation to generation. For example, the wife of Si-jae, Yu Hang-gŏm's ancestor of seven generations above, was from the Chŏnju Yu clan, and she was a daughter of Yu Yŏng-kyŏng, a former Chief State Councillor.[204] Although his family had not been too successful in attaining prestigious government posts, he was nationally reknowned for the fortune he had accumulated,[205] and thus was able to establish marriage relationships with noble families of the time.

Yu Hang-gŏm's son, Chung-ch'ŏl married Yi Yun-ha's daughter Yi (Lugartha) Sun-i, and they are known for dying as martyrs in 1801 while maintaining their chastity. The two families already had a history of intermarriage over several generations. Yu Sŏk-chun, Yu Hang-gŏm's ancestor of eight generations above, had married the daughter of Yi Hi-ch'ŏm of Kyŏngryŏngun branch of the Chŏnju Yi clan. She was also the elder sister of Yi Su-kwang.

Yu Chung-tae, who, along with Yu Hang-gŏm, had participated in the movement to invite Catholic priests from abroad, was Hang-gŏm's first male cousin once removed and was married to the niece of Yun Chi-ch'ung's younger brother Chi-hŏn's wife. As mentioned previously, Yun Chi-ch'ung's mother and Yu Hang-gŏm's mother were the daughters of Kwŏn Ki-jing and were the paternal aunts of Kwŏn Sang-yŏn. Therefore, Yu Hang-gŏm and Yun Chi-ch'ung are cousins through the mother's sister, and with

---

[203] Edward Wagner, "The Civil Examination Process as Social Leaven: The Case of the Northern Provinces in the Yi Dynasty," A paper prepared for the International Sympositum commemorating the 30th Anniversary of Korean Liberation, Aug 11-20, 1975, Seoul, Korea.

[204] Chŏnju Yu-ssi chokpo.

[205] *Sahak chingi*, Vol.1, p.28.

Kwŏn Sang-yŏn, they were cousins by their father's sisters.

Yu Hang-gŏm and Yun Chi-ch'ung were cousins on the mother's side, and Yun Chi-ch'ung and Chŏng Yag-yong were cousins by a paternal aunt as well as a maternal cousin. At the same time, even if it had not been for Yun Chi-ch'ung, it is likely that Yu Hang-gŏm was already directly acquainted with Kwŏn Il-sin's family and Chŏng Yag-yong's family. This is because he himself was a *Namin* and also because before his family moved to Chŏllado, the residence of the family had been Yŏju and Yangju of Kyŏnggido since his great-great-grandfather's time and his eldest uncle's family continued to live in these towns,[206] where Kwŏn Il-sin's family resided.

It is assumed that Yu Hang-gŏm and Tasan maintained a close relationship through Yun Chi-ch'ung. From a citation from the *Sahak chingi*, "how could the request for the dispatch of ships be deliberated when Hang-gŏm was without Yag-yong,"[207] it can be inferred that the two had had a close relationship.

It is recorded that Yu Hang-gŏm first came in contact with Catholicism in the year Sinhae, 1791, through Catholic books lent by Yun Chi-ch'ung, and came to have belief in the religion.[208] Another record shows that his younger brother Kwan-gŏm converted to Catholicism in the Year Kyŏngsul, 1790.[209]

The Kwŏn Ch'ŏl-sin Family

The Andong Kwŏn clan is closely associated with the early Chosŏn Catholic church. Among the members, the most illustrative lineage was that of Kwŏn Ch'ŏl-sin and Il-sin (17th generation descendant of Po) who was a

---

[206] Chu Myŏng-jun, *op.cit.*, p.76.

[207] *Sahak chingi*, p.378.

[208] Sahak choein Yu Hang-gŏm tng ch'uhan, 48-49

[209] *Sahak chingi*, p.231.

descendant of Ko, the third son among the five sons of Po. Another lineage was of the descendants of the fourth son of Po, Wang-ku, which later became a highly distinguished Tanong Kwon clan. Tanong Kwŏn Si established a relationship with Song Si-yŏl through marriage, and he became known throughout his generation by having Yun Chng (1629-1714), the Third State Councillor, as his son-in-law (also his former student). Moreover, the son-in-law of Yun Kk-chi (1538-1592) was the Second State Councillor, Wŏlsa Yi Chŏng-kwi(1564-1635) and brother-in-law of Tanong, who was son-in-law of Tk-ki, was the Chief State Councillor prime minister Sim Chi-wŏn(1593-1662), and competed heavily to marry into the family of Kwŏn Kk-in's brothers.[210]

Kwŏn Ch'ŏl-sin was a famous scholar of the study of *kyŏngsŏ* and *yesŏ,* and his younger brother Kwŏn Il-sin was also a leading figure among *Namin,* Yu Hang-gŏm visited them in Yanggn, learned of Western Learning, and was baptized. The Yu Hang-gŏm's maternal great-grandfather in law was Kwŏn Ki-ching of the Andong Kwŏn-ssi, and although he was a distant relative of Kwŏn Ch'ŏl-sin (1736-1801) and Il-sin (1751-1792), they were all of one family. Therefore, as a maternal grandson of Kwŏn Ki-ching, it was natural that Yu Hang-gŏm was close to the family of Kwŏn Il-sin.

In fact, there was much intermarriage among the Yu and Kwŏn families. Yu Hang-gŏm's son, Chung-chŏl married Yi Sun-i, whose mother was also from the Kwŏn family. The brothers, Kwŏn Ch'ŏl-sin and Il-sin's maternal uncle was Hong Kyo-man of Namyang Hong clan. He lived in P'och'ŏn, Kyŏnggido, and when the Kwŏn family joined the Catholic organization, his son In became a Catholic first, and then encouraged his father Kyo-man to join the church. Later during the Sinyu Persecution in1801, both the father and the son died martyrs. Hong Ik-man, Hong Kyo-man's cousin and his son Hong P'il-chu all died martyrs in 1801, and Ik-man's son-in-law Yi Hyŏn, nephew of painter Yi Hi-

---

[210]Kang Chu-jin, *Yijo tangjaeng yŏn'gu*, p.133.

yŏng, also died a martyr in 1801.[211]

Yu Hang-gŏm and Hong Nag-min (1740-1801) of the P'ungsan Hong clan kept in close touch. Hong Nak-min originally lived in Yesan, Ch'ungch'ŏngdo, but upon becoming a *Chinsa*, he moved his residency to Seoul, and afterwards, he passed the Munkwa examination in 1789. It is assumed that he first came in contact with Catholicism in 1784 through Yi Chae-chang.[212] As one of the leaders in the early stages of the founding of the Chosŏn Catholic church, he was a priest of the false ecclesiastical hierarchy.

Nag-min's older brother was Nak-kyo, and his son Kap-yŏng married the daughter of Yi Yun-ha. Thus, Yi Yun-ha established a relationship with the Nak-kyo brothers. Another daughter of Yi Yun-ha married Yu Hang-gŏm's son Chung-ch'ŏl. Based on such relationships, Yu Hang-gŏm was related to Hong Nag-min and Yi Yun-ha's family through marriage.

Hong Nag-min's second son Chae-yŏng is the son-in-law of Chŏng Yag-yong's older brother, Yak-Hyŏn. Yak-Hyŏn's other son-in-law was Hwang Sa-yŏng. Yu Hang-gŏm was already an in-law to Chŏng Yag-yong through his relationship with Yun Chi-ch'ung, and through his in-law relationship with Yi Yun-ha; he also became related to Chŏng Yag-yong and Hwang Sa-yŏng through marriages.

With such connections, Yu Hang-gŏm was intimately related to Kwŏn Il-sin, Chŏng Yag-yong, Yi Ka-hwan, Hong Nag-min, Yi Yun-ha and Yi Sŭng-hun through direct and indirect marital ties, and thus he was able to acquire a substantial amount of information on Catholicism and convert to Catholicism.

The Chŏng Yag-yong Family

It is difficult to find a family during the early part of

---

[211] Han'guk Kat'ollik tae sajŏn, Appendix, (Seoul: Han'guk kyohoesa yŏn'guso, 1985), p.193.

[212] Chu Myŏng-jun, *op.cit.*, p.101.

the Chosŏn dynasty whose members can match the substantial contribution to Korea and the numerous kinship relationships of Tasan and his two brothers of the Naju Chŏng family of Kyŏnggido Kwangju, Majae: Chŏng Yak-chŏn (1758-1816), Chŏng Yak-chŏng Augustine (1760-1801), and Chŏng Yag-yong John the Baptist (1762-1836).[213] Because the poet Chŏng Yun-jong had lived in Ap'hae, the Naju Chŏng-ssi is sometimes referred to as Ap'hae Chŏng-ssi.

The Chŏng family had lived in Hwanghaedo Paekch'ŏn until the end of the Koryo dynasty, and then as the Chosŏn dynasty became firmly established, they moved to Hanyang. Among their ancestors, there were Su-gon (Munkwa 1472) and Su-kang (Munkwa 1477). In the middle of the Chosŏn dynasty, Chŏng Yun-bok passed the civil service examination in 1567 and served as *Taesahŏn* (Inspector-General).[214] Among seven sons of Chŏng Yun-bok, three of them had successfully passed the civil service examination, and Tasan is the 11th generation descendant of Hosŏn who passed the examination in 1602.

Chŏng Si-yun, Tasan's ancestor of the fifth generation above, passed the civil service examination in 1690 and served as *Chami* of Board of Punishments. After Sukchong's reign, he led a life far removed from government affairs in Kyŏnggido Kwangju Majae, for he was *Namin*. The Chŏng family moved back to Seoul when Tasan's father Chŏng Chae-wŏn became *Chwarang* (Assistant Section Chief) of the Board of Taxation. Tasan received most of his education from his maternal great-grandfather Hong Hwa-bo.[215]

Chŏng Chae-wŏn married the daughter of Nam Ha-

---

[213] Although Tasan was the youngest of the three, since his name is widely known, the Tasan three brothers are often referred to as Chŏng Yag-yong and his brothers.

[214] *Chŏng Tasan chŏnsŏ*, (Seoul: Munhŏn p'yŏn ch'an wiwŏnhoe, 1960), p.325.

[215] *Yŏyudang chŏnsŏ* (Supplement), p.662.

dŏk and had a son, Yak-hyŏn. Upon the early death of his wife, he married the daughter of Yun Tŏk-yŏl who was also the granddaughter of Yun Tu-sŏ. She was the sister of the very first martyr in Korea, Yun Chi-ch'ung. His second wife gave birth to four sons and a daughter - Chŏng Yak-chŏn, Yak-chŏng, Yag-yong, and Yi Sŭng-hun's wife. In addition, Chŏng Chae-wŏn had two daughters and a son from his concubine, among which the first daughter married Hong-kn, a concubine's child of Ch'ae Che-gong, the Chief State Councillor at the time; the second daughter married Yi Chung-sik; and the son is Yak-kwang.

Chŏng Myŏng-nyŏn, a daughter of Tasan's eldest brother, Yak-hyŏn, married Hwang Sa-yŏng, who was famous for the *Paeksŏ* ("Silk Letter") Incident in 1801. Hwang Sa-yŏng was from the Ch'angwŏn Hwang clan, but little was known of his lineage of descent. Furthermore, Yi Ch'i-hun, the younger brother of Yi Sŭng-hun, married the daughter of Kwŏn I-kang, and since Kwŏn I-kang was Chŏng Yag-yong's maternal great-grandfather, Yi Sŭng-hun and Tasan were closely related through overlapping inter-marriages.[216]

The Tasan family was thus intimately related to Catholicism. Living in Kwangju and Yanggn over many generations, they exchanged academic correspondence and established marital ties with *Namin* families of the region. Tasan's older sister married Yi Sŭng-hun, the very first Chosŏn individual to be baptized and also the nephew of Yi Ka-hwan, who was a great-grandson of the leading *Silhak* scholar of the generation, Yi Ik. In addition, Tasan's eldest son, Hak-yŏn, married the sister of Yi Sŭng-hun, who was in fact the older sister of his paternal uncle, and became twice in-laws.

Tasan's mother, Yun-ssi, was the daughter of Yun Tŏk-nyŏl and Yun Chi-ch'ung's paternal aunt who died a martyr during the Rites Controversy of 1791. Subsequently, Tasan and Yun Chi-ch'ung were related through their fathers and mothers. Through these blood ties, Yun Chi-ch'ung

---

[216] *Ibid.*, Ap'hae Chŏng-ssi Kasngpyŏn, p.662.

was able to come in contact with Catholicism in the country side, far from Seoul.

Yu Hang-gŏm of Chŏnju, who played a critical role in the dissemination of Catholicism in Chŏllado, and Yun Chi-ch'ung both married the daughters of Kwŏn Ki-ching, and thus were cousins through their mothers' line.

Kwŏn Sang-yŏn, who died a martyr along with Yun Chi-ch'ung during the *Chinsan* incident, was the nephew of Yun Chi-ch'ung's wife from the Kwŏn clan, and therefore the two are related through their father and mother's lines. It follows from this that Yu Hang-gŏm and Kwŏn Sang-yŏn are also cousins by both paternal and maternal lines.

Furthermore, Tasan and Hong Nak-min (1740-1801) who had passed the civil service examination and who died a martyr were also in-laws. Hong Nak-min's son Hong Chae-yŏng was Chŏng Yak-hyŏn's son-in-law, and thus was a brother-in-law to Hwang Sa-yŏng.

Tasan and the very first Chosŏn Catholic believer Yi Pyŏk were also related. Tasan's eldest brother Chŏng Yak-hyŏn married the daughter of Yi Po-man, Yi Pyŏk's elder sister. Yak-hyŏn had seven sons-in-law, but two, Hong Chae-yŏng and Hwang Sa-yŏng, died martyrs. It is rather strange that there was no kin relationship, despite the numerous writings that proposed "extermination" of the Chŏng Yag-yong brothers, who must have been regarded as authoritarian in their views in the field of history.

Tasan's half sister married the only son, though that of a concubine, of Ch'ae Che-gong's direct line, who was Hong-kn. Although they had no direct relations to Catholicism, one of the reasons for Ch'ae Che-gong's possessing all kinds of books on Catholicism was probably due to his relationship with both families.

Chŏng Yak-chŏn (1758-1816) passed the civil service examination of Chngkwangsi in 1790 and married the daughter of Kim Sŏ-ku. He rose to the government post of *chwaryang* of the Board of Military.[217] Upon converting to Catholicism, he devoted himself to the

---

[217] Naju Chŏng-ssi chokpo kwŏn 7, p.4.

religious life as a Catholic.

It was illuminated in his memorial to the king in 1797 that Chŏng Yak-yong developed his interest in Western Learning mainly from his curiosity in the various new fields of Western scholarship such as astrology, manufacturing, agriculture, and mathematics.[218]

Yi Pyŏk's elder sister who married Chŏng Yak-hyŏn died early. Due to relationships such as this, Chŏng Yagyong, Yak-chŏn brothers came into contact with and learned about Catholic doctrines through Yi Pyŏk. On the fifteenth day of the fourth month of 1784, when Tasan was 23 years old, he was on his way back from the fourth anniversary of the death of his elder brother Yak-chŏn's (1751-1821) wife, Kyŏngju Yi -ssi (1750-1780). On the ship headed back to Tumihyŏp, Tasan first heard about Catholicism through Yi Pyŏk. The fifteenth day of the fourth month of 1784 was only 20 some days after Yi Sŭng-hun had returned from Beijing, baptized and with books on the Western religion.[219]

It is recorded that upon hearing his elder sister-in-law's younger brother explain the Catholic doctrines on the concepts of heaven and hell, creation of the world, man and god, and life and death, Tasan became shocked and fascinated. Then he followed Yi Pyŏk to his house and borrowed "The True Meaning of the Lord of Heaven" and "The Seven Overcomings," to which he became devoted.[220] However, it is reasonable to assume that he had already heard about the Western Religion at the Ch'ŏnjinam and Chuŏsa meeting in 1779, but that it was not

---

[218] *Chosŏn wangjo sillok*, Chŏngjo 21year.6th month. Kyŏngin day, p.26.

[219] Chŏng Yag-yong, "Chach'an myojimyŏng," *Chŏng Tasan chŏnsŏ*, (Seoul: Munhŏn p'yŏnch'an wiwŏnhoe, 1960), p.326 & "Sŏn chungssi myojimyŏng," *Ibid.*, p.324.

[220] *Ibid.*, p.324.

until 1784 that he came to have a religious faith.[221]

Among Tasan's family members, his father Chae-wŏn and his eldest brother Yak-hyŏn did not believe in Catholicism, and his mother Yun-ssi never had the chance to come in contact with Catholicism since she had died when Tasan was only nine years old.[222] Besides these individuals, almost every other member of the Chŏng family had some relationship to Catholicism.

In 1784,[223] the same year Chŏng Yag-yong was baptized, his second elder brother, Chŏng Yak-chŏn was baptized by Yi Sŭng-hun at Yi Pyŏk's house.[224] Meanwhile, Chŏng Yak-chong, who was the most ardent Catholic of all three brothers, admitted that he learned Catholicism from his elder brother Yak-chŏn in 1786 and thus became a devout Catholic. However, it is understood that he had also heard and known about the Western Religion in the past, but only came to be baptized then.[225]

Although Chŏng Yak-chong converted to Catholicism much later than his two brothers, Yak-chŏn and Yag-yong had, he led a religious life of the most firm conviction and with greatest determination. Although in the third month of 1786, influenced by brothers, his two brothers left the church due to the persecution accompanying the Sinhae Chinsan Incident, Chŏng Yak-chong remained undeterred from his pursuits.[226]

---

[221] Chu Myŏng-jun, "Chŏng Yag-yong hyŏngje dl i ch'ŏnjugyo sinang," *Chŏnju sahak* I, 1984, p.82.

[222] Chŏng Yag-yong, *op.cit.*, p.326.

[223] Chu Myŏng-jun, *op.cit.*, p.84.

[224] "The Trial record Yi Ka-hwan and others, Statement of Yi Sng-hun."

[225] "The Trial record Yi Ka-hwan and others, Statement of Chŏng Yak-chong," Chu Myŏng-jun *op.cit.*, p.83.

[226] "The Trial record Yi Ka-hwan and others, Statement of Chŏng Yak-chong," *Hwang Sayŏng Paeksŏ*, 36th line, (trans. by Yun Chae-yŏng), p.46.

Although only one wife, Yi Su-chŏng's daughter, is recorded in the Yu Hong-nyŏl edition of *Nambo* , Yak-chong had three wives in total, the other two being members of Kyŏngju Ch'oe clan and Munhwa Yu clan. Being well versed in the Catholic doctrines, Yak-chong published the very first book of Catholic doctrines, called "*Chugyo yoji* (Essentials of the Lord's Teaching) in 1790's, and made a significant contribution to the advancement and the proliferation of the Catholic Church. This book was even praised by priest Chou Wen-mo.[227] In addition; he devoted all of his effort and enthusiasm in teaching these doctrines.

Chŏng Ch'ŏl-sang (-1801) , the eldest son of Yak-chong and his wife Yu Cecilia (1761-1839) died a martyr and Yak-chong's second son, Ha-sang, also died a martyr after submitting an entreating *"Sangchae sangsŏ"* (Letter to the High Minister). Even his daughter Chŏng Chŏng-hye (1797-1839) died a martyr, from which it can be inferred that due to the strict doctrinal education within his family, the family members came to adhere firmly to Catholicism.

The Yi Pyŏk family

Yi Pyŏk's great- grandfather, Yi Kyŏng-sang (1603-1647) was a member of the *Sigangwŏn* (Crown Prince Tutorial Office) who had accompanied Crown Prince Sohyŏn when he was taken as a hostage to Ch'ing China during the Mongol Invasion, and it is said that he even met Adam Schall with the Crown Prince, in their way coming into contact with Catholicism.[228] Yi Pyŏk's grandfather was Yi Tal (also written Yi Kŏn)(1703-1773), who had been promoted to middle rank military officer and served as a Chŏlla *pyŏngma chŏltosa* (Commander in Chief), who married the daughter of Kwŏn Hu-sang, a *chinsa* of the Andong Kwŏn clan. His father was Yi Po-man (1727-1812)

---

[227] *Hwang Sa-yŏng Paeksŏ*, 37th line.

[228] Kim Ok-hi, *Han'guk ch'ŏnjukyo sasangsa* I, (A history of Korean Catholic thought), (Seoul: Sunkyo i maek, 1990), p.12.

and his mother was the daughter of Han Chong-hae of the Ch'ŏngju Han clan. Between them were born three sons and three daughters. Their first daughter was Han Ch'i-yŏng. The second daughter married Chŏng Yak-hyŏn, an older brother of Tasan, and it was a marriage by which a family connection was established and by which she even engaged in academic interchange with Tasan. The third daughter was married to Hong Yun-ho of the P'ungsan Hong clan. Yi Pyŏk's older brother, Yi Kyŏk, and younger brother, Yi Sŏk, were military officers who had successfully passed the military service examination. Yi Pyŏk, on the other hand, was solely interested in academic scholarship.[229]

Yi Pyŏk's first marriage was to the daughter of Kwŏn Ŏm (1729-1801)[230] of the Andong Kwŏn clan. However, upon her early death, he remarried a woman from a Haeju Chŏng lineage.

The Yi Sŭng-hun Family

Yi Sŭng-hun, Korea's founding father of the Chosŏn Catholic church along with Yi Pyŏk, is of the P'yŏngch'ang Yi clan. The founder of the clan was Yi Kwang, and his fifteenth generation descendant, Yi Ok, was a Chief State Councillor during the first year of Sŏnjo. Afterwards, however, not too many of such successful individuals were born and their status as *Namin* drove their descendants to live in hiding.

Although his clan belonged to the *Namins*, the time from which his family had been registered as *Namin* is unknown.[231] In 1766, the Pyongsul year during the reign

---

[229] *Ibid.*, p.12.

[230] Following the decree prohibiting Catholicism, he became extremely frustrated with his son in law, Yi Pyŏk, to the point that he participated in the "63 men Petition" in the spring of 1801.

[231] Yu Hong -nyŏl, "Yi Sng-hun kwa k husondl i sunkyo," *Hakuk sahoesasangsa nongo*, (Seoul: Ilchogak, 1980), p.208.

of Yŏngjo, Yi Sŭng-hun's father, Yi Tong-uk passed the civil examination and served in the post of the mayor of Uiju.

Yi Sŭng-hun's mother was Yi Yong-hyu's daughter, the grandniece of Sŏngho Yi Ik, and also the elder sister of Yi Ka-hwan.[232] His wife was the daughter of Chŏng Chae-wŏn, Tasan's elder sister.[233] He established in-law relationships with the Naju Chŏng family through his own marriage and with the Yŏju Yi family through his father's marriage.

Strongly urged by his father's request, at one point, he burned several books on Western Learning and even left a piece of writing as if he had abandoned the Catholic Church.[234] However, in the 11th year of Chŏngjo, Chŏngmi year (1787), along with Chŏng Yak-chŏn and Kwŏn Il-sin, he revived the movement for the Catholic Church. In the fifteeth year of Chŏngjo, 1791, they even gathered at Kim Sŏk-tae's house in Panch'on with the excuse that the purpose of the meeting was to write poetry, but read together books on Catholicism, which caused trouble.[235]

The Yi Ki-yang Family

Yi Ki-yang (1744-1802) was from the Kwangju Yi clan and was a seventh generation descendant of Yi Tŏk-hyŏng, a former Chief State Councillor under Sŏnjo and Kwanghae-kun. In 1774, he passed the *Chinsa* examination and in 1795, he passed the civil service examination. His father was Yi Chong-han and his mother was Chŏng Hyŏn-sŏ's daughter. Although his parents did not convert to Christianity, his son and daughter became Christian. Their

---

[232] *Chosŏn wangjo sillok*, *Sunjo* wŏnyŏn 2nd month, Imsin(26).

[233] *Naju Chŏng-ssi chokpo*, p.7-

[234] *Chosŏn wangjo sillok* Chŏngo15th year 11th month Kimyo.

[235] *IbidI.*, Chŏngjo 15th year11th month Kapsin.

son, Pang-ŏk married the daughter of Yi Ka-hwan, and another son, Ch'ŏng-ok married the daughter of Kwŏn Ch'ŏl-sin. Their daughter married the son of Hong Nak-min, Paek-yŏng. Yi Ki-yang's younger brother, Yi Ki-song became a Catholic.

The Yi Yun-ha family

Chibong Yi Su-kwang, who is considered to be the father and the pioneer of *Silhak*, introduced the situation of the Western empire and Catholicism to Koreans. Among his eighth generation descendants, Yi Yun-ha became a follwer of Catholicism, and oddly, among his ninth generation descendants, three siblings, Yi Kyŏng-do, Yi Sun-i and Yi Kyŏng-ŏn, all died martyrs.[236]

Among Chibong's direct descendants, the eldest son, Sŏng-ku (1584-1644) passed the civil service examination (1608) and even served the post of Chief State Councillor, and his second son, Min-ku served as the Second Minister of Board of War. Thus up to the fifth generation, descendants of Yi Su-kwang were successful in attaining high government posts, but starting with the sixth generation descendants, successful ones became few. Among the seventh generation descendants, there is Kk-song, who served as a Hyŏnkam (county magistrate) and Ik-sŏng who served as Ch'ŏmji (associate initiates).

The apparent reason behind the lack of successful individuals of the sixth generation stems mainly from the timing, at which point the party strife against the *Namins* reached its pinnacle, and *Namin lost* their political power in the twentieth year of Sukchong (1694). Afterwards, they abandoned their efforts at entering the political field and led the lives of a recluse.[237]

Possible supporting evidence for the above inference is Chibong's seventh generation descendant, Yi

---

[236] Yu Hong-nyŏl, *Han'guk sasangsa nongo* p.177.
[237] *Ibid.*, p.192.

Kk-sŏng, who spent eighty years of his life in the local region of Kyŏnggido Kwangju, pursuing academic scholarship and writing *Tangp'yŏngch'aek* . He was a *Namin* who refused to accede to Yŏngjo's calling to serve a high government post, and who was the son-in-law of Sŏngho Yi Ik, the great scholar of *Silhak*.

Yi Sŏng-ho's son-in-law, Yi Kk-sŏng's adopted son was Yi Yun-ha,[238] the active Catholic who attended the conferences at Ch'ŏnjinam Chuŏsa during the early stage of the Chosŏn Catholic church and who even retrieved the holy images from the Board of Punishments during the Incident of Detection of the Catholics in 1785.[239]

Yi Yun-ha married a daughter of Kwŏn Ŏm, who was the father of the leader of the early stage of Chosŏn Catholic church, Kwŏn Ch'ŏl-sin. In other words, he became the brother-in-law of Kwŏn Il-sin, who was very active in the early Catholic movement.

Yi Sŭng-hun was Yi Yun-ha's nephew. Yi Sŭng-hun was the nephew of Yi Ka-hwan, Yi Ik's great-grandson, who was his elder sister's husband. Yi Yun-ha's adoptive mother was Yi Ik's daughter, and thus Yi Sŭng-hun is a maternal nephew of Yi Yun-ha.

Among Yi Yun-ha's five children, Yi Kyŏng-do (Charles) and Yi Yu-hi were executed during the Sinyu Persecution of 1801, and Yi Kyŏng-ŏn died a martyr in prison in Chŏnju during the Chŏnghae Persecution in 1827.[240]

The background of Yi Yun-ha's conversion to Catholicism and his three daughters and three sons' deaths contains the influence of Matteo Ricci's "The True Meaning

---

[238] Although Yi Yun-ha was Yi Kk-sŏng's adopted son, because of his Catholic faith, with Yi Yun-ha's children, his name is not even mentioned in the family geneology.

[239] Yi Ki-kyŏng (ed.) *Pyŏkwip'yŏn,* kwon II.

[240] This lineage was not completely recorded in the family geneology as described here, and the information was obtained from documents such as Dallet and *Pyŏkwip'yŏn*.

of the Lord of Heaven" which was in Yi Su-kwang's possession at that time, and wrote about Catholicism in his *Chibong yusŏ*. Exposed to the Western books handed down by his ancestors and to Yi Ik's statement on "The True Meaning of the Lord of Heaven," and also influenced by the Kwŏn Il-sin and Kwŏn Ch'ŏl-sin brothers, who were his maternal brothers-in-law, as well as leaders in founding of the Catholic church, Yi Yun-ha became a critical figure in the early Chosŏn Catholic church.

The Yun Yu-il Family

Yun Yu-il (1758-1795), who was flogged to death during the *Sinbu yŏngip Incident (*priest invitation incident), was from the P'ap'yŏng Yun clan, and his name recorded in the family genealogy book was Yun Che-baek. His father was Chang and his grandfather was Sa-hyŏk. He had initially lived in Kyŏnggido Yŏju, but then followed his father to Yangkn where Kwŏn Ch'ŏl-sin was living at that time and became his father's student.[241] He learned about the Catholic doctrines from Kwŏn Ch'ŏl-sin and Chŏng Yag-yong [242] and was baptized by Priest Raux in Beijing.[243] He then convinced his father and his younger brother Yu-o to convert to Catholicism.

Convinced by his missionary efforts, Yun Yu-il's uncle, Yun Kwang-su also converted to Catholicism and was martyred in 1801. Yun Hyŏn's family including his wife Im-ssi and Yun Sŏn's family both converted to Catholicism and Yun Sŏn's daughters, Yun Chŏm-hye, and

---

[241] Chŏng Yag-yong, Nogam Kwŏn Ch'ŏl-sin myojimyŏng (The Epitaph of Kwŏn Ch'ŏl-sin), *op.cit.*, p.324.

[242] *Ch'uguk ilgi* (Trial Diary), *Kaksa tngrok* 78, (Seoul: Kuksa p'yŏngch'an wiwŏnhoe, 1994), p.259.

[243] Charles Dallet, *op.cit.*, (I), p.327.

Yun Un-hye both were martyred in 1801.[244] Yun Un-hye's husband, Chŏng Kwang-su also died a martyr in 1801.

Yun Yu-il was martyred in 1795 during the priest invitation incident, and his father and younger brother Yun Yu-o were arrested in 1801 during the Sinyu Persecution, upon which his father was banished to Imjado Island and his young brother was beheaded in Yangkn. His three uncles, Kwan-su, Hyŏn and Sŏn and their families, twelve people in total, were arrested and sentenced, among whom five were martyred.

Hong Yu-ho (1726-1785), who can almost be considered as the very first Catholic believer in Korea (his former name was Yu-han and his pen name was Nongn), was a member of the P'ungsan Hong clan, the Munkyŏnggong-kye Chigyegong branch. Among the members of his family, seven of them, Hong Yu-han, Nag-min, Chae-yŏng, Pyŏng-ju, Yŏng-ju, Pong-ju and Nak-kyo, were recorded as Catholic believers and five of them were martyred.

Hong Nak-kyo's son, Kap-yŏng married Yi Ik's maternal granddaughter, who was also Yi Yun-ha's daughter, [245] and Hong-Nag-min's son, Chae-yŏng married Chŏng Yak-hyŏn's daughter, thus became in-laws with Hwang Sa-yŏng (Hong Nag-min was the husband of the sister of Hwang Sa-yŏng's wife). Hong Nag-min's eldest son, Paek-yŏng married the daughter of Yi Ki-yang, who was a seventh generation descendant of Yi Tŏk-hyŏng.

The Yi Ka-hwan (Yŏhng Yi clan) Family

Sŏngho Yi Ik's nephew, Yi Ka-hwan (1742-1801) was a highly regarded figure who was even considered as a potential successor to Chae Che-gong as Chief State

---

[244] Kim Chin-so, "Chu Mun-mo sinbu sŏnkyo hwaltong chŏnhu i sunkyojadl," *Kyohoesa yon'gu* 10 (1995), p.112.

[245] Chŏng Yag-yong, Chŏnghŏn myojimyŏng, *Yŏjudang chŏnsŏ*, pp.22b-23a.

Councillor. Corresponding regularly with the key figures of the early Chosŏn Catholic church, Yi Pyŏk, Kwŏn Ch'ŏl-sin and Chŏng Yag-yong, Yi Ka-hwan actively participated and cooperated in the activities of the church, though he had never been baptized as the others had. During his service at various government posts, as a Puyun in Kwangju and as a Yusu in Kaesŏng, he even suppressed Catholic Church members at times. However, he was accused by the opposition party as the ring leader of a religious cult[246] and died in prison during the Sinyu Persecution.

Yi Ka-hwan was also related to the Yu Hang-gŏm family of Chŏllado. Among Yu Hang-gŏm's ancestors,[247] Yu Hŏn-jang's son-in-law was Yi Yong-hyu, the nephew of Sŏngho Yi Ik of the Yŏhng Yi clan. Yi Yong-hyu's son was Yi Ka-hwan, and his daughter married Yi Tong-uk of P'yŏngch'ang Yi clan and gave birth to Yi Sŭng-hun. Yi Sŭng-hun was Yi Ka-hwan's nephew and Chŏng Yak-hyŏn's brother-in-law.

Yi Ka-hwan's daughter married Pang-ŏk, the son of Yi Ki-yang who was one of the early Catholics, and thus the two became in-laws. Yi Ki-yang's son, Ch'ong-ŏk, also became a Catholic and married Kwŏn Ch'ŏl-sin's daughter. Hong Nag-min's son, Paek-yŏng became a son-in-law of Yi Ki-yang. Sin Yŏ-kwŏn, one of the early fellow church members, was Yi Ka-hwan's elder sister's son.[248]

As the investigation of the above families of several active *Namin Sip'a faction* members of the early Chosŏn Catholic church demonstrates, the families were closely tied to each other through manifold inter-marriage relationships, through memberships in similar factions and through relationships based on school ties. It is most likely that

---

[246] Yi Man-ch'ae (ed), *Pyŏkwaip'yŏn*, kwŏn 4, (Seoul: Yŏlhwadang (Reprinted), 1971), p.264.

[247] He is from the Chinju Yu clan, and in Sukchong Sinyu year (1681), he passed *Munkwa* and became *Chami* of the Board of Punishments.

[248] *Sahak chingŭi*, p.43.

dissemination and proliferation of Catholicism occurred with relative ease precisely because of these intertwined kinship relationships among the distinguished and highly reputable families.

Kwŏn Ch'ŏl-sin's maternal uncle, Hong Kyo-man, lived in Kyŏnggido P'och'on, and as Kwŏn's family joined the Catholic Church, he followed suit and contributed substantially to spreading Catholicism in his hometown. Hong Nag-min was from Ch'ungch'ongdo Yesan, and upon his success at the *Chinsa* examination, he moved to Seoul and married into the families of Yi Ki-yang and Chŏng Yag-yong, who led him to believe and practice Catholicism around 1784-85.

Having been influenced by Yi Pyŏk, Kwŏn Ch'ŏl-sin was successful in converting his own relatives and friends. His father-in-law, An Chŏng-bok, however, ignored and refused to accept the new religion to the very end[249] and openly opposed the Western Learning such as *Ch'ŏnhak mundap* and *Ch'ŏnhakko*.

Overall, the large family structure of Chosŏn contributed to the acceptance and dissemination of Catholicism. However, at the same time, it contained aspects that were hindrances to the process. For example, if one family member, especially the father, opposed the belief, then the dissemination effort within this family became difficult. It can be understood that because of the so-called family persecution, the spreading of Catholicism suffered much restriction.

Catholicism placed a Supreme Being above everything and required an absolute faith. This was a threatening challenge to the traditional Chosŏn society whose structure revolved around a patriarchic system. The father held the ultimate authority within his family and functioned as a tie that maintained the cohesion of the family, and it was often within the family that the strong reactions against its teaching occurred.

The persecution of a family signified the very first

---

[249] Yi Man-ch'ae, Pyŏkwuip'ŏn, kwŏn 2, 3.

point at which Catholicism was oppressed, and throughout the entire period of the Catholic Persecution, it was perhaps the most dangerous enticement. This was because the denial of the familial kinship relationship implies not only potential divisions within families, but also the risk of driving families into social ruin. Subsequently, the persecution families arose from the effort to prevent the fall of oneself and one's family, rather than from an ideological conflict.

In the case of Yi Sŭng-hun's family, it was his father Yi Tong-uk, and in the case of Chŏng Yak-chŏn and Chŏng Yag-yong, it was their father Chŏng Chae-wŏn, who, upon learning of their sons' conversion to Catholicism, were shocked and visited their relatives' homes to persuade their sons to repent and declare that they had renounced it. Yi Sŭng-hun was made to apologize through a writing that denounced Western Learning.[250] Chŏng Yag-yong's family members, the father and the sons, suffered from much frustration arising from mutual distrust, and the Chŏng brothers even despised their father as if he were an enemy for his forbiddance of their studies.[251]

Furthermore, even for Yi Pyŏk, who was the most ardent leader of the new religious organization, his father's attempt at suicide caused him great agony. Because he was a *yangban*, in whom the values of loyalty and filial piety had been inculcated, pressure from others caused him much anguish, and he died young at age 33 in 1786, without having attained his dream of religious accomplishments.[252]

Yi Ig-un, a *Namin* inspector of Kyŏnggido, was so adamantly opposed to Catholicism that he poisoned his son, Yi Myŏng-ho, who was a Catholic with the baptismal name

---

[250] Yi Man-ch'ae, *op.cit.*, p.106.

[251] *Chosŏn wangjo sillok*, Sunjo, The first year, 2nd month Muo.

[252] Charles Dallet, *op.cit.*, (I), pp.320-321.

of John, in his attempt to uphold the honor of his family.253

An epochal point of the dissemination of early Catholicism in Korea was aided by the crumbling of the social class system. Yi Pyŏk paid visits to and spread the Catholic teachings to those *yangban* scholars such as Yi Ka-hwan and Kwŏn Il-sin with whom he usually kept friendly relations. In addition, he transcended the boundaries of social distinctions, a forbidden practice at the time, and conducted his mission directly among the *chungin*. He succeeded in converting translator Kim Pŏm-u, and other *chungin*, Kim Chong-kyo, Chi Hwang, Ch'oe Ch'ang-hyŏn, Ch'oe In-gil.254 They had already been exposed to foreign culture and materials during their trips to Beijing, and thus their relative open mindedness allowed them to accept Yi Pyŏk's invitation

2. Catholic Incidents during the Chŏngjo Reign

Political Background: The Division of the Sip'a and Pyŏkp'a

After the first major division into Easterners (*Tongin*) and Westerners (*Sŏin*) in 1575, factional alignments and realignments became a characteristic feature of Chosŏn politics. The Easterners split again, into Southerners (*Namin*) and Northerners (*Pugin*), and then there were further subdivisions as the Southerners splintered into an Old Doctrine (*Noron*) and a Young Doctrine (*Soron*). The Old Doctrine was to prove most tenacious in clinging to power and came to dominate political decision making for several generations, until Yŏngjo (1724-1776), in an attempt to weaken their grip on power, instituted his policy of

---

253 *Chosŏn wangjo sillok,* Sunjo, the first year fourth month Kyŏngo.
254 Charles Dallet, (trans.), *op.cit.*, I, pp.308-316.

impartiality (*T'angp'yŏngch'aek*). At this point the Southerners, who had been, as noted above, the first and most eager proponents of Western Learning, began to return to the political arena and participate more fully in government.[255]

Factional strife again erupted after Yŏngjo ordered the execution of his son, Crown Prince Changhŏn, in 1762, with the major factions splitting into subfactions depending on whether they approved of the King's act (The Party of Principle, *Pyŏkp'a*) or deplored it (The Party of Expediency, *Sip'a*). After the accession of the unfortunate Crown Prince Changhŏn's son as Chŏngjo in 1776, he showed his gratitude to those who had sympathized with his father by allotting important government positions to the members of the party of Expediency, most prominently the Southerner Ch'ae Che-gong, who rose to the rank of Chief State Councillor.

Throughout Chŏngjo's reign, struggle and competition among the various factions continued. In his 14th year on the throne, 1790, religious outlook became the fault line as the Southerners, so many of whom had shown sympathetic interest in Catholicism, split into *Chaedang* (*Sinsŏp'a*, Pro-Western Faction) who believed in Catholicism and *Hongdang* (*Kongsop'a*, Anti-Western Faction) who did not believe in Catholicism.[256]

The members of the *Sinsŏp'a* were scattered throughout the nearby regions of Seoul, with Seoul as their central focus, such as P'aju, Yangju, Yangŏn and Kwangju of Kyŏnggido. They gathered from time to time to exchange and discuss opinions and to broaden their

---

[255] cf. Yu Pong-hak, "Sipp'al seki Namin ŭi punyŏl kwa Kiho Namin haktong ŭi sŏngnip." *Hansin Taehak nomnunjip* 1, 1983.

Ishii placed great emphasis on the relation between the persecution of Catholicism and factional strife, to the extent that he relied on it to explain the demise of the Chosŏn dynasty, claiming that it proved the superiority of Japan and inferiority of Korea, and thus legitimized Japan's role as colonizer.

[256] Yi Nŭng-hwa, *op.cit.*, p.43, pp.56-57.

scholarship, continuing to further their understanding of Catholicism.

The following key figures in the founding of the Chosŏn Catholic church all were *Namin* in their party affiliation: Yi Pyŏk, Yi Ka-hwan, Yi Sŏng-hun, Chŏng Yak-chŏn, Chŏng Yak-chong, Chŏng Yag-yong, Kwŏn Ch'ŏl-sin, Kwŏn Il-sin, Hwang Sa-Yŏng and others. [257]

Although the Western Learning was studied also by people such as a *Soron* member Kim Kŏn-sun, it was widely known and understood that its study was mostly monopolized by the *Namin* scholars. Their devotion to this scholarly agenda was so uniform and strong that[258] An Chŏng-bok, a scholar during Yŏngjo and Chŏngjo's reigns who was devoted to the Western Learning, wrote a letter to the Chief State Councillor, Ch'ae Che-gong, expressing his concern that the pursuit of Western Learning by individual *Namin* scholars might be exploited in the political arena, potentially leading to their defeat and every demise as a party.[259]

When Western Learning at last made its attempt to be aware of organized religion practiced in the open and thus supposedly heedless of public rebuke or private concern, to the contrary it found itself the target of barrage of vituperative criticism. *Namin Pyŏkp'a* members such as Hong Nak-an, Yi Ki-kyŏng, Mok Man-chung and others loosed an attack focusing on Catholicism. [260] They attacked even the head of the *Namin Sip'a*, Ch'ae Che-gong. This was because there had been an earlier confrontation with Cha'e Che-gong dating back to Hong Nak-an's father,

---

[257] In addition there were other *Namin* scholars who in the beginning studied the Western Learning along with the above members, but later opposed it, such as Hong Nag-an (Hi-un), Sŏng Yŏng-u, Yi Ki-kyŏng, Kang Chun-hŭm, and An Chŏng-bok.
[258] Yi Man-ch'ae, *Pyŏkwip'yŏn*, kwŏn 2.
[259] *Ibid.*, p.112.
[260] Hwang Sa-yŏng paeksŏ, 17th line.

Hong Su-bo. Hong Nak-an wrote a letter to Ch'ae Che-gong, informing him that "the bright and intelligent members of *yangban* background were all immersed in Catholicism so that we may expect to see repetitions of Chinese style popular rebellions in the near future."[261] This dangerous pronouncement was targeted at the figures close to Chŏngjo, in particular at Yi Ka-hwan, Chŏng Yag-yong and Yi Ki-yang of the *Namin*. As the head of the faction in power, Ch'ae Che-gong faced a perplexing situation given the conflicts then raging among the *Namin* themselves. King Chŏngjo had entrusted him with the task of bringing the factional strife under control, but he could do no better than employ expedient measures that likely would be ineffective. Subsequently, the fact that figures such as Yi Ka-hwan and Chŏng Yag-yong were treated rather generously owes undoubtedly to Ch'ae Che-gong. Furthermore, he did not treat harshly the Catholic and other beliefs. Discontented with such a situation, the *Kongsŏp'a* waited for a chance to destroy the *Namin Sip'a* power.

The Incident of Detection of the Catholics in 1785 (Ŭlsa Year)

Persecution of the Chosŏn Catholic church began in 1785, the year after its founding. In order to practice their faith, those who accepted the new religion early on gathered regularly at the house of *chungin* translator Kim Pŏm-u (1751-1787), who had converted to Catholicism after being a member of Yi Pyŏk's mission. He lived in a secluded valley near Namsan, where church activities were likely to escape notice.

In the spring of 1785 (Ŭlsa Year), several months after the religious meetings began, the gathering place was discovered by an officer from the Board of Punishments who had been patrolling in the capital. Passing by Kim Pŏm-u's house and suspicious that drinking and gambling might be taking place; the officer entered his house, upon

---

[261] *Chosŏn wangjo sillok*, Chŏngjo 15th year 10th month Kapja.

The Growing and the Persecutions of the Early Period

where he discovered a group of men with powdered faces, blue scarves over their heads, and behaving strangely. The officer arrested them and confiscated several items including an image of Jesus and books, which were submitted to the Ministry of Justice.[262] The individuals present at this gathering were Yi Pyŏk, who was explaining the doctrine, Yi Sŏng-hun, the three brothers of Chŏng Yak-chŏn, Chŏng Yak-chong, and Chŏng Yag-yong, and Kwŏn Il-sin and Kwŏn Sang-mun, father and son.[263]

The Board of Punishments, Kim Hwa-jin showed leniency toward the *yangban* participants, gently reproving them and sending them home, but *chungin* Kim Pŏm-u he imprisoned.[264] Meanwhile, Kwŏn Il-sin and his son, Yi Yun-ha (Yi Su-kwang's eighth generation descendant), Yi Ch'ong-ŏk (Yi Ki-yang's son and Yi Tŏk-hyŏng's an eighth generation descendant), and Chŏng Sŏp (Yi Ki-yang' maternal grandson), went to the Board of Punishments to petition for the return of the holy image.[265] Taken aback by such a demand, Kim Hwa-jin rebuked them and sent them home. When the *chungin* Kim Pŏm-u, however, refused to abjure Catholicism after much advice and coercion, Kim Hwa-jin sent him in exile to Tanyang, where he died of injuries received after torture for refusing to recant. Besides Kim Pŏm-u, sixty other church members were arrested and ten were executed.[266]

---

[262] Yi Man-ch'ae, *op.cit.*, pp.105-107.

[263] *Ibid.*

[264] *Chosŏn wangjo sillok*, Chŏngjo 15th year 11th month Kimyo.

[265] Yi Man-chae, *op.cit.*, p.106.

[266] This is referred to as the Prosecution of the Catholic Meeting by the Board of Punishments. Ch'oe Sŏg-u, *Han'guk ch'ŏnju kyohoe ŭi yŏksa*, (Seoul: Han'guk kyohoesa yŏn'guso, 1982), p.99. At a royal banquet in the Sinhae year (1791), Kim Hwa-jin recalled that when he condemned those severely deluded individuals to exile in 1785 while serving in his position at the Board

After the incident involving Kim Pŏm-u and his fellow worshippers, the Board of Punishments proclaimed Catholicism to be an evil doctrine and a heresy. In the third month of 1785, a student at the National Confucian Academy, Yi Yong-sŏ, wrote and circulated a petition demanding that his institution "expel these five or six Catholic believers as barbarians."[267] This was the very first document repudiating Catholicism written by a Confucian scholar. At this time, the government also expressed its intention to prohibit Western Learning.[268]

In the next month, Changryŏng (Third Inspector) Yu Ha-wŏn presented a memorial to the king stating, "So called Catholicism only recognizes the existence of heaven, but not the king and those who serve him. It seduces the public with its theory of heaven and hell, so that the resulting harm is worse than that of a flood or a fierce animal. Hence, it must be further prohibited through an appropriate government bureau."[269] Chŏngjo responded to such request saying, "It shall be executed as suggested."[270]

Consequently, Catholicism became prohibited as an evil doctrine by the law.[271] The following year in 1786, even the importation of Western books from Yenching was prohibited following Taesahŏn (Inspector-General) Kim I-so's memorial to the king.

This public condemnation of the Catholic faith by the authorities caused the families of several religious leaders to put pressure on them to renounce their faith. One of the church founders, Yi Sŏng-hun could not withstand his

---

of Punishments, ten or so others also voluntarily requested to be exiled.

[267] Yi Man-ch'ae, *op.cit.*, kwŏn 2, p.1b-2a.

[268] *Sahak chingŭi*, p.378.

[269] *Chosŏn wangjo slilok*, Chŏngjo 9th year 4th month Muja.

[270] *Ibid.*

[271] *Chosŏn wangjo sillok*, Chŏngjo 10th year first month Chŏngmyo.

father Yi Tong-uk's pressure and composed a written recantation of Catholicism, although he later disavowed it.[272] Chŏng Yag-yong's father Chŏng Chae-wŏn also visited his relatives and encouraged them to repent and to publicly recognize their error.[273] The father of Yi Pyŏk attempted to commit suicide after learning of his son's involvement and Yi Pyŏk eventually abandoned his belief.

Such oppression within one's family or clan was the most difficult one to withstand in the patriarchal Chosŏn society, and it was repeatedly applied during persecutions that followed these incidents. The *yangban* class faced relatively more severe oppression when compared to other classes.

Panch'on Incident in 1787

After the banning of Catholic meetings by the Ministry of Justice in 1785, they gathered secretly. In 1787, the 11th year of Chŏngjo (Chŏngmi year), Yi Sŏng-hun, Chŏng Yag-yong and Kang Yi-wŏn had lectured on Catholicism at Kim Sŏk-t'ae's house in Panch'on, near the national Confucian Academy.[274]

Yi Ki-gyŏng, a member of the of *Kongsŏp'a* (The Anti-Western faction), who had originally studied Catholic teachings with Yi Sŭng-hun and Chŏng Yag-yong, but recently had taken to denouncing Catholicism,[275] eventually reported the circumstances of the Panch'on gathering to Hong Nag-an, who then relayed this information to Chŏngjo, recommending that the participants be

---

[272] Yi Man-ch'ae, *op.cit.*, kwŏn 2, Ŭlsa ch'ujo chŏkbal.

[273] *Ibid.*

[274] *Chosŏn wangjo sillok*, Chŏngjo 15th year 11th month Kapsin. Yi Man-ch'ae, ed. *op.cit.*, p.113.

[275] Yi Man-ch'ae, *op. cit.*, Yi Ki-gyŏng's letter.

punished.276 No action was taken, but the Confucian scholars repeatedly submitted memorials to the king, describing Catholicism as a heresy that did not acknowledge the authority of one's father or one's king.

Chŏngŏn (Fourth Censor) Yi Kyŏng-myŏng, alarmed by what had come to be referred as the Panch'on Incident, presented a memorial to the king in the eighth month of the 12th year of Chŏngjo (1788), entreating him to prohibit Western Learning.277

At a gathering of Chŏngjo's cabinet members, *chwaŭichŏng* (Second State Councillor) Yi Sŏng-wŏn proposed a strict prohibition278 and *uŭichŏng*, (Third State Councillor) Ch'ae Che-gong argued that Western Learning corrupted ethical morality and the theory of heaven and hell bewitched ignorant country people, but designing a prohibitive measure was a difficult task.279 While Ch'ae Che-gong's knowledge of Western Learning was substantial and his relationship with its proponents intimate, and was implicitly sympathetic to them, in public he assumed a repudiating attitude.

After listening to the arguments made, Chŏngjo adhered to his previous stance stating, "In my opinion, I believe that if we ourselves gain further enlightenment and a just scholarship is made apparent by God's will, then such wicked academic theory will become extinguished on its own after a short life.280

---

[276] He passed the civil service examination in 1790. His father was Pok-ho, his son Wŏn-mo, cha; Inbaek. He is from the P'ungsan Hong clan, *Kongsŏp'a* (The Anti Western faction).

[277] *Chosŏn wangjo sillok*, Chŏngjo 12th year 8th month Sinmyo.

[278] *Chosŏn wangjo sillok*, Chŏngjo 12th year 8th month Imsin.

[279] *Ibid.*

[280] *Ibid.*

The Rite Controversy in 1791 (The Sinhae Chinsan Incident)

In the 15th year of Chŏngjo (1791), Yun Chi-ch'ung, a literati living in Chinsan in North Chŏlla province, and his maternal cousin, Kwŏn Sang-yŏn created a scandal when it became known that they had renounced the practice of ancestral worship and burned the ancestral tablet. When Yun Chi-ch'ung's mother Kwŏn-ssi had passed away in the fifth month of 1791, a funeral was held out, but a temporary spirit tablet and ancestral tablet were not used, and the ancestral worship ceremony was not conducted.[281]

In the spring of *Kyemyo* year (1783), Yun Chi-ch'ung had passed the chinsa examination, and the following year, went to a relative Chŏng Yag-yong's house in Seoul to continue his studies. While there he began to participate in the meetings at Kim Pŏm-u's house and became a convert to Catholicism.[282] Later, when he accompanied Chŏng Yak-chŏn on a diplomatic mission to China, he received the baptismal name of Paul and became a member of the Catholic Church. Kwŏn Sang-yŏn borrowed books from his maternal cousin Yun Chi-ch'ung and also came to believe in Catholicism.[283]

In the midst of increasing social criticism of the new religion, Bishop Alexander de Gouvea's statement that ancestral worship must not be conducted and ancestral tablets must not be preserved reached the members of the Chosŏn church through Yun Yu-il, who went to Beijing as a secret envoy in 1789 and 1790. Thus Yun Chi-ch'ung had acted in compliance with the Bishop's decree and his mother's request that her funeral not be performed in a superstitious way.[284]

---

[281] Yi Man-ch'ae, *op.cit.*, kwŏn 2, p.122.

[282] *Chosŏn wangjo sillok*, Chŏngjo 15th year 11th month Kimyo.

[283] *Chosŏn wangjo sillok*, Chŏngjo 15th year 11th month Muin.

[284] The third letter of the Bishop de Gouvea, August 15th, 1797, *Kyohoesa yŏn'gu* 8, 1992, p.192.

Through words of mouth of those who came to give their condolence at the funeral, the news was spread that Yun Chi-ch'ung had failed to conduct the appropriate funeral rites. This prompted Hong Nag-an, who had been urging rejection heterodoxy since the Panch'on Incident of 1787, to write letters to Prime Minister Ch'ae Che-gong and Chinsan magistrate Sin Sa-wŏn demanding that Yun be punished and criticized Chinsan Magistrate for delaying in taking action.[285]

> "That band of Chi-ch'ung's is a combination of savages and animals, forwhom the enunciation of ancestor worship was not sufficient that they did not even use a temporary spiritual tablet nor receive ancestral tablet. What's more, he burned and buried his father's ancetral tablet. When the people who were unaware of his conduct made a call of condolence, he at once responded to them, 'It is an event to celebrate not to lament.'[286] Could there be such an extraordinary misdeed since they were not punished by execution, there will no longer be a place where we may find the three bonds and five moral rules in human relations, and our land of propriety that has endured through four thousand years of Korean history will fall into the hands of beasts and savages."[287] He had come to believe that the Western Learning was a religion that deluded the world and deceived the peoples with its

---

[285]*Ibid.*, p.126.

[286]*Chosŏn wangjo sillok*, Chŏngjo 15th year (1791) 10th month Kapja.

[287]Yi Man-ch'ae, *op.cit.*, p.130.

theory of immortality.288

Subsequently, Hong Nag-an urged , *chwaŭichŏng* (Second State Councilor) Ch'ae Che-gong that to avert a disaster befalling the country, Yun Chi-ch'ung and Kwŏn Sang-yŏn must be punished as rebels, and must not only be executed, but their heads chopped off and hung on the street, their houses nailed up, and their village burned.289

When the content of Hong Nag-an's lengthy letter became known, memorials to the king by the intellectual class as well as by members of the government and the general public urging punishment continued to come forth. Five individuals including *Chinsa* Ch'ae Cho circulated a statement renouncing Yun Chi-ch'ung's rejection of ancestor worship as a horrible and wicked deed.290 During the tenth month of 1791, they distributed additional petitions asking that informing the king convene an indignation meeting in order that Western Learning might be eradicated at its root.291

Treatment - Process of Investigation

When Yun Chi-ch'ung's rejection of ancestor worship, even though it had taken place in the remote countryside, generated an enormous amount of controversy within Chosŏn society. The Chinsan magistrate Sin Sa-wŏn searched Yun Chi-ch'ung's house, upon which he found only empty jars of ancestral tablet. He reported this to the Office of Province, and an order to arrest Yun Chi-ch'ung and Kwŏn Sang-yŏn was given.

The two of them had originally fled, but returned and confessed before the magistrate on the 26th upon knowing that Yun Chi-ch'ung's uncle Yun Chŏng had been

---

288 *Ibid.*, p.127.

289 *Chosŏn wangjo sillok*, Chŏngjo 15th year 10th month Kapja.

290 Yi Man-ch'ae, *op.cit.*, p.134.

291 *Ibid.*, p.135.

imprisoned. They were then sent in custody to the office of Province and were interrogated.

In his interrogation, Yun Chi-ch'ung clearly articulated his rejection of ancestor worship. He argued that an ancestral tablet was prohibited by Catholicism, and thus he buried it in his yard and did not conduct the ceremony. He claimed, however, that the rumor that he refused to receive calls of condolences and he had disposed of his mother's corpse was not true. He appealed to his questioners by saying, "How is it that I could ever dare to treat carelessly the mourning observances for my mother when Catholicism dictates much more elaborate funerals? He further testified that:

> Even if I am deprived of my *yangban* title because of my belief in Catholicism, I do not wish to commit a sin against the Lord. It is prohibited by Catholicism to offer drinks and food to the dead. I further believe that since there is no strict law in this country that punishescommon people for not having an ancestral tablet and since there is no strict punishment of a scholar so poor, he is not able to conduct the ritual, it is therefore not in conflict with the law of the nation notto have an ancestral tablet and not to conduct the ritual, and nor is it against the Law to believe in Catholicism.[292]

Having been informed of the Chŏlla governor's report, on the eighth day of the eleventh month of 1791, Ch'ae Che-gong, who had all along shown a lukewarm

---

[292] *Chosŏn wangjo sillok*, Chŏngjo 15th year 11th month Chŏngch'uk. In Muin year of Chŏngjo's reign (1758), there had been a similar incident of refusing to conduct the ancestor worship ritual in Haesŏ Kwandong area, but the individual was merely warned harshly without further action. Yi Nŭng-hwa, *op.cit.*, p.56.

attitude towards punishing Yun Chi-ch'ung and Kwŏn Sang-yŏn, proposed an extremely severe one at the final conference, held on the disposition of their case,[293] declaring that, "They must be beheaded in front of many people, regardless of the time of the day, and their heads must be hung for five days, demonstrating to the world the importance of ethics and that they need to take extreme precautions not to be influenced by Western Learning."[294] It is likely that he arrived at this decision, because he feared the public opinion if he were to show leniency, and wished to protect his own reputation, his social position and his family.

Thirty some memorials demanding punishment were received by the government,[295] and they were beheaded and martyred outside the Chŏnju P'ungnamun on the 13th day in 11th month of the Ŭlsa year, 1791. Yun Chi-ch'ung was 33 years old and Kwŏn Sang-yŏn 41 years old. This was the very first official manifestation by the government of its resolve in dealing with Catholic Church members who repudiated ancestor worship. Due to the Chinsan Incident, besides execution of Yun and Kwŏn, the Chinsan magistrate Sin Sa-wŏn was discharged from his position and the government office there downgraded.[296]

Hong Nag-an, Mok Man-chung, and Yi Ki-kyŏng, also members of *Namin* and who exposed the Chinsan Incident and instigated the punishment, presented an anti-heterodoxy memorial to the king and prosecuted the heads of the Catholic church, leading to the government's declaration of the prohibition order. Oppressive measures against Western Learning became harsher, banning the importation of Western books and burning all of the already existing

---

[293] *Chosŏn wangjo sillok*, Chŏngjo 15th year 10th month Muin.
[294] *ibid.,*
[295] cf. Yi Man-ch'ae, *op.cit.*, kwŏn 2.Sinhae Chinsan
[296] *Chosŏn wangjo sillok*, Chŏngjo 15th (Sinhae) year 11th month Ŭlmyo.

Western books at Hongmungwan.[297]

The severity with which the Sinhae Persecution took place is acknowledged by Hwang Sa-yŏng himself in his Paeksŏ written before his own incident broke out. "Even if there is no more persecution in the future, Catholic organization will be demolished on its own within only ten years."[298] As such, persecution grew worse throughout Seoul, and even Chŏnju, Naep'o and other regions that the organization which just barely took shape was in danger of collapsing.

Subsequently, changes were seen among the Catholics and the leaders of the church. To the Catholics belonging to the social class of scholars and intellectuals, rejection of ancestor worship rituals became a boundary that could not be crossed nor compromised. When they began to be oppressed by their families and clans, there was a much more distinct trend of renunciation of Catholicism than there was for other social classes. As a result, *chungin* class emerged in great numbers to fill the void as the new leaders of the Catholic Church.

They accepted the characteristics of the Catholic faith in their pure form, and further strengthened the authority and absoluteness of the church. They repudiated the perspective of supplementing Confucianism adhered to thus far, and created an opportunity to solidify the church as a new communal organization that pursued a positive understanding of the Catholic doctrine, that obeyed the command of the church and that was willing to go as far as martyrdom for faith.

After accepting the order prohibiting ancestor worship, the Chosŏn church members who had remained with the church abandoned other customs and tradition without hesitation. They were occasionally martyred and some refused to conduct ancestor worship rituals in the

---

[297] *Chosŏn wangjo sillok*, Chŏngjo 15th year 11th month Kimyo, Kyemi.

[298] Hwang Sa-yŏng paeksŏ, 88th line.

spirit of a martyr.

Abiding by the order prohibiting the ancestor worship ritual was a kind of a confession of faith with a mind that was prepared for imminent persecution. It was a choice for the hardship, of suffering ensuing from family, clan and society, and of abandonment of human attachment and parents or children. Such choice was a decision that sprouted from a purified and refined faith.

When the Chosŏn church members were undergoing hardship over the ancestor worship issue, unlike in China, there was no missionary such as Matteo Ricci who was aware of and understood neither the indigenous culture nor a group that supported their action.

What was the source of their strength in even risking death and abandoning ancestor worship? The church members devoted all of their effort in prayer and the sacraments rather than the ancestor worship valued by Confucianism. They brought in many prayer books, memorized them, created a pseudo ecclesiastical hierarchy modeled upon the genuine Catholic institution and performed the sacraments. The early believers probably assumed the conduct of sacraments as a pious act in place of ancestor worship in the Confucian tradition, and as an act of worshipping the Lord.[299] In other words, they believed that the prayer and sacraments were the means of praising heaven and one's ancestors, and this is the reason for which they had abandoned the old customary practices and actively participated in the new religion with much hope.

The Attempted Arrest of Priest Chou in 1795

Chou Wen-mo, the very first priest to arrive in Korea, worked in secret for the first six months. His whereabouts were unknown to the authorities until a new church member, Han Yŏng-ik, visited the priest and thereafter informed the older brother of Yi Pyŏk, Yi Sŏk, who despised Catholicism. Yi Sŏk informed Second State

---

[299]Charles Dallet, *op.cit.*, (sang), pp.322-326.

councilor Ch'ae Che-gong who in turn reported to King Chŏngjo about the priest's underground activities.

On the 11th day of the 5th month of 1795, a police chief named Cho Kyu-jin received an order and with his policemen raided the house of Ch'oe In-gil where Father Chou was residing. By then, the priest had already fled to the house of a female church member, Kang Wan-suk, but the policemen arrested Ch'oe In-gil, mistaking him for Chou Wen-mo. Realizing that they had been deceived, the police bureau also arrested Chi Hwang and Yun Yu-il, who had invited the priest, and interrogated and tortured them. However, all three of them had no knowledge of Father Chou's whereabouts, and as a result, were flogged to death and their corpses thrown into the Han River.[300]

The anti-Catholic faction, including Mok Man-chung, interpreted the summary execution of those three individuals as the government's effort to conceal the fact that a Chinese priest had secretly entered the country.[301] On the 6th day of the 7th month, Taesahŏn (Inspector general) Kwŏn Yu presented a memorial to the king stating that because the three people were executed too quickly, Chou Wen-mo's whereabouts could not be determined, and he blamed it on the chief of the police bureau.[302] Perhaps because he recognized that Kwŏn Yu's memorial was indirectly targeting Ch'ae Che-gong, Chŏngjo took no notice of the memorial.

Those opposed to Catholicism continued to present memorials. One of the issues they raised was that Chŏng Yak-chŏn had written 'the four elements', a notion found in Catholic doctrine, rather than 'the five elements' at the civil examination in Kyŏngsul year, but that Yi Ka-hwan had selected him regardless.[303] Pak Chang-sŏl asserted that the

---

[300] Chŏng Yag-yong, *op.cit.*, p.327-328.

[301] Yi Man-ch'ae, *op. cit.*, 3:15a-16b.

[302] *Sŭngchŏngwŏn ilgi.*, Chŏngjo 19th yer 7th month 4th day.

[303] Chŏng Yag-yong, *op.cit.*, Chach'an myojimyŏng, p.328.

responsibility lay with Yi Ka-hwan and Chŏng Yag-yong, and presented a memorial asking for them to be blamed for failing to arrest Chou Wen-mo. Pak Chang-sŏl, in fact, received a sentence of exile because of this memorial.[304]

Memorials impeaching Yi Ka-hwan, Yi Sŏng-hun and Chŏng Yag-yong were continuously presented, an indication that they were targeted to be overthrown by *Sŏin* and *Namin Pyŏkp'a*. In the end, Yi Ka-hwan was transferred to the position of Ch'unju magistrate, Yi Sŏng-hun was exiled to Yesan, and Chŏng Yag-yong demoted to the post of *Kŏmjŏng ch'albang*.[305]

The government's intention was to harass the Catholic converts, of whom there were relatively many in Kŏmjŏng, Yesan and Ch'ungju, and to prevent further conversions.[306] They did in fact persecute the Catholics in line with the government's intention and Yi Ka-hwan in particular, who was not an official church member yet was criticized as one, forced the converts to renounce Catholicism by using extremely cruel tortures such as leg screws. However, not surprisingly none of them promoted again.[307]

In the case of Yi Ka-hwan, even though he was not baptized and even though he acted against the Catholics at his new post, the *Pyŏkp'a* faction continued to exclude him accusing him to be the head of the Catholics. Clearly, their behavior was driven by factional motives.

Subsequently the fever of the witch hunt subsided temporarily in Seoul, but an arrest for Chu Mun-mo was ordered throughout the nation, and persecution in the regional areas worsened again.[308] Chŏngjo ordered an individual named Cho Hwa-jin to convert to Catholicism in

---

[304]*Ibid.*

[305]*Chosŏn wangjo sillok*, Chŏngjo 19th year 7th month Kapsul and Ŭlhae.

[306]Chŏng Yag-yong, *op.cit.*, p.328.

[307]Hwang Sa-yŏng paeksŏ, 49th and 50th lines.

[308]Hwang Sa-yŏng paeksŏ, 12th line.

disguise, and then reveal and report the houses of the church members and in Kimi year (1799), a persecution in Ch'ŏngju occurred, killing many dedicated Catholics.[309]

In Ch'ungch'ŏngdo Naep'o, Hongju, Haemi and Chŏngyang regions, it was reported that over a hundred people died during the two years, 1798-1799. In the 3rd month of Kyŏngsin year (1800), a persecution occurred in Kyŏnggido Yŏju. At Chŏng Chong-ho's house, as the Easter mass was finishing, eleven church members were arrested and imprisoned. On the 24th day of the 5th month in Kimi year, Taesagan Sin Pong-jo presented a memorial accusing Kwŏn Ch'ŏl-sin and Chŏng Yak-chong to be the key leaders of the Catholic church members, and thus the two families of Yangkŏn became the direct target of an attack.

In Kyŏngsin year (1800), Kwŏn Ch'ŏl-sin was informed of the fact that the evil faction members of Yangkŏn were planning to steal an ancestral tablet of the Kwŏn family and blame him for the act, and so he moved the tablet to another place. When the thieves noticed that it was already gone, they spread a rumor that Kwŏn Ch'ŏl-sin had burned it. The magistrate Yu Han-ki declared the act innocent, but then he was later discharged from his post, the reason being that he had defended an evil doctrine.[310] A new magistrate was posted, and when he again raised the old incident, Kwŏn Ch'ŏl-sin took his aged body and fled to Seoul.[311]

In the 6th month of Kyŏngsin year (1800), a renegade Kim Yŏ-san discovered Priest Chu's dwelling and reported it to the authorities. At that time, Priest Chu, who had been in hiding at Kang Wan-suk's house, already had received the news and fled to another place, again avoiding arrest. A few days afterward, King Chŏngjo died, and Priest Chu confessed during the Sinyu Persecution.

---

[309] Hwang Sa-yŏng paeksŏ, 5th line.
[310] Hwang Sa-yŏng paeksŏ, 12th line.
[311] *Ibid.*

The causes behind the persecution subsequent to the Ŭlmyo year (1795) were not only that Chŏngjo was suspicious and fearful of Priest Chu and thus determined to arrest him. It rather was because the *Noron* (Old Doctrine faction) despised and were jealous of *Namin* (Southerners), and attempted to drive them to ruin. Because Yi Ka-hwan, for his writing, and Chŏng Yag-yong, for his talent and wit, had won Chŏngjo's trust that they wished to destroy them.

Policy towards Catholicim of Chŏngjo and Chae Chegong

As Catholicism came to be accepted and practiced as a religion, the government found itself in a position of having to respond to it. The following directive issued by the Office of the Censor-General after the Prosecution of Catholic Meetings in the Board of Punishments Incident indicates that initially the alarm of government officials prompted them to order only the destruction of books:

> Recently, the Western Learning is claiming fortune and misfortune under the pretext of empty matters, and thus the words of its pursuers are nonsensical, their meaning dangerous, for it is no more than a collateral sect of Buddha. The theories preached in the books are those of heaven and hell, flesh and soul, and its extreme impiety may well be known. Alas! How could one replicate so easily the form of the Divine Being that is so faraway and silent and orderless. What other crime can be more desecrating than the crime of worshipping a portrait of another human being in place of the Divine Being and calling it "Jesus." The books in the possession of these fools everywhere and the portrait that they worship must all be either burnt or thrown into water so to prevent further

misdeeds in the future..[312]

Western Learning initially came to the court's attention in the 12th year of Chŏngjo (1788) when *Chŏng'ŏn* (Fourth Censor) Yi Kyŏng-myŏng submitted a memorial criticizing it,[313] which prompted a series of discussions of the dangers it represented and appropriate policy to be taken.

In general, Chŏngjo and his officials assumed that the popularity of Western Learning was a temporary phenomenon and that it would eventually fade on its own. "If we elucidate clearly our (Confucian) Way and prove the superiority of the orthodoxy, then even though heterodoxy such as this may arise, will soon disappear. Thus people's lives shall be spared but their books shall be burned."[314] "If we are to enlighten ourselves through a legitimate scholarly inquiry, we will eradicate such wicked ideas, and then inappropriate books should naturally disappear on their own."[315] Nevertheless, he ordered the officials "to throw those books stored in people's houses into water or burn them, and to punish all those who violate this order." Furthermore, he stated that:

> If no single Sadaebu (literati) becomes polluted then the naive common people, whose minds have been made restless by this talk of disaster and fortune will realize and repent on their own. Thus, there is no need for the government to spend much effort in this matter.[316]

In charging that the loss of vitality in the Confucian

---

[312] *Sahak chingŭi*, p.378.

[313] *Chosŏn wangjo sillok,* Chŏngjo 12th year 8th month Sinmyo.

[314] *Ibid.*, Chŏngjo 12th year 8th month Imjin.

[315] *bid.*, Chŏngjo 12th year 8th month Ŭlmi.

[316] *Ibid.*

school was owing to the rise of the evil doctrine, Chŏngjo said: "Besides the leftist Tao, the ideas of Western Learning are not the only ones that have deluded the public. In China, there have been the Lu-Wang School, Buddhism and Taoism, yet was there ever a need to prohibit them? It must be that our Confucian scholars have not done their reading."317

Thus, Chŏngjo's attitude towards Western Learning was a much more moderate one than that of the Confucian literati who advocated prohibition through harsh sentences. He forsaw potential social conflict among scholar-officials if a prohibition of the Western Learning were to be enforced. In other words, he was concerned that if individuals from the *Namin Sip'a*, which was closely involved with the Western Learning at that time, were removed, then the balance of political power must undergo a substantial change.

During the Chinsan Incident (Abolition of Ancestor Worship) of 1791, Hong Nag-an urgently called for anti-heterodoxy and through punishment in a lengthy letter. The justification for his argument was that Western Learning was as dangerous as the "Huangjin Pailien (the White Lotus Society and Yellow Turban Rebels)" and that it was particularly evil influence on the lower classes, women and children, and thus should be considered treason.318 His actual purpose, however, was to attack his political enemies.

The Office of the Inspector-General and the Office of the Censor-General proposed repeatedly that Yun and Kwŏn, the two *yangin*, be sentenced at once and suggested that it was a mistake to leave in the hands of the local Chinsan office such an unprecedented incidence of neglect of ethical responsibilities, but Chŏngjo initially made no special appointment.319

Chŏngjo saw the attack on Western Learning as

317*Ibid.*, Chŏngjo 12th year 8th month Imjin.

318*Ibid.*, Chŏngjo 15th year 10th month Kapja.

319*Ibid.*

motivated by factional politics, an attempt to create problems for members of the Sip'a (Party of Expediency) rather than a defense of Confucianism, and his policy of impartiality was devised to allay these tensions. He further understood the anti-Western Learning argument as an attempt to destroy the impartiality policy (T'angp'yŏngch'aek). But at the same time, he could no longer condone teachings which called for the abolition of ancestor worship and unconditional protection of those scholars who believed in Catholicism. Therefore, when he decreed the executions of Yun Chi-ch'ung and Kwŏn Sang-yŏn, he also sentenced Hong Nag-an to exile, punishing both sides.

In 1795 (Chŏngjo's 19th year) when the government was attempting to arrest the Chinese priest Father Chou Wen-mo, who had secretly entered the country, a student at the National Academy submitted a memorial criticizing Western Learning: not only did it not recognize the authority of one's King and one's father, but it did not recognize the distinctions between social classes and men and women, thus constituting a grave challenge to domestic stability, and thus it must be treated as treason.[320]

Chŏngjo's response to this and other similar petitions was:

> It has been several hundred years since books on Western Learning have entered Korea, and it is well known to all that they have been preserved in History Archives and in the court since the earlier times, not only during the present days. But now, orthodoxy has become obscure and its evils are worse than those of heterodoxy and beasts. Therefore, there is no better way to prevent such wickedness in our days than to

---

[320] *Ibid.*, Chŏngjo 19th year 7th month Kyeyu.

enlighten orthodoxy.³²¹

On the other hand, after failing to capture Priest Chou Wen-mo in 1795, Chŏngjo tightened inspection and toughened sentences. He also secretly ordered and implicitly approved persecutions in local regions, resulting in an increase of tyranny by the local government offices. Ch'oe Sŏg-u pretended to be unaware of the situation, and so by inducing the minds of the Catholic believers to be lax, he attempted to capture the priest in secret, thus bringing the incident to a conclusion.³²²

As a ruler of a nation during a period when the Western Learning was being accepted as a religion and evoking much criticisms from the society, Chŏngjo did not possess a concrete knowledge of Catholicism, but merely learned indirectly from Ch'ae Che-gong.³²³ His view on Catholicism, therefore, was much shaped through Ch'ae Che-gong. He acceded to Ch'oe Che-gong's advice "not to read any nonsensical books, in fear of dissipating one's energy."³²⁴

Such a moderate stance by Chŏngjo appears to have been partially initiated by his positive attitude towards Western science. He gave Chŏng Yag-yong a copy of *Ch'i-ch'i-t'u-shuo* (Description of Ingenious Devices) edited by Jean Terrenz and had him use a crane in building a fortress at Suwŏn. Whenever an incident had to be dealt with concerning Western Learning, Chŏngjo resorted to "removing a government official from his office" or "relegation to exile", which temporarily quieted the political rancor.³²⁵ He did

---

³²¹Ch'oe Sŏg-u , *Han'guk kyohoesa ŭi yŏksa*, p.68.

³²²Ch'oe Sog-u, *Han'guk kyohoesa ŭi yŏksa*, p.68

³²³ *Chosŏn wangjo sillok*, Chŏngjo 12th year 7th month Imjin.p.68. cf. Cho Kwang. *Chosŏn hugi ch'ŏnjugyosa*. p.210.

³²⁴*Ibid.*, Kapsul.

³²⁵ Some examples are Yi Ka-hwan who was relegated to the position of Ch'ungju *Moksa* (magistrate), Chŏng Yag-yong who

not officially or publicly persecute Catholicism, adhering to his basic policy not to focus attention on it unnecessarily. He feared that an order of persecution might instigate an uprising, and thus did not wish to oppress Catholicism through official decree. Accordingly no massive persecution occurred during his reign.

Ch'ae Che-gong's Perspective on Western Learning

What was the perspective on Western Learning of Ch'ae Che-gong - the head of the *Namin* and the official in Chŏngjo's court who directly handled the problems related to the introduction of Catholicism, from the founding of the church in 1784 until his death, Ch'ae Che-gong's position in regards to Western Learning was that of "burn the books but save men's lives," as expressed by Chŏngjo himself using Han Yu's words. He even informed Chŏngjo that if things are done in this way, then heterodoxy will perish on its own.[326]

Ch'ae Che-gong proposed a heavy penalty for those who studied Western Learning but also expressed a concern that its importance was unduly magnified because of factional strife, which might lead to the suffering of innocent victims, stating that "it would truly be a difficult problem to resolve if the people who accuse irrelevant individuals for the sake of attacking them are the same individuals who used to work here before."

In year 1791, 10th month 24th day, Ch'ae Che-gong described his position on Western Learning in a communication presented to the king. He stated:

> "...I have detested the theories of the Western Learning, and early on, I clearly argued against it in writing, even being appropriately cautious whenever meeting

---

was downgraded to Kŭmchŏng *Ch'albang* (Superintendent) where Catholics were prevalent, and Yi Sŭng-hun who was forced to publicly declare a rejection of Catholicism.

[326] *Ibid.*, Chŏngjo 15th year 10th month Pyŏngjin.

people. Not only that, two years ago, I repeatedly testified at a face-to-face meeting wishing to permanently prevent its origin.[327]

Ch'ae Che-gong also criticized the Catholic Church members' refusal to practice ancestor worship, saying,

> "They claim that after people die, those who were good go to heaven while those who committed sin go to hell. Therefore, even if an ancestor worship were performed, those in heaven will certainly not desire to return while those in hell will not be able to return, and thus it is not necessary to conduct an ancestor worship. That a country of proper etiquette such as ours is deluded by such wicked theory is a truly embarrassing matter."[328]

Chŏngjo responded to the communication and delegated responsibility and authority to Ch'ae Che-gong saying,

> "The reason that I appointed you to this position is because I regarded the principles that you advocate[329] to be not incorrect in an attempt to wash away the shame of the past one hundred years. Since the theories of the heterodoxy emerged while you were the Chief State Councillor, you must know all of those who attack and those who believe. If you are unable to control this situation, how can the condition are

---

[327] *Ibid.*, Chŏngjo 15th year 10th month Ŭlch'uk.

[328] *Ibid*, Chŏngjo 15th year 10th month Pyŏngin.

[329] This refers to the principle that only those clearly identified as Catholics were punished.

avoided? The means to bring the situation under control depend on you, and so it is imperative that you reject this heterodoxy, and eradicate its roots ..."330

As a proponent of Practical Learning (Silhak) who significantly influenced its doctrinal development, 331 Ch'ae Che-gong was allied with the group among the disciples of Yi Ik (the Sŏngho School) who opposed Catholicism, referred to as the Right Branch (Up'a), which included such scholars as Chŏng Ch'an-hŏm (1740-1824), Yu Ha-wŏn (1740-1824), and Ch'oe Hŏn-chung (1747-) had all rejected Catholicism.332 He most likely gained an understanding and formed a critical perspective on Western Learning throughcontacts with these individuals. It appears that he was influenced from early on by his friend Yi Hŏn-kyŏng, who at one point held the post of Chief Magistrate of Seoul under Chŏngjo and was the author of several anti-Catholic writings including *Ch'ŏnhak mundap*.333 As head of the *Namin* (the Southerners), he was wary of Catholicism just as other *Namin* elders such as An Chŏng-bok had been, but at the same time, he sought to protect the members of his faction associated with Catholicism and so urged a policy of moderation upon Chŏngjo.

Unlike most of the anti-heterodoxy proponents, Ch'ae did not reject Catholicism in its entirety. During a meeting with Chŏngjo, he is reported to have said, "Among the theories of Catholicism, there are some positive aspects from time to time, and one is that *Sangche* (God) will descend to be with and watch over the people in order to

---

330 *Ibid.*

331 cf. Han U-kŭn, *Sŏngho Yi Ik yŏn'gu* (Seoul: Seoul taehankkyo, 1980), pp. 28-72.

332 Cho Kwang, *Chosŏn huki ch'ŏnjukyohoesa yŏn'gu,* p.200.

333 Cho Kwang, *op.cit.*, p.201.

help them,"³³⁴ and further stated that "the true intention of Catholicism is grounded on performing good deeds and avoiding evil."³³⁵

It was probably through Matteo Ricci's *The True Meaning of the Lord of Heaven* that Ch'ae Che-gong first came in contact with Catholicism. He once said, "I too read the book *The True Meaning of the Lord of Heaven*, since the theories of the so called Western Learning are quite popular,"³³⁶

Ch'ae Che-gong believed that it is possible to utilize to their advantage the ideological trends of not only Catholicism but also of Buddhism or other heterodoxies if they can positively contribute to managing the family and governing the country.³³⁷

Once when he was conversing with Yi Ki-kyŏng (1756-1819), a member of *kongsŏp'a*, after the Chinsan Incident in 1791, he reminded him that Chu Hsi also was knowledgeable about Buddhism as well as Taoism. "One can reject Catholicism," he said, "only after having read its texts and understood its truths and immoral principles, and hence I also read *Ch'ŏnju silŏi*.³³⁸

He criticized Catholicism on several points. The first point is the lack of a father and king in Catholicism. As he told Chŏngjo, "A key example of how they neglect ethics and overturn tradition and customs, lies in whom they hold worthy of respect: for them, first there is God, then there is Jesus and then there is one's own father. This is the same as

---

³³⁴*Chosŏn wangjo sillok*, Chŏngjo 12th year 7th month Sinmyo.

³³⁵*Ibid.*, Chŏngjo 15th year 10th month Pyŏngin.

³³⁶*Chosŏn wangjo sillok*, Chŏngjo 2th year 7th month Sinmyo.

³³⁷ Pak Kwang-yong, "Yŏng Chŏngjo- dae Namin seryŏk ŭi chŏng ch'i chŏk wich'i wa sŏhak chŏngch'aek (Political position of *Namin* power during the King Yŏngjo and Chŏngjo and policy on the Western Learning). *Han'guk kyohoesa nonmunjip*, II, (Seoul: 1985), p.28.

³³⁸Yi Man-ch'ae, *op.cit.*, 2:37a.

having no father at all."³³⁹

Because Catholicism did not recognize the authority of the king as father of his people, "its harm is truly greater than that done by the famous Chinese philosophers Yang-tzŏ and Mo-tzŏ by a hundredfold, and thus I despise it as I despise an enemy."³⁴⁰

On this basis he also criticized Catholicism as an institution. He understood the Catholic practice of electing a Pope as that of electing a king, saying "It had been the custom of their nation not to have a king, and thus they had no king to begin with. Therefore, they selected an unmarried man from the common people and designated him as their king. This is a deplorable matter."³⁴¹

A second issue that he considered to be a problem was the Catholic belief in life after death.³⁴² He told Chŏngjo that the Western Learning claims the theory of heaven and hell, which is extremely similar to Buddhism,³⁴³ and even though we reject Buddhism,³⁴⁴ the heaven and hell theory is derived from certain Buddhist beliefs.

The third issue that he considered to be problematic was that the doctrine was not rational. "According to the Catholic books *Sangje* (God) descended to earth, and became Jesus, which is similar to Yao and Shun of China. But his opening of a blind man's eyes and causing a cripple to walk are exceedigly irrational. Furthermore, how can one believe the story that he opened the door of heaven and

---

³³⁹*Chosŏn wangjo sillok*, Chŏngjo 15th year 10th month Pyŏngin day. There is an instance before in which he expressed a similar view, *Chosŏn wangjosillok* Chŏngjo 12th year 7th month Imjin.

³⁴⁰*Chosŏn wangjo sillok*, Chŏngjo 15th year 10th month Ŭlch'uk.

³⁴¹ *Chosŏn wangjo sillok*, Chŏngjo 15th year 10th month Pyŏngin.

³⁴²*Ibid.*

³⁴³*Ibid.*

³⁴⁴*Ibid.* Chŏngjo 12th year 7th month Imjin.

flew in?"³⁴⁵

Such arguments on the part of Ch'ae Che-gong were denounced and scorned by the opposition group of *Sinsŏp'a* of the *Sip'a* faction and *Kongsŏp'a* of the *Pyŏkp'a* faction. As a result, the conflict between Ch'aedang under Ch'ae Che-gong and Hongdang under Hong Nak-an worsened, preventing Ch'ae Che-gong from resolving the Yun Chi-ch'ung incident according to his wish.

Having noticed in Hong Nak-an's letter that books on Western Learning had been published, *Taesagan* Kwŏn Yi-kang submitted a memorial demanding that Western Learning be uprooted.³⁴⁶ Ch'ae Che-gong had sent his son Hong-wŏn to inquire of Hong Nag-an on the identity of the publisher of those books, but as Hong Nak-an did not know, it may have been that he attempted to attack Hong Nag-an's group by having the same faction member, Kwŏn Yi-kang, submit a memorial.³⁴⁷

As the issue over the publication of Western books drew attention, Hong Nak-an evaded a definitive answer by stating that he had heard of it from the former Sŏngji (Royal Secretary) Yi Su-ha, but at the same time, testified that the fundamental source was the books brought back by Yi Sŏng-hun from Beijing ³⁴⁸ and that Yi Ki-kyŏng had witnessed those banned books in Yi Sŏng-hun's possession at the 1787 Panch'on meeting.³⁴⁹ He further claimed that Kwŏn Il-sin was the founder of the religion.³⁵⁰ As a result, Yi Sŏng-hun was exiled to Yesan and Kwŏn Il-sin was first

---

³⁴⁵*Chosŏn wangjo sillok*, Chŏngjo 12th year 7th month Imjin.

³⁴⁶*Chosŏn wangjo sillok*, Chŏngjo 15th year 10th month Sinmi.

³⁴⁷ Chin In-kwŏn, Sinyu saok-e kwan-han yŏn'gu, (Study of Sinyu illicit imprisonment), Ph.D. dissertation, Sŏnggyungwan University, 1986, p.34.

³⁴⁸*Chosŏn wangjo sillok*, Chŏngjo 15th year 11th month Sinmi.

³⁴⁹*Ibid.*, Kapsul.

³⁵⁰*Ibid.*, Pyŏngja.

exiled to Chejudo then his punishment was mitigated to Yesan, but died on the way.

3. The Sinyu Persecution (1801)

Background of the Sinyu Persecution of 1801

In 1799, Ch'ae Che-gong died, and in the 24th year of Chŏngjo (1800) 6th month, Chŏngjo also died unexpectedly. Chŏngjo had pursued a moderate policy towards Catholicism and mediated among the *Namin Sip'a* factions, and his death was a disastrous misfortune for the Catholic believers and *Namin Sip'a* members.

The political situation underwent a dramatic change upon Chŏngjo's death. The son who succeeded as Sunjo was only eleven years old, and a regent was appointed for him, Yŏngjo's second wife, Queen Dowager Kim-ssi. She was the younger sister of Kim Ku-ju, one of the leading figures in the events surrounding the death of the Crown Prince Changhŏn as a member of the Party of Principle (*Pyŏkp'a*), which supported Yŏngjo's act. Kim Ku-ju had been sent into exile and died there. Jumping at the good opportunity created by Chŏngjo's death and Sunjo's accession, the *Pyŏkp'a* began their conspiracy to expel the *Sip'a* with the support of Queen Dowager Kim.

Assuming administrative authority from behind the scenes, Queen Dowager Kim replaced high ranking officials from the *Sip'a* with *Pyŏkp'a* members, including Sim Hwan-ji as the Chief State Councillor.[351] Even during

---

[351] According to Sim Hwan-ji's request, her elder brother Kim Kwan-ju (1743-1806) was promoted to the Minister of the Board of Personnel. Mok Man-chung of the *Namin Pyŏkp'a* was appointed as the Inspector General. Sin Tae-hyŏn was appointed as the police chief of the left, and Yi Han-p'ung was appointed as the police chief of the right, taking control over the police department of Seoul. Hwang Sa-yŏng pointed out that when Queen Dowager Kim "unexpectedly came to wield political power, she at last

Chŏngjo's reign, the *Pyŏkp'a* had been envious of the appointments to high office of Ch'ae Che-gong, Yi Ka-hwan and Chŏng Yag-yong, and fretted at learning that Ch'ae Che-gong had named Yi Ka-hwan and Chŏng Yag-yong as his possible successors. Thus, members of the *Pyŏkp'a* made an attempt at every opportunity to drive Yi Ka-hwan and Chŏng Yag-yong out from political power by linking the two people to Western Learning.352 Pigeon-holing Catholicism as heterodoxy was a merely superficial action, for the underlying intention was to redress their wrath at having been excluded from political power, in other words, this was a typical political revenge set in an arena of factional strife.353

Having acquired a justifiable cause as well as an opportunity, Sim Hwan-ji, head of the *Noron Pyŏkp'a*, denounced Hong Nag-im and the late Ch'ae Che-gong as the leaders of Catholicism. Finally, Queen Dowager decreed the prohibition of Catholicism in 1801 first month 10th day.354

The Beginning

Government action to contain the spread of Catholicism had been taken from time to time. In 1798 Fourth Inspector (Chip'yŏng) Yun Ham submitted a memorial stating, "The minds of those who live in Ch'ungch'ŏng province are becoming polluted, and this

---

expelled all of the members of one of the *Sip'a* factions immediately following the funeral of the former king (in Kyŏngsin year (1800) 11th month), and the royal court thus became half vacant..."

352 Hong I-sŏp, "Chosŏn hugi e issŏsŏ sahoe chŏk pyŏndong." *Hong I-sŏp chŏnchip 3* (Seoul: Yŏnsei University Press, 1994), p.245.
353 *Ibid.*
354 Yi Nŭng-hwa, *op.cit.*, p.113.

must be stopped."[355] Thus, at Ch'ae Che-gong's order, persecution began in Ch'ungch'ŏng province, and its harshness was such that "most of the devoted Catholics in Ch'ungch'ŏngdo died and the church became almost extinct.[356]

Sixty three people including Chisa Kwŏn Ŭm submitted a memorial denouncing the Chŏng Yag-yong brothers, Yi Ka-hwan, Yi Sŏng-hun, Hong Kyo-man and Kwŏn Ch'ŏl-sin[357] As members of the *Pyŏkp'a*, Mok Man-chung and Hong Nag-an[358] had been all along attacking Catholic members of the *Sip'a* since Chŏngjo's time, and as the state of affairs changed suddenly, they spread the canard that Yi Ka-hwan was inciting a rebellion, thus aggravating public opinion.

Once the period of the national mourning for Chŏngjo ended, action began to be taken against Catholics. In Kyŏngsin year (1800) 12th month 17th day, the *Chungin* and a Hoejang (lay leader), Ch'oe P'il-gong was convicted and on the 19th day, his younger cousin P'il-je was arrested. Because the previous arrest of Ch'oe P'il-gong that was brought to suit had not been resolved, his arrest was not unexpected, and the Catholic members were not disturbed.

Early in 1801, as a result of Kim Yŏ-sam's in-forming, the *chungin* Ch'oe Chang-hyŏn, *hoechang* of Seoul, was arrested. The continuing arrests of the *chungin* leaders of the Catholic Church illustrate the fact that Catholicism was propagated widely among the *chungin* class and that due to the Sinhae Chinsan Incident and Ŭlmyo Incident (an attempt to capture Priest Chou), the

---

[355] *Chosŏn wangjo sillok, Chŏngjo* 22nd year 5th month Ŭlyu.

[356] *Ibid.*,

[357] *Ibid.*, Sunjo, the beginning year, 2nd month, Imsul.

[358] Even his father Hong Su-po had a hostile relationship with Ch'ae Che-gong and was an anti-Catholic, whereas Nag-min (His father Hong Hwa-po; Chŏng Yag-yong's father in law) was a member of the *Sinsŏp'a*.

leadership of the church had been transferred from the *yangban* class to the *chungin* class.

After she publicly declared the persecution of Catholicism, Queen Dowager Kim stated that "Inspectors and county officials should persuade those pursuing heterodoxy to abandon it to make non-believers afraid, and to be cautious... And after strictly prohibiting it in this way, if there still remain those who have not recanted, they should be treated under the law of treason."[359] And at the same time, they instituted a law mandating the organization of households into units of five (*oga chakt'ong pŏp*), to ensure the reporting of every Catholic church member.[360]

Queen Dowager Kim now came to wield power and she called for the extermination of the Catholic Church members, for they were considered a herd of animals lacking in ethics. Thus she justified the decree of prohibition and persecution.

> "Men are men because there is morality, and a country is a country because there is civilization. Presently, this so-called Catholicism has neither king nor father, falsifying morality and betraying civilization, and its followers resemble barbarians and beasts"[361]

To stop the spread of Catholicism, an order was given first to change the minds of converts through persistent persuasion, and if they still continued to disobey, then they were to be imprisoned for treason.[362] The law of treason was applied because the Catholic Church members

---

[359] *Ibid.*, Sunjo, the beginning year 1st month Chŏnghae.

[360] *Ibid.*

[361] *Chosŏn wangjo sillok*, Sunjo, the beginning year, first month Chŏnghae.

[362] *Ibid.*

were regarded to have disturbed the ethics and order of society, to have contravened orthodox teachings, and to be allied with foreign forces.

The persecution accelerated with the arrest of Im T'ae-in. Chŏng Yak-chong, the leader of the Myŏngdohoe had moved from Yanggŏn to Seoul in the 5th month of 1800 in his attempt to avoid persecution, and when arrests increased, he had Im T'ae-in move the trunks containing his crucifix, Catholic manuals and letters from Father Chou Wen-mo to a safer place. On his way to Hwang Sa-yŏng's house in Ahyŏn on the 19th day 1st month in 1801, Im T'ae-in was arrested by an official of the Seoul Magistracy, and the trunks were confiscated.[363] As a result, the activities of Chou Wen-mo and of Catholic Church members were exposed.[364] The newly appointed Chief Magistrate, Sin Tae-hyŏn, released all those who abandoned Catholicism, such as Ch'oe P'il-kong, Ch'oe P'il-che and Ch'oe Ch'ang-hyŏn.[365]

Such lenient treatment so angered Pak Chang-sŏl of the *Sobuk* faction,[366] Yi Sŏ-gu of the *Noron*, and Ch'oe Hyŏn-jung of *Namin* that they presented a memorial demanding an extermination of heterodoxy. An equally furious Queen Dowager Kim had Sin Tae-hyŏn imprisoned and transferred the responsibility punishing of Catholics from the police to the State Tribunal (*Ŭigŏmbu*), signifying that Catholics were being considered to have committed treason.[367]

The Office of the Inspector General proposed that

---

[363] Hwang Sa-yŏng paeksŏ 26-27th lines.

[364] Hwang Sa-yŏng paeksŏ, 27th line.

[365] *Ibid.*, 28th line.

[366] He was on friendly terms with Mok Man-chung of the *Pyŏkp'a*, and in the 7th month of 1795, he had submitted a memorial to Chŏngjo assailing Yi Ka-hwan and Chŏng Yag-yong for having fallen into heterodoxy.

[367] *Ibid.*, 29th line.

since Yi Ka-hwan, Yi Sŏng-hun and Chŏng Yag-yong were the origin of the spread of heterodoxy, which would destroy the country and its families, they should be rigorously interrogated by the State Tribunal, exposing the true state of affairs, and that they be quickly dealt with under national law.368 Accordingly, Queen Dowager Kim gave an order to handle the situation in a strict manner and to arrest these individuals, and subsequently, on the 9th day of 2nd month, Yi Ka-hwan, Yi Sŏng-hun and Chŏng Yag-yong were arrested.369

On the 11th day (Chŏngsa), Kwŏn Ch'ŏl-sin and Chŏng Yak-chong were also arrested and on the 18th day, Hong Nak-min and others were arrested.370 In addition the Catholic Church members who had been released by the Chief magistrate Sin Tae-hyŏn were recaptured.371 The arrested Catholics filled the prisons of the State Tribunal, the two police departments and the Board of Punishments, and they became so crowded that there was no more room to accept additional arrests.372

Arrests of Catholics began in the provinces as well. Yi Chon-ch'ang was jailed in Naep'o in Ch'ungch'ŏngdo,373 and from Chŏllado, Yu Hang-gŏm, Yun Chi-hŏn and Kim Yu-san were transferred in custody to Seoul for the crime of writing a letter to the Catholic church

---

368 *Ibid.*, Ŭlmyo.

369 *Ibid.*

370 *Ilsŏngrok*, Sunjo Sinyu year 2nd month 5th day.

371 Hwang Sa-yŏng Paeksŏ, 30th line.

372 At that time, as the judiciary institutions of Chosŏn, the police department of the left and the right handled thieves in the Seoul area; the Board of Punishments handled the crimes committed by *yangban* without government official titles and *pyŏngmin*; and the StateTribunal handled those disturbing the politics of the country.

373 *Ilsŏngnok* Sunjo Sinyu year,2nd month, 5th day (Sinhae).

in Beijing and requesting a large ship to be sent.[374] The arrested Catholics were to be convicted for the crime of treason, and interrogations given to serious criminals by the State Tribunal continued from the 10th day to the 26th day of 2nd month.

When *Yŏngbusa* (First Minister) Yi Pyŏng-mo, the Second State Councillor Yi Si-su and others requested an immediate resolution of the situation, Queen Dowager Kim instructed:

> If we were to apply the provisions of the law simply to those individuals without having exposed the den of the founders of the religion, then the person who is the true founder of the religion will blame his crime on this individual. However, according to the principles of handling criminal incidents, we must never apply the provisions of the law in haste. He must be rigorously interrogated so that the den of the founders of the religion is ultimately exposed, and only then should they be sentenced according to the law.[375]

This was in contrast to the lenient handling of the three individuals related to the attempted capture of Chou Wen-mo in 1795, which had provoked the public criticism. A thorough eradication of the source of evils was being sought.

On the 26th day of the 2nd month in 1801, the proposal of *Ch'ukukchŏng* (Office of Trial Processes) recommended the execution of Chŏng Yak-chong, Ch'oe Ch'ang-hyŏn, Ch'oe P'il-gong, Hong Kyo-man, Hong Nag-min, and Yi Sŏng-hun in front of the Sŏsomun Gate for the crime of treason. Kwŏn Ch'ŏl-sin and Yi Ka-hwan had

---

[374] *Chosŏn wangjo sillok*, Sunjo, the beginning year 5th month Sinmyo.

[375] *Ibid.*, Muo.

already died while in prison and brothers Chŏng Yak-chŏn and Chŏng Yag-yong were in exile. Yi Chon-ch'ang was executed in Kongju.[376]

In the provinces, every person imprisoned in Yŏju and Yangkŏn of Kyŏnggido was executed. In Yŏju, Yi Chung-bae, Im Hŏi-yŏng, Cho Tong-sŏm, Wŏn Kyŏng-do and others were beheaded, and in Yangkŏn, Yun Yu-o and Yu Han-suk were beheaded. Yi Hŏi-yŏng, a talented artist, was executed for the crime of drawing and spreading the picture of Jesus and disseminating books and words of the evil doctrine.[377] The first day of the fourth month, the son of Chŏng Yak-chong, Chŏng Ch'ŏl-sang, Yi Hak-kyu, Ch'oe P'il-gong's younger cousin, P'il-che, Chŏng In-hyŏk, and Chŏng Un-hye were executed for the crime of disseminating books and words of the evil doctrine.[378] On the 22nd day (chŏngyu) of 5th month, Kang Wan-suk, Ch'oe In-chŏn, Kim Hyŏn-u, Ko Kwang-sŏng, Yi Kuk-sŏng, Kim Yŏn-i, a former court lady Kang Kyŏng-bok, a court lady Mun-Yŏng-in, Han Sin-ae, Yi Hyŏn, Hong Chŏng-ho, Yun Chŏng-hye and Sun-mae and others were executed.[379]

Yu Hang-gŏm was accused of conspiring with Chou Wen-mo, communicating secretly with foreign countries and collecting funds to request a ship from Beijing, and as a result he was convicted as a traitor to the country. Yun Chi-hŏn as well was convicted for secretly communicating with foreign countries and sending letters to Westerners three times, and also for participating in the conspiracy to request a ship. Yi U-jip, as Yu Hang-gŏm's relative, was accused of not reporting the conspiracy, and Kim Yu-san was also

---

[376] *Ibid.*, Imsin.

[377] *Chosŏn wangjo sillok*, Sunjo, the beginning year, 3rd month, the holy image, and they were used at mass celebrating, being representative in expressing the faith and art of the early Catholic Church. Pae ŭn-ha, *Yŏksa ŭi ttang, Paeum ŭi ttang Paeron*, (Seoul: Sŏng Paolo ch'ulp'ansa, 1992), p.60.

[378] *Ibid*, Sunjo, the beginning year, 4th month, Chŏngmi.

[379] *Ibid.*, 5th month, Chŏngyu.

convicted of being a traitor for secretly communicating with the Catholic church of Beijing by delivering letters.[380]

Towards the end of this year, on the 26th day of 12th month, Mujin day, Chŏng Kwang-su, Hong Ik-man, Kim Kye-wan, Son Kyŏng-yun, Kim Hŏi-ho, Song Chae-ki, Kim Kwi-dong, Ch'oe Sŏl-ae, Kim Il-ho, Chang Tŏk-yu, Pyŏn Tŏk-chung, Yi Kyŏng-do, Hwang Il-kwang, Han Tŏk-un, Hong In, Kwŏn Sang-mun (son of Kwŏn Il-sin), Yun Un-hye (wife of Chŏng Kwang-su) and others were executed.[381]

During this persecution period, the target of oppression consisted of the leading figures among the church members at that time, and the members of the *Sip'a* (especially *Sinsŏpa*) who had been treated with favoritism by the late king Chŏngjo. In eliminating the opposition faction, even those who were not Catholic believers but were in the slightest doubt, and those against whom personal grudges were held were arrested on the charge of "heterodoxy" and sentenced harshly.[382] These were acts of political revenge, in which even the non-Catholic family members of Catholic believers were punished.

For example, Yi Tong-uk lost his government position due to the fact that his son Yi Sŏng-hun had brought back books on Western Learning on his trip to Beijing, and senior envoys, Ch'ang Sŏng-ŏi and Hwang In-chŏm, who had accompanied the entourage, also were deprived of their official titles.[383]

Memorials continued to be submitted, demanding the dismissal of Yi Kyŏk, the older brother of Yi Pyŏk, from his official position.[384] Before the end of this year, along

---

[380] *Ibid.*, 9th month Ŭlyu.

[381] *Ibid.*, 12th month Mujin.

[382] Chin In-kwŏn, *op.cit.*, p.65.

[383] *Chosŏn wangjo sillok*, Sunjo, the beginning year 3rd month Kimyo.

[384] *Ibid*, Chŏnghae, Kich'uk and Sinmyo.

with the *yangban* Catholic Church members, the leaders of the church and the active members of the church were all executed. It seemed at the time that the Church organization had been entirely destroyed.

Surrender of Chou Wen-mo

The government exerted every effort to capture Father Chou Wen-mo, the central figure in the dissemination of Catholicism. Beginning in 1795 it was learned that he arrived in Seoul, and an order of arrest was issued. During the following six years, he worked in secret. When persecution worsened in 1801, he fled as far as Hwangju of Hwanghaedo, but he confessed on the 12th day 3rd month of Sinyu year (1801).[385]

Priest Chou Wen-mo had spread a heretical religion that was banned and created a cell organization called Myŏngdohoe. Furthermore, Chou Wen-mo's letter to the Bishop in Beijing attempted to attain missionary freedom in Chosŏn by having the king of Portugal establish diplomatic relations with the king of Chosŏn.[386]

In his confession, Chou Wen-mo named his associates, most of whom had already been sentenced by the Ch'ugukchŏng. The rest, Kim Kŏn-sun, Kang I-ch'ŏn, Kim Yŏ, Kim I-baek and others were all arrested for meeting with Chou Wen-mo and receiving doctrinal teachings.[387] In interrogating these individuals, persecution went beyond the level of a mere political faction and they were seen as associating with foreign forces and challenging the authority of the government. Kim I-baek was Kim Kŏn-sun's relative through a concubine's child, and while

---

[385] *Chosŏn wangjo sillok*, Sunjo, the beginning year 3rd month, Sinmyo.

[386] Charles Dallet, *op.cit.*, (sang), p.386, *Sinyu sahak choein Yu Hang-gŏm ch'uan*, Yu Kwan-gŏm kongch'o (statement).

[387] *Chosŏn wangjo sillok*, Sunjo, the beginning year 3rd month Imjin.

residing at Kŏn-sun's house, he had cooperated with Kang I-ch'ŏn, Kim Yŏ, Kim Sŏn and other like figures. He related what he had heard while corresponding and drinking with Kim Kŏn-sun and Kang I-chŏn: "There was an island in the middle of the ocean, and its form was that of the Chinese character Pum, and the soldiers and the horses were strong and energetic...There was also a person in the middle of the ocean who had mastered the 'way,' and he knew the ways of fortune telling and magic." Such stories had been spread. In actuality, he was very interested in obtaining the sending of a Western ship.[388]

When Queen Dowager Kim was concerned about the sentencing of Priest Chou Wen-mo, First Minister Yi Pyŏng-mo informed her:

> Kim Kŏn-sun told Priest Chou 'In the future, I want to build a large ship and take armor and weapons, and build a capital on the big ocean. Then I want to find and enter an offshore area in the outskirts and immediately attack that country on the other side to wash away our past disgrace of the Manchu Invasions of Pyŏngja year (1636). Priest Chou responded, 'That will never be successful in any way. I have a way that can be taught to others, so you ought to stop what you intend to do and learn from me.'[389]

Having concluded that Chou Wen-mo was colluding with foreign forces, the Chosŏn government was even more concerned about his contact with the members of the royal family. When a female servant in the house of

---

[388] Sinyu sahak choein Yi Ki-yang tŭng ch'uan 3, 3rd month, 15th day.

[389] *Chosŏn wangjo sillok*, Sunjo, the beginning year, 3rd month, Kyemyo.

Kang Wan-suk, the *Hoejang* of the female Catholics, was interrogated and tortured, she disclosed that Chou Wen-mo had stayed at Kang Wan-suk's house, and he visited the Yanghŏi palace, the residence of the wife of Chŏngjo's illegitimate brother, the Ŭnŏnkun and her daughter-in-law, he found that they had become converts, as had a significant number of palace women.

Many statesmen submitted memorials requesting that not only First Minister Yi Pyŏng-mo and the Ŭnŏnkun (In), but also Hong Nag-im, the son of the former the Chief State Councillor, Hong Pong-han should be punished for the crimes of treason and heterodoxy.[390] The Chief State Councilor Sim Hwan-ji also urged that these be considered cases of treason and that sentencing take place immediately, stating:

> When one speaks about this criminal incident related to a wicked learning, the criminal incident of Seoul and Hosŏ area are not simply due to the wicked doctrine. In order to carry out an evil scheme by colluding with a heretical group, they relied on a den of wicked learning in any way possible and attempted to enter it, and this is entirely because the two traitors still remain alive. In addition, there is no denying the fact that the spreading of false rumors and wicked sayings is all fabricated by these people.[391]

The Second State Councillor, Yi Si-su and the Third State Councillor, Sŏ Yong-bo, agreed with Sim Hwan-ji's opinion and urged a decisive conclusion, refusing to

---

[390] *Chosŏn wangjo sillok*, Sunjo, the beginning year 4th month, Kisa.

[391] *Chosŏn wangjo sillok*, Sunjo, the beginning year, 4th month Kyeyu.

back down until the proposed decree was approved.[392] Seven-hundred nine Confucian students of the Sŏnggyungwan, including Yi Ŭi-sil, seven-hundred fifteen Confucians including Yi Ik-hŏi, and sixteen people of the colleges including Yi To-myŏng jointly signed a proposal, and the Inspector-General and the Censor-General also submitted a similar entreaty.[393]

In response, Queen Dowager Kim gave an order written in Korean. She instructed that Ŭnŏnkun be exiled to Kanghwa Island, his son to be relocated and prohibited to make any contact with the outside and that Hong Nag-Im be exiled to Cheju Island.[394] Not satisfied by the decree, Yŏngbusa Yi Pyŏng-mo, the Chief State Councillor Sim Hwan-ji, the Second State Councillor Yi Si-su and the Third State Councillor Sŏ Yong-bo again argued that Ŭnŏnkun and Hong Nag-im should be executed, using as an excuse the report to the king by Hwang Sŏng-wŏn, the Yusu(Commandant) in Kanghwa. In addition to the traitors' case, they continued to attempt a purge of *Sip'a* by involving religious issues, saying "sly wives and wicked daughters-in-law communicated with the Westerners in secret."[395]

At first, Queen Dowager Kim was unable to come to a decision as to how to punish the members of the royal family. But due to the repeated submissions of such memorials, she eventually ordered an execution by poison of Ŭnŏnkun and Hong Nag-im (1741-1801).[396] Hong Nag-im was Hyegyŏng-kung (Crown Prince's wife)'s younger brother and Hong Pong-han's son as well as a member of *Sip'a*. The denunciation of them as Catholics was merely a

---

[392] *Ibid.*

[393] *Chosŏn wangjo sillok*, Sunjo, the beginning year, 4th month, Kyeyu.

[394] *Ibid.*

[395] *Ibid*, 5th month, Kyemyo.

[396] *Ibid*, Kapjin.

convenient excuse, the real objective being to purge members of an opposing faction.[397] After the execution of Ŭnŏnkun and Hong Nak-im, a recommendation was made to put their children to death as well.[398]

Authorities were at first suspicious of Chou Wen-mo's voluntary surrender after eluding capture for so long.[399] The *Sunjo sillok* indicates that Yŏngbusa Yi Pyŏng-mo reported to the king that his voluntary surrender was due to several reasons: because so many converts had been purged, it was difficult for him to find anywhere to hide, and also because he was not proficient in Korean, it was difficult for him to pursue his work; furthermore, if he had been caught, then he would certainly have been executed, and so by voluntarily confessing, he attempted to avoid death.[400] However, the same record also states that when asked to identify him, Chou Wen-mo declared, "I am an upholder of the teachings of Catholicism, and from what I hear; the court has strictly prohibited its teachings and killed many innocent people. Being alive is meaningless, and thus I came to ask that my life also be ended."[401]

The remaining question was how to handle Chou Wen-mo. Yi Pyŏng-mo proposed that he be treated according to the military law.[402] Chief State Councillor Sim Hwan-ji proposed that since he is no different from our own people, there is no need to consider where he is from and he should simply be executed. [403] The Second State

---

[397] *Ibid.*

[398] *Ibid*, 6th month, Kimyo.

[399] *Ibid*, 4th month, 11th.

[400] *Chosŏn wangjo sillok*, Sunjo, the beginning year, 3rd month, Sinmyo.

[401] Hwang Sa-yŏng paeksŏ, 79th line.

[402] *Chosŏn wangjo sillok*, Sunjo, the beginning year, 3rd month, Kyemyo.

[403] *Ibid.*

Councillor Yi Si-su expressed a concern stating that "He has been in our country for quite some time and is considered as father by the followers of heterodoxy, and thus there is nothing that he does not know about our country's affairs and customs. If a public announcement is made and he is sent back to China, there is the potential for harmful confrontation."[404] The Third State Councillor Sŏ Yong-po argued that there was no harm in treating him under the legal provisions for thieves, since he had been living in hiding just like a thief.[405]

Queen Dowager Kim was concerned that if the military law was applied, then the Ching authorities might hold Chosŏn responsible and thus she wanted to avoid possible future conflicts.[406] Chou Wen-mo was beheaded and gibbeted on the 19th day of the 4th month of 1801 according to the military laws.[407] During the six years of his missionary activity, he had gained converts in Seoul, Kyŏnggi, Ch'ungchŏng and Chŏlla provinces. He further systemized the church, wrote and taught catechisms, and performed masses.

Hwang Sa-yŏng's Silk Letter

On the 25th day of the 9th month of 1801, the Sinyu Persecution entered a new phase with the arrest of Hwang Sa-Yŏng, who had been hiding in Paeron, Chech'ŏn in Ch'ungch'ŏng province.[408] At the time of his arrest, the long letter he intended to send to the Bishop in Beijing was confiscated, and its contents titled "Hwang Sa-yŏng's

---

[404] *Ibid.*
[405] *Ibid.*
[406] *Ibid.*
[407] *Ibid*, 4th month, Pyŏngin.
[408] Sinyu sahak choein Hwang Sa-yŏng ch'uan, 10th month, 3rd day.

Declaration (Paeksŏ),"[409] aroused the government.

Hwang Sa-yŏng (1775-1801, Alexander) came from the Ch'angwŏn Hwang-ssi.[410] At 16 years of age, he passed the Chinsa examination, and by marrying the daughter of a prominent *Namin,* Chŏng Yak-hyŏn, he came in contact with and came to have deep faith in Catholicism. He studied its teachings with Chŏng Yak-chong and even studied under Chou Wen-mo as his disciple. And after 1791, when many Catholic *yangban* members had left the church due to the fury over the rites incident, he continued to practice the religion.

When the Sinyu Persecution erupted, Hwang Sa-yŏng had fled to Paeron in Ch'ungch'ŏngdo. He directly witnessed the mass slaughter of fellow Catholics and heard about others. Meanwhile, from Hwang Sim, he heard in detail about the situation of the persecution including the beheading of Priest Chou Wen-mo. These events motivated him to write his Declaration.[411]

He composed this letter on a piece of silk with the intention to inform Bishop Gouvea in Beijing of the tragic situation of the Chosŏn church and to request help to leave a record for posterity of those who died as martyrs during the persecution, and to quickly bring an end to the persecution thereby attaining freedom of belief.

The letter also detailed the development of the Sinyu Persecution and the actitivities of the martyrs of the previous persecutions of 1791 and 1795; the role that factional strife had played in the recent persecution; and his

---

[409] Charles Dallet I, p.567. This Paeksŏ was written on a piece of white silk, measuring 62cm in width and 38cm in length. It contains 122 lines, each of 110 characters, for a total of 13,311 characters. The original is currently preserved in the Archives of the Papal Court in Rome.

[410] His father Sŏk-pŏm passed Munkwa in1771.(Mansŏng Taedongpo, B208B4a.)

[411] Ch'oe Sŏg-u, *Han'guk kyohoesa ŭi t'amgu,* p.76.

plan to revive the Chosŏn Catholic church.[412] Hwang Sa-yŏng's letter also included a request that the Ch'ing emperor instruct Chosŏn to allow Westerners and missionaries to enter Chosŏn, as well as the following proposals: the building of an "office of pacification" for people between P'yŏngyang and Anju and sending a letter to a Western country, requesting that several hundred ships, fifty to sixty thousand soldiers, and powerful weapons such as cannons be sent to Chosŏn in order to intimidate the government so that it would not prohibit Western Learning.[413]

Hwang Sa-yŏng's name had been mentioned several times in the testimonies of many fellow church members, and on the 11th day of the 2nd month of 1801, he was reported to the State Tribunal and an arrest order was issued. But since he had already fled, the arrest had been delayed.[414] From Seoul where he had been visiting the church members' houses, on the 15th day of the 2nd month, he fled to the house of Kim Kwi-dong in Paeron, about 30 *li* from Chech'ŏn, Ch'ungch'ŏng province. There, he claimed himself to be a member of the Yi-ssi clan from Seoul.

Hwang Sa-yŏng was taken in custody to the State Tribunal and was interrogated from the 9th day through the 15th day of the 10th month, and he confessed that the content and the handwriting of the Paeksŏ were both his. He also stated that the reason for his borrowing Hwang Sim's name was because Hwang Sim was already acquainted with the Western missionaries in Beijing.[415]

While the trials of Hwang Sa-yŏng and others continued, *Chipŏi* (Second Inspector) Hong Nag-an and *Hŏnnap* (Third Censor) Sin Ku-jo jointly submitted a

---

[412] Hwang Sa-yŏng Paeksŏ, 1-112th line.

[413] *Chosŏn wangjo sillok*, Sunjo, the beginning year, 10th month, Musin.

[414] *Chosŏn wangjo sillok*, Sunjo, the beginning year, 2nd month, Imsin.

[415] Sahak choein Hwang Sa-yŏng tŭng ch'uan, *op.cit.*, p.731-799.

The Growing and the Persecutions of the Early Period

petition saying that as to the matters of Hwang Sa-yŏng's Paeksŏ, there must have been others who were involved in giving the order and in the conspiracy to deliver the letter. Thus they requested that those in exile such as Chŏng Yag-yong, Chŏng Yak-chŏn, Yi Ch'i-hun, Yi Hak-kyu, and Shin Yŏ-kwŏn be summoned and interrogated in order to reveal the truth.[416] In response, Queen Dowager Kim ordered Chŏng Yak-chŏn, Chŏng Yag-yong and Yi Ch'i-hun to be captured and brought to Seoul,[417] and also ordered the arrest of Yi Hak-kyu and Sin Yŏ-kwŏn the next day.[418]

On the 5th day 11th month, Hwang Sa-yŏng was sentenced to death by dismemberment for the crime of treason (*taeyŏkbudochoe*). The conclusion of the Tribunal's finding was as follows:

> Hwang Sa-yŏng the criminal, who is Chŏng Yak-chong's nephew by marriage, became infatuated by impure magic. After Chou W, and was baptized with a baptismal name. When an order of arrest waenmo's arrival, he considered him as his teacher, called him a priest s issued, he had already sensed the situation, upon which he fled and remained hidden in the mountain valleys, where he plotted a rebellion. Subsequently, actively cooperating with Hwang Sim and Ok Ch'ŏn-hŏi, he attempted to send a letter on silk cloth to a Catholic church where there were Westerners. Every word in this writing reflects the evil mind of a traitor to the king and constitutes a scheme to treat our country as an enemy. Sentence was passed

---

[416]*Chosŏn wangjo sillok*, Sunjo, the beginning year ,10th month, Pyŏngjin.
[417]*Ibid*, Muo.
[418]*Ibid*, Kimi.

naming him as guilty of high treason.[419]

On the 23rd day 10th month of 1801, Hwang Sim, and Kim Han-bin were both hanged outside the Sŏso gates, Hwang for abetting a traitor,[420] and Kim, for the crime of concealing their plans.[421] Hwang Sa-yŏng was pressed hard to say that Chŏng Yak-chŏn and Chŏng Yak-chong had been involved in the writing of his letter, but no evidence was found. On the 5th day 11th month, Hwang Sa-yŏng was executed for "the crime of the most brutal and wicked treason," outside the Sŏso Gate.[422]

On the other hand, Yi Ch'i-hun was exiled to Chejudo, Chŏng Yak-chŏn to Hŏksando, Chŏng Yag-yong to Kangjin, Yi Hak-kyu to Kimhae, Sin Yŏ-kwŏn to Kosŏng and Yi Kwan-ki to Changhŏng.[423] They had been interrogated concerning their involvement in Hwang Sa-yŏng's letter, but since none was confirmed, only the places of their exile were changed.

The police officer who arrested Hwang Sa-yŏng was appointed as a commander in a popular region.[424] After the execution of Hwang Sa-yŏng, an order was issued in Seoul and local regions to strictly observe the practice of combining five households into one unit for the purpose of mutual surveillance, and to report at the end of every month

---

[419] *Ibid*, Muin.

[420] *Ibid*, 10th month, Pyŏngin.

[421] *Ibid*.

[422] *Ibid*, Muin. Ok Ch'ŏn-hŭi and Hyŏn Kye-hŭm were also executed for not reporting the knowledge of Hwang Sa-yŏng's request for ships from abroad. Hyŏn Kye-hŭm received a judgement for the crime of going along with the request of large ships and not reporting it, and was also executed.

[423] *Ibid*.

[424] *Ibid*, 11th month, Sinsa.

anybody involved in heterodoxy.425

Although Hwang Sa-yŏng in his confession described his request for an armed force to invade the country as mere bluster designed to frighten the government into backing down on its prohibition of Catholicism, there is no doubt that it fueled a sense of alarm at court and among the common people at that time. 426

The Government's Denunciation

Tosa chumun (1801)

Faced with the upcoming Winter Solstice Embassy in 1801, the court discussed whether the situation of the Catholic persecution should be reported. The execution of Chou Wen-mo had been recorded in Hwang Sa-yŏng's letter, and the court believed his execution had already been reported since it was only recently that Ok Ch'ŏn-hŏi had visited Beijing. Afraid that they would be reprimanded for the execution of the priest, Queen Dowager Kim decided to dispatch a *chinjusa* (envoy to present a memorial to the Chinese emperor).

The Court officials did not want it known that they were aware of Chou Wen-mo's Chinese identity when they executed him. Cho Yun-dae suggested that in the beginning they executed him thinking that he was a Korean, and they came to learn of his Chinese identity only later through Hwang Sa-yŏng's statement that he was Chinese. Subsequently, *Taechehak* (Director) Yi Man-su devised *Tosajumun* (Edict for the Punishment of heterodoxy) and the "Hwang Sa-yŏng Paeksŏ" was to be accompanied as evidence of the content of the *jumun*, (incantation) but with the problematic words deleted.427 As a result, the content

---

425 *Ibid.*

426 Sahak choein Hwang Sa-yŏng dŭng ch'uan, *op.cit.*, p.732.

427 *Chosŏn wangjo sillok*, Sunjo, the beginning year,10th month, Kyŏngo.

of Hwang Sa-yŏng letter was altered, and a "false letter" created.

On the 27th day of 10th month of 1801, *chinjusa* Cho Yun-dae was dispatched to deliver a petition called a *Tosajumun* to China. Its content included a historical account of the introduction of Catholicism and the beginning of persecution with the Rites Controversy Incident in 1795 (the 15th year of Chŏngjo), saying that Yun Chi-ch'ung and Kwŏn Sang-yŏn were executed for their refusal to conduct ancestor worship, thereby committing a serious violation of the basic ethical principles by which the country was ruled. It also described Hwang Sa-yŏng's letter, emphasizing its conspiratorial and treacherous intent. Lastly, with regard to the execution of Chou Wen-mo, it reported that because he illegally crossed the border and there was no evidence of his Chinese identity, and further because he could not be distinguished from a Chosŏn man in his speech and appearance, he was executed as the principal propagator of a dangerous heterodox belief. It also claimed that his Chinese identity was mentioned only in the confession of Hwang Sa-yŏng, and that the rumor was difficult to prove even to this date.[428]

Ch'ing China evidently regarded both the execution of Chou Wen-mo and Hwang Sa-yŏng's letter as internal matters and did not respond.

T'osa gyomun (The Edict for the Punishment of Heterodoxy)
As Sinyu year (1801) came to a close, a congratulatory ceremony was held to celebrate the punishment of those who pursued "impure scholarship." At this gathering, a *T'osakyomun* was proclaimed, which was written again, by *Taechehak* (Director) Yi Man-su, summarizing the position of the Chosŏn government on the Sinyu Persecution, and affirming what were perceived as fundamental tenets of Confucianism.[429]

---

[428] *Ibid.*

[429] *Ibid*, 12th month, Kapja.

In a summary, it stated:

...(1) Catholic dogma "deceives" the world with its doctrine of heaven and hell; (2) the Catholic appellation of the "spiritual father" and "bishop" constitutes excessive worship; (3) the Ten Commandments and the so-called Seven Cardinal Virtues are a kind of falsehood analogous to prognostication and sorcery; (4) to enjoy life and hate death is human nature, and yet the Catholics regard a big sword and saw as if they are delightful to lie down upon; (5) to long for the distant past and to repay one's debt of life to one's parents is moral rectitude, and yet the winter and autumn ancestral sacrifices are despised and rejected; (6) entangled with the fallen families and the disclaimed, who bear grudges against the nation, and the despondent, and gaining their influence as a band, the Catholics gathered a multitude of the merchants, peasants, and women, and confounded moral obligations and violated public morals; (7) by means of two or three mysterious calligraphic characters each of them names himself for identification. With indecent paintings they secretly decorate their caves and dens. In the middle of the night in hidden rooms they crowd themselves and recite their books and preach. Sometimes speaking aloud in broad daylight, they agitate the crowd gathered in the middle of the street.[430]

Subsequently, Sunjo discarded Chŏngjo's policy of moderation and proclaimed his decision to adopt harsh

---

[430]Yi Man-ch'ae, *op.cit.*, Kwŏn 5, (English translation by Grant S. Lee, *Korea Journal*, Jan. 1988, p.20.)

measures of punishment.[431] For the persecution that occurred afterwards, the *Tosakyomun* became the fundamental legal prescription for the prohibition order of Catholicism.

The Nature of the Sinyu Persecution

The number of people known to have been executed or who died in prison as a result of torture during the Sinyu Persecution was over three hundred.[432] Over one hundred more lost their lives because of their association with Hwang Sa-yŏng, and over four hundred were exiled.

In addition to the human casualties, the church also suffered from the collapse of its organizations, while its books, holy items, and holy images were confiscated and burned.[433] During Chŏngjo's regime, 'defending orthodoxy' had been promoted and the issue was dealt with under a prohibition order. However, from Sunjo's reign, Catholics were treated under the principle of 'rejecting heterodoxy' and were regarded as anti-society and anti-nation, in short, as guilty of the crime of treason.[434]

Commander Kang Hŏi-ok submitted a memorial stating that a loud cry of thunder was heard in the winter which was a warning sign from the Heaven rebuking the dismissal of Ch'ae Che-gong from his official position and urging that they must respond to the warning.[435] On the 24th day of 12th month (Pyŏngin day), *Taesagan* Yu Han-nyŏng also presented a memorial, which stated that Ch'ae Hong-wŏn's house, Ch'ae Che-gong's illegitimate son by a concubine became the hiding place for Catholics in flight. The memorial also requested that because according to Yi Tong-uk's son-in-law, Kim Hŏi-ch'ae, when Yi Sŏng-hun

---

[431] *Ibid.*

[432] Yu Hong-nyŏl, *op.cit*, p.129.

[433] Pae Ŭn-ha, *op.cit.*, p.60.

[434] *Sŭngjŏnwŏn ilgi, 97chaek*, p.288.

[435] *Ibid*, 10th month, Ŭlch'uk.

visited Beijing in 1784 as *anhaeksa* he did not pay reverence to Confucian shrines, he ought to be exiled. Based on the joint petition submitted by *the Offices of the Censor-General and Inspector-General* proposing that the late *Yŏngbusa* Ch'ae Che-gong should be deprived of his official title since he is the root of evil treason.[436] Queen Dowager Kim allowed the matter to proceed and he too was removed from his government position.[437]

On the contrary, as the persecution was extended nationwide, it also certainly became an opportunity for the common people to become aware of Catholicism. First, when the church members fled from persecution from one place to another, they came to create a group of church members living together in hiding, and pursuing an even more devout religious life.

The persecution concentrated mainly on literati believers, Yi Ka-hwan, Kwŏn Ch'ŏl-sin, Yi Sŏng-hun, and Chŏng Yak-chong who were executed, and Chŏng Yag-yong who was exiled. But in many cases their children and wives continued to hold to their faith. Furthermore, believers of the *chungin* class came to solidify their position as the leaders of the church.

The active church members during the Sinyu Persecution were mostly those below the *chungin* class, in terms of social class standing. They pursued Western Learning as a popular religion, lacking in religious passion, or intellectual conviction, and thus the government was astonished and felt a sense of crisis at their relationship with Western forces.

---

[436] *Ibid*, 12th month, Kyŏngsin.
[437] *Ibid*.

Jai-Keun Choi

CHAPTER IV

Rebuilding of the Chosŏn Catholic Church and Establishment of a Korean Vicariate Apostolic

1. Formation of Kyouch'on (The Village of the Brethren)

Following the Sinyu Persecution, the Chosŏn government believed that the roots of heterodoxy had been eradicated. When Chou Wen-mo left them without a single priest, the Chosŏn Church would not have another priest until 1834.[438] The founders of the church contributed to its advancement by encouraging other church members and participating in church activities themselves. Nearly all the converts from the *yangban* class had been executed, and

---

[438] Ch'oe Wan-gi, "Pakhaegi Han'guk ch'ŏnju kyohoe wa p'yŏngsindo undong." *Han'guk kyohoesa nonmunjip, II*, 1985, pp.258-260. During approximately 100 years starting from the founding of the church in 1784 up to the end of persecution in 1876, the only periods during which a priest was present in Chosŏn were 1794 to 1800 with Chou Wen-mo, 1835 to 1838 with Liu Fang-chi, and 1846 to 1865 with a French priest. During all other times, the church was that of lay men without a priest.

their property confiscated, so that the remaining family members had no other choice but to leave their hometown.[439] Though the church members of the commoner class were persecuted less severely, they remained isolated, and did not communicate with each other. Since Catholic texts and religious relics had all been destroyed, the only activity left to them was prayer.

Church members, who had left their families behind as they fled the persecutions went into the mountains in the countryside, came together one by one and, as a result, a group called Kyouch'on (village of brethren) emerged spontaneously. The Korean Catholic Kyouch'on was in a very real sense a product of persecution.[440]

In 1798, Hwang Il-kwang, who became a Catholic after accompanying Yi Chon-ch'ang's mission, moved from Hongju to the Yŏngnam region with his younger brother in order to freely practice the Catholic faith,[441] and this is evidence that a Kyouch'on had existed even before the persecution of 1801. But it is only after the persecution of 1801 that the Kyouch'on began to take shape.

Where were these Kyouch'on formed? In his letter written in 1801, Hwang Sa-yŏng wrote, "there were many Catholic followers in the three areas of Kyŏnggi, Ch'ungch'ŏng and Chŏlla, and many had fled to Kyŏngsang and Kangwŏn, and thus secret government agents roamed about in these five provinces,"[442] indicating that Catholic groups had already been formed there even before the persecution. The locations were mainly in deep mountains where there was minimal contact with the outside.

Catholic followers who left their hometowns for the

---

[439] Charles Dallet, (tr), *op.cit.*, (chung), pp.51-52.

[440] Alan Pate, Catholic Persecution and Catholic Survival: The Korean Kyouch'on and Popular Catholicism in Nineteenth-Century Korea, M.A. Thesis, Harvard University, 1990, p.2.

[441] Charles Dallet, *op.cit.*, (sang), p.473.

[442] Hwang Sa-yŏng paeksŏ, 94th line.

anonymity also fled to Seoul. Among the 290 Catholics who were arrested and interrogated in the Seoul region during the Sinyu Persecution, 58 were from the countryside.[443] This fact posed a kind of challenge to the traditional order of authority. Nevertheless, the majority joined Kyouch'on in mountainous areas in the countryside.[444] Even after a Kyouch'on was established, on many occasions, they had to move because of the imminent threat of persecution.

> "At times, when the Catholic followers had cultivated a piece of land for over two to three years and came to believe that the land was sufficiently fertile, they had to abandon it and move to another place. At several other times, even with the harvesting season ahead, they had to desert everything and flee with no set place to go, relying only on God whom they believed would not let even one bird in the sky to die of starvation."[445]

The formation of Kyouch'on witnessed by Sin T'aebo (1768-1839) following the Sinyu Persecution is recorded in Charles Dallet's work, and the following portion clearly illustrates the economically difficult situation of Kyouch'on:

> Before we knew it, the time for farming had passed, and the winter had arrived, and the snow began to accumulate and wiped out all of the trails. We had no

---

[443] Cho Kwang, Sinyu pakhae ŭi punsŏkchŏk koch'al. *Kyohoesa yŏn'gu I*, p.61.

[444] For example, Pakkok-village of Chinch'ŏn-county in Ch'ungchŏng province was found to have approximately twenty Kyouch'on.

[445] Yi Wŏn-sun, Hŏ Yŏn(ed.), *Kim Tae-gŏn ŭi sŏhan*, p.206.

acquaintances in the area; [it was] impossible to even communicate with the neighbors, and we were about forty people all exposed to hunger and the cold...the children cried continually, asking for food; the adults themselves became anxious and impatient. Almost no provisions remained; each day appeared gloomier, and we began to succumb to the temptation of complaining, of hating the faith which was the cause of such horrible sufferings, to criticize ourselves for even having believed in God.[446]

In a Kyouch'on, the leader of the village automatically became the Hoejang who taught doctrine to others, while prayer took place communally. In addition, collective allocation of food among the Catholics was possible with their Christian love. In other words, they not only united religiously and emotionally, but together they cultivated agriculture through the fire-field farming method and created their own practical economic occupations, such as producing potteries and coal and cultivating tobacco that can be grown in the mountains. They also established relationships with other Kyouch'on through trading of local produce and pottery, which was also convenient for sending messages. Later when the missionaries entered Chosŏn, they formalized the organization of Kyouch'on. In a letter written by Father Chastan in 1837, it is recorded that the missionaries visited Kyouch'on, and they either created or supplemented the organization of Catholic groups by appointing or giving approval to the chief of the village and prescribing rules on various practices of Catholicism, such as baptism of children, wedding, funeral, observance of

---

[446]Charles Dallet, *op.cit.*, (chung), pp.13-14. (English trans. from Alan Pate's, M.A. Thesis pp.24-25).

Sunday, gatherings on feast days.[447] This is an illustration that regulations different from those of the general society were applied to Kyouch'on, which later on transformed into *Kongso* (mission stations).

Since there were only a few priests and the sphere of their activities was limited, Priest Le Gendre organized a presidential system called *Hoejang kyujŏng* (Regulations for the Catechist) in order to manage the Catholic followers.

The Hoejang (catechist) gathered the followers on Sundays and feast days as well as leading the meetings. At the gathering, they prayed in communion, and read doctrinal dialogues, gospel Bible and biographies of saints, and afterwards, the catechist provided an interpretation of the materials.[448]

While it was the several members of the intellectual class who promoted the movement to invite priests from abroad, the leaders of the *Kongso* fellowship which in leading the Kyouch'on in each region disseminated the doctrine. Having been persecuted by their own families, the Catholic followers strived to form a religious family system on their own as a new communally operated organization. As Consor-General Mok Man-chung described in a memorial that Catholics "...consider their own parents and siblings, if they do not convert to Catholicism, as enemies for life, while strangers from all sorts of places are considered as kin once they join the Catholic church... ."[449]

2. Introduction of Priests

The rebuilding of the church organization was the work of the second generation of those initially involved in

---

[447] Charles Dallet, *op.cit.* (chung), p.359.
[448] *Ibid.,* (chung), p.335.
[449] *Ibid*, 2nd month 18th day.

the founding of the Catholic church. They were Kwŏn Ch'ŏl-sin's nephew Kwŏn Yo-han (Kwŏn Ki-in), Hong Nak-min's son Hong U-song, Chŏng Yak-chong's son Chŏng Ha-sang, and Yi Yŏ-chin and Sin T'ae-bo of Ch'ungch'ŏngdo Naep'o. Sin T'ae-bo in particular united and encouraged the scattered fellow believers, reproduced and distributed catechisms, and strived to collect funds to operate the church.[450]

In 1811, the Chosŏn Catholics sent a letter to J. Souza-Saraiva (1744-1818), the Bishop of Beijing, as a part of their plan to reconstruct the church.[451] Their principal request was that a priest be sent who could conduct liturgical rites, but they also said:

> Fellow believers who were talented in the business of living all died during the mass persecution. Those whose lives were spared from execution and those who live in hiding are all frightened and have become almost witless. They lost all of their family wealth and their possessions, and now merely sustain their lives by begging. No one is self-sufficient. What is more, the suffering is so severe that many people's intentions have changed and they have become more fearful and doubtful.[452]

---

[450] Yi Wŏn-sun, *Chosŏn sŏhaksa yŏn'gu*, p.79.

[451] Width 11 cm, length 23 cm, 28 pages in total, with each page consisting of 9 lines and each line consisting of 25 characters. The translated version of Portugal, French and Italian are preserved in the consultant's library of the Pope, and the original version in Chinese characters was recently discovered. Yun Min-ku, Sinminyŏn (1811) e Chosŏn ch'ŏnjugyo singadŭli pukkyŏng chugyo egye ponaen p'yŏnji e taehan yŏn'gu. *Suwŏn Kato'llik taehak nonmunjip*, 2, 1990, p.40.

[452] "Pukkyŏng chugyo ege ponaen Chosŏn kyou ŭi sŏhan (1811)." *Mannam kwa midŭm ŭi kilmok esŏ*, p.102.

In 1811, Kwŏn Ki-in, Sin T'ae-bo, Cho Tong-sŏm and others sent Yi Yŏ-chin as a secret envoy to Beijing to earnestly request dispatch of a priest, writing,

> Because of our sins, we sent our spiritual father to his death... Please extend to us the hand of salvation to help us free ourselves from this wretched situation that we have fallen into! Our tears and wailing refuse to cease and we pray to the Lord day and night. The only reason for our wish to continue living is simply to be able to participate in the mass and sacraments and to relish the happiness of confessing ousins... .[453] Writing a letter to the Pope exceeds our capability given our situation. We request that our letter be translated and sent to the Pope. This is a small token of filial piety expressed to the one who is in place of the Lord in our world of humble people and who is the source of our happiness. We are hoping to inform him or our situation in detail and encourage him to have sympathy towards us.[454]

They further requested from the Bishop that the regulations be relaxed a bit to allow those living along with non-Catholics without being accused as a Catholic believers. They professed to abide by the instruction prohibiting ancestor worship, in relation to the first commandment, but requested that for those involved in compulsory labor and military service, the practice of fasting and abstinence

---

[453] *Ibid*, pp.99-100.

[454] "Pukkyŏng chugyo ege ponaen Chosŏn kyou ŭi sŏhan (1811)." *Mannam kwa midŭm ŭi kilmok esŏ*, p.107.

related to the third commandment be relaxed.[455] Since the religious relics and books had all been confiscated and burned, they also requested that they receive Catholic books printed in small letters as well as religious relics.[456] Another request was the sending of the promised ships. This was a request that had been made continuously ever since the early stage of the church, and they perceived the request as the dispatch of a peaceful envoy through when they would attain freedom of missionary activities rather than military intervention.[457] Another request was to establish a locale near Beijing at which they could communicate with the Beijing parish. At the time the prohibition order forbade the Chosŏn envoys to Beijing from visiting Western individuals at the Catholic churches.[458]

The secret envoy who delivered this letter was Yi Yŏ-chin, a *yangban* who disguised himself as a servant in the group accompanying the Winter Solstice envoy.[459]

> It seems appropriate that the Pope and the king of Portugal send gifts and a respectful letter to our king. We suggest that you indicate in the letter that the intention of the Pope and the king of Portugal is to praise the one and only Lord, to spread the holy religion, to allow all people to enjoy freedom and to establish peace among the people of the nation. The ways of Catholicism should also be explicated clearly, and in all good faith and propriety, the letter should be persuasive of the fact

---

[455] Yun Min-ku, *op.cit.*, p.70.
[456] *Ibid.*
[457] *Ibid*, p.44.
[458] *Ibid*, p.72.
[459] Charles Dallet, *op.cit.*, (chung), p.18.

that the missionaries' arrival is in their pursuit of charity, not to invade Chosŏn. If done in such manner, our fellow countrymen may open their eyes and suspicion would disappear on its own, so that they may be able to understand the true way.[460]

It is worth noting that perhaps having in mind the controversy surrounding the Hwang Sa-yŏng Paeksŏ, they proposed a peaceful diplomatic measure rather than a military one.

The Bishop in Beijing, Father Gouvea, who had understood the situation of the Chosŏn church, had died, and his successor, as Bishop of Beijing, Bishop Saraiva, was residing in Macao. The letter written by the Chosŏn church members was delivered to a delegate in the Beijing Parish, Priest Riverio, who sent the letter on to Macao.

Upon the eruption of the Chinese Rites Controversy, the Beijing church was also the victim of a persecution policy against Catholicism, such as the 1805 order prohibiting missionary work, publications by Westerners, and in 1811 a further prohibition of mission work. Thus, in actuality, Beijing itself was short of clergymen and was unable to dispatch one to Chosŏn.[461]

Having received the letter from the Chosŏn Catholic church members, Bishop Saraiva in Macao was deeply moved and devised a way to send a missionary to Chosŏn, there translating the letter and sending it on to the Pope in Rome. Although the Papal Court received the letter in 1815, because of the chaotic situation in Europe following the French Revolution and Napoleon's reign of ten years after 1804, Pope Pius VII was imprisoned in Fontainebleau and was unable to address their request.[462]

---

[460] *Ibid*, p.111.

[461] Chalrles Dallet, *op.cit.*, (chung), pp.37-39.

[462] Charles Dallet, *Ibid*, (chung), p.38.

Rebuilding of the Chosŏn Catholic Church

Movement for Invitation of Priest by Chŏng Ha-sang and Yu Chin-gil

Though they did not receive a single priest after their request to the Bishop in Beijing and the Papal Court in Rome, the Chosŏn church members were not dissuaded and went to Beijing in 1813 to ask for dispatch of a clergyman. Chŏng Ha-sang, Chŏng Yak-chong's second son, also went to Beijing in 1816 accompanying Yi Yŏ-chin.

When the Chosŏn church members saw that there was no progress even after numerous requests for a priest, they decided to send a letter directly to the Pope in Rome. In 1825, Chŏng Ha-sang [463] and Yi Yŏ-chin , Yu Chin-gil and others wrote:[464]

> We humbly suggest the following two proposals to the Pope, and we believe the two are equally necessary. Furthermore, these two issues are inseparable from each other. If a person does not eat for many days, he will die from lack of energy. Though food may be arriving for him in one month, if he does not receive food immediately and relieve his hunger, what use would the later arrival of food have? On the other hand, if no food is to be given to him in the next month, then what would

---

[463] At age six, Chŏng Ha-sang lost his father and the family fortune, and with his widow mother Yu So-sa and his sister, he was residing at his uncle Chŏng Yag-yong's house in Majae, Kwangju, Kyŏnggido. Pressured to renounce the religion by his relatives, he left his residence in Majae and continued to practice the faith while living with a poor fellow Catholic. When he learned that Cho Tong-sŏm (1738-1830) from Yanggŭn was living in exile in Musan, Hamgyŏngdo, he visited him and learned the Catholic doctrine and Chinese. Persuaded by Cho Tong-sŏm, he decided to travel to Beijing in order to reconstruct the Chosŏn church.

[464] Charles Dallet, *op.cit*, (chung), p.105.

be the use in his eating today? Likewise, there is no doubt that the dispatch of a priest is a great grace and joy to us. At the same time, if our desire is not permanently fulfilled and no measure is devised to guarantee the salvation of the souls of our posterity, then it will be a matter of great indignation.[465]

In this letter of request, they stated, "In order to produce a positive result, a priest must first be sent to oversee our exigent situation, and then have the priest receive the requested ships. This is the best method for allowing freedom to practice Catholicism."[466] They not only requested the dispatch of a priest, but also proposed a peaceful measure in order to attain religious freedom, and this demonstrates their cautiousness in devising a solution for their problem.

Establishment of Korean Vicariate Apostolic

As the Nanjing Diocese was established in 1660, the Chosŏn church was established as a district within the Paris Foreign Mission Society by the Sacred Congregation for the Propagation of the Faith of Roman Curia. At that time the Bishop was Ignace Cotolendi, who continued until 1690 when the Beijing Parish was established.[467] When Yi Sŭng-hun, Yi Pyŏk and others created a Catholic communal organization on their own and requested a dispatch of missionaries in 1784, the Chosŏn region was under the personal protection and guidance of Bishop Gouvea of the Beijing parish.

---

[465] Kyohwang sŏngha ege ponaen sŏhan (1826). *Mannam kwa Midŭm ŭi kilmok esŏ*, p.117.

[466] *Ibid.*

[467] Pae Se-yŏng, "Pari woebang chŏngyohoe ŭi Han'guk sŏngyo chŏngch'aek." *Kyohoe wa yŏksa*, 102, Dec. 1982, p.7.

Along with interpreter Yu Chin-gil, Chŏng Ha-sang, who visisted Beijing and made a request for a priest on nine occasions, again requested a priest and entreated the Beijing Bishop to take measure in regards to the Chosŏn church. The Chosŏn church members' letter was sent to Priest Umpierres in Macao, and in 1826, with the help of Priest L. Lamiot, the letter was translated into Latin and sent to Rome with Father Umpierres' opinion attached, which was that what the Chosŏn church needs is a religious order that can take exclusive responsibility for it, and further that it is appropriate that the Chosŏn church be separated from the jurisdiction of the Beijing Bishop, and that the Jesuits should undertake a ministry in Chosŏn.[468] The Chosŏn Catholics' letter was delivered to Pope Leo XII in 1827 [469] and, having been impressed by its presentation, he made a decision to establish an independent ecclesiastical jurisdiction in the territory of Korea, to have it belong directly to the Holy See (Roman Curia), and to delegate the missionary work to the Paris Foreign Mission Society (La Sociéte des Mission-Étrangères de Paris).[470]

However, the matter came to a standstill as the Paris Foreign Mission Society hesitated to accept the Chosŏn church as a region of mission. In 1829, Priest Barthelemy Bruguière, who was pursuing missionary work in Thailand, at that time volunteered to become the missionary to the Chosŏn ecclesiastical jurisdiction. The Holy See (Roman Curia) took this opportunity to commission the Paris Foreign Mission Society to select a missionary to lead the missionary work in Chosŏn, and subsequently, it decided to appoint Father B. Bruguière, who was already well aware of the persecution of the Chosŏn church and their request for a priest.[471]

---

[468] Charles Dallet, (tr.) *op.cit.*, (chung), p.216.
[469] *Ibid*, pp.211-215.
[470] *Ibid*, p.216.
[471] *Ibid*, pp.220-223.

The one who showed the greatest enthusiasm toward the mission in Chosŏn was Cardinal Capellari of the Prefect of the Sacred Congregation for the Propagation of the Faith. While he was promoting the dispatch of a missionary to Chosŏn, Pope Leo XII passed away and Cardinal Capellari was elected to the Holy See and acceded as Gregory XVI in 1831.

Due to Bruguière's volunteering to be the missionary to Chosŏn, along with the Chosŏn church members' repeated efforts, Pope Gregory XVI issued a proclamation on the 9th day of 9th month in 1831 (31st year of Sunjo), not even a year since his accession, establishing the Chosŏn Vicariatus Apostoricus. "With accurate knowledge, and after much consideration and with the full official authority of the Pope, I declare an immediate establishment of the Chosŏn kingdom as a new parish through the issuance of this message, and declare an appointment of the head of the parish, entirely independent from the Bishop in Beijing."[472]

Upon the establishment of the Chosŏn parish, a papal's breve appointing Bishop Bruguière (1792-1835) as the Bishop of the Chosŏn church was proclaimed.[473] The patron saint of the newly established Korean Vicariate Apostolic approved by Pope Gregory XVI on the 22nd day of August of 1841 (solar calendar) was the Blessed virgin Mary.

In 1791, according to the wish of Bishop Gouvea (1751-1808) and the instruction of Pope Pius VI, the society for the Propagation of the Faith (Sacra Congregatio de

---

[472] *Ibid*, (chung), p.235. A Vicar Apostolic is a titular bishop who rules a territory called a vicariate apostolic as a delegate of the Holy See. Vicars Apostolic have no territorial diocese, cathedral church or chapter of canons, and their name is not mentioned in the canon of the mass; but they usually exercise by delegation the same powers as diocesan bishops. Kim Chang-mun & Chung Jae-sun (ed.), *Catholic Korea Yesterday and Today*, (Pusan: Catholic Korea Publishing Co., 1988), p.128.

[473] *Ibid.*, p.237.

Propaganda Fide) had given Beijing the authority to supervise Chosŏn, a new ecclesiastical jurisdiction. Since at that time the Beijing parish was under the missionary responsibility of Portugal, this meant the Portugese society claimed authority over Chosŏn as well. But the Pope was concerned that the Portugal missionary group would not dispatch a priest promptly, so he transferred responsibility for Chosŏn to the Paris Foreign Mission Society.

A Chinese Priest, Liu Fang-chi, was dispatched to the Chosŏn kingdom, under papal order, to prepare to greet the arrival of Bruguière. With the help of Chosŏn church members such as Yu Chin-gil and Cho Sin-ch'ŏl, Father Liu successfully entered Chosŏn in 1834. However, acting according to the view held by the Beijing diocese and the suzerain authority of Ch'ing China, he intervened in Chosŏn church matters and so delayed the arrival of the Bishop for three years.[474] Father Liu had wanted to keep the Chosŏn parish under the governance of the Beijing bishop.[475] In addition, he had another independent goal, to train the youth of Chosŏn as clergymen. Bishop Bruguière arrived in China in July of 1832 and eventually made his way to Manchuria from which he made several unsuccessful attempts to enter Chosŏn. But he failed and died in October of 1835.[476] In August of l936, the Pope appointed his assistant, Laurent Marie Joseph Imbert (Korean name: Pŏm Se-hyŏng) (1796-1839) to take his place.[477]

The very first Western priest to arrive in Chosŏn following the establishment of the Chosŏn parish in 1831 was a French Priest, Pierre Philibert Maubant (Korean name: Na Paek-darok). He arrived in Seoul in the 1st month of 1836 under the guidance of Chŏng Ha-sang and Cho Sin-ch'ŏl, and immediately he confirmed the misdeeds

---

[474] Yu Hong-nyŏl, *op.cit.*, (sang), pp.286-287.

[475] Charles Dallet (tr.), *op.cit.*, (chung), p.322.

[476] *Ibid.*, p.324.

[477] *Ibid.*, p.377.

of Priest Liu Fang-chi and decided to banish him to China. In the 1st month of 1837, Priest Jacques Honorè Chastan (1803-1839) arrived and Bishop Imbert arrived in the 12th month.

Revival of the Church (1830-'s1840's)

With the establishment of the Chosŏn parish and the arrival of the missionaries from the Paris Foreign Mission Society, the number of the church members increased measurably: from 6,000 at the time of Priest Maubant's arrival in 1831 to to 9,000 by 1838.[478]

The cultural and language barrier facing the black-robed priests were enormous. But, they learned Korean, visited church members scattered around various regions in the countryside, teaching and providing texts and using funds sent from their headquaters in Paris. In 1843 a French priest, Jean Joseph Ferréol (1808-1853) was appointed as the third Vicar Apostolic of Korea (Vicaire Apostolique de Corée). [479] After six years of failed attempts to enter Chosŏn in October of 1845, Ferréol finally entered Chosŏn together with a priest named Father Daveluy and a Korean Father, Kim Tae-gŏn. At that time, the number of believers amounted to approximately 4,000, and they were scattered throughout the country. He spent the next eight years, until his death in 1853, in establishing groups such as the Maekoehoe (Society of the Rosary) and Sŏngŭihoe (Confraternitas sacri scapularis). He strived to expand the organization of the church as well as strengthening the relationships among the fellow church members. He also wrote "Kihae Ilgi"(Diary of the perseqution of 1839) and edited "Pyŏngo Ilgi." (Diary of the persecution of 1846)

His replacement as Vicar Apostolic of Korea was Simeon-Françoise Berneux (Korean name: Chang Kyŏng-il) (1814-1866), who arrived in Hwanghae province in

---

[478] *Ibid.,* p.377.

[479] *Ibid.*, p. 263.

1856.[480] French priests continued to enter Chosŏn, and in the 7th year of Chŏlchong, Pyŏngchin year (1856), there were five French priests and one Korean, the largest number of Catholic clergymen the Chosŏn Church had ever had.

The fifth Vicar Apostolic of Korea, Bishop Marie Antoine Nicholas Daveluy (1818-1866) arrived in 1845, and for 21 years until 1866 when he died a martyr, he pursued missionary work in Chosŏn and became the most knowledgeable about Korean language and customs among all the missionaries. He edited a Korean-Chinese-French dictionary and a chronological table of Korean history. His significant contribution was the collection and editing of materials related to the history of the Chosŏn church, and providing the historical materials for Charles Dallet's writing of *Histoire de l'Eglise de Corea*.[481] He further devised regulations for the activities of churchmen, and structured the activities of the Chosŏn parish.

In 1857, Father S. Féron (1827-1903) entered Chosŏn. In 1861, Priests J.M. Landre, P.M. Joanno, F.C. Ridel, and A.N. Calais, and in 1863, Priest P. Aumaitre entered Chosŏn. In 1864, four Western priests also entered Korea. They were Simon-Maie Antonio-Just Ranfer de Berteniere (1838-1866), Bernard Louis Beaulieu (1840-1866), Pierre-Henri Dorie (1839-1866), and Martin-Luc Huin (?-1866).

Consequently, by 1836, thirty years after the arrival of Priest Maubant, twenty priests from the Paris Foreign Mission Society had come to Chosŏn. Three of them, Imbert, Maubant and Chastan had been martyred during the Kihae Persecution of 1839; and five priests, Jansou, Ferréol, Maistre, Joanno, and Landre died of illness while pursuing missionary work in Chosŏn. Nine were martyred during the Pyŏngin Persecution of 1866: Berneux, Petitnicolaus,

---

[480] Charles Dallet, *Ibid.,* (chung), p.402. In 1852, Priest Ambroise Maistre entered Chosŏn through the coast of Chŏllado. In 1854, Priest F. S. Jansou arrived in Chosŏn.

[481] Charles Dallet, *Ibid.,*, (ha), p.259.

Pourthie, Aumaitre, Bretenieres, Huin, Beaulieu, Daveluy and Dorie. Three others, Féron, Ridel, and Calais escaped the country.

The Beginning of Theological Education

Since foreign priests were able to enter Chosŏn only with great difficulty, and those priests already residing in Chosŏn could not communicate in Korean, the Paris Foreign Mission Society had already adopted a policy of cultivating native clergymen to meet the demand for priests.

When Priest Maubant arrived in Chosŏn at the end of 1836, he selected three young men, Kim Tae-gŏn, Ch'oe Yang-ŏp, and Ch'oe Pang-je,[482] and sent them to the Paris Foreign Mission Society in Macao to be educated. They were guided to the border by Chŏng Ha-sang and Cho Sin-ch'ŏl.

Bishop Laurent Marie Joseph Imbert (1769-1839), who entered Chosŏn in 1837, recognized the immediate need for Korean clergy, and considering the length of time it would take for the students in Macao to complete their training, he decided to institute a shorter, but intensive training process and ordain priests within Chosŏn.

He had chosen unmarried individuals who frequented Beijing and participated in church activities, such as Chŏng Ha-sang, a 42 year-old widower, Yi Mun-u, Yi Sun-kyo and Ch'oe Peter. By 1838, they were already able to read in Latin and were studying theology through books in Chinese translation, and Bishop Imbert planned to give them ordination within three years.[483] But Bishop Imbert was arrested in the persecution of 1839, before that could be accomplished.

In the 8th month in 1845, Priest Kim Tae-gŏn (1821-1846) was ordained, becoming the very first Chosŏn

---

[482] *Ilsŏngnok*, Hŏnjong 5th year (1839), 8:7.

[483] Charles Dallet (tr.), *op.cit.,*(chung), p.384. Pae En-ha, *op.cit.*, p.127.

priest.[484] Father Ch'oe Yang-ŏp (1821-1861), having been ordained and returned to Chosŏn in 1849, assumed the responsibility for overseeing Tonggol Kyouch'on in Chinch'ŏn-gun Paekŏk-myŏn in accordance with the order of Bishop Berneux. He translated Bishop Perréol's French translation of "Pyŏngo ilgi" into Latin, and simplified the "Ch'ŏnju sŏngkyo ilgwa," a year round prayer book, (completed in 1858) so that it was easier to understand. He composed a song (in the 4-4 rhyming pattern of a traditional Korean song form) called "Ch'ŏnju kasa (Song of Heaven), and facilitated the learning of doctrine.

As the persecution was relaxed upon the accession of Ch'ŏlchong (1849), three seminary students were sent to the Collège Generale Penang in the 3rd month of 1854.[485] They became the second group of Chosŏn people to go abroad to study. In 1858, three more were sent, but for health reasons related to an epidemic disease, they were unable to stay longer and all returned to Chosŏn by the year 1863. Afterwards, persecution prevented further dispatch of students, and it was not until 1882 that more were sent abroad.[486]

There were problems in sending seminary students abroad for priesthood training, such as their inability to adapt to the climate and deaths from epidemic diseases. Furthermore, theological education within Chosŏn became slowly feasible, with government hostility lessened, and already ten or so French priests were active in the country who could provide training. Father Ambroise Maistre (1808-1857), who was the Vicar Apostolic of Korea at that

---

[484] Ch'oe Pang-je (? - 1861) of Hongju, Ch'ungchŏngdo died of fever while studying theology in Macao and never returned to Chosŏn. He was a cousin of Priest Ch'oe Yang-ŏp.

[485] Charles Dallet, *op.cit.,*(ha), p.206, p.296.

[486] Pae En-ha, *op.cit.*, p.128.

time, founded Korea's first theological school in Paeron[487] in 1855,[488] the *St. Joseph Theological School,* [489]

When the Pyŏngin Persecution occurred in 1866, the president, teachers and the financial director were all martyred, and the school closed of its own accord as theological education could no longer be continued. Among the subjects taught at the school, Latin was taught so thoroughly that Oppert found it almost odd that he was able to communicate with a seminary student in Latin when robbing the grave of the Taewŏngun's father.[490]

Later, with the end of persecution in 1885 theological education in Korea began again with the establishment of the Sacred Heart of Jesus in Wŏnju by Bishop Blanc Paek.

4. Doctrinal Training in Practice

Before he was arrested and executed in the 9th month of 1839, Chŏng Ha-sang presented a letter called *Sangjae sangsŏ* to the Third State Councillor Yi Chi-yŏn. He had written the article in defense of the Catholic doctrine criticizing the prohibition of the Western Learning and anti-

---

[487] Currently Ch'ungbuk, Chech'ŏnkun, Pongyang-myŏn Kuhak-ri.

[488] Charles Dallet (tr.), *op.cit.*, (ha), pp.269, 324.

[489] The president of the school for the next ten years was Charles Antoine Pourthié (1830-1866) (Priest Kap). Michel Alexandre Petitnicolas (1828-1866) (Father Pak) was the only teacher, Ch'ang Chu-gi was the financial director and Yi Kyŏng-ju (Vincencio) was the Chinese language teacher. It was in the home of Chang Nak-so (Chu-gi). In 1855, there were three students; in 1856, there were four students; and by 1859, there were nine students. In addition to Latin, philosophy and theology, the subjects taught were zoology, botany, geology, science, and history.

[490] Ernst Oppert (tr.), *op.cit.*, pp.163-165.

heterodoxy stance of the Chosŏn government.

The content of the *Sangjae sangsŏ* was an appeal to the authorities not to reject Catholicism as an evil doctrine, and cause the sacrifice of many lives. It was writing of supplication that demonstrates an attempt to awake the Chosŏn government from its misunderstanding and ignorance of Catholicism. During the time when the government pursued the policy of authorized oppression through punishment, it was subjected to theoretical refutations which revealed the unsoundness of its ideological foundation.

He criticized Buddhism, and the logic of anti-Buddhism was that Buddhism had neither parents nor king and thus was barbarian. A Buddhist concept of leaving one's home and entering the mountains to practice asceticism and pursue priesthood violated the virtue idea of reality. He argued that deserting one's parents and family and living in the mountains to seek priesthood was the same as having neither a father nor a king. Although he renounced Buddhism, he viewed the Confucian ideologies to be in concordance with the Catholic doctrine in their origins. For example, he explained that there was no difference between the Ten Commandments and the Confucian ethics. He also briefly introduced the existence of God, immortality of soul and judgment after death, and in particular, argued the unreasonableness of the practice of ancestor worship.

Sangjae sangsŏ was a short document of 3,400 words, and it was written concisely enough that Bishop Kao John of Hong Kong used it as a material for his doctrinal education for the Chinese people. While Hwang Sa-yŏng had turned his focus to outside forces and asked to be saved, Chŏng argued to the king and to the public counrymen that one could be a Catholic believer without neglecting the duty of loyalty to one's country.

Ch'ŏnju kasa (Song of God/Heaven)

Because of the ban on Catholic books, materials

written in Korean or Chinese were difficult to get hold of. Under these circumstances, one effective means of spreading doctrinal teachings was by word of mouth through the composition of songs, composed in the traditional *kasa* form, a rhyming pattern of parallel lines in two groups of 3 or 4 syllables, called *Ch'ŏnju kasa*, which became popular after the middle of the 19th century due to the persecution and oppression. Church members could learn the song and sing along during the mass led by the Hoejang (cathechist) of Kyouch'on even when a clergyman was not present. The *kasa* form had appeared by the end of the Koryŏ dynasty and had been used for personal expression but also occasionally to celebrate Confucian virtues or memorialize Buddhist teachings. [491]

Furthermore, "Ch'ŏnju kasa" written by Priest Ch'oe Yang-ŏp during the persecution period were more profuse, and they were handed down as songs among the common people of the culture, making a marked contribution to the Catholic mission.

Around this time, the secret Sunday gatherings of twelve to fifteen Catholics had been continuing, conducting rituals and learning doctrinal dialogues (catechisms) themselves at the same teaching them to their children.[492] The Kyouch'on Catholics educated their children regarding the Catholic doctrine and prayer, and emphasized the glory of martyrdom, instilling in the children an ardent desire for martyrdom. This was precisely the content of the "Ch'ŏnju

---

[491] Some scholars claim that "Ch'ŏnjugasa" had been written since the founding of the Catholic church and that two of those early pieces exist today: Yi Pyŏk's "Ch'ŏnju Konggyŏngga" (The Lyrics in Praise of the Lord) and Chŏng Yak-chŏn's "Sipkyemyŏngga" (Ten Commandments Lyrics). Both were said to have been composed after the Chuŏsa conference led by Kwŏn Ch'ŏl-sin during the winter of year 1779. However, issues regarding these early songs remain problematic.

[492] Charles Dallet, *op.cit.*, (ha), p.252.

kasa."[493] "Ch'ŏnju kasa" continued to be sung even after the persecution had ended and lasted until the 1930's.[494]

The greatest number of "Ch'ŏnju kasa" catechisms in Korean and other Catholic books were written or printed around 1860. In 1864, a woodblock printshop waa established and thirteen catechisms in eight versions were published.[495] The individuals involved in the translation, editing and publication of catechisms in mid 19th century were Ch'oe Yang-ŏp, Ch'oe Hyŏng, Kim Chang-un, Chang Chu-gi and Hwang Sŏk-du.[496]

Sŏnggyo yori mundap was the very first catechism that the Korean Catholic church adopted. In 1864, Bishop Berneux had it published in Chnese. This was a Korean catechism of the *Sŏngsa yori* written in Chinese by the French priest d'Ollières. The time of the transmission of the

---

[493] Kim Ok-hŭi, Ch'oe Yang-ŏp Sinbu ŭi ch'ŏnju kasa I, *op.cit.*, p.27.

[494] Pak Che-wŏn's Sogyŏng chat'anga (Lamentational song of a blind person) is said to be the last "Ch'ŏnjugasa." It is said that the discovered pieces alone numbered to be 186 in kinds. "Ch'ŏnju gasa," *Kyohoe wa yŏksa*, 66, Feb. 1989. "Chugyo yoji" written by Chŏng Yak-chong during the earlier period was published in its original script. The following books were the major catechisms published from 1864 to 1865, *Sŏnggyoyorimundap, Ch'ŏnjusŏnggyogonggwa, Ch'ŏnjusŏnggyoryegyu, Sinmyŏngch'ohaeng, Hoechoechikchi, Yŏngsedaeŭi, Chugyoyoji, Chyunyŏnch'ŏmryekwangik, Ch'ŏndangchikno, Sŏngkyojŏlyo* and others. These books were mostly Chinese trans-lations of Western books that had been translated into Korean, and read by many church members at that time. The Christian gospel could be much more easily spread among the mass due to the Korean translations, and as a result, the Korean language also became popularized.

[495] Yu Hong-nyŏl, *op.cit.*, (ha), p.548. The first woodblock prinshop was established in 1859.

[496] Yi Pyŏng-yŏng, Mokp'anbon ŭl chungsimhan *Ch'ŏnju sŏngkyo kongkwa*, sogo." *Han'guk kyohoesa nonmun sŏnjip*, (Seoul: Han'guk kyohoesa yŏn'guso, 1976), p.294.

Chinese translation, *Sŏngsa yori* into Chosŏn is unknown, but it is only speculated that it must be before the Sinyu Persecution of 1801.

The 36 chapters of the book contain questions and answers on four basic topics: baptism (yŏngse, 70 questions), confession (kohae, 37 questions), eucharist (sŏngch'e, 24 questions), and confirmation (kyŏnsin, 23 questions). Although it was first printed in 1864, even before this time, reproduced copies had already been in use and were used as the sole catechism during the persecution period. The reproduced edition, the woodblock edition, and the printed edition all were of the same order and content.

For example, Chosŏn's second priest Ch'oe Yang-ŏp's father Ch'oe Kyŏng-hwan, Francisco (1805-1839) was arrested along with forty other family members and friends, and it was during the hottest part of summer when they followed the police officials to Seoul to be martyred, walking for a long period of time during which there were women and children who were unable to walk and fell down. At these moments, he led the way, yelling out and encouraging them saying "Fellow brothers, have courage! See the Lord of heaven measuring and counting your each step with a gold yardstick! See Jesus Christ ascending to Calvary ahead of you."[497]

It is also said that when her young children whined in complaint while moving to a far place, Priest Ch'oe Yang-ŏp's mother Yi Maria told them the stories of Virgin Mary and Joseph fleeing to Egypt and of Jesus climbing up the Calvary mountains.[498] *Chunyŏn ch'ŏmrye kwangik*, a bibliography of saints which introduces 93 saints and their feast days, was in 43 volumes, and its first volume was translated by Bishop Daveluy and published in 1865.

---

[497] Im Ch'ung-sin, Ch'oe Sŏg-u (tr.), *Ch'oe Yang-ŏp sinbu sŏhanjip*, (Seoul: Han'guk kyohoesa yŏn'guso, 1984), p.143.

[498] *Ibid*, p.147.

5. Korean Catholic Church in the 1860's

King Hŏnjong died without an heir and was succeeded by Ch'ŏlchong (1849-1864), during whose reign the church was able to grow within a relatively peaceful environment. As mentioned before, Ch'ŏlchong was the grandson of Chŏngjo's illegitimate brother, the Ŭnŏn-kun, who was killed during the Sinyu Persecution, and Song Maria: hence he pursued a policy of moderation towards Catholicism.

Year		Number of Catholics
1850	Kyŏngsul	11,000[499]
1853	Kyech'uk	12,775
1855	Ŭlmyo	13,638
1857	Chŏngsa	15,206
1859	Kimi	16,700
1861	Sinyu	18,035
1863	Kyehae	19,748[500]
1865	Ŭlch'uk	23,000

Increase in the Catholic Population

In the 10th month of 1861, Bishop Berneux divided the entire country of Chosŏn into eight dioceses,[501] so that missionaries had exclusive responsibility for their districts. That can be considered as the beginning of the formation of a systematic structure that centered around the churches, which had been fellowships led by lay people. At the end

---

[499] Charles Dallet, *op.cit.*, (ha), p.361, p.384, p.389, p.434, p.452, and p.475.
[500] Yi Mun-kŭn, "Christianity in Korea. "*Korea its Land, People and Culture*, p.338.
[501] Pae En-ha, *op.cit.*, p.114.

of this year (1849), the Korean priest Ch'oe Yang-ŏp returned to Korea and began to pursue the callings of his mission. By the end of the following year, the 1st year of Ch'ŏlchong (1850), the number of Catholics had increased to over 11,000 people.[502]

Upon entering Korea, Bishop Daveluy translated the Chinese catechisms. He was very active in publishing books related to Catholicism, not to mention the catechisms themselves, and began the process of compiling a Korean-Chinese-French dictionary for the sake of future missionaries.[503] He also gathered and compiled materials on the martyrs. The materials that Priest Daveluy gathered on the martyrs, as well as those on the Chosŏn Catholic church were critical supporting evidence to the declaration by the Roman Pope of the eighty two martyrs of the Kihae and Pyŏngo Persecutions as the venerable ones. These materials were also used as the primary source in the compilation of *Histoiré de lEglise en Corée* by Charles Dallet.[504] Priest Daveluy translated the fundamental catechism of Catholicism, *Sinmyŏng ch'ohaeng* and wrote preparatory mass books for those who were confessing such as *Hoechoe jikji, Ryŏngse daeŭi,* and *Sŏngch'al kŭiryak,* [505]

Daveluy left behind the following report:

> Though it may be that one knows how to read the dialogues of the doctrine, doctrine can only be learned slowly... When I explain the truths of Catholicism, they become moved and drawn to absorb it, and so they come to regard even the most difficult sacrifices lightly. However, when the details

---

[502] *Ibid.*

[503] Charles Dallet, (tr.) *op.cit.*, (ha), p.209.

[504] Ch'oe Sŏg-u, "Dallet chŏ, Han'guk ch'ŏnju kyohoesa ŭi hyŏngsŏng kwajŏng. "*Kyohoesa yŏn'gu* , 3, pp.120.125.

[505] Charles Dallet, (tr.) *op.cit.*, (ha), pp.363-364.

of each truth are closely examined, they do not understand the explanation so easily, especially the women and the ignorant men.[506]

In general, during the middle part of the 19th century, which was the latter part of the persecution, even if one did become a Catholic, most people around him were non-believers, and opportunities to study its teachings thoroughly were rare.[507] During the middle part of the 19th century, the Catholic catechisms were mostly those translated from Chinese. *Sŏngkyo chŏlyo* and *Sŏngkyo yorimundap* that were used in the 1840s also were translated from Chinese.[508] In the beginning catechisms were re-produced and distributed by hand, but by 1864, woodblock printeries were established in two places in Seoul, making it possible for printing and distribution on a massive scale to occur.[509] In 1864, the two woodblock printers published four different newspapers and in 1865, they published three types of books, one volume of *Kyorimundap* and four volumes of *Kidosŏ* and one volume of *Ŭisiksŏ*.[510] In addition to Daveluy's works and translations, the following catechisms were published: *Sŏnggyo yorimundap, Ch'ŏnju sŏnggyo konggwa, Yŏnjung sŏnggyo ryekyu, Chugyo yoji, Ch'ŏndang chikro, Chyunyŏn chŏmrye kwangik,* and *Sŏnggyo chŏlyo.*

The printing and provision of Korean catechisms did not merely serve as tools in dissemination of the Catholic religion, but brought about a new flourishing of

---

[506] Charles Dallet, (tr.) *op.cit.*, (ha), pp.364-365.

[507] *Ibid.*,p.367.

[508] Pae Hyŏn-suk, *op.cit.*, p.8 & p45.

[509] Charles Dallet, *op.cit.,* (ha), p.363.

[510] *Ibid*, (ha), pp.363-364.

Korean culture.[511] Since its creation in the 15th century, the Korean writing system had been neglected by the intellectual class that valued the Chinese language and thus had not been able to establish its roots in the traditions of the national culture, being regarded as a merely peripheral cultural artifact. Having been neglected by the *yangban* and the government official class, the Korean alphabet had persisted as the language of the women and the commoners. It was this language that the Catholic church actively adopted, and by being the writing system in which all church related books in Korea were published, the Korean alphabet came to contribute not only to a native literature but also to the flourishing of native Korean culture. By actively adopting and employing the Korean language, the Catholic church was able to appropriately respond to the transformation that was occurring pronouncedly after the Sinyu Persecution, which was the change in the social class of the church members from *yangban* and *chungin* to *sangmin* and commoners. Using Korean and not Chinese, which was the language of a minority intellectual class, made it possible for the church to pursue a mass-oriented mission and to create an opportunity for the common people to flourish as the principal support group of the church.

At the rumor that there would be religious freedom in Chosŏn, four priests, Dorie, Bretniere, Huin and Beaulieu entered Korea on the 27th day, 5th month, 1865 with many silver ingots and other support materials. As a result of the proselytizing activities of the twelve French priests now on the scene in Chosŏn, the church members' numbers increased to over 23,000.

---

[511] Ch'oe Sŏg-u, *Hankuk kyohoesa ŭi t'amgu*, pp.414.415.

CHAPTER V

The Persecution of the Later Period

1. Persecution during the 1830's and 1840's

Political Background of Sedo chŏngch'i (In-law Government)

The three kings at the end of the Chosŏn dynasty, Sunjo, Hŏnjong and Ch'ŏlchong, all acceded to the throne at young ages, and it was their royal grandmothers who wielded the actual power from behind the scenes. Accordingly, their relatives eventually seized control of political power. Influential families, the Andong Kim clan and the P'ungyang Cho clan, dominated the political scene during the three generations and sixty years of the era of so-called in-law government (*sedo chŏngch'i*), and at times fierce struggles erupted between the two families.

In-law government was a form of political rule that excluded the royal house from the forefront of politics and whose actual authority was exercised by a few interrelated elite families. In contrast to the factional strife of the previous period, in-law government was a struggle for political power among a small number of clan lineages. Seizure of political power was no longer determined by family lineages but by clans. Moreover, it was not determined by the level of the positions of government officials but wielded by a group that won the king's favor. As a result, the concentration of power in the hands of king's in-laws was inevitable, and their abuse of power undoubtedly became the source of political and social corruption during the late Chosŏn society.

The origin of this type of in-law government dates back to the succession of Chŏngjo upon the death of his grandfather, Yŏngjo. At that time, Hong Kuk-yŏng (P'ungsan Hong lineage) came to wield enormous power due to his achievement in protecting Chŏngjo from the group that opposed and conspired to harm Chŏngjo. This era, however, was short, and it was only after Sunjo that its ills became fully apparent. Kim Cho-sun of the Andong Kim clan was a *Sip'a* figure who had the capacity to confront Queen Dowager Kim of the Kyŏngju Kim clan and the *Pyŏkp'a*. Even Chŏngjo, who had firmly established his authority, was wary of the Kyŏngju Kim clan that continued to persist as a powerful lineage group. Thus, he had left a will with Kim Cho-sun of the Andong Kim clan to protect the young crown prince - later King Sunjo. In order to protect the crown prince, it was necessary to have a powerful group that could confront the Kyŏngju Kim clan, the maternal family of the royal house. In spite of the opposition of the Kyŏngju Kim clan, Kim Cho-sun installed his own daughter as the queen to stand against the force of the Queen Dowager Kim. Kim Cho-sun was a member of the *Sip'a* of the Old Doctrine faction. At first when the proposal to select his daughter as the queen was raised, Kwŏn Yu of the *Pyŏkp'a* of the Old Doctrine opposed the proposal. But with the support of Pandonryŏng Pusa Pak Chun-wŏn, who was Sunjo's maternal grandfather and had exerted much effort to protect him, and *Tongji Chungch'u Pusa* Pak Chong-bo, Kim Cho-sun's daughter was invested as the queen.

Although Kim Cho-sun's daughter had become the queen, the *Pyŏkp'a* of the Old Doctrine faction still remained in power, and moreover, the Queen Dowager continued to reign, so that Kim Cho-sun was not able to exert much influence. In the 4th year of Sunjo (1804) he reached the age of fifteen, and the Queen Dowager Kim had to withdraw from control behind the scene. She passed away in the first month of the following year in 1805, the 5th year of Sunjo. Consequently, the political force of *Noron Pyŏkp'a* surrounding the Queen Dowager Kim gradually began to wane, and before long it lost its political power.

Upon the ending of Queen Dowager Kim's regency, Kwŏn Yu, who opposed Kim Cho-sun's daughter becoming the queen, died while being interrogated for the crime of treason (in the 6th month of the fourth year of Sunjo[512]). Kim Tal-sun (1760-1806), the third state Councillor, was executed, and Kim Kwan-chu (1743-1806) was demoted from his position and died on his way to exile. Later Sim Hwan-ji (1730-1802), who had held the position of Chief State Councillor as well as the head of *Noron*, was also removed from his official position.[513] It is worth noting here that, at this point, those who constituted the leading force behind the Sinyu Persecution all had been eliminated.

On the other hand, Kim Cho-sun of the Andong Kim clan, a member of the *Noron Sip'a* and Sunjo's father-in-law, now seized political power upon the death of Queen Dowager Kim. The emergence of Kim Cho-sun signifies not only *Sip'a*'s regaining of political power, but also the beginning of the so-called in-law government by the Andong Kim clan. During the period of the Andong Kim clan's reign, the Catholic persecution was eased. Again, this is illustrative of the fact that the Sinyu Persecution was driven not merely by religious causes, but also by an element of political revenge. In addition, Sunjo, even at a young age, hesitated to execute Catholic followers, and the new queen's alignment with Sunjo's attitude further contributed to the easing of the persecution.

During the in-law government by the Andong Kim

---

[512]*Chosŏn wangjo sillok*, Sunjo 4th year, 5th month Imin.

[513]*Chosŏn wangjo sillok*, Sunjo 6th year, 4th month Kyŏngjin & Imo.

clan, however, persecution of Catholicism nevertheless persisted. In the 17th year of Sunjo, persecution occurred in Kyŏngsangdo and Kangwŏndo, and in the 27th year of Sunjo, it also occurred in the regions of Hosŏ, Honam and Yŏngnam. Among them, the persecution in Chŏnju was the most severe. However, while persecution occurred in almost all regions, the number of martyrs was very few. Following the Sinyu Persecution, although the anti-heterodoxy group achieved an absolute victory in both the political and religious realms, with the emergence of a new political force, the so-called in-law government, it faced a fierce resistance by the *Namin* of the Yŏngnam region who had not participated in politics up to then. Confucians from Kyŏngsangdo numbering 3,877 individuals submitted a memorial requesting that the deceased Ch'ae Che-gong, who had been posthumously demoted, be restored his official title, and that the members of the opposition faction such as Hong Ŭi-ho and Hong Su-bo, father and son, Hong Nak-an, Yi Ki-kyŏng, Yi Hŭi-un and Kang Chun-hŭm all be punished for the crime of conspiracy.[514]

This memorial appears to have been initiated by the *Namin Sip'a* members who had been sentenced to exile during the Sinyu Persecution, such as Yi Ch'i-hun and Yi Hak-kyu, who now were instigating the Confucians of the Yŏngnam region, reflecting their pride in the *Namin* tradition.[515] Again, one can get a glimpse of an element of political revenge here. The group led by Hong Ŭi-ho had once sent a long letter to Ch'ae Che-gong, through Hong Nag-an, during the Chinsan Incident, thus creating an uproar. In addition, during the Sinyu Persecution, Hong Nag-an had sent a memorial arguing that Hwang Sa-yŏng 's paeksŏ was not his effort alone, but rather that Yi Ka-hwan, Yi Sŭng-hun, and Chŏng Yag-yong and his brothers were all involved, and therefore that they should all be arrested and interrogated.

---

[514] *Chosŏn wangjo sillok*, Sunjo 18th year, 9th month Ŭlmyo.

[515] *Ibid*, Sunjo 18th year 9th month, Chŏngsa.

Thus interconnected, they became close with one another, and when Kim Cho-sun of the *Noron Sip'a* seized power, they attempted to use this opportunity to take revenge against the *Pyŏkp'a*. Due to the memorial, the group led by Hong Ŭi-ho felt advantaged, and although they submitted a memorial through Chichungch'u Pusa claiming their innocence,[516] the general trend was already leaning in favor of the *Sip'a*. *Pyŏkpa* members including Hong Ŭi-ho were forced to retreat from the core of political power, and subsequently, the government's policy towards the Catholic Church became more moderate.

Political authority rotates in cycles. Towards the end of the Sunjo's regime, the Andong Kim clan was challenged by the rising influence of the P'ungyang Cho clan. The change in the political scene seemed to occur as the daughter of Cho Man-yŏng of the P'ungyang Cho clan was selected as the wife of Sunjo's son Crown Prince Hyomyŏng (posthumously named Ikchong, the father of Hŏnjong). It was Sunjo's plan to hold the Andong Kim clan in check, and that is why he put forward a P'ungyang Cho clan member, Cho Man-yŏng's daughter, as the wife of Hyomyŏng and employed individuals from the P'ungyang Cho clan such as Cho In-yŏng. Furthermore, he had Crown Prince Hyomyŏng take control of the government as a regent, in place of himself, thereby attempting to restrain the forces of the Andong Kim clan. However, political power was not easily transferred to the P'ungyang Cho clan because the Crown Prince died unexpectedly in 1830.

When Kim Cho-sun's daughter became Hŏnjong's queen (Queen Hyohyŏn) in 1837, the P'ungyang clan was pushed out by the Andong Kim clan forces. In the 4th month of 1832, Kim Cho-sun died and power was handed over to his son Kim Yu-kŭn (1785-1840). With the death of Sunjo in the 11th month of 1834, his grandson Hŏnjong acceded to the throne at age eight, and Queen Dowager Kim (the widow of King Sunjo, Andong Kim clan) wielded authority from behind the scenes.

---

[516] *Ibid.*

Because Sunjo's wife, Queen Dowager Kim, sympathized with Catholicism and had influenced Sunjo, when she held the regency for Hŏnjong, she pursued a policy of moderation towards Catholicism, as was done during Chŏngjo's reign. Sunjo was also grateful that Chŏng Yag-yong had once cured his son, Prince Hyomyŏng, with medicine, and when Crown Prince Hyomyŏng passed away, Sunjo had wondered whether the death had been divine retribution for the persecution of Catholics.

Moreover, Kim Yu-kŭn, who took charge of political power with Queen Dowager Kim, himself was in favor of Catholicism. He was an intimate of Yu Chin-gil, a Catholic follower and a high level official translator, and before he died in the 12th month of 1840, he was even privately baptized by Yu Chin-gil. Thus, under the circumstances, it was not so surprising for the Chosŏn Catholic church to become solidified under the leadership of French priests who entered Chosŏn after 1836, and for the number of followers also to increase to ten thousand people.

On the surface, because Queen Dowager Kim oversaw political matters and Kim Cho-sun's son Kim Yu-kŭn remained active, the Andong Kim clan appeared to wield political power without interruption. However, internally, the Andong Kim clan was quite unstable.[517] This was because Kim Yu-kŭn was stricken with paralysis in 1836 and could not regularly oversee political affairs, and, subsequently, authority was transferred to Yi Chi-yŏn (1777-1841), the Third State Councillor. Seizing this opportunity, he cooperated with the P'ungyang Cho clan to bring about a Catholic persecution, at the same time attempting to snatch political authority from the *Sip'a* Andong Kim clan.

Following the death of Sunjo and with the accession of Hŏnjong at age eight, his grandmother Sunwŏn Queen Dowager Kim came to govern from behind the scenes, and, although the power of the Andong Kim clan continued to persist with the support of Queen Dowager, it was

---

[517]Yu Hong-nyŏl, *op.cit.*, pp.312-316.

challenged by the P'ungyang Cho clan. The P'ungyang Cho clan was a family of influence that rose to power with the support of Hŏnjong's father Crown Prince and after Hyomyŏng's Queen Cho, and after Crown Prince Hyomyŏng came to exercise authority in place of his father, in obedience to a decree in the 27th year of Sunjo. At every opportunity, the Cho clan devised secret schemes to purge the Kim clan. As Sunwŏn Queen Dowager Kim's relative, Kim Cho-kŭn's daughter became Hŏnjong's queen in the 3rd year of Hŏnjong, the P'ungyang Cho forces, led by Cho Man-yông, were wary that the Kim clan force would become strengthened, had no choice but to struggle in confrontation. Finally in 1839, Cho Man-yŏng became the Director of the Office of Special Councillors, which administered the government decrees. Cho In-yŏng became Minister of the Board of Personnel; and his nephew Cho Pyŏng-hyŏn became Minister of the Board of Punishment. In addition, as Third State Councillor Yi Chi-yŏn also came to align his interests with those of the P'ungyang Cho clan[518].

The Kihae Persecution of 1839

Having risen to power in such manner, the P'ungyang Cho clan criticized and condemned the Andong Kim clan's Catholic policy of moderation, and attempted to drive out the Kim's forces by persecuting the church. In 1839, the 5th year of Hŏnjong, a persecution more severe than the Sinyu Persecution erupted, and it is called the Kihae Persecution. The P'ungyang Cho clan, together with Chief State Councillor Yi Chi-yŏn, persistently requested punishment of Catholicism, and though it was not her true intention, the Queen Dowager was unable to withstand the persistent pressure and issued a persecution order. Even before this formal measure, there had been arrests. Yi Ho-yŏng had been arrested in Ich'ŏn of Kyŏnggido in 1835 and died in prison in the 11th month of 1838, while awaiting

---

[518] Yi Wŏn-sun, *Han'guk chŏnju kyohoesa yŏn'gu*, p.132.

execution. Police officials arrested Catholic followers in parts of Seoul. In the 1st month of 1839, along with Kwŏn Tŭk-in's arrest in Seoul, many others were arrested at various places. Prisons came to be filled with Catholic followers. Cho Pyŏng-hyŏn, Minister of Board of Punishments at that time, urged them to apostatize so that their lives could be spared, but this effort did not succeed. The issue then was the question whether to stop the arrests, or to free the imprisoned Catholics, or to execute them. The Minister of the Board of Punishments reported the situation to Third State Councillor Yi Chi-yŏn, and Yi Chi-yŏn argued to Queen Dowager Kim that the converts should be executed to eradicate the roots of Catholicism.[519] It is said that Hŏnjong, even at his young age, had no intention to wholly accept the request of the Third State Councillor.[520] Queen Dowager Kim alone agreed to the proposal. The Queen Dowager was not known to have consulted even her older brother Kim Yu-kŭn, and her unexpected condemnation of the heterodoxy took those present by surprise.

On the 18th day of 4th month, the order for execution of heretics was decreed and the persecution officially started.[521] Queen Dowager Kim was not at all personally opposed to Catholicism, and actually was in favor of the religion. However, pressured by the rising force of the P'ungyang Cho clan, she had no choice but to give the persecution order.[522]

The decree asserted that the Catholic followers were a group of traitors who had neither father nor a king, and thus there was no alternative to turning the matter over to the police authorities for intensive investigation. It was also mandated that the accused be executed in the presence of other arrested Catholics who refused to renegade on their

---

[519] *Chosŏn wangjo sillok*, Hŏnjong 5th year 3rd month Sinch'uk.
[520] *Ibid.*
[521] *Chosŏn wangjo sillok*, Hŏnjong 5th year 3rd month Sinch'uk.
[522] Charles Dallet, *op.cit.*, (chung), pp.143-144.

conversion. And the five family mutual surveillance law was to be put into effect throughout Seoul and adjacent regions so that no one would be allowed to escape. At that time, Queen Dowager Kim stated that if the Catholic followers were left alone, then not only would the country be destroyed but the human race would become extinct. She criticized the religion more severely than did the officials, stating that though it is said that the oppression of the Sinyu year (1801) was perhaps a bit too excessive, now that she looked back, it was rather not harsh enough. In addition, in regards to a court lady who was arrested but not even mentioned in the official report, she instructed that those who are and were once court ladies be reported to their appropriate superior and arrested if evidence of Catholicism is confirmed. On the topic of religious relics, she also ordered that if such materials were found, their source must be traced and that even if the possessors are not Catholics, they must be severely punished.[523]

Fifteen days had passed since the Queen Dowager's instruction to arrest all Catholic church members, but no key figures had been apprehended. *Chipŭi* (Surrogate) Chŏng Ki-hwa submitted a memorial saying that if the original key figures were not caught, then Catholicism could not be exterminated. He stated that though not a great number of Catholics has been caught thus far, the original evil ones had not yet been arrested. How could the translating of books and making of equipment be the work of a band of thoughtless people of low class? It must have been that there were people of some wealth who secretly traveled to Beijing and acquired these items, and distributed them among many people. Therefore, unless the den of these people is found and wiped out, just executing those who have been arrested will not bring about the end of Catholicism.[524]

Yi Chi-yŏn reported to the Queen Dowager that

---

[523] *Pipyŏnsa tŭngnok*, Hŏnjong Kihae year 3rd month 5th.

[524] *Chosŏn wangjo sillok*, Hŏnjong 5th year 3rd month Pyŏnjin.

during the investigation by the police officials there often were evil groups that caused trouble, and thus when they were put behind bars, the number of arrested Catholics was not substantial. The Queen Dowager criticized the way in which the situation was handled by saying, "How is it that the conduct of the police is in such a manner? If the criminal's family wealth is confiscated first, then it is probably difficult to return it when he does repent later on. Since each district and town has its own chief in charge, why is it that the confiscated properties are not left in the chief's possession until they are returned?" It can be inferred from the above conversation between the Queen Dowager and the Third State Councillor that the number of arrested Catholic followers was not significant, and especially that one of the main reasons for failing to arrest the key individuals was the barring of the police officials from searching out their family treasures and extorting family wealth.[525]

According to the report by the Minister of the Board of Punishments on the 20th day of the 3rd month, there were forty three prisoners transferred from the police bureau to the ministry of justice, and among them, fifteen had already renounced the religion and been released. Of the twenty-eight who remained in police custody, all but nine declared their renunciations in the following weeks, and those nine, including Nam Myŏng-hyŏk and a court lady, Pak Hŭi-sun were executed.[526]

Along with the second minister of the Board of Punishments, Cho Pyŏng-hyŏn resigned from his post, conscience-stricken at the slaughtering of Catholic followers. Upon their resignation, Hong Myŏng-chu was appointed as minister and Im Sŏng-ko was appointed as second minister. At the time of the arrest of Father Kim

---

[525] *Sŭngchŏnwŏn ilgi*, Tokwang, 19th Ŭlhae year, 3rd month 20th day.

[526] *Ibid*, Tokwang 19th Kihae year, 4th month 12th day. Those who were executed also include Kwŏn Tŭk-in, Yi Kwang-hŏn, Pak Hŭi-sun, Yi Agatha and Kim Ŏp-i

Tae-kŏn in 1845, Second Minister Im Sŏng-ko treated him rather generously, to the point that he himself came under suspicion of being a Catholic.[527] As persecution became more moderate, even Bishop Imbert, who had hastily arrived in Seoul to prepare against the persecution, considered that it was no longer necessary for him to stay in Seoul and left for Su-wŏn on the 22nd day of 4th month.

Meanwhile, Cho Pyŏng-ku seized political power at the court at the end of a struggle for power with the Andong Kim clan. He was a maternal uncle of Hŏnjong and a central figure of the in-law government of the P'ungyang Cho clan. His official position was Kŭmuitaechang (Commander of the Capital Garrison), but he wielded absolute power from behind the scenes. Cho Pyŏng-ku was known to have personal hostility towards Catholicism, and shortly after his assumption of office, he proposed and declared a new law to seek out Catholics.[528]

As the arrest of Catholics progressed very slowly, the Queen Dowager announced an even stricter decree as follows: "Ever since the forbidding of searching and extortion of Catholics' possessions in their houses, the police officers have not made any arrests and this is because the police chief did not apply the new law zealously. Thus they must be punished for failing to perform their duties strictly."[529] Starting with the execution on the 24th day of the 5th month outside the Sŏsomun Gate of Nam Myŏng-hyŏk, arrests and executions of Catholics took place in Seoul, Chŏnju, Hongju, Kongju and Wŏnju.[530]

After the death of Kim Yu-kŭn of the Andong Kim clan, an extremely powerful figure who had a positive attitude towards Catholicism, the Catholic leaders were

---

[527] Charles Dallet, *op.cit.*, Tome II, p.155. (tr), *op.cit.* (chung), pp.421-422.

[528] Charles Dallet, *Ibid*, (chung), p.424.

[529] *Chosŏn wangjo sillok*, Hŏnjong 5th year 5th month Kimi.

[530] Charles Dallet, *op.cit.*, (chung), pp.407-421.

arrested on the basis of reports by Kim Sun-sŏng, who pretended to be a Catholic. Yu Chin-gil, a leading figure in reconstruction of the church as well as a high level official translator, was arrested along with Chŏng Ha-sang and Cho Sin-ch'ŏl.[531] Bishop Imbert, in hiding in Suwŏn at the time, also turned himself in to the police bureau on the 3rd day of the 7th month when a fellow church member, who was deceived by Kim Sun-sŏng, revealed his whereabouts.

The arrest of Bishop Imbert surprised the court. Third State Councillor Yi Chi-yŏn recommended that since this was rather a serious case it should be handled by the State Tribunal, not by the police bureau. He also requested that police officers should be sent to Namp'o to arrest the other two Western priests. The Queen Dowager claimed that the trial at Kukch'ŏng is not an urgent matter and thus should be left to the police bureau for now to be investigated, while instructing an immediate dispatch of police officers to arrest the Western priests. When they were not promptly taken into custory, she issued an order for establishing a five-family mutual surveillance unit in Ch'ungch'ŏngdo.[532] Meanwhile, Bishop Imbert believed that the confession of the two priests would bring an end to the punishment of church members, and sent a note urging them to give themselves up and accompany him to martyrdom. The two priests, Mobant and Chastan, then presented themselves to Son Kye-chang, the head of the group of police officers sent to Hongchu from Seoul, upon which they were sent to Seoul in custody.[533]

Meanwhile, interrogation and arrest of Catholics continued.[534] On the 25th day of 7th month, the court

---

[531] *Ibid*, pp.425-426.

[532] *Sŭngchŏngwŏn ilgi*, Tokwang 19th year 7th month 5th day.

[533] *Ilsŏngnok*, Hŏnjong, Kihae year 8th month 3rd day.

[534] On the 10th day of 6th month, seven Catholics including Yi Kwang-yŏl and a female church member were executed outside the Sŏsomun Gate. On the 25th day of 7th month, five people

issued an order prohibiting importation of even miscellaneous materials from Yenching.[535]

From the 5th day to the 15th day of the 8th month inquiries were held by the Office of Trial Procedures (*kukch'ŏng*), and the leading figures of the church at the time, Yu Chin-gil and Chŏng Ha-sang, and the three missionaries underwent a trial interrogation. To the police chief's question inquiring from where and for what purpose they came to Korea, the missionaries responded by saying that as Westerners, they voluntarily came to Chosŏn to spread Catholicism, and that they could not give information on who their guides and church members were for they would be harmed. But they agreed when the police chief asked them whether it was Yu Chin-kil's silver coins that paid for the traveling expense to Korea and whether it was Cho Sin-ch'ŏl who was their guide.

On the 7th day of 8th month, an order was issued to move the inquisition to the State Trubunal (ŭigŭmbu), and the missionaries were transferred there, where they were tried along with those who were known to have been their guides, Yu Chin-kil, Chŏng Ha-sang and Cho Sin-ch'ŏl.[536] During the interrogation, the judge attempted to persuade the missionaries that if they told the truth, then they would be sent back home. But after more than 10 beatings, they refused to give any information about those who had helped them. "Your claim to be missionaries is only a pretense," Bishop Imbert was told, "From your trip to Beijing and your cooperation with Chosŏn people who held grudges against their own country, it appears that you have an ulterior motive. Isn't this true?" Bishop Imbert answered by saying that they had no other motive except to pursue missionary work, and then he defended the Catholics by claiming that even if there were some resentful individuals towards their

---

including Pak Hu-chae and another female church member were also beheaded outside the Sŏsomun Gate.

[535] *Chosŏn wangjo sillok*, Hŏnjong 5th year 7th month Muo.

[536] *Ilsongnok*, Hŏnjong, Kihae year 8th month 5th-7th day.

country, those believing in Catholicism are all good at heart and no one is inherently evil, and thus it was impossible for a Catholic to become a traitor.

The Office of Trial Procedures concluded that further torture would kill the missionaries and that it was difficult to expose the true state of affairs. Subsequently, the Queen Dowager issued an order, one that was similar to that in the Chinese priest Chou Wen-mo's case, to have them beheaded and to hang their heads from a high place to serve as a warning to the people. On the 14th day of the 8th month the three French priests, Pierre-Philibert Maubant, Jacques-Honoré Chastan, and Laurné-Marie Joseph Imbert, were beheaded and their heads hung up high by the Saenamtŏ near the Han River.[537] They were the first Westerners in Chosŏn to be executed for religious reasons.

Yu Chin-gil, Chŏng Ha-sang and Cho Sin-ch'ŏl underwent interrogation for bringing in Westerners, for they were found to be involved in Hwang Sa-yŏng's "Silk Letter" incident. Thus they were accused of conspiracy for bringing in foreign ships and of treason. On the 8th day of 8th month, Yu Chin-kil claimed during the trial process at the State Tribunal that missionaries were brought to Chosŏn because they were indispensable to the Catholic church and that their activities related exclusively to the church, and therefore they could not be accused of being traitors. He also defended the missionaries, countering questions, asking how could they declare a religion if they had an intention to commit treason, and claimed that this religion was not one which leads an army of soldiers and invades the royal palace. He said that everything arose from nothing more than the procedures of practicing the law of the religion. Furthermore, in response to the accusation that he was relying on the evil tricks of Hwang Sa-yŏng, he defended himself, saying, "I am also a human being and aware of the existence of king and father as well as of the law of our country. Hence, how could I even dare to attempt to commit an act such as bringing in enemies from across the

---

[537] Charles Dallet, *Ibid*, (chung), pp.428-463.

sea?" He claimed that his deeds were nothing but merely to respect and serve God and thereby save his soul, so that he may attain eternity after death. He repeatedly emphasized that his activities could never alter the customs of one's country and become an unrighteous religion.[538]

In response to the question whether his deeds were practicing and teaching others a foreign religion and thereby bringing confusion and violating the law of the country, Chŏng Ha-sang stated that all people have an obligation to obey God who is the creator of all things. He also said that God is the origin of all nations and since they comprise a family, he is the father of all nations, and thus no one from any nation could be foreign to anyone. He was then asked whether he therefore believed that it is not right for the king and ministers to ban this religion. He responded by saying that he has nothing to say to such a manner of attacking his motives and that he simply awaits for death as a Catholic.[539] Furthermore, the judge mentioned the incident of inviting the Western priests, and expressed the view that since Ha-sang's father Chŏng Yak-chong, was executed for the crime of treason, the son must also be one of those resentful individuals towards their country. In addition, the judge regarded their activities of practicing and fulfilling the plans proposed in the Hwang Sa-yŏng Paeksŏ, and accused him of treason. Ha-sang responded saying, "Even if I had no resentful feeling towards the country, at this point, all I wish for now is to die soon." At the same time, he added that there is nothing in the teachings of Catholicism that condones calling in foreign forces in order to harm one's own country.[540] He composed a *Sangchae sangsŏ*. document and submitted it to the Chief State Councillor. In it Chŏng Ha-sang criticized the injustice of religious

---

[538] Ŭigŭmbu Ch'inguk, Togwang 19th Kihae year 8th month 7th, 8th, 9th, and 12th day.

[539] *Kihae ilgi*, p.49-50.

[540] Ŭigŭmbu Ch'inguk, Togwang 19th Kihae year 8th month 8th, 9th, 12th, 13th, and 14th day.

persecution by questioning how could it be that the court could declare Catholicism to be a heresy without having investigated the origin and tradition of Catholicism and simply handling it by issuing death sentences. In his *Sangchaesangsŏ*, Chŏng Ha-sang attacked the doctrine of Buddhism, arguing that the Catholic faith is not similar to the Buddhist doctrine, and attempted to prove that it was harmless and just. First, he argued that Christianity was practical and emphasized that its ethical practicality was sufficiently extensive to the point that it could even become the governing principle of a nation. He mentioned the Ten Commandments as evidence for his assertion. The Ten Commandments rendered Catholicism the most virtuous religion, since it embraced loyalty, forgiveness, filial piety, humility, generosity, justice, propriety, and wisdom, and he demonstrated that Catholicism did not lack in any aspect even from the point of view of an ideology that supervises families and rules the country. In addition, he provided evidence of the appearance of Christian church society during the Wu Dynasty in China, and testified that during the T'ang Dynasty, even scholars such as Wei Chang and Fang Hsüng-ling studied Western Learning under the protection of the emperor. He also wrote that during the Ming and the Ch'ing dynasties, missionaries were able to carry out various activities under the protection of the court. Thus, by proving the truthfulness of Christianity through historical investigation of Christianity in China, and at the same time by emphasizing the fact that Christianity existed under the protection of the court, he attempted to disprove the claim that Christianity was barbarian.

Chŏng Ha-sang declared in his *Sangchae sangsŏ* that Catholicism does not violate the orthodoxy of Confucius, Mencius, Chuangtzu and Chu Hsi, and that the Bible, in instructing men to praise heaven, was no different from the four Chinese classics. Lastly, he insisted that the Catholic church members had not abandoned their country. He was mindful of the fact that Chosŏn was a country in the Orient which respects etiquette, and he was careful to show that the doctrines of Catholicism were compatible with the most cherished Confucian values. He further emphasized that Catholicism does not lead to abandonment of one's country and is loyal to orthodoxy, and that it is within the traditional ethics of Chosŏn. He entreated as a Christian and a faithful civil servant. He appealed by asking, "Don't you think that only those who believe in this holy religion are truly the children of kings?"

On the 15th day of the 8th month, the Chosŏn court found Yu Chin-gil and Chŏng Ha-sang to be traitors, and they were summarily put to death on the execution ground of Sŏsomun.[541] On the 19th day of the 8th month, nine others including Cho Sin-ch'ŏl were executed at the same place.[542]

The persecution did not come to an end with the execution of the missionaries and active Catholic church members. Kim Sun-sŏng continued to seek out Catholics and report them to the authorities under the justification of extinguishing Catholicism. As Third State Councillor Yi Chi-yŏn was replaced and a new figure, Cho In-yŏng emerged, persecution became even more intensified. He instructed that the imprisoned Catholic churchmen should be executed by hanging in closed rooms. This was because he viewed public execution as countereffective rather than being a lesson to the crowd. On the 25th day of the 9th month in Kihae year, a fourteen-year old son of translator Yu Chin-gil, Tae-ch'ŏl kept his faith to the end, and he was victimized by a sentence of execution by hanging during his imprisonment.[543]

Afterwards, the government proceeded to bring an end to the situation by secretly executing by hanging the remaining church members who were yet to be tried. It was decided that on the 24th day of the 11th month, six female church members including Ch'oe Ch'ang-hŭp were to be

---

[541] *Ilsŏngnok*, Hŏnjong, Kihae year 8th month 14-15th day.

[542] *Sŭngjŏngwŏn ilgi*, Hŏnjong Kihae year, 8th month 15th and 19th day.

[543] *Kihae ilgi*, p.107.

executed, and on the 27th and 28th of the 12th month, ten others including Pak Chong-wŏn and Yi Mun-ŭi were to be executed at a place called Sajang Tangkokae.[544]

As public opinion turned against the government because of the brutal executions of the Catholic church members, *Ch'ŏksa yunŭm*, an edict banning heterodoxy (written by Cho In-yŏng) was declared on the 18th day of the 10th month (lunar calendar) in order to justify the legitimacy of the persecution as well as to announce an end to it. It was Hŏnjong's first public declaration:

> "King Chungjong [Chŏngjo], my predecessor, was a man blessed of Heaven, and yet he was annoyed by this Sung Heung [Sŭng-hun] who purchased every sort of Western book that he could lay his hands on, calling them the "Religion of God." Wholly unauthorized by any use in the past, with all manner of subtlety, and in a way no Sage was ever thought of, this cult increased and grew so as to fascinate and deceive the people till it brought upon us a world of barbarians and wild beasts. King Chungjong, seeing this and fearing what the end might be, severely punished the leaders, but the leaders only, letting others go free in the hope that their love of life might induce them to turn to a better way. He could not possibly have shown more leniency. Even swine and monsters of the deep, yes, owls and wolves, would have been moved by this to repent, but these people, having lost all conscience, and being incapable of reform, continued until the year *shinyu* (1801), when they were dealt with according to their evil ways. Be careful, I beg of you, my people, my ministers. As a parent teaching a child,

---

[544] *Ilsŏngnok*, Hŏnjong Kihae year 12th month 27th and 28th day.

or an older brother a younger, I address you. Study how to lead these people away from their place of danger, and those, not wholly dead, urge and counsel them. Those who will not listen, let them be destroyed as a warning to the world, so that this evil may never show its head again."[545]

The motivation behind the message was to address the ideological attack of the *Sangchae sangsŏ* during the Kihae Persecution and to persuade the people with the message as they faced the final stage of the persecution, and thereupon declared was *Ch'ŏksayunŭm*.

The first part of the message was a presentation of the Confucian way of praising Heaven in response to the doctrine of the Western Learning.[546] This was also a theoretical response to the doctrinal defense in the *Sangchae sangsŏ*. It concluded and stipulated that the Catholic way of praising Heaven was unacceptable from the viewpoint of Confucianism.[547] Secondly, it is said that Jesus was executed as the most atrocious criminal, and this fact is obviously an unquestionable testimony to the evilness of the religion, and that those who believe in such a religion are indecent and foolish. Thirdly, Catholicism was a kind of fanaticism, deluding the people, pointing to the greater prospering of Catholicism among women and naive commoners. Fourth, it addressed the theory of Christianity, arguing that one could not discern whether the so-called

---

[545] Grant S. Lee, "Persecution and Success of Roman Catholic Church in Korea," *Korea Journal,* Vol. 28. No. 1, p. 21. *Ch'ŏksayunŭm* was written in both Chinese and Korean, which was an unusual practice for the government at that time, and is illustrative of the fact that Catholicism had widely spread among the lower class, women and children and commoners.

[546] Yi Ma-ch'ae p'yŏn, kwŏn 7, 18th day of 10th month, (tr.) pp.358-363.

[547] *Ibid.*

Jesus was a human being or a ghost or fake or real. This was because the story of Jesus descending from Heaven to become a man and then resurrecting upon his death and ascending to Heaven was unbelievable. Fifth, it argued that the principle of husband and wife is eternally fixed and that rejecting marriage under the pretext of virtue among the church members meant the human succession would come to an end, and that filial piety was seriously threatened. Moreover, the mingling together of the men and women followers of the lower class, indicated a slackness of discipline and lack of morality. In conclusion, it entreated the Catholics to reform and stated that if they abide by the lessons of sages and observe the laws of Heaven, wisdom and nature, then the heterodoxy will surely disappear on its own.

Persecution of 1846 (Pyŏngo)

After the Kihae persecution the church organization began to revive rather quickly. In the 8th year of Hŏnjong, Imin year (1842), the Opium War erupted in China, and as a result, the pride of the Chinese was damaged. A secret envoy from the Chosŏn church was sent to Beijing to restore communication with the French priest Jean Joseph Ferréol (1808-1853).[548] In the following Kyemyo year (1843), the Pope appointed Priest Ferréol as the Vicaire Apostolique de Corée, the third Bishop in Korea.[549] He also appointed Priest A. Maistre and Priest Yi as missionaries and instructed them to go to Korea.

Kim Tae-gŏn (baptismal name: André), who had left in 1836 to study in Manila, was ordained in Shanghai as the first Korean priest. He arrived in Korea on the 12th day of 10th month in 1845, accompanied by Bishop Mgr. Ferréol and the newly appointed Marie-Antoine-Nicholas

---

[548] Charles Dallet, (tr. Ch'oe & An), Tome II, p.245.
[549] Charles Dallet, II p.263.

Daveluy (1818-1866).[550] Immediately upon arriving in Korea, Father Ferréol and Daveluy began missionary work in Seoul and Ch'ungch'ŏngdo. Kim Tae-kŏn concluded that the strict supervision rendered it impossible for Priest Maistre of Manchuria and Father Ch'oe Yang-ŏp to enter Korea via land, and thus in order to search out a sea route, he went to the West coast and then to the island Paekryŏngdo of China where he surveyed the area. But he was arrested in Sunŭido[551] and was brought in custody to Seoul.

In the 12th year of Hŏnjong (1846), the Chosŏn court used the occasion of Kim Tae-kŏn's arrest to carry out another persecution.[552] At this time a commander of the French Navy, Admiral Cécil, appeared with three battleships in the sea nearby Hongju, and presented a royal message decrying the executions of Bishop Imbert, Priest Maubant and Priest Chastan during the Kihae Persecution. When a court meeting was held, Chief State Councillor Kwŏn Ton-in said that there must have been a Chosŏn person who had been communicating with the Frenchmen for these French battleships to have arrived.[553] The court viewed the admiral's protest as a military provocation and decided to find and execute all thos who had colluded in bringing the

---

[550] He arrived in Korea through Ch'ungch'ŏngdo Kangkyŏng. The passage to secretly enter Korea through Manchuria and Ŭiju that had been used upto then was closed to them due to the government's strict surveillance, and hence they had used a sea route from Shanghai and directly landed on the West coast. Charles Dallet, (tr. Ch'oe & An), *op.cit.*,pp.80-88.

[551]Charles Dallet, *op.cit.*, Tome II, pp.308-309, (chung) pp.100-111.

[552]Ilsŏngnok, Hŏnjong, Pyŏngo year 5th month 20th - 21st day. Charles Dallet, (tr. Ch'oe & An, *Ibid*, (chung), pp.112-121.

[553]*Chosŏn wangjo sillok*, Hŏnjong 12th year 7th month Musul.

foreign ships to Chosŏn shores.554

At the final court meeting, in discussing the sentencing of Kim Tae-kŏn, who was arrested at a time of great confusion, Kwŏn Ton-in argued for severe punishment in order to clearly demonstrate the authority of the court. Otherwise, unexpected events in fighting would erupt, and then the band of the heterodox and the barbarians "would no longer be distinguishable from each other even if it was true that they were actually one and the same." In this manner, he rebuked the heretics including Kim Tae-kŏn on their communicating with foreign forces and asked the police officials for their opinions.555 Third State Councillor Pak Hae-su stated, "We should not hesitate even for a minute because no one knows how high the heretics' influence might reach and how much more arrogant they may become," and advocated capital punishment.556 Finally, Kim Tae-kŏn was sentenced to execution by hanging, and his head hung as a warning to the people. The execution took place on the 25th day of 7th month by the Han River.557 In addition, several *chungin* who had survived the Kihae Persecution, including Hyŏn Sŏk-mun, president Nam Kyŏng-mun, Han Yi-hyŏng and Im Kun-chip were all executed.558

A total of 79 church members were martyred during the persecution of Kihae and Pyŏngo years.559 The Kihae Persecution, which started from the beginning of 1839 (5th year of Hŏnjong), resulted in approximately 200 martyrs,

---

554*Ibid*, 7th month 15th and 25th day. Charles Dallet (chung), p.319, (ha), p.118.

555*Ilsŏngnok*, Hŏnjong, Pyŏngo year 7th month 25th day.

556*Ibid*, Hŏnjong Pyŏngo 7th month 25th day.

557*Chosŏn wangjo sillok*, Hŏnjong 11th year 6th month Musul.

558Charles Dallet, (tr. Ch'oe & An), *op.cit.*, (ha), pp.123-141.

559In 1925, they were beatified as the Blessed and canonized as saints in 1984.

including the three French priests of the Paris Foreign Mission Society and Chŏng Ha-sang, Yu Chin-gil and Kim Che-jun. Meanwhile, a significant number of others were arrested in various regions and imprisoned in the provinces, Honam in particular. During the Kihae Persecution, a *chungin* Catholic believer named Hyŏn Sŏk-mun (1799-1846) gathered the materials of the martyrs into a collection titled *Kihae Ilgi* and finished the manuscript in 1842. It was partially unearthed by Bishop Mutel and published in 1905.

This record relates that at the end of the persecution in the 12th month of 1840, 54 Catholic had been beheaded, while those who were hanged, beaten to death or died of an illness in prison numbered more than 60. Apostates who were released numbered 450.[560] During the Kihae Persecution, there were no individuals whose social status or wealth were substantial enough to incite envy in the opposition party or to provoke political revenge. The most active figures were Chŏng Ha-sang and Yu Chun-kil. But Chŏng's family had virtually reached extinction from the previous generation, while Chun-gil, was a *chungin* translator.

On this occasion there were few memorials submitted by Confucian scholars or high officials. This implies either that the persecution lacked political nature, or that they were entirely disinterested in the measures taken by the government, or that they were reluctant to disturb the troubled status quo.

Hŏnjong's Policy on Catholicism

The Kihae and Pyŏngo Persecutions took place nationwide relative to the earlier persecution. It was severe in Seoul and the Kyŏnggi region and took place throughout the south portion of the peninsula, Kangwŏndo, Chŏllado, Kyŏngsangdo, Ch'ungch'ŏngdo. This constitutes evidence to the fact that by now Catholicism had disseminated throughout the entire nation. Everytime a persecution

---

[560]*Kihae ilgi*, p.9.

occurred the church lost its leaders from the *yangban* class and the intellectual class. But in fact, since the church membership came to include the commoners, its numbers actually grew even more.

The following changes in the social classes of believers occurred around the time of the earlier persecution and also around the time of the Kihae and Pyŏngo Persecutions.[561] In the religious aspect, the church became popularized, changing from a religion of intellectuals emphasizing Confucianism and ethics to a commoner's religion that was evangelical and apocalyptic. Moreover, whenever a persecution occurred, the believers left the city areas and moved into the deep mountains, and as a result, Catholicism that first began as a metropolitan religion gradually changed to a rural religion, emphasizing the other world. The enthusiasm of the earlier church to eliminate the evils of the old society and to reform it into a new society based on the principles of Catholicism gradually disappeared within the Catholic church. Among the people who suffered misfortune due to social and political reasons, many sought a Catholicism that would give them hope for the other world. But as persecution intensified, their pessimism was further exacerbated and they came to avoid reality even more. Those who had fled to the mountains to avoid the persecution attempted to develop the wilderness and construct an idealistic society.

When compared to the time of the Sinyu Persecution, the proportion of the *yangban* class that made up the population of believers had fallen while that of the commoner class increased sharply. An increase in the number of women believers was also obvious.[562] Such evidence indicates and illuminate the gradual shift in the core leadership from the intellectual and *yangban* class during the early stage of the church to the *chungin* class,

---

[561] Ch'oe Yong-gyu, "Kihae Pyŏngo kyonangi ch'ŏnju kyodo ŭi punsŏkjŏk koch'al." *Kyohoesa yŏn'gu*, 6: 1988, p.242.

[562] Ch'oe Yong-gyu, *op.cit.*, p.237.

commoners and women. Such a lowering in the social classes of the believers continued past the Kihae Persecution, and during the Pyŏngin Persecution the uneducated, poverty-stricken and lower class people came to dominate the main strata of the church members.[563]

2. The Pyŏngin Persecution of 1866

Political Dimension

As the last persecution of the century-long persecution period, the Pyŏngin Persecution of the Pyŏngin year of King Kojong (1866) was the most extensive persecution of the Chosŏn Catholic church in all aspects, in size, duration, severity of punishment and number of victims. The political background of this persecution was also extensive. Every time political power changed hands, policy on Catholicism also changed accordingly. Shifts in political power and the Catholic persecution were inseparably related. As Chŏlchong died and Kojong acceded to the throne, persecution of the Catholic church was launched once again.

As noted above, the Kihae (1839) and Pyŏngo (1846) Persecutions both erupted in the midst of political situations forged by the P'ungyang Cho clan's in-law challenge to the Andong Kim clan in-law forces. Through these persecutions, the P'ungyang Cho clan succeeded to a certain extent in driving the Andong Kim clan from power. However, the initiator of the persecution, Chief State Councillor Yi Chi-yŏn was dismissed from his position and died while in exile, and the key figure of the P'ungyang Cho clan, Cho Man-yŏng, became blind in 1843 and died unexpectedly in 1846. His younger brother Cho In-yŏng also lost power and was banished in 1849 and died in 1850. Cho Pyŏng-hyŏn, the key leading figure in the persecution as the Minister of Justice, was also exiled and died in 1849.

---

[563] *Ibid.*, p.276.

As a result, the in-law force of the P'ungyang Cho clan came to ruin.564

One of the reasons for the rapid fall of the P'ungyang Cho clan from power was the unexpected death of Hŏnjong. When Hŏnjong died without an heir, the authority to decide who would accede to the throne lay in the hands of Sunwŏn Dowager Queen Kim of the Andong Kim, whose power until then had been restrained by the P'ungyang clan force. She seated on the throne the grandson of the Ŭnŏnkun as Ch'ŏlchong.565 Chŏlchong (1831-1863), the 25th king of Chosŏn (reigned from 1849 to 1863), and the grandson of the Ŭnŏngun Yi In as well as the third son of the Chŏnkyegun Kwang. He was appointed as Tŏkwŏngun in 1849 and acceded to the throne at the age of 18. The Sunwŏn Queen Dowager herself came to oversee state affairs from behind the scenes.566 She also made her close relative Kim Mun-kŭn's daughter as Ch'ŏlchong's wife in the 9th month of 1851. Queen Dowager Sunwŏn transferred ruling authority to Kim Mun-kŭn on the 28th day of the 12th month in 1851, and retreated from the political scene, but until the 4th day of the 6th month in 1857, she discreetly exerted much energy in protecting Catholicism. Ch'ŏlchong himself also pursued a relatively generous policy on Catholicism until his death on the 8th day of the 12th month in 1863, and as a result, there was no massive persecution of Catholicism. In addition, the Andong Kim clan that was in power at that time took a moderate stance on Catholicism. Subsequently, under the rule of the Andong Kim clan's in-law government, the Chosŏn Catholic church thrived dramatically as the priests from the Paris Foreign Mission Society arrived and pursued

---

564 Yu Hong-nyol, *op.cit.*, (sang), pp.498-499, pp.513-515.

565 Ch'ŏlchong's family tree: between the Ŭnŏnkun and his wife from the Song clan, there was Sang gyegun Tam, who married Chŏn gyegun Hwang, and had three children, P'ung gyegun Tang, Ch'oe Pyŏnggun Myŏng and Ch'ŏlchong.

566 *Chsŏn wangjo sillok*. Hŏnjong 15th year 6th month Imsin.

their missions in Korea. Along with the change in political power, the Ŭnŏnkun couple and their daughter-in-law, who had been executed during the Sinyu Persecution in 1801 for the crime of being associated with Catholicism, were exculpated from the accusation. Yi Sŭng-hun, who was also executed in the Sinyu year for the being associated with Catholicism, was also exonerated from all charges in accordance with the request of his son, Yi Sin-kyu.[567]

    The in-law government by the Andong Kim clan produced all kinds of evils towards the end of Ch'ŏlchong's rule. The Andong Kim clan monopolized all political, economic and cultural rewards and conducted a politics of corruption and depravity. After losing his son in 1859, Ch'ŏlchong led a dissolute life and neglected to oversee state affairs. In 1857, Sunwŏn Queen Dowager Kim, who was the backbone of the Andong Kim clan force, died and Ch'ŏlchong's father-in-law, Kim Mun-kŭn also died in 1863. Chŏlchong himself died in 1864 without an heir (8th day of the 12th month of 1863, lunar calendar).

    Upon the death of Ch'ŏlchong, a king needed to be brought in from outside the palace. At that time the most powerful figure in the palace was Sinjŏng Queen Dowager Cho, who was the leading figure of the Kihae Persecution and the mother of Hŏnjong, as well as the daughter of Cho Man-yŏng. She had the second son of Hŭng Sŏn-gun Yi Ha-ŭng, Myŏngbok, accede to the throne at age 12 as the 26th king of Chosŏn. Because of his young age, Sinjŏng Queen Dowager Cho was involved in overseeing state affairs.[568] Queen Dowager Sinjŏng and the Hŭngsŏn Taewŏn'gun, who harbored enmity towards the Andong Kim clan's power, came to seize political power upon the accession of Kojong, immediately dismissing the Andong Kim clan force. This signifies the fall of the *Sip'a*, faction, which centered around the Andong Kim clan and had

---

[567] Yu Hong-nyŏl, *op.cit.*, p.515.

[568] *Chosŏn wangjo sillok*, Ch'ŏlchong 14th year 12th month Kyŏngjin.

traditionally pursued a moderate policy towards Catholicism, and a victory for *Pyŏkp'a,* which centered around the P'ungyang Cho clan that had pursued a stringent policy towards Catholicism.

In the beginning, the P'ungyang Cho clan assumed the key posts in the government, but starting from 1865; the Taewŏngun employed the force of his in-laws, the Min clan of Yŏhŭng, and challenged the Cho authority. In 1866, he installed the daughter of Min Ch'i-rok as the queen of Kojong and inveigled Sinjŏng Queen Dowager to retire from politics, thereby successfully seizing the actual political authority for himself. [569] As soon as the Taewŏn'gun assumed power, he attempted to overcome social discontent and injustice by pursuing a reform policy. He abolished *sŏwŏn*, the Confucian academies, which were the source of the long lasting factional strife, and began to reconstruct the Kyŏngbok palace that was destroyed during the Japanese Invasion and had been neglected ever since. However, his radical reform policy did face considerable opposition. The abolition of the *sŏwŏn* was resisted by the conservative force of Confucian scholars, *yurim*, and the removal of the *Mandongmyo* of the Ming (the Shrine to honor Ming China), which was the symbol of "the ideology of Cherishing China" during the 2nd year of Kojong's rule, was also resisted by Confucians nationwide. Fundraising for reconstruction of Kyŏngbokkung became a scheme to exploit the people and to sell government positions for money.[570] As a result, it was criticized by the people and led to much political unrest.

International Political Situation

Every Catholic persecution was associated with the domestic political situation at the time. During the Sinyu Persecution there was factional strife between the newly

---

[569] Yu Hong-nyŏl, *Kojong chiha sŏhak sunan ŭi yŏn'gu,* (Seoul: Ŭlyu munhwasa, 1962), pp.30-31.

[570] Yu Hong-nyol, *op.cit.*, (ha), pp.26-27.

formed *Sip'a* and *Pyŏkp'a*, while the Kihae Persecution was associated with the greed for political power stemming from in-law government. During the Pyŏngin Persecution, another political factor was involved, which went beyond internal politics and was related to the international political scene. Chosŏn was now becoming the target of imperialist Western forces, bent on "opening" Korea to Western military and commercial intercourse. This gave rise to the most extensive, the largest and the longest persecution of Catholicism in history.

The battleships of the Western colonial powers began to arrive along the coast of Chosŏn from the middle of the 19th century, and their requests for trade were a source of social instability as well as of Catholic persecution.

Taewŏngun's Policy on Catholicism

The attitude towards Catholicism adopted by the majority of the nation, ranging from the key government figures including Queen Dowager Sinjŏng, down to the local authorities, was rejection of foreign ideologies and anti-Western Learning. Queen Dowager Cho, who had been overseeing state affairs from behind the scenes, had always been conservative with respect to Catholicism, and as a firm adherent of the P'ungyang Cho clan's attitude toward Western Learning, she hated the Western Religion as well as Western Learning.[571] During the three years since Kojong had come to the throne, in the early years of the Taewŏn'gun's grasp of power, the Taewŏn'gun was considerably tolerant of Catholicism. According to Bishop Mutel, the Regent Taewŏn'gun's wife was said to have inclined to Catholicism for some time, to such an extent that she once asked a French priest, Simon-François Berneux, to

---

[571] Yi Sŏn-kŭn, *Han'guksa,* ch'oekŭnsep'yŏn, p.237.

pray for her son, the future King Kojong.[572] Since Kojong's nursemaid Pak was a baptized Catholic believer (baptismal name: Martha),[573] the Taewŏn'gun appeared to have implicitly allowed some Catholic believers to exist around him. The Regent Taewŏn'gun also seemed to have had wide contact with the *namin*, many of whom had fallen out of the political sphere during the earlier persecutions but could be categorized as hereditary Catholics.[574] Upon the accession of Kojong, the Kyŏngpyŏng-gun (Yi Se-bo), who had been exiled for the crime of heterodoxy, was released under the order of the Queen Dowager.[575]

So lenient a policy of the Taewŏn'gun towards Catholicism underwent a drastic change, becoming a harsh policy, and this transformation arose from Russia's "southern perimeter strategy". When Russia appeared along the northern region of Chosŏn and requested trade relations, the Catholic believers proposed an alliance with France as a anti-Russian policy through those who were close to the Taewŏn'gun, such as Sŭngji Nam Chong-sam and others, thinking that this was a chance for them to attain religious freedom. At that time, the Taewŏn'gun decided to meet with Bishop Berneux, and asked Nam Chong-sam to arrange the meeting. However, the bishop was in the midst of making visits to the countryside, with the result that the Catholic Church members were in a state of excitement and were unable to respond promptly. As the situation was carelessly disclosed to the public and became a source of rumor, the Taewŏn'gun canceled the meeting with the bishop and afterwards administered a severe policy of oppression and persecution.

---

[572] Choe Chin-young, The rule of the Taewŏn'gun, 1864-1873, (Cambridge, Mass: Harvard University Press, 1972), p.95. Calais Sinbu ŭi sŏgan, Feb. 13, 1867.

[573] Yi nŭng-ha, *op.cit*(ha), p.32.

[574] Choe Chin-young, *op.cit.*, p.95.

[575] *Chosŏn wangjo sillok*, Kojong 1st year 12th month 20th day.

If he had inherently been so inclined he could easily have initiated a persecution from the beginning of his seizure of power. What could be the reason behind his adopting a policy of persecution only after a period of two years had passed? Why did he all of a sudden change into the most brutal persecutor of Catholicism? What led to the change in the Taewŏn'gun's attitude from that which even initiated a meeting with the French bishop as an anti-Russian policy?

This was partially due to the bold character of the Taewŏn'gun, and partially because he regarded the pace set by Nam Chong-sam and Catholic believers to be too slow.[576] His personality and way of thinking were both rooted in the political ideologies of Confucian East Asia, and he was a firm believer in an absolutism based on a concept of unlimited royal authority.[577] Up until then, the Taewŏn'gun had been sympathetic towards and understanding of the unfortunate Catholic believers. But his understanding of Catholicism was very limited just as it had been for the past persecutors of Catholicism, and this is evinced by his question to Nam Chong-sam, who approached him on adopting an anti-Russian policy and who wished for religious freedom for Catholicism asking "Why don't the Catholics practice ancestor worship?"

As for Regent Taewŏn'gun, Bishop Daveluy wrote as follows:

> So far Regent Taewŏn'gun, the father of the young king, has not bothered himself either with us or with the Christians, but how long will this state of affairs last? He has a violent and cruel nature, despising the people and placing no value on human life: if he ever attacks religion, he will do it in a terrible manner... This will be a hard winter.

---

[576] Yi Sŏn-kŭn, *op.cit.*, p.236.
[577] Yi Sŏn-kŭn, *Ibid.*, p.238.

> The drought first of all, and then floods, and then in autumn violent gales destroyed the crops and caused a shortage of food. Already many of the poor are starving. Experience teaches us that it is in time of famine that vexation and persecutions of Catholics begin to take place. We offer an easy prey to all marauders and to the pillaging hangers-on of the magistrates. Pray constantly for us...[578]

Priest Ch'oe Sŏg-u claimed that the Taewŏn'gun's drastic change of mind was because shortly after the occupation of Beijing by the armies of Britain and France, the situation reversed itself and Britain and France withdrew their forces, and as a result, the threat of invasion of Chosŏn became less imminent.[579]

Development of the Pyŏngin Persecution

The Pyŏngin Persecution (the 3rd year of Kojong, 1866) did not occur just during that one year, but continued for six years until the Taewŏn'gun retired from his position. This period of persecution can be divided into approximately four stages: the first stage being 1866 in relation to Russia's southern invasion; the second stage being the latter part of 1866 surrounding the execution of French priests and the invasion by the French warships; the third stage being the period between 1866 to 1870; and the last stage being the "foreign disturbance of 1871" -- the attack on Kanghwa Island by an American vessel in 1871. Therefore, in light of its association with the Western forces at the time and not simply with the internal political situation, the Pyŏngin Persecution deserves an interpretation from the

---

[578] *Catholic Korea Yesterday and Today,* p.240.

[579] Ch'oe Sŏg-u , *Pyŏngin Pakhae charyo yŏn'gu,* (Seoul: Han'guk kyohoesa yŏn'guso, 1968), p.17.

perspective of world history as well.

Russia's Policy of Expansion of the Southern Region and Catholic Persecution

The beginning of Pyŏngin year was the first stage of persecution during which a measure to befriend Catholicism was first adopted in order to address the southward movement of Russian forces, and then a drastic change in course occurred, leading to a full-scale persecution. It was a period of massive slaughter, during which most key figures in the Korean Catholic church were executed.

Russia's Southward Expansion and the Persecution of Catholicism

In the first year 2nd month of Kojong, five Russians arrived in Kyŏnghŭng and requested to establish trade relations from County Magistrate Yun Hyŏp,[580] and in the 9th month of 1865, several tens of Russians arrived in Kyŏnghŭng and proposed a meeting with the governor.[581] In the 12th month of the same year they requested a meeting on two additional occasions, but Kyŏnghŭng County Magistrate Yun Hyŏp disregarded their requests and sent them back.[582] To the Chosŏn people at that time, Russia appeared as having interest in taking over the land of Chosŏn. It was widely known in Korea that Russia had taken the entire area of Siberia and the state of Yŏnhae from Ch'ing China. In fact, Russia was building warships in Vladivostok and preparing for a southward expansion policy. As Russia proceeded with this policy and the occurrences of crossing the border and requesting for trade relations

---

[580] *Chosŏn wangjo sillok,* Kojong 1st year 3rd month 2day, 7th month 22nd day.

[581] *Chosŏn wangjo sillok,* Kojong 2nd year 11th month 10th and 11th day.

[582] Yi Sang-baek, *Han'guksa, kŭnse hugip'yŏn* (Seoul: Ŭlyu munhwasa, 1965), p.386.

became more frequent, the Chosŏn government began to feel a sense of crisis. It also became a convincing motivation behind the massive persecution of Catholicism in the Pyŏngin year.

Hong Pong-ju (Thomas), in whose house Bishop Berneux resided,[583] and other Catholic believers confessed at the trial interrogation that Bishop Berneux was wary of the threat posed by Russia and thus proposed the solution of an alliance with France as an effecive anti-Russian policy.[584] Their confession demonstrates their considerable knowledge of international affairs. They had been able to learn about world affairs through clergymen in Korea or as envoys to China. Hong Pong-ju, Kim Myŏn-ho (Kyeho), Yi Yu-il and others concluded the situation at the time to be a good opportunity to attain religious freedom and so they decided to propose an anti-Russian policy of their own. They decided to deliver a letter to the Taewŏn'gun, a letter proposing an alliance among Korea, Britain and France as the ideal measure, suggesting that the task could be easily accomplished through Western priests.[585] This letter of proposal was delivered to the Taewŏn'gun by the father-in-law of the Taewŏn'gun's daugher, Cho Ki-jin.[586] When the Taewŏn'gun did not give any response, Kim Myŏn-ho became nervous and went into hiding on his way back. However, while waiting curiously for the Taewŏn'gun's response, they received a message from Queen Min through Kojong's nursemaid Pak Martha, instructing to "have priests come to Seoul at the earliest opportunity and meet with the

---

[583] He was the grandson of Hong Nag-min who died a martyr during the Sinyu Persecution. His father was Hong Chae-yŏng, who was martyred during the Kihae Persecution. His mother was Chŏng Yak-hyŏn's daughter.

[584] *Pyŏngin kukan*, Pyŏngin year, 1st month 16th and 19th day. *Kojong sillok*, Kojong 3rd year 1st month 18th day.

[585] Yi Nŭng-hwa, *op.cit.*, p.32.

[586] Yi Nŭng-hwa, *op.cit.*, (ha), p.33.

Taewŏn'gun to discuss the anti-Russian policy." [587] Encouraged by the message, Hong Pong-ju and Kim Myŏn-ho informed Nam Chong-sam, a key figure in the church, of the message and asked him to take an active role in the negotiation. Immediately, Nam Chong-sam rewrote their letter and personally delivered it to the Taewŏn'gun. The following day, the Taewŏn'gun called upon Nam Chong-sam and confirmed his belief of "the ability of the missionaries in preventing the invasion of Russia," after which he ordered the missionaries to come to Seoul and arrange a meeting thereupon.

Because the Taewŏn'gun was afraid of the southward expansion of Czarist Russia, as a preventive step, he had attempted to approach the Catholic church members, whose religion thus far had been branded as "evil doctrine that has neither father nor king." Having heard the news from Nam Chong-sam that the Taewŏn'gun was willing to meet with French priests, the Catholic church members believed that their long-cherished desire of religious freedom had already been fulfilled, and intoxicated with bliss, rather than promptly taking action, they even informed the believers in the countryside and gathered in Seoul to perform a mass of gratitude. Bishop Berneux as well as priests were in the midst of visiting the countryside regions, and thus could not quickly respond to the Taewŏn'gun's order. Subsequently, as Kim Myŏn-ho appeared again and urged them on, it was only then that Nam Chong-sam attempted to seek communication with Bishop Berneux and Daveluy in Naep'o. However, this time, he had difficulty in gathering funds from the poverty-stricken Catholics to bring the priests to Seoul, and after several days of delay, Cho Ki-chin provided the expenses and the priests were able to come to Seoul. Bishop Daveluy, who also had been making visits to the countryside regions, returned to Seoul on the 25th day of the 1st month in 1866, and Bishop Berneux followed suit afterwards. On the 15th day of the 2nd month, Nam Chong-sam visited and

---

[587] Yi Sang-baek, *op.cit.*, p.387.

informed the Taewŏn'gun of the bishops' arrival. In an angry voice, the Taewŏn'gun, however, reproached Nam Chong-sam for the delay as well as for insincerity, saying, "Haven't you yet gone down to the countryside? I thought that you had gone to visit your father ... Now that there is nothing urgent, let's see what happens. Send my regards to your father when you see him."[588] Upon being scolded by the Taewŏn'gun in such manner, Nam Chong-sam returned in disappointment.[589]

At the time, the political forces around the Taewŏn'gun and the Confucian scholars had been raising objections to the Taewŏn'gun's moderate policy and apparent tolerance of Catholicism. Concurrently, Russia's effort at military maneuvering seemed to have waned, and with the news that Ch'ing China had changed its policy to one of greater permissiveness, the spirit of anti-Western religious sentiment was plainly gaining strength.

Subsequently, the Taewŏn'gun suddenly changed his policy of tacit approval of Catholicism, which was owing to pressure from Queen Dowager Cho and her high officials. On the 5th day of 1st month in 1866 (3rd year of Kojong), he had Chŏn Chang-un, Ch'oe Hyŏng and Bishop Berneux's attendant Yi Sŏn-i arrested, and thus began the full-scale Pyŏngin persecution.[590] Due to Yi Sŏn-i's report, the priests under Bishop Berneux (Mgr. Siméon-Francois Berneux) who had not taken flight from the expanding persecution, and Hong Pong-ju (Thomas) were arrested.[591] The powerful officials including Chŏng Wŏn-yong, Kim

---

[588]Charles Dallet, *op.cit.*, (ha), p.388-389.

[589]Yi Nŭng-hwa, *op.cit*(ha), pp.34-35.

[590]*Chōsenshi* Vol.6, Jan.5-9. Tongchi 5th year 1st month 5th day. The Catholic persecutions in the past have always begun on the new year's day of lunar calendar, most likely because it was an occasion for families to gather together at one place and thus easier to arrest and take them into custody.

[591] *Up'odoch'ŏng dŭngrok*, Pyŏngin year 1st month 9th day. *Sŭngjŏngwŏn ilgi*, Tongchi 5th year 1st month 11th day.

Chwa-kŭn, Cho Tu-sun, and Kim Pyŏng-hak submitted a memorial to the king urging arrest and punishment of the representative figure of Catholics, Nam Chong-sam. Puhogun Nam I-ryun, Hojo Nam Sŏng-kyo, and Pusŭngji Nam Chong-sun of the Nam clan were imprisoned for assisting the Catholics.[592] Starting from the 16th day of the 1st month, nine among the already arrested twelve missionaries and other church members were transferrred to the Ŭigŭmbu (State Tribunal) and interrogated for trial. Bishop Berneux was directly interrogated by the Taewŏn'gun himself, who strongly encouraged him to apostatize and leave Chosŏn, but as he refused to betray his faith, he was beheaded on the Noryangjin execution ground. On the same day, Nam Chong-sam and Hong Pong-ju were also beheaded, on the execution ground outside the Sŏsomun Gate.[593]

In the name of Queen Dowager Cho, a nationwide order was issued to burn all Catholic books, enforce the five-household mutual surveillance system, reward those who report heretics and punish those who hide them, and to strengthen the guarding of the Hwanghae Ch'ungchŏngdo coast.[594] Thus began an unprecedented full-scale persecution of Catholicism throughout the nation. The missionaries who had been caught up to the 7th day of the 2nd month were all executed,[595] and executions were carried out in Seoul and Pyŏngyang and elsewhere in the countryside. In addition to the massive slaughtering of Chosŏn Catholics, the execution of nine French priests, and the deaths of refugees from diseases and starvation, there were many others, who, though innocent, were killed by corrupt and false charges leveled by corrupt government

---

[592]*Chōsenshi*, Vol.6, No.4, Kojong 3rd year 1st month 11th day.

[593]Charles Dallet, *op.cit.*, (ha), pp.400-404. *Chwa p'odoch'ŏng tŭngnok*, Pyŏngin Jan. 21. *Chōsenshi Ibid*, Jan.21.

[594]*Ibid*, Jan.18-24.

[595] *Ibid.*, Jan. 7.

officials. Moreover, the government officials, fake officials accused non-believers as Catholics in avarice for their wealth, resulting in many harmed individuals. This is evidenced by the issuance of an order prohibiting such plunder.[596]

Invasion of the French Fleet

The second stage consists of the latter part of 1866 when the French fleet, having been contacted by the priests who had fled the country, clashed with Koreans on two occasions in their request for communication. Moreover, the Chosŏn government had already learned of the mobilization and sailing of the French fleet through a report from the Ch'ing government before the fleet attacked Chosŏn at Kanghwa Island. Subsequently, the Chosŏn government concluded that they were a brigand seeking to escape the law and thus instructed that the border be strictly regulated. The Pyŏngin yangyo (foreign disturbance of 1866) arose now due to the confrontation with the French fleet, but it was Catholicism that became the victim of the reprisal.

Persecution Instigated by the Pyŏngin Yangyo

The Paris Foreign Mission Society had assumed responsibility for Catholic mission activities in Korea, and had dispatched about twenty missionaries to Korea by the time of the Pyŏngin (1866) Persecution. Among them, three French priests were executed during the Kihae Persecution and nine priests were executed during the Pyŏngin Persecution. It was these executions and deaths of French priests that brought the French fleet to Korea. The three priests who had remained alive during the Pyŏngin Persecution, Ridel, Feron, and Calais, met in secrecy and decided to inform the French embassy of their plight. Father Ridel took the responsibility, and with eleven Chosŏn Catholic believers, acquired a fishing boat, and

---

[596]*Ibid*, March 7.

arrived in the Shandong Province port of Chefoo, where he met Admiral P.G. Roze and informed him of the situation in Korea. Having learned what had happened, French ambassador minister Henrie de Bellotrot ordered a military action to be taken against the Korean peninsula.[597] The Ch'ing government of China informed Chosŏn of this independent decision of the French ambassador minister. The Chosŏn court sent a reply to China to the effect that they had condemned the clandestine activities of the missionaries and that they had submitted a petition in all sincerity in regards to the compensation for damaged foreign ships.[598]

The French fleet commanded by Admiral Roze was somewhat delayed, but on the 10th of the 8th month (solar calendar, 16th day of the 9th month), he led three warships, *Primauget, Tardif* and *Déroulède*, and with Priest Ridel and three Chosŏn Catholics as translators as well as navigators, departed from Chefoo, China and headed for the Korean peninsula.[599] The flotilla passed Kanghwa Island and entered the Sŏgang River, but perhaps because they felt their position to be at a disadvantage, they retreated without any demonstration of armed force.[600] At that time, Father Ridel requested that at least one warship be left behind so that he could rescue his two fellow priests, but his request was denied.[601] Shortly afterwards, on the 5th day of 9th month, Admiral Roze again appeared on the coast of Kanghwa Island, this time with a force of seven armed French warships, and demanded an explanation for the

---

[597] Griffis, *Corea the Hermit Nation*, pp.377-378.

[598] *Sŭngchŏngwŏn ilgi*, Pyŏngin year 7th month 6th day.

[599] Charles Dallet, *op.cit.*, (ha), (pp.459-461).

[600] Hulbert, *op.cit.*, II, p.208.

[601] Yi Sŏn-kŭn, *op.cit.*, P.254.

execution of nine missionaries.[602] On the 8th day of the 9th month, they seized the government headquarters building of Kanghwa Island. Around the 30th day, they fought a battle with Chosŏn army defenders, and thoroughly pillaged the island, taking away gold, silver (19 boxes of silver ingots weighing about 888.5 kilograms), books and other cultural items.[603] On the 3rd day of the 10th month, miserably defeated in a battle at Chŏngjoksan fortress and low in spirits, the French army withdrew (on the 5th day of the 10th month). This incident demonstrates not so much the desire of the French for trade relations but rather an intent to chastise the Chosŏn government for executing the French priests. However, because they relied only on their armed force and misjudged the Chosŏn government, they retreated, having even failed to rescue the two remaining missionaries. Even though the French priests from the Paris Foreign Mission Society proselytizing in Chosŏn did not take an active part in the vanguard of the invasion by the French colonial power, [604] the East Asian region at the time was a battleground for the competing Western colonial powers, to the point that it was not out of the ordinary that the Chosŏn government mistook their roles. Through the Pyŏngin Yangyo Incident, they were made unable to avoid the accusation that they were the spearhead of the colonial powers.

After defeating the French warships, the Taewŏn'gun erected *Ch'ŏkhwabi* (Stele Rejecting Reconciliation) throughout the nation and further spurred on the persecution of Catholicism. He swore that the land polluted by the Western barbarians should be washed clean with the blood of pursuers of the Western Learning, and thus he continued to execute numerous Catholic believers. On the

---

[602] *Chōsenshi*, Vol.6, No.4, Pyŏngin year 9th month 5th day, p.103.

[603] *Ibid.*, p.106. *Ilsŏngnok,* Pyŏngin year 9th month 9th day.

[604] No Kil-myŏng, *Catholic kwa Chosŏn hugi sahoe pyŏndong*, pp.182-187.

18th day of the 9th month, even the remaining two priests escaped to Ch'ing China, and consequently, the Chosŏn church was once again left without clergy.

The Oppert Incident

The third stage of the 1866 Persecution lasted for four years of Kojong's reign, from 1866 to1870, a period during which the persecution was reinforced by the Tŏksankulchong Incident instigated by the German adventurer Oppert. This was a scheme hatched by the German merchant-adventurer Ernst Oppert to rifle the tomb of the Taewŏngun's father, holding its remains hostage to the wishes of the marauders.

In a violent rage, the Taewŏn'gun issued a strict order to all government bureaus throughout the nation to destroy the Western barbarians and the evil religion, and to ferret out and slay the believers who had escaped the previous persecution. Approximately 170 people were put to death within eight months.

Foreign Disturbance of 1871

The fourth stage of the final "Persecution of 1866" actually consisted of forty days of revived persecution in 1871, due to the Sinmiyangyo (Foreign Disturbance of l871). With the incident of the merchant ship *General Sherman* in 1866, there began an effort on the part of America to aggressively pursue trade relations with Chosŏn. The Taewŏn'gun's adherence to an isolation policy, nevertheless, remained unchanged. Not to mention those who had confessed to communicating with the enemy, but even those believers who were merely under suspicion of so communicating were all arrested and killed.

In early August (lunar calendar 7th month) of 1866 a heavily armed American merchant ship, the *General Sherman*, left north China for Korea with a crew of Americans, English, Chinese and Malaysians. Also aboard was an Anglican missionary named Robert Thomas.[605] The *General Sherman* sailed along the Taedong River shores and forcibly detained a Korean investigating officer, Yi Hyŏn-ik. When a crowd gathered around, the crew members returned to their ship, at which point they opened fire. Subsequently, under the order of Pak Kyu-su, the governor of the province, the ship was set on fire and those on board all perished.[606]

In search of the *General Sherman*, the *Wachusett* under the command of Commodore R.W. Schufeldt arrived in Korea in the 12th month of Pyŏngin (1866) year, and *The Shenandoah* under the command of Commander John C. Febiher arrived in Korea in the 3rd month of the 5th year of Kojong, but both returned without any success.[607] Accordingly, the U.S. Minister to Beijing, Frederick F. Low, made an attempt at establishing trade relations with Korea by sending a diplomatic letter through the Ch'ing China government offices. However, as there was no positive result, on the 8th day of the 4th month in the 8th year of Kojong (solar calendar 26th day of 5th month), the Commander of the U.S. Asiatic Squadron, Rear Admiral John Rodgers, proceeded into Korean waters with a detachment of five warships, eighty cannons and 1,230 soldiers, along with Priest Ridel as translator.[608] They passed along Yŏngjong Island and appeared at the Kwangsŏngjin fortification where they inquired about the incident of the *General Sheman* and requested trade relations, but the Taewŏn'gun refused. With a small motor boat they were passing through the Kanghwa Strait,

---

[605] Kim Key-hiuk, *The Last Phase of the East Asian World Order*, (Berkeley & LA: University of California, 1980), p.52.

[606] *Chōsenshi* Vol.6, No.4, Pyŏngin year 7th month 4th day, p.92.

[607] Charles O. Paullin, Diplomatic Negotiations of American Naval Officers, 284-286. Quoted from Kim Key-hiuk, *op.cit.*, p.54.

[608] W. E. Griffis, *op.cit.*, p.406.

surveying and reconnoitering the region, whereupon Korean batteries at Sŏndolmok opened fire, leading to an eruption of cannon fire both sides. A battle lasting 48 hours, perhaps the shortest war in the history of American warfare,[609] had occurred in Kwangsŏngpo. The American force withdrew forty days later on the 16th day of the 5th month (solar calendar 3rd day of the 7th month).

At the subsequent negotiations held in 1867 in Beijing the delegate minister of the U.S., Dr. S. Wells Williams acknolwedged the wrongdoings of the *General Sherman*,[610] and he also admitted that Admiral Rodgers' attack in 1871 was a mistake.[611] On the 25th day of the 4th month (solar calendar 12th day of 6th month), on the Korean side, the Taewŏn'gun had *chŏkhwabi*, monument stones incised with admonitions to the Western nations, set up throughout the nation. At the same time, he deplored the reports that there were Koreans who had accompanied the American ships as guides and professed great shock upon learning that Catholic believers visited the American warships every night and attempted to establish communication with the foreigners.[612] Following the Mujin year (1868), the number of arrested Catholics had decreased while those who were being martyred continued to increase. Due to the Kanghwa Island incident in the 8th year of Kojong (1871), the Chosŏn government further hardened its policy on Catholicism. During this one year alone, the number of Catholic believers who had their trial records on the police bureau list was forty two. Due to the General Sherman incident, Yi Yŏn-kyu, Yi Sŭng-hun's great-grandson, Yi Kyun-kyu and others were beheaded at Chemulp'o, the accusation being that their father Yi Chae-ŭi was a Catholic believer and that he had attempted to

---

[609] Yi Sŏn-kŭn, *op.cit.*, p.305.

[610] W.E. Griffis, *op.cit.*, p.394f.

[611] *Ibid*, p.482.

[612] *Kojong Sillok*, Sinmi year 4th month 29th day.

communicate with the American ship. Yi Chae-kyŏm's wife Song Chŏng-nyŏ and his granddaughter Yi Myŏng-hyŏn (Yi Sŭng-hun's Great-great granddaughter on the paternal side) were both executed for the same reason.[613]

In the 10th year of Kojong (1873), the Taewŏn'gun relinquished his power as Regent, and an isolation policy was no longer possible amidst invasions of both Eastern and Western powers. This offered a glimpse of hope to Catholics and it also signified the collapse of the reactionary ruling group. In the 7th month in the 14th year of Kojong (1877), Priest Ridel secretly entered Korea once again, only to be arrested on the 26th day of the 12th month.[614] However, he was released upon the issuance of a letter from the Beijing government instigated by a protest from the French charge d'affaires in Beijing.[615] Hereupon, the persecution of Catholicism finally came to an end in Chosŏn. From the 1870s to the beginning of the 1880s, there were arrests of Catholic believers or priests from time to time, but Kojong's policy on Catholicism was that of appeasement and his foreign policy was that of enlightenment. The arrested French priests were sent back to Ch'ing China and there were no more executions of foreigners. Meanwhile, in 1876, the Pyŏngja and Suho treaties between Korea and Japan had been signed, and Kojong had already been promoting an open-door policy in alignment with the general trend of the world.

In 1880, Kim Hong-jip was sent to Japan as a member of a special government mission. In Tokyo, he met Huang Tsun-hsien, Councillor of Ch'ing China, from whom he acquired a book called *Chao-hsien ts'e lueh* (Strategy for Korea), and trouble arose in Korea upon his return with the book. The content was much the same as that Kim Hong-jip had already heard from Inoue Kaoru, the Japanese

---

[613] *Kojong sidaesa* 1, (Seoul: Kuksa p'yŏnch'an wiwŏnhoe, 1967), p.396. Yu Hong-nyŏl, *op.cit.*, pp.275-347.

[614] *P'odochŏng tŭngnok*, Chŏngch'uk 12th month 26th day.

[615] *Ilsŏngnok*, Muin year 5th month 4th day.

foreign minister, and from the Ch'ing minister to Tokyo, Ha Yŏ-jang. It was a proposal for cooperation among Japan, Ch'ing China and America to prevent Russia's invasion of Korea, for Russia's movements had been suspicious. In response, Confucian scholars presented criticisms, and Yu Wŏn-sik (Section Chief of the Board of War) presented a critical memorial, only to be exiled to a remote district of P'yŏngan province:

> *Chao-hsien ts'e lueh* maintains that Catholicism is in fact one and the same with our religion of Neo-Confucianism. This is a great insult to the sages by those polluted by the evil religion, and thus it must be destroyed. To bring such a book, into this country is a crime. This book must have been produced in a conspiracy between the Catholic believers and foreigners, and such a wicked band must be caught and eliminated.

Thus, the general trend of affairs was disadvantageous to the obstinate Neo-Confucians. Nevertheless, on the 26th day of 2nd month in 1881, Yi Man-son, a Confucian scholar in Yŏngnam, presented a so-called"Yŏngnam maninso," a memorial signed by ten thousand names, to the king in his attempt to drive out Catholicism:

> It has been only ten years since the group of heretics had been exterminated in the Pyŏngin year, and the evil religion is again spreading. Before, it was shared among them in secret, but now it is learned and taught out in the open. It was proper to have eliminated the evil religion in the Pyŏngin year (1866), but today it is treated generously. With what deeds would His Majesty repay the previous kings and with what words would His Majesty address the

posterity?⁶¹⁶

On this issue, Confucian scholars submitted memorials on Catholicism on seven consecutive occasions, and on the 16th day of the 5th month in 1881, Kojong issued an admonition titled*Chŏksa yunŭm* just as it was done during the Kihae Persecution.⁶¹⁷ This was the last *Chŏksa yunŭm* issued by Kojong, and it was also declared in both Korean and Chinese. Its content stated that faithfully abiding by the lessons of Confucianism was the way to defeat Catholicism. The Chosŏn government had been deeply submerged in anti-Western xenophobia, but the Yŏhŭng Min clan, who had been in control of the government, opened its doors and entered into the Kanghwa Treaty with Japan in 1876 and Korean-American Suho Treaty in 1882 through the mediation of Ch'ing China. In entering into a treaty with France, Chosŏn experienced difficulty, because France proposed freedom of mission while the Chosŏn government rejected it. The French government was already aware of the situation in Chosŏn through a missionary in Korea, Bishop Mutel, who had just returned to France. Moreover, in an attempt to protect its missionaries, the French government wished to enter into a treaty. In the 3rd month of 1886, then, France dispatched François-George Cogordan to Chosŏn. He was able to conclude a treaty on the 5th day of the 5th month of 1883 through a statesman Kim Man-sik and an American, Denny.⁶¹⁸ Due to the Treaty, the persecution of the Chosŏn government on the Catholic Church was officially over.

The Nature of the Persecution of 1866

The Pyŏngin Persecution was enforced throughout the nation for six years starting at the beginning of 1866,

---

⁶¹⁶*Ilsŏngnok*, Kojong Sinsa year 2nd month 26th day.

⁶¹⁷In the possession of the Beineke Library, Yale University.

⁶¹⁸Yu Hong-nyŏl, *op.cit.*, (ha), p.267.

which was the period of the Taewŏn'gun's rule. Approximately eight thousand people were martyred during this persecution. Many factors contributed to origins of the persecution. In addition to the uncompromising self-righteousness of the Hŭngsŏn Taewŏn'gun, the wielder of actual political power at the time, various external factors such as Russia's southward expansion, invasion by a French fleet, the barbaric act of the German, Oppert, and an attack by American ship led to further intensification of the persecution. The continuous arrival of the American, British and French warships and their demands for trade relations as well as their military provocations sparked clashes between foreign and Chosŏn military forces, and this doubtless contributed to the prolonging of the persecution. With the eruption of confrontations against the the armed forces of Western colonial nations, the Catholic persecution became no longer a purely religious persecution but rather took on an element of rebellion against invasion by the forces of Western colonialism.

As it was for the previous persecutions, the fundamental cause behind the Pyŏngin Persecution lay in the confrontation between the Confucian notions of national sovereignty in the latter part of the Chosŏn dynasty and the heterodoxical ideology of the Western Learning, Catholicism. The Chosŏn government perceived Catholicism as an ideology of equality that destroyed the traditional order of Chosôn's social classes, with its concept of equality, rejection of ancestor worship, lack of absolute respect for father and king, gender equality and desegregation of men and women. And thus it was seen as destructive to the ethics and morality of Chosen society. Not merely these domestic considerations alone, but the Catholics' open conspiracy with Western forces and the ensuing military and economic threats clearly put the sovereign authority of Chosŏn at great risk. Accordingly, a direct cause of the persecution was Russia's southward expansion and the anti-Russian policy called *Yiyicheyi* (using barbarians to control barbarians) of Catholicism. One of several peripheral reasons for the persecution was that, as the Taewŏn'gun lacked funding for reconstructing Kyŏngbok palace; he attempted to extort substantial contributions from Bishop Berneux. The nature of the internal affairs of Chosŏn was another factor contributing to the persecution. The corruption of the in-law government was worsening, and due to the disorder in the "three administrations" people's suffering mounted. The Chinju Uprising of 1861 ignited a succession of similar outbreaks of peasant uprisings throughout the nation. These uprisings signified a popular rebellion against "politics as usual."

Then, in 1860, Ch'oe Che-u began to propound a new native doctrine called *Tonghak* (Eastern Learning), which had an immediate appeal, to the downtrodden peasants and common people. Afraid of the consequences of unregulated proselytizing, the Chosŏn government arrested Ch'oe Che-u, put him on trial, and executed him in 1864. This *Tonghak* upheaval led to the further hardening of the Catholic persecution for the reason that it sowed discord in the society and led to the easy argument that all "evil doctrines" must be suppressed. Those in power were incapable of adequately responding to the social discontent of the common class, and such incapability itself was an additional factor in exacerbating the causes of other discontent.

Amid the influx of Western forces and the pressure from their demand for trade relations and missionary freedom, the Taewŏn'gun had felt a sense of crisis and thus had pursued an exclusion policy, and it was this period in which he also enforced the Pyŏngin Perscution.[619] Internally, this was a policy that promoted solidarity and mobilization within the nation, and externally, it was of a policy of resistance to demands for creating ties to the outside. Although the Taewŏn'gun's exclusion policy is often evaluated as a hindrance to the general historical development of Korea, it must have been unavoidable in the situation at that time for the sake of self-protection and the strengthening of his authority. The largest group that

---

[619] Kŭm Chang-tae, " Ch'ŏnjukyo taeŭng ch'aek." p.14.

supported the Pyŏngin Persecution was not the original ruling class, but rather was composed of the Confucian intellectuals who had been kept out of government positions.[620] They vehemently denounced heterodoxy and adhered to their traditional beliefs. In cooperation with the ruling class, they suppressed the Catholic group, which was related to the foreign forces and composed of mainly the lower non-ruling class, and also suppressed the spontaneously formed *Tonghak*, which was supported by the commoners. They had instigated the Pyŏngin Persecution as the last measure in their unwavering faith and theoretical conviction in Confucianism.

The Pyŏngin Persecution was truly tragic. Hulbert wrote, "The tales of that terrible time remind one of the persecutions under the Roman Emperors or the no less terrible scenes of the Spanish Inquisition."[621] For example, P'yŏngyang inspector, Chŏng Chi-yong arrested the Catholic believers, and among them, he released those who apostatized while he had the one hundred apostates beat Yu Chŏng-nyul (1837-1866), who did not renounce to the very end, each three times until he died.[622]

In 1866, Kojong issued a *Chŏksa yunŭm* (Reject Heresy Pronouncement) aimed at Catholicism. It pointed out the Catholic believers' firm religious conviction that was difficult to control through punishment, and it recognized that Catholics learn and teach each other the evil books and pose a threat to the nation by attracting foreigners. As a counter-measure, it urged the people to abandon Catholicism and firmly establish the Confucian faith.[623]

---

[620] *Ibid*, p.440

[621] Hulbert, *The History of Korea II*, p.211.

[622] This was inscribed in the epitaph of Chŏng Chi-yong erected by the following Pyŏngyang inspector Yi Chae-ch'ŏng in 1876 in Pyŏngyang Pubyŏkru Yŏngmyŏngsa. *Pyŏngin pakhae sun'gyoja chŭngŏnnok, Han'guk Catholic Taesajŏn*, pp.9-04-905.

[623] Yi Nŭng-hwa, *op.cit.*, (ha), pp.57-59.

The *Chŏksa yunŭm* refuted the issues regarding God, parents, men and women, taking its argument from the Catholic doctrine itself. This can be understood as an attempt not so much to enlighten the Catholic believers but to change the views of the common populace through teaching.

Because the Pyŏngin Persecution was initiated by complex and diverse factors, its size and extent could only be greater than those of any other persecutions in the past. The persecutions before the Pyŏngin Persecution were brought to an end within one to two years, while the Pyŏngin Persecution began in 1866 (3rd year of Kojong) and lasted for eight years until 1873 when the Taewŏn'gun relinquished his power. However, it can be claimed to have lasted until 1878 (15th year of Kojong), because the persecutions continued regionally. The persecution was also carried out throughout the entire nation. The fact that the persecution was enforced for such a long period of time throughout the entire nation testifies to the fact that the Catholic believers had expanded widely throughout the Korean peninsula in the meantime. Its size at the same time was substantial, resulting in an estimated eight thousand to twenty thousand martyrs.[624] A *Ch'imyŏng ilgi* (The Diary of Martyrdom) was published, in which were recorded seventy-seven martyrs who were active from 1890 to 1895, and twenty-four of them whose credentials were reviewed by the Roman Papal Court were blessed in 1964. In 1984, they were canonized as Saints.

Although it is referred to as the Pyŏngin (1866) Persecution, there were a greater number of martyrs and arrested believers in the Mujin year, 1868. It is nevertheless called the Pyŏngin Persecution. But since it started in the Pyŏngin year (1866), and the Catholic Church, which had been on the rise under the relatively tolerant policy pursued by the Andong Kim clan under Ch'ŏlchong, was greatly shocked by the sudden persecution and the loss of key church figures. Generally there had been more apostates

---

[624] Yu Hong-nyŏl, *op.cit.*, (ha), p.44. Hwang Hyŏn, *Maech'ŏnyarok*, Kaboijŏn, p.7

The Persecution of the Later Period

than those who maintained their faith, but during the Pyŏngin year, there were more believers who maintained their faith. Furthermore, many male believers were executed.[625] In addition, in the Pyŏngin year, three priests among the twelve French priests, Ridel, Féron, and Calais all fled to China, while the remaining nine priests were all executed.[626]

---

[625] Iwai Hisao, *op.cit.*, p.199.

[626] Charles Dallet, *op.cit.*, II, pp.563-576. As a result, international events occurred with the Oppert incident and the invasion of Kanghwa Island by French warships, and the persecution intensified.

Chapter VI

The Causes of the Persecution

1. Ideological Causes

Western Learning as Heterodoxy
When the Chinese translations of books on Western Learning were transmitted to Chosŏn in the 17th century, the initial response of the Confucian scholars was that of academic curiosity, as they strove to understand and grasp the nature of Western Learning as well as its principal dogma. Essentially, it became an academic subject from the persepective of intellectual curiosity. Most of the books they read, such as *Ch'ŏnju silŭi* and those included in the *Ch'ŏnhak ch'oham (T'ien-hsueh ch'u-han chi)* (1629) edited by Li Chih-tsao (1565-1630), were mostly written with a view toward avoiding ideological conflict with Confucianism. These books were mainly translated or written by the Jesuit missionaries working in China, who believed that the best approach to propagating the Catholic faith was to adapt it so that it seemed consonant with traditional beliefs.

As the doctrinal content of Catholicism became better understood, intellectuals began to criticize it. The first criticism came from Yu Mong-in. He explicated *Ch'ŏnju silŭi* in detail and criticized its teachings on heaven and hell and the practice of celibacy as improper, and further condemned the religion for deluding people.[627] Yi I-myŏng, who had held discussions with the Jesuit Priests Joseph Sauerz and Ignatius Kögler in Yenching during Sukchong's reign, opined that Catholicism and Confucianism were of the same status, and both were above Taoism or Buddhism. He praised the Western missionaries' evangelical enthusiasm and sense of mission, but suggested that it would be very difficult to reform the world with the theory of incarnation of Jesus and the theory of heaven and hell of Catholicism.[628]

As investigation into Western Learning became more extensive, a movement affirming the orthodoxy of Confucianism and condemning Christian doctrine as *idan* (heterodoxy) [629] began among some of the Confucian literati, including Sin Hu-dam, An Chŏng-bok, and Hong Chŏng-ha. An Chŏng-bok generally regarded the Western Learning as *idan*, stating that "although there may be more than one true way of the world, anything that is not Confucianism is *idan*."[630] He asserted that the Catholic teachings were the same as Buddhism, but under a different name: the ten commandments of Catholicism and the seven commandments of Buddhism were similar, and both ignored the importance of the ethical obligations between king and people, father and son, and husband and wife.[631] In a memorial submitted by Censorate official

---

[627] Yu Mong-in, *Ŏuyadam,* kwŏn 2, "Sŏgyo."

[628] *Ibid.*

[629] Its literal meaning is "a different thread," meaning that it violates the sages of ancient China. Chŏng Yag-yong, *Chŏng Ta-san chŏnjip* II, 7:31a.

[630] *Sunam munjip*, kwŏn 2, Sang Sŏngho sŏnsaeng pyŏlji, Chŏngch'uk.

[631] *Ibid.*

(Changryŏng), Yu Ha-wŏn in 1785,[632] it is stated that,

> ...It has been already many years since the Western books have been entering Chosŏn through translators (*yŏkkwan*) and the occurrences of deceiving the populace, as well as those who believe, have increased. So called *Tao*, the true way, recognizes only heaven, and it not only ignores the existence of parents, but it also deludes the people and tempts the world with the theory of heaven and hell. Thus its poison is worse than that of a large sea monster or vicious beast. It must be prohibited even more strictly through the government bureaus in charge of legal matters.

Three years later another Censorate official, Yi Kyŏng-myŏng also submitted a similar memorial:[633]

> This so-called "Western Learning" among the populace is truly a seriously outrageous phenomenon. Although his Royal Highness has given clear instructions of strict punishment this year, as time passed, its seed matured gradually and came to be transmitted from the capital city to the countryside, tempting people. Consequently, even the extremely ignorant farmers and uneducated countrymen copied these books in Korean and worshiped them as gods, claiming never to regret even in the face of death. If this is not stopped immediately, such wicked theory will spread and we would not be able to know the extent of its harm. It should be strictly

---

[632] *Chosŏn wangjo sillok,* Chŏngjo 9th year 4th month Muja.
[633] *Chosŏn wangjo sillok,* Chŏngjo 12th year 8th month Sinmyo.

controlled by the order of the court through the inspectors and governors of the several provinces and thereby to have no more spreading of the evil.

Besides the above memorials, there were those submitted by Hong Nag-an,[634] by Taesagan Sin Ki in the 10th and 11th months of 1791,[635] by Chip'yŏng Han Yŏng-kyu,[636] by Taesagan Kwŏn Yi-kang, [637] and a student of Sŏng'gyun'gwan Song To-chŏng, [638] and all of their assertions were similar in content. They branded Catholicism as a collection of dangerous ideas that brought confusion to the populace, especially its theory of heaven and hell and as damaging as the Ch'eng-Chu school.

When the Incident of Detection of the Catholics occurred in 1785, the 9th year of Chŏngjo, the students of the National Confucian Academy circulated a flyer proclaiming that if the evil heterodoxy is not expunged, they are afraid that its evil would be greater than that of the barbarians disturbing the Middle Kingdom.[639] When the Panch'on Incident, a study group for Catholic doctrine, arose in 1787, students of the Confucian Academy Yi Ki-kyŏng and Hong Nag-an publicly denounced Western Learning as heterodoxy and advocated its repudiation.[640]

The Neo-Confucians came to conclude that Western Learning was a threat to the ideology of the Chosŏn kingdom, and to the Confucian spirit, and they demanded the renunciation of the pursuers of Western Learning for

---

[634] Yi Man-ch'ae, *Pyŏkwip'yŏn*, kwŏn 2.

[635] *Ibid.*

[636] *Ibid.*

[637] *Ibid.*

[638] *Ibid.*

[639] Yi Man-ch'ae, *Pyŏkwipyŏn*, "Ŭlsa ch'ujo chŏkpal."

[640] Yi Man-ch'ae, *Pyŏkwipy'ŏn*, kwŏn 2.

they were the same as Huang Jinzei and Bai Lianjiao of China.[641] Those in power were emphasizing the possibility of an uprising by the practioners of Western Learning, and thus had expressed a wish for an immediate extinction of the heterodoxy. All criticisms were based on Mencius' theory of anti-heterodoxy, which claimed that the Yang- Chu's egoism was heterodoxy because they denied relationship between the king and the people, which is a social standard and thereby denied the king. Mencius' theory of Anti-heterodoxy regarded as heterodoxy Mo-tzu's universal love theory, because it essentially ignores one's own father, thereby denying fatherhood. Thus, these heterodoxies were denounced as evil doctrines that deserted humanity and brought in the world of birds and beasts.[642] Furthermore, declaring that the purpose of their renunciation of Yang Mo was to abide by the Tao of the sages, they established the logic for anti-heterodoxy.[643]

At the time of the Chinsan Incident in 1791, Hong Nag-an had written a long letter to Ch'ae Che-gong, the Second State Councillor at the time, and this culminated in the formation of a prohibition policy with respect to the study of Western Learning. In the 15th year of Chŏngjo (1791) as the nationwide prohibition order aimed at Western Learning hardened and acquiring or possessing at home books on Western Learning was prohibited, a formal channel of approaching and studying Western books became closed to the literati class. As a result, their approach from the perspective of theoretical criticism declined in quality, while what remained was only their repudiation of underground religious activities. Due to the court's political decision to pursue an anti-heterodoxy stance, the Christians of the Chosŏn dynasty were accused of placing priority on revering God rather than on loyalty to the king and to the

---

[641] Yi Man-ch'ae, *Pyŏkwpy'ŏn*, kwŏn 2, "Chinsa Hong Nag-an taechin chaekmun."
[642] Mencius, Tŭngmungkong, ha, 9.
[643] *Ibid.*

doctrine of filial piety. Thus it was that key doctrinal positions were rejected one-sidedly without an opportunity to exchange ideas on ideologies with the Confucians.

Among the *Silhak* scholars, the members of the *Pukhak*, (as opposed to the *Sŏngho* school), Hong Tae-yong, Pak Chi-wŏn, Pak Che-ka and others argued for adopting the civilization of Ch'ing China, for the remnants of the traditional pro-Ming policy still remained. Although they actively expressed curiosity for Western science and technologies, they simply adopted a critical attitude without understanding Catholicism. Around the time of the introduction of *Silhak* and *Sŏhak* (Western Learning), Chosŏn was abiding by the perception that China is the center of the world, a perception that stemmed from the *sadae* (serving the great) relationship with Ming China, which Chosŏn had established at the time of its founding. Chosŏn considered itself as a "small China," but with the invasions of the Manchus in 1627 and 1636 and the establishing of the Ch'ing Empire, Chosŏn came to despise and reject a country founded by a Jurchen people as a country of barbarians, and continued to adhere to its original pro-Ming stance.[644] The view on Western Learning held by the *Pukhak* faction was different from that of the *Sŏngho* School. On the one hand, they highly praised Western Learning for its utilitarian worth for the sake of the public welfare. On the other hand, however, they were not merely disinterested but were critical towards the Western Religion. During the period in which Catholicism and Westerners were regarded as evil and suspect, regarding Catholicism as nothing more than Buddhism, they simply acknowledged the advantage of the Westerners' science and technology.

At first those among the Confucian literati who condemned Catholic teachings did so only on the grounds that they contravened Neo-Confucian orthodoxy. With the events surrounding the persecution of 1839, however, they came to associate Western religion with the threat of foreign domination, and as the literati confirmed their fear of a link

---

[644]Kang Chae-ŏn, *Chosŏn ŭi sŏhaksa*, p.13.

between foreign missionaries and Western military intervention, they came to perceive Catholicism as a threat to national security. Consequently, their nationalistic attitude of self-sufficiency was distilled in the theory of "rejecting heterodoxy and accepting orthodoxy." *Hwasŏ* Yi Hang-no (1792-1868), who can be considered as the representative advocate of the theory of rejecting heterodoxy, viewed Catholicism not so much as a heterodoxy that challenged the Neo-Confucian tradition but as puppetry in which the Western forces played the role of invaders:[645]

> What other objectives could the Western foreigners have in secretly entering our country and spreading the evil doctrine? It is only to plant their own gangs into our soil, to correspond within and without, and to investigate our weaknesses, after which they plan to invade our country with their armies, to pollute our cultural institutions, to plunder our wealth and talented men, and thereby seize our mountains and rivers in order to fulfill their greedy ambition."[646]

Therefore, he argued that since they could not become friends, they must be fought against and defeated. This was also consistent with the foreign policy of the ruling figure of that time, the Taewŏn'gun, who had proclaimed an isolation policy, labeling Korea as the Forbidden Country. In 1839, Yi Chŏng-kwan wrote *Pyŏksa pyŏnchŭng*, in which he reevaluated the theory of rejection of Western Learning by Yi Ik and An Chŏng-bok, and thereby reinitiated the rejection of Western Learning. Following the year 1848 (14th year of Hŏnjong) Yun Chong-ŭi wrote the *Pyŏkwisinp'yŏn* (in seven volumes), proposing measures to address the armed threat of the West in addition to the theory of

---

[645] Yi Han-no, *Hwasŏjip*, kwŏn 2, Ŏlok.
[646] *Ibid.*, kwŏn 3.

"rejecting heterodoxy". However, since it digressed from the ideological nature of the theory of "rejecting heterodoxy and accepting orthodoxy," it failed to attract people's interest.[647] Kim Chi-jin presented criticisms of Western Learning that were more substantially based on theoretical premises. Since circumstances did not permit him to obtain books on Western Learning, he converted in secret. After having understood the Catholic doctrine, he wrote *Chŏksaron* (1856).[648] Around this time, the literati could not obtain books on Western Learning due to the government prohibition policy, and thus it was not possible to criticize the specific doctrines of the learning. All they could do was to presume it to be an anti-government group and to criticize it for conspiracy with Western forces by associating the religion with the frequent appearances of Western ships. Their criticisms were extremely simple theories which claimed that doctrine other than Neo-Confucianism was an evil religion and heterodoxy.

The Concept of Divinity

Upon arriving in China, the earlier missionaries, including Matteo Ricci, translated the name of God as "Ch'ŏnju (Lord of Heaven)," thereby contrasting it to the "Sangje" of Confucianism and the "T'aekŭk" of Taoism. Confucian scholars, like Sŏngho Yi Ik, who had read the translations of these missionaries, understood the Ch'ŏnju of Catholicism in the same sense as the Sangje of Confucianism.[649] However, the concept of a supreme being as a creator of the universe, and as a being who was incarnated into a human body and resurrected after his death, proved difficult to transmit and to understand.

Chŏng Ha-sang claimed that there must be a creator in order for all sorts of things to be created and maintained,

---

[647] Kŭm Chang-tae, *op.cit.*, p.54.
[648] Hwang P'il-su, Ch'ŏksasŏl.
[649] *Sŏngho sŏnsaeng munjip*, kwŏn 55, Pal Ch'ŏnju silŭi.

just as there is a man building a house using various materials. If one reports that columns, foundation stones, girders, rafters, doors, windows, fences and walls combined with each other and erected themselves into a house, then there is no doubt that the person will be regarded as insane. Heaven, generally speaking, is a large building. How is it possible that flying things, running things, animals, plants, and all kinds of mysterious things could emerge on their own? Even if they had emerged spontaneously, how is it that the sun, the moon and the stars do not cross their ways and how is it that spring, summer, fall and winter do not violate their order? Who could it be that governs prosperity versus perishing and flourishing versus withering, and who could it be that supervises the blessing of the good ones and punishing the immoral ones?[650]

The Confucian scholars of the time who accepted the concept of Ch'ŏnju as that of Sangje did so from the perspective of Neo-Confucianism, and therefore, rather than as a transcendental religious figure, Sangje was accepted more as a concept similar to *t'aegŭk* (T'ai-chi in Chinese), the great ultimate, or as *i* (li in Chinese), principle, under the rules of creation and change or principle.[651] From the Confucian perspective, the concept that God is not a creator, but a governor and a personal figure who was transformed into the image of a particular human being was a contradiction. Yi Ik illuminated the Confucian concept that, though the Sangje of Confucianism is a transcendental being, it is not a religious figure as a personal being. This is an illustration of the inclusion of the traditional concept of religion, which is considerably different from the concepts of Heaven and God that are logically explained by Neo-Confucianism in its latter period.

One of those whose criticisms generally reflect the

---

[650] Chŏng Ha-sang, "Sangjae sangsŏ." *Sunkyoja wa chŭnggŏjudŭl*, p.120.

[651] Yun Sa-sun, "Sŏhak e taehan Han'guk yuhak ŭi taeŭng." *Tongyanghak nonch'ong*, p.405.

tenor of the attacks on Western Learning was Sin Hu-dam. He also understood Ch'ŏnju (Heavenly Lord) as sharing common attributes with Sangje, in that Ch'ŏnju governs the universe and guides all things. However, he rejected it as the creator and as a personal being. Although they put forth the example of a carpenter building a house, I believe that creation of the universe is most likely quite different from a man building a house: the Sangje could never be compared to a carpenter.... The being called Sangje came into existence after the universe was created and was termed as such from the combination of Tao and Chi. This is similar to human beings governing their own bodies with their own mind after being granted life and being born to this world, but unable to create human bodies themselves. Therefore, even though Sangje could be actually governing the universe, there is no logic that leads to the claim that he is the creator of the universe. This is precisely the reason that their theory is false.[652]

Discussions between Confucianism and Catholicism began with Hong Chŏng-ha, Yi Hyŏn-kyŏng and Sin Hu-dam. They argued that Neo-Confucianism regards "Ch'ŏn" as form, but Sangje as ruler, and that is because this is merely a difference in perspectives. Ch'ŏn and Sangje are the same concept, and besides Ch'ŏn, they argued, there is no other God in Confucianism, and moreover, that Ch'ŏn and Sangje were not like the Creator of Catholicism. An Chŏng-bok made a distinction between the two doctrines by suggesting that because Christianity puts emphasis on the other world, heaven, it is private, while Confucianism is public because it stresses the enlightenment of the present world.[653] Hong Chŏng-ha had read various catechisms such as *Ch'ŏnju silŭi* , and he distinguished the Ch'ŏnju of Catholicism from the Sangje of Confucianism in his *Silŭi chŭngŭi* (Reflection on the true

---

[652] Yi Man-ch'ae, *Pyŏkwip'yŏn* kwŏn 1, Sin Hu-dam, Sŏhakbyŏn, Ch'ŏnju silŭi.

[653] *Sunam munjip*, kwŏn 17, Ch'ŏnhak mundap.

doctrine of the Lord of Heaven). He argued that the Ch'ŏnju of Catholicism is for superintendence while the Sangje of Confucianism became "*chu* (Lord)" spontaneously and without much of any particular purpose. To him, Sangje was a metaphor employed to facilitate the understanding of *li*, and not an actual personal figure.[654] Towards the middle of the 19th century, Yi Hang-no asserted that the claim made by the conservative Confucian scholars of that time, that the Ch'ŏnju of Catholicism is the Sangje of Confucianism, is invalid because Sangje refers to Ch'ŏnli, the way of Heaven, and personifying this entity is wrong.[655]

Chŏng Yag-yong accepted the concept of God presented in Ricci's *Ch'ŏnju silŭi* in a broad sense. Since it is based on Confucian doctrine, it cannot be said to have digressed from a Confucian perspective, but his concept of Sangje, nevertheless, was almost the same as the concept of God in Catholicism. To this date, his concept of Sangje continues to be regarded as the most liberal attitude towards Christianity from a Confucian point of view.[656] Chŏng Yak-chong writes in his *Chugyo yoji* (Essentials of the Lord's Teaching) in 1795 that "As a general rule, when man looks up to heaven, he knows that the Master is above there. If he undergoes illness, pains and distress, he looks up to heaven, implores the Lord to heal him and wishes to be delivered. When he faces the thunder and lightning, he remembers his bad sin, and his soul is alarmed and afraid. If there is no Master in heaven, why should each man's soul react like this?[657] Chŏng Yak-chong is identifying the Christian God with the traditional Hanŭnim and adds the Christian understanding of God as trinity; Creator,

---

[654] *Taedong chŏngno,* kwŏn 5.

[655] Yi Hang-no, *Hwasŏjip,* kwŏn 25, Chapjŏ.

[656] Kŭm Chang-t'ae, *op.cit.,* p.65.

[657] Hector Diaz, M.G. *A Korean Theology* (Immensee: Neue zeitschrift für Mission wissenschaft, 1986), p.281.

Redeemer, and Sanctifier.[658] In the middle of the 19th century, Chŏng Ha-sang claimed in his *Sangjae sangsŏ* that the universe and all things in it were not created spontaneously, but that there is a creator, and this is very much analogous to there being a creator behind building a house or producing a piece of artwork, and therefore that there is a creator of all things.[659]

Catholicism and Buddhism

Another criticism of Catholicism was that, like Buddhism, it spoke of the immortality of the soul and the world after death. The view that Buddhist emphasis on the private activity of self-cultivation in solitude mocks the pragmatic values society must uphold, was first articulated by Ch'oe Sŭng-no in the Koryŏ dynasty.[660]

Yi Ik equated the Ch'ŏnju of Catholicism and the Buddha of Buddhism, and saw the figure of Jesus as a missionary and an educator who punished the evil and praised the good, with his theory of heaven and hell. He distinguished between Western Learning and Western Religion, and with discerning eye, he positively acknowledged Western Learning while stating that although the missionaries criticize the transmigrations of Buddhism and advocate the theory of heaven and hell, he criticized both theories as absurd. "Their effort to drive out the teachings

---

[658] Kim Sŭng-hye, "The Concept of the high God and its interpretations in the different religion and social structures of Korea." XVII I.A.H.R. Congress Mexico, August 6-11, 1995. p.15.

[659] Chŏng Ha-sang, Sangjae sangsŏ, in *Sunkyoja wa chŭnggŏjadŭl* (Seoul: Han'guk kyohoesa yŏn'guso, 1983), p.120.

[660] Yi Saek, *Kajŭngjip*, Sinjak simwŏnluki."
He argued that since a Buddhist leaves home, he has no father, and since he enters the mountains, he evades the reality and thus has no king, and finally Buddhism came from a country called India, and thus it is foreign.

of Buddha is remarkable, yet they do not realize that they themselves will eventually end up falling into vain wrongdoings."[661] In his letter to Fathers Joseph Saurez and Ignatius Koegler, Yi I-myŏng wrote that they had a strange statue and fragrant candles placed on the top of the table, and these all seemed just like a monastery in their ritualistic appearance.[662]

In contrast to his teacher Sŏngho Yi Ik's acceptance of the religion with some level of criticism, Sin Hu-dam condemned it as heterodox and fiercely criticized it in his *Sŏhakpyŏn*. The gist of his views was that Catholicism was a complementary discussion of Buddhism and was a religion seeking for blessings which makes people believe in God with its theory of heaven and hell, and therefore, in the end, the basis of Catholicism was rooted in the selfish nature of human beings and violated Confucianism that takes root in sincerity.[663] He understood Western Learning as worshipping of God, immortality of the soul, and the existence of heaven and hell after death, and viewed it as an *idan* (heterodoxy) that adopted the claims of Buddhism. Furthermore, he acknowledged the validity of Matteo Ricci's statement that "Sangje governs the universe," but rejected the idea that a superior being had done all the labor work of creating the universe all by him and refuted the theory that a personalized God was the creator of all things.[664] An Chŏng-bok also ridiculed the concept of immortality of the soul, and the theory of heaven and hell. He derided Catholicism as a brand of Buddhism for its denial of reality[665] and yearning for rewards after death,

---

[661] *Sŏngho sŏnsaeng munjip*, kwŏn 55, *Pa; Ch'ŏnju silŭi*.

[662] Yi I-myŏng, *Sojaejip*, kwŏn 19.

[663] Sin Hu-dam, "Sŏhakp'yŏn, youngŏn nyŏjak" in *Pyŏkwip'yŏn*, kwŏn 1.

[664] *Ibid*, Ch'oe Tong-hŭi, Sin Hu-dam ŭi "*Sŏhakp'yŏn*" e kwanhan yŏn'gu. *Asia yŏn'gu*, vol.15, no.2(1972), pp.9-10.

[665] An Chŏng-bok, "Ch'ŏnhakko." in *Pyŏkŭip'yŏn*, kwŏn 1.

and thus he concluded that it should be refuted as heterodoxy along with Buddhism. Yi Hŏn-kyŏng (1719-1791)[666] judged Christianity as even less worthy than Buddhism, for it is not as profound as, is more peculiar than, and not as old as the Buddhist canon.[667]

The *Pukhak* faction also equated Catholicism with Buddhism. Hong Tae-yong (1731-1783) met and conversed with Catholic priests in Beijing, and expressed interest in astronomy and the Western calendar. However, he stated that Catholicism "stole the name of our Confucian Sangje and disguised it with the transmigrations of Buddhism. It is shallow, worthless and contemptible."[668] Pak Chi-wŏn (1737-1805) of the *Pukhak* faction also sharply criticized Catholicism as "the leftover scraps of Buddhism."[669] Pak Che-ga (1750-1815)[670] was notably insightful, reform-oriented and progressive. He also stated that Catholicism was based on the theory of heaven and hell, and thus was no different from Buddhism.[671]

The anti-Buddhism policy of the early Chosŏn dynasty was pursued by the founding leaders of the new nation for the purpose of forming an ideological background to solidify the foundation of the state. Afterwards, this anti-Buddhism theory was broadly interpreted and used in denouncing the theories of Lao-tzu, Chuang-tzu, Yang-chu and Mo Ti, not to mention the Yangming School. Consequently, they were successful in reaping the fruits of Neo-Confucian ideology solely through the Neo-Confucianism of Yi Yul-gok and T'oegye. But their tolerance for other systems of ideology declined. They failed to

---

[666] Passed munkwa in 1743.

[667] *Pyŏkwip'yŏn*, kwŏn 1, 14a.

[668] *Tamhŏnsŏ*, woechip, kwŏn 2.

[669] *Yŏnamchip*, kwŏn 2, Tapsunsasŏ.

[670] Student of Sŭngji Pak P'yŏng.

[671] Pak Che-ga, *Chŏngnyŏchip*, kwŏn 3, P'yŏngo sohoe.

embrace, repudiating even the Yangming School, which was essentially of the same origin. Thus, not only Catholicism, but *Tonghak* of the late 19th century was also denounced as heterodoxy. The anti-Buddhism policy of the early Chosŏn dynasty was largely influenced by the concepts of Han Yu in China. Starting with the anti-Buddhism arguments of Ch'oe Sŭng-no and Yi Saek in the late Koryŏ dynasty and the pioneer of the Chosŏn dynasty Sambong Chŏng To-jŏn, it solidified its position as the orthodox ideology by the time of Yi T'oe-gye. It was precisely this anti-Buddhist theory that was transformed into a theoretical foundation for rejecting Catholicism when Catholicism entered Korea. Thus, the anti-Buddhism theory and anti-West theory were exactly the same in their logic.

While Confucianism caused the deaths of approximately 10,000 people for more than one hundred years by denouncing Catholicism as heterodoxy, the same Confucianism in the early Chosŏn period, however, did not bring about such persecution of Buddhism, although it had a policy of oppression on Buddhism. What was the reason? The Confucian of the early Chosŏn period who advocated anti-Buddhism policies claimed Confucianism as the ideological foundation for the new dynasty, but since they themselves had been raised in a Buddhist society from the early on, they did not take a harsh action toward Buddhism. The anti-Buddhist policy was not thoroughly pursued even in the reigns of King Sejong and King Sejo. However, when Catholicism entered Korea, the foundation of Confucianism had become stabilized and the anti-heterodoxy movement was intensely pursued. Furthermore as it spread among the members of the *Namin* group, which had been ostracized from political power, Catholicism was exploited in the political strife then raging, causing severe persecutions to continue.[672]

---

[672] Hong I-sŏp, "Chosŏn yuga ŭi ch'ŏksaron e taehayŏ." pp. 7-8.

The Theory of Heaven and Hell

Another issue which led the Confucians to denounce Western Learning as heterodoxy was its views on soul and spirit. Both religions viewed human beings as the union of soul and body. However, in Confucian thought, soul vanishes with the end of the physical body, because the soul is based on the physical body. Accordingly, it refuted the theory of immortality of the soul in Catholicism.[673] It is believed in Confucianism that when *honbaek* (the soul) of Confucianism exists, in which *hon* is a physical entity while *baek* is a spiritual aspect, and human beings are made of *honbaek*, then they become spirits after death and their soul disappears. The Christian doctrine of immortality of the soul directly contradicted this Confucian belief. This doctrine was one of the reasons why Confucian criticized Catholicism as heterodoxy. However, *yŏnghon* (intellectual soul) in Christianity is exclusive to human beings, in contrast to the *saenghon* (vegetable soul) or *kakhon* (sentient soul). It can also be regarded as being different from the *honbaek* of Confucianism, unique to each individual, and instead more similar to the *li* of Neo-Confucianism. If we see the arguments of Confucianism from this perspective, it is clear that the Confucian misinterpreted and wrongly criticized the Christian doctrine.

While the gist of Christianity comprises the immortality of the soul, with the theory of heaven and hell, Confucianism stresses the present life rejecting the concept of a world after death, heaven or hell. Thus, Sin Hu-dam criticized the theory of heaven and hell as luring people:

> On what basis was the unchanging reward in heaven really being spoken? The concept of rewarding the good and punishing the evil exists also in our Confucian doctrine. Only, we refer it to as *li*. Those who follow *ich'i* are naturally bound to be rewarded while those who violate *ich'i* are

---

[673] Sin Hu-dam, "Sŏhakp'yŏn," in *Pyŏgwip'yŏn*, kwŏn 1.

undoubtedly bound to be punished. How could they speak of a Sangje who descends for each human being...Today, what they call scholarship excels only in seeking rewards. It is extremely insincere, and their minds are filled only with yearning for personal gain. Though the various schools of *idan* (heresy) are all very different, yet their origins all emerged from a desire for personal gain.[674]

An Chŏng-bok indicated the cruelty of the idea of hell to be a negation of Sangje's compassionate heart and thus denied the theory.[675] In Hong Nag-an's letter to the Second State Councillor Ch'ae Che-gong, he stated that "the lowly and ignorant women and children are susceptible to temptation, and once they hear such a theory, they throw themselves into the religion and risk their lives, disregarding life and death in the present world and devoting their heart to the theory of everlasting heaven and hell. Thus once they are snared by this delusion doctrine of everlasting Heaven and Hell, there is no way to free them from their delusion."[676] Chŏng Ha-sang declared that the blessings of the present world are incomplete and temporary, while those of Heaven are complete and lasting, and stated that one should rather seek for the lasting blessing of Heaven rather than the fleeting rewards of the present world and subsequently resolutely refuse to surrender even when faced with death.[677]

Because the Catholic religious movement had been oppressed from the very beginning and could only subsist as

---

[674] Yi Man-ch'ae, *Pyŏkwip'yŏn*, Sŏhakpyŏn, Yŏngŏnyŏjak.

[675] An Chŏng-bok, *Sunamjip*, yo Kwŏn Ki-myŏng sŏ, (Kapjin).

[676] *Chosŏn wangjo sillok*, Chŏngjo 15th year 10th month Kapja

[677] Chŏng Ha-sang, "Sangjaesangsŏ," *Sunkyoja wa chûnggŏjadŭl*, pp.129-130.

an underground organization due to the anti-Catholicism policy rooted in Confucian ideology, people became consciously immersed in the doctrine of Heaven and Hell that repudiated the present world and gave promise of redemption after death. It provided the source of power for Catholicism to continue to expand and to survive in such a situation. Although the inclination of the religion towards the next world was a common phenomenon during the persecutions, its denial of the present world led to restrictions on the role of the religion in society. Subsequently, it brought to itself isolation from the rest of society and criticism from the Confucians.

2. Social Reasons

Relationship between Father and Son

Confucians criticized Western Learning as a heterodoxy that destroyed the society's traditional order and moral foundation. The three bonds and five moral rules in human relations in Confucianism can be summarized as follows: the three bonds between father and son, king and people, and husband and wife; the five moral rules of *puja yuch'in, kunsin yuŭi, pupu yubyŏl, changyu yusŏ* and *pungu yusin*. The basic rule through which all others are realized is that of father and son, *puja yuch'in*. In other words, the relationship between parents and children was considered as the most fundamental one and then followed the relationship between king and people. Among the five moral rules, filial piety is the most basic rule. The duty of filial piety extends also to one's family affairs. Mencius wrote, "The root of the kingdom is in the state. The root of the state is in the family. The root of the family is in the individual."[678]

In contrast to Confucianism with its emphasis on the bond between parent and king, Christianity placed

---

[678] James Legge, *The Work of Mencius,* Vol.II, Oxford: Clarendon Press, 1893. Part 2, p.171.

Ch'ŏnju (God) above parent and king,[679] and regarded Ch'ŏnju as the absolute and transcendental being. Thus, Christianity was perceived as destroying the social order. Filial piety in Confucianism was an absolute concept. God or Sangje is not a transcendental being, but rather is embedded in the character of human beings. Living in fulfillment of this character is precisely the Way and practicing this Way is the height of filial piety. This filial piety is not limited only to the period during which one's parents are alive, but must continue even after their deaths, and this is "ancestor worship." Even after their deaths, ancestors continue living in their graves or beside *Sinju* which are their personal figures, and thus require continuous filial piety. The code of filial piety stipulates that the dead ancestors must be worshipped as if they were alive and that, though they no longer exist, they must be treated as if they do, and its fundamental meaning lies in people fulfilling their duties to worship their ancestors.[680]

The Ten Commandments of Catholicism also speak of filial piety, and when the Catholic believers were arrested and interrogated, they also spoke of the Catholic concept of filial piety. However, there is a significant difference between the Catholic concept of filial piety and the Neo-Confucian concept of filial piety. Catholicism placed the command of God above that of parents, and the concept of filial piety was a relative one. In this respect, the officials regarded the Catholic followers to be denying the worth of filial piety itself and thus neglecting humanity.

There had already been a Rites Controversy in China related to the issue of filial piety and ancestor worship. Matteo Ricci viewed the practice of ancestor worship as a continuous expression of love and gratitude to the deceased just as when they were alive, and that it was not because the deceased wanted or ate things offered on sacrifice. What is more, he believed that people did not

---

[679] The first commandment in the Ten Commandments.
[680] *Hyokyŏng*, "Sangch'in-jang."

regard the deceased as god-like, and did not demand anything from them.[681] The Jesuits centered around Matteo Ricci understood the Confucian ancestor worship and worship of Confucius not so much as superstition nor worship of idols, but as a customary memorial ceremony. Longobardi, a Jesuit who inherited the position of Ricci, forbade ancestor worship. He concluded that ancestor worship was superstitious. As the Dominicans joined in the decision, the issue over the ceremony erupted in China. In the beginning, in 1652, Pope Alexander VII of Congregatio de Propaganda fide of the Roman Papal Court (1655-1667) wished to protect the converts and expand the mission by declaring a doctrine in support of the position taken by the Jesuit missionaries of China. Other religious orders such as Franciscan and Dominican were opposed to the declaration, with the result that a lengthy controversy arose, which in the end involved the Pope, the religious orders of the local missionary areas and even the Kang Hsi emperor of China.

The Papal Court concluded the fierce 106-year-long Rites Controversy in China with Pope Clement XI's prohibition letter (Ex illa die) and Pope Benedict XIV's confirming letter (Ex quo singulari), which established that the practice of ancestor worship was in violation of Christian faith and was to be prohibited as idol worship as well as superstition.[682] In 1742, Pope Benedicto XIV decreed the prohibition of Confucian ancestor worship rites. This decree brought about a chronic counter-effect in pursuing missionary work in a Confucian culture.[683] Alexander de Gouvea of the Beijing parish was abiding by this decision by the Papal Court when he sent a rejection in response to the Chosŏn church members' inquiry on

---

[681] Ri Madu, *Chungkuo ch'uan chiao shih*, 1, p.85.

[682] Julia Ching, *Confucianism and Christianity: A Comparative Study* (Tokyo: Kodonsha International, 1977), p.19ff.

[683] Ch'oe Ki-bok, *op. cit.*, p. 116.

attending ancestor worship ceremonies.[684]

Rejection of Ancestor Worship

In 1790 the Chosŏn church faced a new turning point when they received a response through a ministry letter from the Beijing Bishop forbidding ancestor worship. It was no longer allowed to practice the Catholic faith within the Confucian tradition, and they had to reject the Confucian tradition in order to abide by the doctrines of the Catholic religion. To the *yangban* class, this demanded a decision on their part to either abandon their social status or the faith.

During the period in which the Western books translated into Chinese were being studied, as well as in the years in the early period of the Chosŏn Catholic church, no issue regarding ancestor worship arose. As people's understanding of Catholic rituals deepened, they came to doubt whether Confucian ancestor worship and Catholic rituals could co-exist, and eventually had come to the decision to dispatch a secret envoy to Beijing to inquire on the matter. A letter containing inquiries regarding superstitious practices and ancestor worship was delivered to Beijing in the 9th month of 1790 by Yun Yu-il, who accompanied the embassy to congratulate the eightieth birthday of the Ch'ing emperor.[685] The response to the question was an order prohibiting ancestor worship.

In accordance with this prohibition order, Yun Chi-ch'ung and Kwŏn Sang-yŏn refused to conduct the ancestor worship ceremony for the deaths of their mothers in 1791, which resulted in the Rites Controversy. After this incident, the issue of rejecting ancestor worship was claimed as the justification for every persecution regardless of what other

---

[684] Third letter sent to the Vicariate Apostolic by Pope Gouvea (1797), *Manam kwa midŭmŭi kilmok esŏ*, p.148.

[685] *Mannam kwa midûm ûi kilmok esŏ* p.21.

motives there may have been.[686]

The church members who rejected the order by the Beijing Bishop prohibiting the practice of ancestor worship were Yi Sŭng-hun, Kwŏn Il-sin, Kwŏn Ch'ŏl-sin, Chŏng Yak-chŏn, Chŏng Yag-yong, Yi Ka-hwan, and Hong Rak-min. They viewed "ancestor worship" as Koreans practiced it to be the symbolic expression of filial piety which is the core of Confucian ethics, and in consequence, to ban this key family rite was seen as tantamount to destroying the ethical and moral order.[687] Tasan (Chŏng Yag-yong) not only refused to abide by the prohibition order, but he even left the church altogether on this account. He asserted that when he was working diligently serving the church, no one mentioned anything regarding prohibiting ancestor worship,[688] and along with other Confucian, he concluded that refusing to practice ancestor worship would be wrong.[689] In the case of Hong Ik-man, he himself asserted the meaninglessness of ancestor worship, but at the same time, persuaded by his relatives, he did not reject the practice.[690]

If those recorded in *Sahak chingŭi* who refused to practice ancestral rites in accordance with the order of the church, are distinguished among their social classes, there were twenty from the *yangban* class, two from the *chungin* class and seven *yangmin* , twenty-five were men and four

---

[686]*Chosŏn wangjo sillok.* Sunjo The beginning year 1st month Chŏnghae day, 10th month Kyŏngo. *Ibid..*, Hŏnjong, 5th year 10th month Kyŏngsin.

[687]cf. *Ibid.,*. Chŏngjo 15th year 11th month Kimyo.

[688] *Ibid.,* Chŏngjo 21st year 6th month Kyŏngjin.

[689]*Yŏyudang chŏnsŏ*, I-9 44a.

[690]*Sahak chingŭi* , kwŏn I, Chongpŏb choeinjil, Hong Ik-man kongch'o.

were women.[691]

The reason that the Catholic believers agreed to reject ancestor worship was simply that the Catholic Church prohibited the practice of ancestor worship. In 1791, Yun Chi-ch'ung wrote in his testimony that "As long as one praises God as the great parents, disobeying God's command is not the way of worshipping Him. But now that the church prohibits the ancestral tablet of a literati's family, I would rather commit a sin against the literati, and do not wish to commit a sin against God... Moreover, having drinks and food in front of a dead person is also prohibited by the Catholic Church... Therefore, it is only in obedience to Catholicism that I do not put the tablet in its place and practice ancestor worship."[692] Yun Chi-ch'ung said that "the root of filial piety for parents is also a command of Catholicism."[693] Yu Hang-gŏm also testified that "placing an ancestral tablet is forbidden by God."[694] Chŏng Yak-chong too stated that "conducting ancestor worship, bowing in front of their graves, making *honbaek* (departed soul) in the images of parents, and offering sacrifices, all are committing sins against God."[695]

When Yun Yu-il learned of Bishop Gouvea's order

---

[691] *Yangban*: Yu Hang-gŏm, Yu Kwan-kŏm, Chŏng Yak-chong, Chŏng Ch'ŏl-sang, Yun Chi-ch'ung, Yun Chi-hŏn, Kwŏn Sang-yŏn, Hwang Sa-yŏng, Yi Ch'ung-bae, Im Hŭi-yŏng, Chŏng Chong-ho, Yu Han-suk, Yi Ki-yŏn, Han Chŏng-hŭm, Chŏng Kwang-su, Yi Kuk-sŭng, Wŏn Kyŏng-do, Kim Paek-sun; Women: Kang Wan-suk, Yun Un-hye. *Chungin*: Ch'oe Ch'ang-hyŏn, Ch'oe In-ch'ŏl. *Yangin*: Ko Kwang-sŏng, Kim Chŏng-dŭk, Yi Pu-ch'un, Yi Chi-pŏn, Pak Ch'ui-dŭk; Women: Kang Kyŏng-bok, Chŏng Pok-hye.

[692] *Chosŏn wangjo sillok*, Chŏngjo 15th year 11th month Muin.

[693] Charles Dallet, *op.cit.* (sang), p.346.

[694] *Sahak chingŭi*, Chŏlla Kamsa Kim Tal-sun milkye.

[695] *Sinyu Sahak choein Yi Ka-hwan dŭng ch'uan*, 2nd month 12th day, Chŏng Yak-chong, Kongan.

prohibiting ancestor worship, he initially inquired of the Bishop, "Conducting ancestor worship is to pay respect to the deceased, just as we do to the living, and if we cannot believe in Catholicism and conduct ancestor worship at the same time, then this is an extremely difficult dilemma for us. Is there any other way to address the issue?" However, later on, he testified that "Catholicism regards fidelity as the most important element, and preparing and serving food for those even after their deaths is a breach of fidelity."[696] There were those who refused to practice ancestor worship simply because they put respecting God as the foremost priority. Cho Yong-sam stated that "Ch'ŏnju is the great king of all things of the universe that gave life to me and to my parents, and thus we ought to obey the command of Ch'ŏnju rather than that of our parents."[697] Nam P'il-yong also stated that soul and spirit cannot consume food, and thus it is a vain effort to try to conduct an ancestor worship ritual, and subsequently the Catholic believers did not conduct the ceremony.[698]

Hong Chŏng-ha, a retired scholar of Yŏngjo's reign, pointed out that differentiating between the degree of reverence owed to the Ch'ŏnju of Western Learning and one's parents was fundamentally wrong, since paying respect to one's parents is precisely the way of God and that it is also the true way to obey God.[699] Pak Yŏng-wŏn, a Confucian submitted a memorial arguing that by prohibiting the practice of ancestor worship, Catholicism "severed the intimate relationship between the father and the son."[700]

Amid such socially critical public opinion, the early Chosŏn church members who rejected ancestor worship

---

[696] *Sahak chingŭi* kwŏn 2, Ihwan songgil, *Yu Kwang-gŏm kongch'o.*

[697] Charles Dallet, *op.cit.* (sang), p.461.

[698] *Sahak chingŭi* p.284.

[699] *Taedong chŏngno* kwŏn 6, *Sŏngse ch'uyo* chŭngŭi.

[700] *Chosŏn wangjo sillok,* Chŏngjo 19th year 7th month Kyeyu.

obeyed the order of the church, and they maintained, "since priests preach in place of Ch'ŏnju, we would rather disobey the order of their parents, and we absolutely will not disobey the command of the priests."[701]

It was Chŏng Ha-sang who clearly explicated the Christian view on the rejection of ancestor worship ritual by Chosŏn society.

> Placing drink and food in front of the deceased is prohibited by Catholicism. Even while alive, our soul is unable to consume drink and food, and thus how is it that it is able to do so after death? Food is for the mouth of a physical body and morality is the food for the soul. No matter how respectful a son may be, he cannot prepare a delicious meal and place it in front of his parents while they are asleep. It is not the time to neither eat nor drink while one is asleep. If it is such while one is asleep, how different is it when one is asleep forever? Ritual food of all sorts of grain and fragrant fruits is in vain if not fake. As the children of human beings, how can they pay respect to their parents through these meaningless and fake rituals? The ancestral tablet is forbidden by Catholicism. Already pulsation and blood have no relation to parents or to the hard labor of giving birth, or rearing. If one knows how precious the terms 'father' and 'mother' are, how could one dare to call what the craftsman has made, powdered and painted as the true father and true mother? This has no basis in reason, and neither does our conscience allow it. I would rather commit the sin of violating the Confucian literati's duty than to commit a sin against

---

[701] *Chosŏn wangjo sillok.*, Chŏngjo 15th year 11th month Muin.

Catholicism."702

This is an illustration of willingness to protect their religious organization and of personal conviction to die a martyr, refusing to surrender to any sort of persecution. In *Chŏksa yunŭm* (Edict Proscribing Catholicism) declared by King Hŏnjong after the persecution of 1839, the Chosŏn government refuted the Catholics' rejection of ancestor worship stating:

> "Alas! Who is born without a father and who is raised without a mother? They (Catholic followers) call those who gave birth to them as the parents of their physical being while calling Ch'ŏnju as their spiritual parent, but they only love and pay respect to Ch'ŏnju and not to their own parents, thereby cutting themselves off from their parents. Can this really be tolerated?"703

Hŏnjong's proscription decree argued that the position taken by the Catholic believers had no logic, asserting that "the Catholic followers destroyed ancestral tablets and refused to conduct ancestor worship rituals claiming that the deceased has no way of knowing whether ceremonies are being held or not. If this is true, then where could their souls be?" In addition, the decree posed the question that while paying respect to Ch'ŏnju, calling him their spiritual parents, they, on the other hand, distance themselves from their own biological parents. How could this be possible as an ethical human being?704

The prohibition decree made it more difficult for

---

702 "Sangjae sangsŏ," *Sungyoja wa chŭnggŏja dŭl*, pp.135-136.

703 *Chosŏn wangjo sillok.*, Hŏnjong 5th year 10th month Kyŏngjin.

704 *Ibid.*,

the intellectual class to join the church[705] and as a result, new Catholic converts were found mainly in the commoner class. Subsequently, the Chosŏn church became one that centered around a foreign missionary and one that abided by the commands of the church institution. Later on, Chou Wen-mo, the priest who pursued the ministry in Chosŏn as the first priest ever, wrote a letter to the Bishop in Beijing on the 14th day in 9th month of 1796 expressing concern regarding the abandonment of Catholicism by converts due to the prohibition of the practice of ancestor worship.[706] It actually did result in the members of the *yangban* class leaving the church somewhat precipitously.

The Relationship between the King and His People

Chŏng Ha-sang stated the following on the relationship between the king and the people: "There are high and low in status, as well as light and heavy in affairs. In a family, the father of the family is the most important, but higher than a father of a family is the king. The king is the most important person in a nation, but higher than the king is the great king of the universe."[707] This statement argues that one respects the king, but at the level of the universe, God must be placed above the king.

Hong Nag-an (1752-?) vehemently rejected the concept of an authority greater than that of one's king and one's father, saying that it disturbed the country's ethical foundation.[708] Yi Ki-kyŏng, who at one point had a close relationship with Yi Sŭng-hun, and from time to time had read Western books on Catholicism, borrowed a book from Yi Sŭng-hun in order to seek out the reason that Yi Sŭng-

---

[705] Gouvea's letter, *op.cit.*,p.224.

[706] *Ibid.*, *op.cit.*, p.69.

[707] Chŏng Ha-sang, "Sangjae sangsŏ," in *Sunkyoja wa chŭnggŏjadŭl*, p.32.

[708] *Chosŏn wangjo sillok,*.Chŏngjo 15th year 10th month Kapja.

hun became so engrossed in the study of Catholicism. Afterwards, he testified in a memorial that upon reading the passage "the people of the world only know that their parents raised them and do not know that God's caring is greater than that of their parents, and they also only know of the rule of their king and do not know that God's governing is greater than that of their king "he became startled and did not look at the book again.[709] Changryŏng Yu Ha-wŏn submitted a memorial expressing his concern over the absolute concept of God and relative concept of king, stating that Catholicism "only recognizes God and does not recognize the authority of one's king or one's parents, and with its theory of Heaven and Hell, it deceives the people and deludes the world. Its harm is greater than that of a flood or a dangerous beast."[710] These reactions expressed by Yi Ki-kyŏng and Yu Ha-wŏn upon reading the catechisms of Western Learning indicate that the literati were against the superiority of God over king, and they found the Catholics' perception of the sovereign authority to be a relative concept.

The Catholic followers of the time believed that, "God is the great father of the universe and father of all humanity, and that is why we respect him the most of all. We must pay respect to our king, statesmen and parents only after God."[711] During the Chinsan Incident Chŏlla inspector Chŏng Min-si stated as follows: "Even when bleeding and their flesh torn, they did not express the pain on their face nor did they make a moaning sound. They repeated at the end of every sentence that it is the teaching of God and that, though they could disobey the commands of king and parents, they could not disobey the commands of God, even if they were to be executed, and that they would never change their position. They abide by the belief

---

[709] Yi Man-ch'ae, *Pyŏkwip'yŏn,* kwŏn 2, Yi Ki-kyŏng ŭi sangso.

[710] *Chosŏn wangjo sillok,* Chŏngjo 9th year (Ŭlsa) 4th month Ŭlch'uk.

[711] Charles Dallet, *op.cit.*, (chung), p.175.

that dying by a knife blade is an honor."[712] Kwŏn Sang-yŏn also asserted during an interrogation that though he would disobey the king's command and his parents' command, he would certainly never disobey the teachings of God even if he were to receive a death sentence.[713]

The Catholic believers publicly claimed, at the court, that the sovereign authority is not absolute. At the trial, Kim Yu-san stated that "our nation does not realize the advantages of following the ten commandments of Catholicism and thus strictly prohibits it by the law. As a result, many of those people with no heinous crime are being punished and put to death, and this is extremely regrettable,"[714] and in these words he resented the policy of the nation that prohibited the Western Learning. Hwang Sa-yŏng himself believed that Western Learning was not harmful to the people and the nation. He testified that the Chosŏn court nevertheless attempted to restrict Catholicism, and that he tried to devise a counter-measure.[715] On the topic of a king, Chŏng Ha-sang endorsed the concept of loyalty to a king, but regarded a king as being inferior to God, saying that "though I obey the king's commands, disobeying the great king of the universe is an even greater sin that cannot be compared with. Therefore, if praising and believing in God is disobeying the command of the king, it is not by will but by necessity."[716]

A Catholic follower from the countryside, Kim Thomas, who was born in Chŏngyang Ch'ungch'ŏngdo, and served as a P'unghŏn (clerk), regarded the nation, house and

---

[712] *Chosŏn wangjo sillok*, Chŏngjo 15th year 11th month Muin.

[713] *Ibid.*

[714] Sinyu Sahak choein Yu Hang-gŏm ch'uan, Sinyu 4th month 29th day. Kim Yu-san kongch'o.

[715] Sinyu Sahak choein Hwang Sa-yŏng tŭng ch'uan, Sinyu 10th month 19th day. Hwang Sa-yŏng Kongch'o.

[716] Chŏng Ha-sang, "Sangjae Sangsŏ," *Sungyoja wa chŭngŏja dŭl*, pp.132-133.

family as of no significance when compared to the Catholic faith.[717] Yi To-ki, a Catholic believer from Naep'o Ch'ungch'ŏngdo, believed that God is the creator of all things and that God was greater than any social system or any human being.[718] They at the same time continued to emphasize loyalty to the king. When Yi To-ki (1743-1798) was being tortured and interrogated, and was accused of not recognizing the king of the nation nor his parents and also of continuing to believe in the religion despite the national prohibition order, when he was encouraged to apostatize, he responded by saying that filial piety to parents and loyalty to the king are all embodied in the fourth commandment of Catholicism.[719] Priest Chou Wen-mo also claimed during the interrogation that the ways of Catholicism teach the people to be loyal to their king and to love their king.[720] Hwang Sa-yŏng, who was executed for the crime of treason, also commented on the nation and the church, saying that "the Catholic religion stresses loyalty, filial piety and love, and if the entire nation is admired, then that would surely bring wealth and power to the kingdom,"[721] hereby emphasizing the Catholic teaching of love in addition to the traditional Confucian concepts of loyalty and filial piety.

Election of a Pope

Ch'ae Che-gong, a High State Councillor during Chŏngjo's reign, said that "from the beginning there has been no institution of kingship in that country's political culture and thus they pick an unmarried man among the common people to be the king of their nation. This is more

---

[717] Charles Dallet, *op.cit.*, (sang), p.398.

[718] *Ibid*, p.402.

[719] *Ibid*, p.402.

[720] Sahak choein, Kim Yŏ ch'uan, p.416.

[721] Hwang Sa-yŏng paeksŏ, 111th line.

than simply ludicrous."⁷²²

In actuality, Ch'ae Che-gong was describing the system of electing the Pope, as he understood it. In his dissertation on factional politics, *T'angron*, Chŏng Yag-yong opposed the hereditary nature of kingship and the appointment of bureaucrats based on blood lineage. He believed that ministers should be elected by recommendation, and he further made it clear that other government officials should also be selected by the populace, or otherwise they should not be promoted.⁷²³ It seems that the commoner Catholic followers were aware of the practice of "transmitting the ruling power of the Pope to a wise man rather than to his son."⁷²⁴ This concept ran contrary to the Chosŏn dynasty practice, in which sovereign power was transmitted by hereditary blood ties, and many in the ruling class came to view Catholics as a threat to their privileged positions, and a reason in itself that it should be suppressed.⁷²⁵

The Catholic followers who were being tortured stated that "returning to heaven as soon as possible will be the ultimate joy and dying by a knife blade is an honor that surpasses all.⁷²⁶ Although the pursuers of Western Learning claimed that its doctrines were beneficial to the nation,⁷²⁷ the government considered Catholics to be a band of traitors who were opposed overall to the social and political order of the dynasty. It appears that the number of people who were dissatisfied with and bore resentment towards the politics of the nation and the society had been

---

⁷²²*Chosŏn wangjo sillok.* Chŏngjo 15th year 10th month Pyŏngin.

⁷²³ cf, Cho Kwang, "Chŏng Yag-yong ŭi minkwŏn sasang yŏn'gu." *Asia munje yŏn'gu* 56, pp.66-69.

⁷²⁴Sahak choein Hwang Sa-yŏng tŭng ch'uan, p.821.

⁷²⁵Cho Kwang, *Chosŏn hugi Chŏnjugyosa yŏn'gu*, p.132.

⁷²⁶*Chosŏn wangjo sillok,* Chŏngjo 15th year 10th month Kapja.

⁷²⁷Sinyu sahak choein, Yu Hang-gŏm, ch'uan, p.34.

significant, to the point where they "comprised half of the city population."[728] It also appears that the Chosŏn government was concerned over the possibility that ideological heretics and those dissatisfied with the day to day conduct of the government might communicate with each other, and plan some sort of scheme. For example, the wife Sin and daughter-in-law Song of the Ŭnŏnkun, who was in exile in Kanghwa Island for the crime of treason, were residing in the palace, and the fact that Chou Wen-mo had even visited and baptized them and thus spread Catholicism within the palace appeared threatening to the government as a potential point of contact between the pursuers of Western Learning and the rebellious group.[729] Subsequently, the government officials treated a Catholic convert Hong Si-ho harshly merely for approaching Sin and Song.[730] The government even viewed the situation as critical enough to assume that an uprising might erupt at any moment.[731] The Chosŏn government believed that once having been persecuted, the Catholics' ardent desire in the present world would be the collapse of the government that brought the persecution. The pursuers of Western Learning, in fact, were considered to be guilty, a priori, of all sorts of anti-government and anti-social modes of behavior.[732]

Disobedience of the Law

At the same time the early Catholic believers were being enlightened by a new concept of law, they came to understand the "law of the mind" and the "law of the

---

[728] Sinyu Sahak choein Kang I-ch'ŏn tŭng ch'uan, p.23.

[729] Sinyu Sahak ch'oein, Kim yŏ tŭng ch'uan, p.11.

[730] *Ibid*, p.15.

[731] *Pipyŏnsa tŭngnok*, 192 chaek, Vol 19, p.292. Sinyu, 2nd month 9th day.

[732] *Chosŏn wangjo sillok*, Sunjo Sinyu 10th month Kapja, Tosakyomun.

conscience," concepts that had not existed before, and while emphasizing that "the just laws of the nation must be observed,"[733] at the same time they argued for obedience to the commands of God.[734] This produced another breach in the authority of the king. Yun Chi-ch'ung, the primary figure in the Chinsan Incident, replied to a government official demanding observance of ancestor worship rituals that "I would rather commit a sin against the literati than against God,"[735] and chose to die according to God's law. The execution of Yun Chi-ch'ung and Kwŏn Sang-yŏn under the charge of an infamous offense[736] was an exercise of the sovereign power of the nation. However, the pursuers of the Western Learning refused to recognize the legitimacy of the execution and viewed the death of Yun Chi-ch'ung as "*chŏlsa* (death to maintain loyalty)" and did not lose their respect for him.[737] At the same time as they lamented the death of Yun Chi-ch'ung and others, a rumor spread that a church building would someday be erected on their graves.[738] Those people who died during the Sinyu Persecution such as Chŏng Yak-chong,[739] Hong Ik-man,[740] Hwang Il-kwang,[741] Kim Kye-wan,[742] and Ok Chŏn-hi were also viewed as having died for the cause of

---

[733] *Sŏngch'al kiryak*, p.20a.

[734] Charles Dallet, *op.cit.*, (sang), p.407.

[735] *Chosŏn wangjo sillok*, Chŏngjo 15th year 11th month Muin.

[736] *Chosŏn wangjo sillok*, Chŏngjo Sinhae year 11th month Ŭmyo.

[737] *Sahak chingŭi*, p.16.

[738] *Ibid*, p.17, p.231.

[739] Sahak choein Yi Ka-hwan ch'uan p.24.

[740] *Sahak chingŭi*, p.125.

[741] *Ibid*, p.147.

[742] *Ibid*, p.132.

loyalty to their faith.[743] In preparing his "Paeksŏ" Hwang Sa-yŏng stated that "I myself believe that Western Learning is not harmful to the people nor to the country. However, the government wishes to prohibit it regardless, and that is why I have devised such a plan to do my best to sustain Western Learning."[744] Thus Hwang Sa-yŏng gave priority to promoting Catholicism and was only secondarily concerned with obeying a command.

Distinctions between Husbands and Wives and Between Men and Women

In Chosŏn society, it was believed that there must be a differentiation between men and women for there to be affection between father and son, and that if there was no distinction, then humans were no different from birds and beasts.[745] The Neo-Confucian ethical system postulated *samjŏng jido* (the duty of serving father, husband and son) and *ch'ilgŏ jiak* (seven *culpae*). In addition, it emphasized the ethics of a hierarchical relationship between husbands and wives, which required women to obey their husbands, and forbade wives from remarrying after the death of their husbands. Women were prohibited from participating in social activities and treated as individuals who had neither rights nor authority. Fidelity between husbands and wives was the responsibility of the wives, and even when husbands commit a wrongful deed and take a concubine, wives must not show a jealous disposition.

On the issue of distinction between men and women, a traditional Confucian view on women, Dallet recorded as follows: "Women are not men's companions, but are nothing more than slaves and instruments of pleasure for men. The laws and customs do not endow women with any

---

[743] *Ibid*, p.224.

[744] Sahak choein Hwang Sa-yŏng ch'uan, p.733.

[745] 1) disobedience to parents-in-law, 2) inability to have children, 3) adultery, 4)jealousy 5) bad illness 6) talkativeness 7) stealing

right and do not even recognize them as spiritual beings."[746] "They cannot leave the house without permission from their parents or from their husbands and cannot even glance around the streets. Accordingly, with such restricted lives numerous women believers could not participate at all in the performance of sacraments."[747]

Catholic doctrine, based on the idea that God Created men and women as equals, taught equality of all people without distinction of gender. Catholic doctrine further emphasized a relationship that is mutually equal between a husband and a wife.[748]

There were certain obstacles to the spread of Catholic doctrine among women, since traditional Confucian orthodoxy observed strict avoidance of mixed gender gatherings. In the case of Kang Wan-suk, the "president" of the women believers, she let Priest Chou Wen-mo, a man from outside her family, hides in her house, and conducted mass six to ten times in a month with men and women gathered together, and she communicated with the *Namin* literati men. These actions were unthinkable in a Confucian society, and signified liberation of women.

In Confucianism, issues regarding men and women were delicate and strict, so that as soon as a child became aware of the opposite sex, so-called *"namnyŏ 7 ch'ilse pudongsŏk"* - forbidding a boy and a girl from sitting together when they reach the age of seven - became the standard policy for distinguishing male from female. In such a society, the Catholic believers were relatively liberal and held meetings with men and women together. Here, as men and women, elders and young ones, *yangban* and commoners, and the destitute and the rich, all sat together in one place almost entirely without any distinction. Inevitably this was raised as an issue at a trial, "when Ch'oe Ch'ang-hyŏn, Ch'oe P'il-che, Hong Mun-kap, Hwang Sa-

---

[746] Charles Dallet, *op.cit.* (sang), p.183.

[747] Charles Dallet, *Ibid.,.*(sang), p.184.

[748] *Sŏngch'al kiryak*, pp.14b-15b, 22a-24b.

yŏng, Kim Paek-sim and others gathered at Hong Mun-kap's house, women from various regions also joined them and sat together in one row with the men"[749]

Conducting a mass and a doctrinal education session with men and women gathered in one place was considered immoral. "As relationships between men and women became dissipated, ethics of husbands and wives became corrupt and ... as the roles of a husband and a wife were no longer differentiated, adultery came to flourish..."[750] Performing a mass with men and women in one place was criticized as not differentiating men and women.[751] In addition, men and women residing together in one room in their naked bodies was censured as an act that even birds and beasts would not commit.[752] It was further perceived that wives were shared communally among men.[753] In the face of these social criticisms, the Catholic believers defended themselves by claiming that these criticisms were unfounded and pointed out the ten commandments of Christianity that forbade adultery, luring other men's wives and the mingling of men and women. They also argued that during the mass, there were separate seats for men and women.[754] Nevertheless, men and women sitting together in one place were socially denounced as a defilement of ethics that corrupted the education of the public morals.[755]

At the same time the Catholics criticized the practice of taking a concubine as a violation of the teachings

---

[749] *Sahak chingûi*, p.70.

[750] *Chosŏn wangjo sillok*, Chŏngjo 19th year 7th month Kyeyu.

[751] *Sahak chingŭi*, pp.73, 108, 122, 145.

[752] *Nulam kiryak*, p.5a.

[753] Charles Dallet, *op.cit.*, (sang), p.410, 447, (chung), p.148, 497.

[754] *Sahak choein* Yi Ki-yang tŭng ch'uan, pp.213-214.

[755] *Chosŏn wangjo sillok*, Hŏnjong 5th year, Kihae, 10th month, Kyŏnjin Ch'ŏksa yunŭm.

of God, and further as a fulfillment only of the selfish desires of individuals.[756] Thus, if one did not give up his concubine, his religious pursuits were not acknowledged by the church.[757] However, because traditional ethics prescribed that giving birth to a son, and thereby continuing the family lineage and practicing ancestor worship were the basic elements of filial piety, the system absolutely required having a son, and as a result, the Catholic prohibition of the concubine became problematic.

Marriage relationships and methods also raised issues and became controversial. The church did not prohibit remarriage by widows and acknowledged them to be legitimate. Furthermore, due to the law of the church requiring marriage among only the Catholic believers, it was difficult to find an appropriate partner during the persecution period, and thus it was inevitable that marriages among close relatives prevailed in the *kyouch'on* of Pyŏkch'on, marriage which was undoubtedly a subject of criticism. There was a case of a woman who, in accordance to her parents' suggestion, married a man irrespective of his social status, a widower of a humble trade yet a devout Catholic.[758]

One of the aspects of Catholic belief that the early Chosŏn church adopted was the practice of celibacy. In a Confucian society, staying unmarried was a rejection of an ethos which stressed the centrality of family life and the importance of descendants.[759] An Chŏng-bok criticized the practice by saying that "the Catholic Church teaches that chastity is more complete than marriage, and this would bring about the extinction of mankind"[760] The virgins

---

[756] *Songse ch'uyo*, Idan p'yŏn.

[757] Charles Dallet, *op.cit.*, (sang) p.48.

[758] Charles Dallet, *op.cit.*, (chung) p.516, *Kihae ilgi*, 91b-92a.

[759] Kim Ok-hŭi, *Han'guk ch'ŏnjugyo yŏsŏngsa I* (Seoul: 1983), pp.121-122.

[760] An Chŏng-bok

recorded in *Sahak chingŭi* were six *yangban* in total, and they were Yun Chŏm-hye (Yun Yu-il's cousin), Chŏng Sun-mae (Chŏng Kwang-su's sister), Kim Kyŏng-ae (daughter of a widow), Cho To-ae (Cho Sop's daughter), Pak Chŏng-yŏm, and Yi Duk-im (Yi Hap-kyu's siter). In order to avoid being criticized by society and at the same time maintain their chastity, they either called themselves widows or pretended to be someone's wife. Yun Chŏm-nye, Yi Tuk-im and Pak Sŏng-yŏm called themselves widows, while Chŏng Sun-mae and Kim Kyŏng-ae falsely claimed themselves to be the wives of a man named Hŏ and Cho To-ae claimed herself as wife of O. The character Hŏ was taken because of its meaning of emptiness.[761] During the early Chosŏn church, unmarried status was viewed as a virtue. A communal life of women believers, who refused the command of their parents to marry and left their homes in pursuit of a free religious life, became the norm within the church after the Sinyu Persecution. This was denounced as a contradiction in Catholicism for God created both men and women, at the same time those who remained unmarried were praised.[762]

Concept of Equality Relationship among Social Classses

Chosŏn society was a caste society in which social ranks were divided into and restricted by *yangban*, *chungin*, *yangin* and *ch'ŏnin* classes. In regards to the issue of social status reformation in the Chosŏn dynasty, Yi I and Cho Hŏn requested redemption of slavery [763] and Yu Hyŏng-wŏn proposed abolition of the hereditary transmission system for slaves, yet no actual reformation took place.

The fundamental ideology in Christianity was that

---

[761] *Sahak chingŭi*, p.107, 110, 341, 346-7, 355.

[762] *Taedong chŏngno,* kwŏn 5, "Silŭi chŭngŭi."

[763] James B. Palais, *Confucian Statecraft and Korean Institution* (Seattle: University of Washington, 1996), p.234.

all men are equal before God. The principle underlying the Catholic concept of equality stems from practicing 'love' as a core principle. The *Sinmyŏng ch'ohaeng*, which had been widely read since the early period states: "Because all men are the children of God, they must treat each other as brothers, and as all men are created equal by God they maintain the 'status of being human, and it is taught that they all must love each other."[764] The Confucian were most wary of this concept of equality.[765] The idea that not only men and women were equal, but all people were equal in the eyes of God was shocking. As *yangban who* comprised the ruling class, it was inevitable that they felt their social status to be at risk.

On the other hand, the emphasis on a religious brotherly love by Western Learning, transcending social classes, was welcomed by the repressed lower class. The *yangban*-oriented society and the nation-state system were deeply suspicious of the *yangban* force that cooperated with Western Learning.[766] Accordingly, the authorities adopted a stringent attitude towards the *yangban* believers.[767] The most severe punishment was proposed for not only *yangban* believers but all those who adhered to the Western religion.[768] Such a policy became one of the inducements that drove *yangban* from the church. The principle of social equality was practiced early on in the establishment of the church. *Yangban* Confucian such as Yi Sŭng-hun and Kwŏn Il-sin or local gentry such as Yu Hang-gŏm and translators such as Ch'oe Ch'ang-hyŏn, and local *yangin* such as Yi Chon-ch'ang transcended the social boundaries and actively

---

[764] *Sinmyŏng ch'ohaeng,* ha, 64b-65a.

[765] Yun Sa-sun, "Sŏhak e taehan Han'guk yuhak ŭi panŭng," p.416.

[766] *Sahak chingŭi,* p.89, *Ibid,* p.97, Sinyu Sahak choein, Yi Ka-hwan tŭng ch'uan, p.80, *Sahag chingŭi,* p.101.

[767] *Pipyŏngsa tŭngnok* 192 kwŏn, p.291.

[768] *Ibid,* p.289.

participated in the early church organization as priests. The Catholic Church members demonstrated in their actions that all men were in actuality equal beings, and they pursued relationships among each other as equal fellow church members without any restrictions as to their social classes, whether they be *p'yŏngmin* or *ch'ŏnmin*. In Chosŏn dynasty society the lowest social position was *paekchŏng*, and when Hwang Il-kwang converted to Catholicism as a *paekchŏng* he was treated as an individual and as a brother with love. He was emotionally touched, and even stated that there were two heavens, one on earth and one in the next world.[769]

In regards to the unequal social system, the Catholic believers propagated the new communal organization with a confidence that was based on the principle of equality of men. Sin T'ae-bo, who was martyred in 1839, said to his friend that "Catholicism is a very fair religion, and no distinction is made between children, adults or *yangban* or *sangnom*."[770] It was also attempted to eliminate any discrimination based on economic differences. After having been baptized, Yu Kun-myŏng and others who were arrested in Ch'ungchŏngdo Tŏksan donated their income to the destitute and the unfortunate, and also liberated all of the slaves in their possession.[771] A *Soron* Kim Kŏn-sun who was martyred in 1801, said that he came to believe in Catholicism because in Catholicism followers shared their wealth and could associate together regardless of their social classes.[772]

There was neither active movement nor struggle for abolition of the social ranking system, nor was there a movement for social equality. It was only through their

---

[769] Charles Dallet, *op.cit.*, (sang), p.473.

[770] *Ibid*, p.388.

[771] *Ibid* (chung), pp.47-8.

[772] Sahak choein Yi Ki-yang tŭng ch'uan, *Ch'uan kŭp kukan*, p.63.

efforts to put into practice what they learned through the catechisms. Catechisms, however, could not deny entirely the social ranking system itself.[773]

  The class that responded most eagerly to the introduction of Catholicism into Chosŏn society was the *chungin* class. Since the founding of the Catholic church, a *chungin* translator Kim Pŏm-u, and other *chungin* such as Ch'oe Ch'ang-hyŏn had actively pursued church activities. And as Western Learning became subjected to suppression by the government and criticisms by the society, with the eruption of the rejection of ancestor worship issue during the Chinsan Incident in Sinhae year (1791), there was a clear trend of *yangban* church members leaving the church, while the *chungin* class emerged as the leading force within the church. King Chŏngjo believed that the members of the *chungin* class had many complaints regarding the fixed nature of the social ranking system and that this is why they joined the new religion of Catholicism.[774] In the *Ch'ŏksa yunŭm*, Hŏnjong argued that "if Catholicism is an enlightening and a correct religion, then how is it possible that sons of concubines, people who have lost hope and resent their own country, the ignorant and mean people and those who covet others' wealth all mingle together as one group?"[775]

  The wives of the literati taught Catholic doctrine to their female slaves and awakened in them a sense of equality for all people. They attended sermons and participated in baptism together with their slaves and taught them to memorize Bible verses. The female slave of Ch'ŏn Il-sin, Pok Chŏm played an active role, making visits to Yi Yun-ha and Yi P'ansŏ's homes in Hanrimdong, Pak Saengwŏn's home in P'idandong, Yi Ch'amp'an's home in Hwakkyo, Cho Ye-san's home in Sukumunnae, Chŏng Chinsa's home

---

[773] cf. *Sŏng ch'al kiryak*, 17a-b.

[774] *Chosŏn wangjo sillok*, Chŏngjo 23rd year 5th month, Imsul.

[775] *Ibid.*, Hŏngjong 5th year 11th month Kyŏngjin.

in Tojŏdong, and Nam P'ansŏ's home in Naengjŏndong.[776] As for the Catholic believers' disregard for the differences in economic and social status, and their treatment of even slaves as brothers, the *yangban* at the time commented that "from the very beginning, there never was a differentiation of high and low in Western Learning and, therefore, even slaves are connected to everyone just like 'the intestines in a human's body.'"[777] It is written in *Nulam kiryak* that the pursuers of Western Learning view all people who join the religion, whether they be slaves or *ch'ŏnin*, as their own siblings, thereby failing to recognize the differences in the social status, and this is a trick that deludes ignorant people.[778] Male slaves often were in charge of overseeing the communications among the church members.[779] In the case of Kim Yu-san, a *ch'ŏnmin* by birth, he traveled to Beijing in 1798 and in 1799 as a member of the retinue and took charge of establishing communication with the church in China. He was also responsible for maintaining the contact between Yu Hang-gŏm, a wealthy Catholic believer in Chŏnju and Chŏng Yag-yong's family in Seoul.[780] Ch'oe P'il-gong, who was martyred in 1801, also stated that "intellectuals without a doubt believe in Catholicism, and those among the commoners with a slight amount of knowledge also follow the Catholic faith."[781]

---

[776] *Sahak chingŭi*, pp.370-373.

[777] *Sahak chingŭi*, p.259.

[778] *Nulam kiryak*, p.12a.

[779] *Sahak chingŭi*, p.359.

[780] Chu Myŏng-jun, *op.cit.*, pp.136-137.

[781] Sahak choein, Yi ka-hwan tŭng ch'uan, p.28.

3. Political Causes

Because politics and religion were entangled with one another in the Chosŏn dynasty, the persecution of Catholicism was exploited and sacrificed to the power struggle among factions yearning for political power. The 1801 persecution resulting from the factional strife between Sip'a and Pyŏkp'a factions, the 1839-1845 persecution resulting from the in-law politics of the Andong Kim clan and P'ungyang Cho clan, and the 1866 persecution resulting from the Taewŏn'gun's personal greed for power have all been already examined. Another political cause of the persecutions was the perception that the Catholic Church and its members were secretly communicating with foreign forces. Such a fear was confirmed following the Hwang Sa-yŏng Paeksŏ incident, and upon the initiation of the movement to invite priests from abroad, French missionaries smuggled themselves into Korea and pursued their missions, accompanied by armed forces. Thus the Catholic Church members were accused as 't'ongoe punja' (individuals who collude with foreign nations). Because of the decree prohibiting Catholicism, the church acquired the character of an underground church, and as a result, Catholicism could only be propagated in secret. Subsequently, they were assailed as a group of individuals who held grudges against the state,[782] who yearned for reform of the world,[783] who entertained thoughts of rebellion,[784] and who were further associated with the mass uprisings in China such as Yellow Turban Rebels (*Hwang Kŏn-jŏk*) or White Lotus society (*Paekyŏnkyodo.*).[785] There were many who left their hometowns to avoid the persecution,

---

[782] Sahak choein, Kim Yŏ tŭng ch'uan, p.14.
[783] *Sahak chingŭi*, p.14.
[784] Sahak choein, Kang I-ch'ŏn tŭng ch'uan, p.91.
[785] *Sahak chingŭi*, pp.70, 135.

such as those who left their homes and went into hiding,[786] those who wander hither and thither, [787] and those who drift from one place to another.[788] The government was apprehensive of the potential formation of bandits or rebellious bands by these individuals hiding in the mountains.[789] When a French fleet arrived in Korea to inquire about the French missionaries who had been executed during the Kihae Persecution in 1839, King Hŏnjong believed that there was a Chosŏn individual who had been communicating with the French force. [790] Therefore, the Catholic Church members were persecuted and accused as people who communicate with foreign forces,[791] bands who call themselves thieves,[792] and individual who communicate in secret with foreign nations.[793]

Request for Large Ships

Rampant Rumor and Yearning for Utopia

At the end of the 18th century, a rumor that "the propitiousness of the time will not last for long" ran rampant, foretelling the demise of the Chosŏn dynasty.[794] Immediately preceding 1800, a rumor had swept through Ch'ungch'ŏng province that a thousand ships would arrive

---

[786] *Sahak chingŭi*, p.168.

[787] *Ibid*, p.158.

[788] *Ibid*, p.89.

[789] *Ibid*, p.14.

[790] *Chosŏn wangjo sillok,* Hŏnjong 12th year 7th month Musul.

[791] *Kojong sillok*, Kojong 3rd year 8th month 16th day.

[792] *Ilsŏngnok*, Kojong Mujin 4th month 27th day.

[793] *Kojong sillok*, Kojong 3rd year 1st month 24th day.

[794] Sinyu sahak choein, Kang I-chŏn tŭng chu'an, *Ch'uan kŭp kukan* 25, (Seoul: Asea Munhwasa, 1983), p.307.

between Inchŏn and Pup'yŏng to hail the dawning of a holy era, and subsequently the rumor had taken on a concrete meaning.[795] This was seen to be similar to a prophecy in the *Chŏnggamnok* that ten thousand ships would sail the river between Kanghwa and P'yŏngt'aek.[796] The year 1800 was the year of the 1800th anniversary of the birth of Jesus and thus was considered to be a holy year, but some Catholic Church members who had hoped for the arrival of the Western ships became doubtful when no news of such a coming reached them.[797] In addition, at the time of Chŏngjo's sudden death, a rumor that he had been poisoned spread among the believers as well as common people,[798] and government officials such as Hong Nak-in, Yu Hŭi-yŏng and Kim Hŭi were convinced of its truth.[799]

Along with the prophecies, Utopian fantasies also became popular. For example, among the prophecies that sprouted in the Ch'ungch'ŏng region there were stories of a utopian island nation in the middle of the ocean. Although the notions of utopia varied considerably, they generally involved an island that had a leader called Chŏng'gu who ruled the ocean, that this was an independent nation with many talented men, and a powerful armed force.[800] There were also some Catholic Church members who awaited a new society governed by the Roman Pope to appear. Yu Kwan-gŏm and Ch'oe In-kil testified that a book entitled

---

[795] Sinyu sahak choein, Yu Hang-gŏm tŭng ch'uan, 19.

[796] *Chosŏn pikyŏl chŏnŏ,* (Seoul: Kyuunkwak), p.21.

[797] *Sahak chingŭi,* p.247.

[798] Chŏng Yag-yong, *Yŏyudang chŏngsŏ,* I, 17:36b.

[799] *Pipyŏnsa tŭngnok* 19ch'aek, Sinyu 1st month 5th day.

[800] Sahak choein, Yi Ki-yang tŭng ch'uan, 112. Kim I-baek kongch'o. Sahak choein, Kim Yŏ tŭng ch'uan 65 & 82, Yi Chu-hwang kongch'o, Kim Yŏ kongch'o.

The Causes of the Persecutions

Sŏhakpŏm[801] expounded that the Western Learning was divided into liberal arts, religion, medicine and science, all centered around the one individual Pope, and talented men were educated within each field and were promoted according to their ability.[802] Other prophecies had it that the traditional emperor of China would be replaced by the Pope from the West to set up a new suzerain state, and that the priest appointed by the Pope would assume the seat of the Chosŏn king. And it appears that because of such beliefs, Catholic Church members, along with the concept of Chŏnju, were seen as denying the royal authority. Furthermore, the Catholic believers expected a large ship loaded with treasure to arrive in Korea and build a Catholic church.[803] This seems to have stemmed from the statement made by priest Chou Wen-mo as he passed by the tomb of Yun Chi-ch'ung in Chŏllado that a Catholic Church building will be erected on the ground above his grave.[804]

Yu Kwan-gŏm anticipated that the "currency of Chosŏn" that was based on the *sangp'yŏng* coins would not be used when erecting a church building in Chosŏn.[805] Kang I-ch'ŏn also said that *sangp'yŏng* coins, would become worthless in the future and therefore they must be exchanged for and kept in silver.[806] Such a theory of the worthlessness of *sangp'yŏng* coins likely represents the dreams of only a few believers yearning for a new world,

---

[801] A book written in Chinese by P. Julius Aleni (1582-1649) priest for the purpose of introducing the education and academica system of the West to the Chinese society.

[802] Sinyu sahak choein, Yu Kwan-gŏm tŭng ch'uan, Yu Kwan-gŏm kongch'o, *Sahak chingŭi*, p.80.

[803] *Sahak chingŭi*, p.17.

[804] *Ibid*, p.233.

[805] *Sahak chingŭi*, Kim Tal-sun changye, Yi U-jip kongch'o.

[806] Sinyu Sahak choein, Kim Yŏ tŭng ch'uan 48, Yi Kuk-hwang kongch'o.

but to the government authorities, it could only be interpreted as a scheme to bring on an upheaval to the Chosŏn dynasty.

The First Request for Western Ships
Chosŏn's Catholic Church members had sent secret envoys to Beijing on numerous occasions to request a dispatch of priests and to request ships. The fact that such a request had been made stirred up a serious controversy within the court when it was made known. The very first secret envoy was Yun Yu-il. In the 10th month of the Kiyu year (1789), he accompanied the Beijing Winter Solstice envoy, Yi Sŏng-wŏn, in 1790 and arrived safely in Beijing. Yun Yu-il met with Bishop Gouvea and delivered the letter written by Yi Sŭng-hun and Yu Hang-gŏm. The letter contained a request for a dispatch of priests to Chosŏn and questions regarding the institution of the church. Subsequently, Yi Ka-hwan, Hong Nak-min, Yi Sŭng-hun and Chi Hwang repeatedly requested dispatch of priests in 1790, and a request for a large Western ship was made at the same time.[807] The Catholic believers at the time were aware of the fact that the Western missionaries traveled throughout the world in large ships in order to propagate Catholicism. Therefore, they believed that if a large ship arrived in Chosŏn, they could then build a church and disseminate the religion and that they would no longer be persecuted.[808]

In the 9th month of 1790, Yun Yu-il accompanied the entourage of Envoy Hwang In-chŏm to Beijing on the occasion of the eightieth birthday of the Ch'ing emperor. His task at that time was to request a Western ship for the first time in addition to requesting a dispatch of priests. If it is agreed that the purpose of those involved was "only to bring in priests", then the original purpose in requesting a large ship lay in inviting many missionaries. Korean converts believed that if a large ship was sent to Chosŏn,

---
[807] *Sahak chingŭi*, p.218.
[808] *Ibid*, p.232.

then propagation of Catholicism would be permitted easily, as it was in China. However, their attempt to attain religious freedom with help from the outside unfortunately earned them only misunderstanding and suspicion the part of the government.

The Second Request for a Large Ship

Another attempt to request a large ship and a priest was made in 1796 by Yi Sŭng-hun, Hong Nak-min, Yu Kwan-gŏm, Kwŏn Il-sin, Ch'oe Ch'ang-hyŏn, and Hwang Sa-yŏng, following the entrance of priest Chou Wen-mo. This was after Yun Chi-ch'ung and Kwŏn Sang-yŏn had been martyred in 1791 for refusing to conduct the ancestor worship ceremony, and also after Ch'oe In-kil, Chi Hwang and Yun Yu-il had been executed for their involvement in the incident of the attempt to arrest Father Chou Wen-mo in 1795. Due to the refusal of many converts to conduct ancestor worship, persecution worsened, and the church members asked Father Chou Wen-mo to request a large ship to help secure the church and freedom of missionary activity.[809] Father Chou took and partially edited the letter signed by the church members, and sent it to Beijing through Hwang Sim in 1796.[810]

Upon receiving the letter, the Beijing Bishop responded that he had sent the request to the Pope, but had received a response of rejection from the Papal Court, for the Papal Court would not dispatch a large ship to Chosŏn despite the prohibition on Catholicism, because the related expense would be too costly.[811] As to the second objective in requesting a large ship, the record offers several possibilities since the original letter has never been found. One common assertion is that, "it was solely for the purpose of

---

[809] *Sahak chingŭi*, pp.25-26.

[810] *Sahak chingŭi*, pp.239-240.

[811] *Sahak chingŭi*, p.235.

propagating Western Learning throughout." [812] Many church members believed that if a large ship arrived, the prohibition of Catholicism would be abolished, [813] and, further, the issue of Chou Wen-mo's personal safety would be resolved.[814]

Yu Hang-gŏm's testimony that "even if Western ships do arrive, if the Chosŏn kingdom refuses to accept Catholicism, then a war is unavoidable,"[815] stirred serious alarm. Seen from his statement that "a large ship has many holes through which guns are fired, and there is no one who would not be afraid once guns begin to fire,"[816] his "ship" refers to a battleship and thus it would appear that Korean Catholics were prepared to attain religious freedom through armed force if necessary. Even afterwards, the Chosŏn church continued to request large ships from abroad. Yi Chon-ch'ang who had been imprisoned in Kongju, sent Kim Yu-san as a secret envoy to Beijing on two different occasions, in 1798 and again in 1799. Yi Chon-ch'ang told Kim Yu-san that "if a large ship comes to Chosŏn, then everything will be fine,"[817] and it can be inferred from this statement that the purpose of his trip was to deliver a letter to the Beijing Bishop requesting dispatch of a large ship.

The Third Request for a Large Ship
Hwang Sa-yŏng Paeksŏ (silk letter) Incident

The Chosŏn church members' yearning for a large ship resulted in repeated requests and eventually led to the Hwang Sa-yŏng Paeksŏ Incident during the 1801 Persecution. The controversial element of the Paeksŏ Inci-

---

[812] *Sahak chingŭi*, p.238.
[813] *Ibid*, pp.25-26.
[814] Sinyu Sahak choein, Yu Hang-gŏm ch'uan, 48.
[815] *Sahak chingŭi*, pp.229-230.
[816] *Ibid*, p.246.
[817] *Sahak chingŭi*, pp.30-31.

dent was the direct request for assistance from Western armed forces, "We request that a large ship be sent to our country, carrying several hundred small ships with fifty to sixty thousand soldiers, and potent weapons such as cannon."[818] He also wrote that "if the requested number of ships and men can be sent, then nothing could be better. But if the force is insufficient, then several tens of ships and five to six thousand soldiers would do."[819] At the same time the Hwang Sa-yŏng Paeksŏ was composed, a full-scale persecution had been launched by Yŏngjo's Queen Dowager Kim, and the Pyŏkp'a officials, and attaining religious freedom was not even considered a possibility. Hwang Sa-yŏng's colleagues and relatives had all been martyred and he alone composed the letter in Paeron, Ch'ungch'ŏngdo. Hwang Sa-yŏng was also one of the individuals who had signed the second letter requesting a large ship.

Just as he said, his intention was "to follow the Catholic propagation format in China and enable Western Learning to flourish in Chosŏn, and with the force of the large ship, to abolish the prohibition order in Chosŏn and to have people develop faith in Western Learning,"[820] He said that he had heard about the appearance of the large Western ship through Hyŏn Kye-hŭm.[821] He believed that "not only does a country that is the size of a bullet alone refuse to obey a command, but its refusal also brutally harms the holy religion, kills priests...therefore there is nothing wrong if their sin is investigated by mobilizing armed force."[822]

---

[818] Hwang Sa-yŏng paeksŏ, 110-111th lines.

[819] *Ibid*, 112th line.

[820] Sinyu Sahak choein, Hwang Sa-yŏng dŭng ch'uan, p.732.

[821] *Ibid*, p.733. Hyŏn Kye-hŭm (1762-1801)had visited English ship the *Broughton* that was banked on the eastcoast in 1797.

[822] Hwang Sa-yŏng paeksŏ, 116th line.

Jai-Keun Choi

Appearance of Foreign Ships and Individuals who secretly communicated with Foreign Nations

Arrival of the French Missionaries and Appearance of Strange Ships

After the Sinyu Persecution, the Chosŏn Catholic Church members continued to request a dispatch of priests from the Beijing parish and the Pope. From the point of view of the Chosŏn goverment, this was seen as secret communication with a foreign power. The movement to invite priests continued beyond 1811, and the Chosŏn church members led by Chŏng Ha-sang repeatedly made the request in 1813 and again in 1816. In 1816, Chŏng Ha-sang accompanied Yi Yŏ-ching to Beijing, after which point, Chŏng Ha-sang had traveled to Beijing on a total of nine different occasions in an attempt to bring priests to Chosŏn. It was through such contact that a Chosŏn parish was established and missionaries from the Paris Foreign Mission Society entered Chosŏn one by one. Consequently, in 1836, the French missionaries launched full-scale activities in Chosŏn. Until that time, the Western Learning as a religion and scholarship had been transmitted indirectly through books or through Chinese people. However, with the arrival of the French missionaries, Catholicism was promoted by Western priests secretly entering and working in Korea. Along with the incident of the Catholic believers' requesting foreign ships, appearances of strange ships from time to time throughout the first half of the 19th century was viewed as evidence that foreign powers intended to invade Korea. There was a survey of Cheju Island and Ullŭng Island by a group of men led by a French navigator La Perouse in 1787 (11th year of Chŏngjo).[823] In 1816 (16th year of Sunjo), there also occurred an incident in which two British ships "Alceste" and "Lyra" commanded by Captain Basil Hall approached the west coast of Korea, surveyed the

---

[823] H.N. Allen, *Korea: Fact and Fancy*, (Seoul: Methodist Publishing House, 1904), p.150.

shore and drew up a map.[824]

Appearance of Strange Ships and People who Communicated with Foreign Countries Secretly

    The Chosŏn court's alarm about the foreign ships that appeared sporadically increased even further, in the 6th month of 1846, when three French vessels under the command of Captain Cecile appeared in waters off Hongju, Ch'ungch'ŏngdo. They delivered a letter demanding an explanation for the execution of the three French missionaries in 1839 (5th year of Hŏnjong) and threatening Chosŏn that if no sincere reply is received, "it will not be able to avoid a great disaster."[825] The court came to be convinced that the French were keenly aware of the internal affairs of Chosŏn and that Chosŏn individuals had been colluding with them.[826] The next year, in 1847, two French vessels, the "La Glorie" and "La Victorieuse" under Captain Pierre's command arrived in Korea seeking a reply to the previous letter of Captain Cecile .[827] However, as one of their ships was wrecked along the shore, they fled Korea without receiving an explanation. In 1856, the French vessel "Virginia" appeared along the west coast of Chosŏn and demanded that trade relations be established. The arrival of a French vessel naturally instilled a sense of fear in the minds of the Chosŏn people as well as in the government, and prompted them to view the Catholic Church members as puppets of the Western nations.

---

[824] *Chosŏn wangjo sillok,* Sunjo 16th year 7th month Pyŏngin day. Horace N. Allen, *op.cit.*, p.151.

[825] *Ilsŏngnok* Hŏnjong 12th year 6th month Pyŏngja day. H.N. Allen, *Korea: Fact and Fancy*, (Seoul: Methodist Publishing House, 1904), p.152.

[826] *Ibid.,*

[827] *Ibid.*, p.152. *Sŭngjŏngwŏn ilgi,* Hŏnjong 13th year, 8th month, 11th day.

Catholic Believers who Communicated Secretly with Foreign Nations

During the Pyŏngin Persecution that took over eight thousand lives and that was carried on for six years starting in 1866, the Catholic Church members were regarded as a group of people who brought in foreign thieves and secretly communicated with foreign nations to sell the country. Thus the Chosŏn government understood the Catholic believers as a national threat and launched a full-scale persecution. This was because Russia's request for trade relations, invasions by French vessels, Oppert's grave robbery and invasion by American ships were all either directly or indirectly related to the Catholic Church. It was for the purpose of defending itself against invasion by the Western forces that the court had pursued a policy of persecution.[828] Even the proposal to prevent a Russian invasion, which stemmed from the belief that "barbarians must be used to control barbarians" was seen as a collusion with foreign forces, and in the document of the sentence of Nam Chong-sam, who was beheaded, it is said that "we dared to scheme a plan to sell our country by conspiring to secretly bringing in thieves."[829] In 1866 when the invasion of Kanghwado by the French fleet erupted because of the 1866 foreign disturbance, Ki Chŏng-chin (1798-1876) wrote in a memorial to the king that "...they coveted our land without restraint and attempted to annex our country. They covet the goods produced by our country and intend to possess our countrymen as slaves and rape our women and treat our people as beasts...[830] and thus he argued that it was impossible to enter into friendly relations with the Western nations and that those who collude with the Western nations

---

[828] cf. Kim Wŏn-mo, "Sinmi yangyo e daehan hangjŏn," pp.233-260. cf. Yi Wŏn-sun, "Pyŏngin Yangyo wa taebul hangjŏn," Han minjok toknip undongsa 1 (Seoul: Kuksa p'yŏnch'an wiwŏnhoe, 1987), pp.203-232.

[829] Pyŏngin Sahak choein, Chŏngsam Pongju tŭng kukan, p.1.

[830] *Kojong sillok*, Kojong 3rd year 8th month 16th day.

should be punished for the crime of facilitating robbery. Yi Hang-no, the lead signatory among the Confucian literati who submitted a memorial to reject heterodoxy on three occasions during the 1866 foreign disturbance, stated that "the nation's ideologies are split into two camps, one of which is comprised of those who propose to fight and the other is made up of those who propose to establish peace. The proposal to fight the Westerners is made by those on our side, while the proposal to coexist peacefully is put forward by those on the enemy's side. Those on our side maintain the traditional values and those on the enemy's side are falling into the state of beast."[831] Thus, he regarded the situation as critical for the life and death of the nation.

The Queen Dowager viewed the entire group of Catholic believers as secretly communicating with foreign forces, and she ordered to seek out and interrogate all Catholic believers, and to first behead them and then to report that fact.[832] During the Pyŏngin Persecution of 1866, the Chosŏn government came to believe that the Catholic believers and France were secretly colluding.[833] In other words, although the missionaries of the Western colonial powers at the end of the 19th century were not aware of it themselves, the end result of missionary activity was that the Catholics played the role of puppets for Western colonialism. And in actuality Chosŏn was invaded by France, and Henri de Bellonnet, French charge' d'affaires in Beijing, did say threateningly that "the day the king of Chosŏn attacks the French people will be the last day of his rule."[834] And the missionaries in Chosŏn also argued that France must demonstrate to Chosŏn its great power and

---

[831] *Kojong sillok* Kojong 3rd year 1st month 24th day.

[832] *Ilsŏngnok* Kojong 3rd year 7th month 8th day.

[833] Hanbul charyo (1866-1867), *Kyohoesa yŏn'gu 2*, p.205.

[834] *Kyohoesa yŏn'gu* I, pp.178-187.

determination.[835]

In a word, the efforts by the Catholic Church members to establish diplomatic contact between France and the Chosŏn kingdom were mistakenly regarded as efforts to bring about secret collusion with foreign forces, but this misinformed conclusion not only characterized the thinking of the government officials. It also represented a Confucian conception of politics that had all along put forward the traditional theory of upholding orthodoxy and rejecting heterodoxy. This all too easy dogmatism was matched by the facile suspicions of government authorities as to the motives behind the activities of the Korean Catholics. In the end, then, the Western powers were easily drawn into their Korean adventure.

---

[835] *Ilsŏngnok,* Kojong 5th year 4th month 27th day..

CHAPTER VII

Comparison of the 1801 and 1866 Persecutions: Changes, Continuations and Survival

The Sinyu Persecution of 1801 was the first nationwide one, while the Pyŏngin Persecution of 1866, in which over 8000 people died as martyrs, was the last and the largest persecution of Catholicism in the Chosŏn dynasty. This chapter explores the impact of the persecutions and the state of the Church before and after the persecutions, from a sociological perspective, by examining the changes in social status of the church members, the changes in the ratio of male to female believers, the changes in habitation, the changes in economic situation, and the motivations for conversion of the believers during the periods of the first and the last persecutions.

1. Comparison of the 1801 and 1866 Persecutions

Researchers who have examined the structure and characteristics of Chosŏn society and the Catholic Church of this period through statistical analyses are: Kim Han-gyu, "*Sahak chingŭi lŭl t'onghaesŏ pon ch'ogi han'guk ch'ŏju kyohoe ŭi myŏtkaji munje* (Some questions about the Early Korean Catholic church in light of the *Sahak chingŭi)*" ; Ishii Hisao, "Ritai ÿch® no Ch®sen Tenshukyo to sono hakugai (The Korean Catholic Church and the Persecution of King Kojong's reign)"; Cho Kwang, "*Sinyu pakhae ŭi punsŏkchŏk koch'al* (An analysis of the causes of the 1801 Persecution)"; and his book, *Chosŏn hugi ch'ŏnju kyohoesa yŏngu* (A Study on the history of the Catholic Church in later Chosŏn) ; Ch'oe Yong-gyu, "*Kihae Pyŏngo Kyonan'gi ch'ŏnju kyodo ŭi punsŏkchŏk koch'al:1802-1846 nyŏn ŭl chungsim ŭro*" (Analytical investigation of the Catholic converts during the religious persecution years of 1802 - 1845); Ko Hŭng-sik, "*Pyŏngin Kyonan'gi sindodŭl ŭi sinang* (Faith during the 1866 Persecution)."

Cho Kwang's analysis of the Causes of the 1801 Sinyu Persecution will be referred to as A; his book, *Chosŏn hugi Ch'ŏnju kyohoesa* as A'; Kim Han-gyu's research on the Early Korean Catholic Church as B; Ch'oe Yong-gyu's research as C; Ishii Hisao's research as D; Ko Hŭng-sik's research as E. Comparison of these analyses reveals clearly the changes in the early period of the persecutions and the post-persecution period. Research C is examined to understand the intervening years.

The estimated number of believers at the time of the Sinyu Persecution was 10,000,[836] and the names of 592 people (5.92% of the total number of believers) were recorded in various government documents, *Sahak chingŭi, Sinyu sahak choein ch'uan,* and *Sungjŏngwŏn ilgi* ; a church document, *Hwang Sa-yŏng paeksŏ*; and Dallet's *Chosŏn kyohoesa.*

In *Chosŏn hugi ch'ŏnjugyosa*, Cho Kwang identified one hundred more people than in his previous research. Thus, a total of 692 people (6.92% of the whole believers)

---

[836] C. Dallet (tr.), *op. cit.,* (sang) p. 393.

were analyzed.[837] Kim Han-gyu's book on the Sinyu Persecution is a statistical approach, which analyzed 146 people in the *Sahak chingŭi* and compared the results with his previous research A.[838]

In Research B, Ch'oe Yong-gyu analyzed 441 people, 4.41% of the total believers,[839] on the basis of Charles Dallet's *Han'guk ch'ŏnju kyohoesa, Sunjong Hŏnjong Sillok, Ilsŏngnok, Sŭngjŏngwŏn ilgi, Chwau p'odoch'ŏng tŭngnok, Ch'uan gŭp kukan, Pibyŏnsa tŭngnok, Yi Man-ch'ae's Pyŏgwip'yŏn,* and *Hyŏn Sŏk-mun's Kihae ilgi*.[840]

Ishii Hisao analyzed ten missionaries and 407 people who were arrested during the period of 1866 through 1878, based on the *Chwau p'odoch'ŏng tŭngnok* (Records of the Police Station of the Left and Right Divisions). Since the jurisdiction of *Chwau p'odoch'ŏng* was only the capital, this document does not show any significance for the persecutions in other regions. Particularly, Ishii tried to reveal the nature of the faith of the believers, the motivations of conversion and the reasons for apostasy by analyzing the ratio of male to female, occupation, habitat, and age of the believers.

Ko Hŭng-sik analyzed 444 people whom he identified as converts from 1866 to 1879 on the basis of two documents, *P'odoch'ŏng tŭngnok* (Police Records) and *Ch'imyŏng ilgi* (Diary of Martyrs).[841]

The Changes in the Social Classes

One way to understand the Catholic Church within

---

[837] Cho Kwang, *Chosŏn hugi ch'ŏnju kyohoesa yŏngu*. p. 33.

[838] Kim Han-gyu, B. p.52.

[839] Ch'oe Yong-gyu, *Kihae pyŏngo kyonangi ch'ŏnju kyodo ŭi punsŏkchŏk koch'al* p. 234.

[840] *Ibid.,* p. 234. French priests and children were excluded.

[841] Ko Hŭng-sik, *Pyŏngin kyonangi sindodŭl ŭi sinang*, p. 277.

Chosŏn society, in which social classes were distinctively divided, is to examine what classes of the society accepted this new Western religion, and in what way they contributed to the growth of the Church.

The following table summarizes the distribution of the converts by social classes as analyzed by six researchers:

Period	Researchers	Yangban	Chungin	Sangin	Ch'ŏnmin	Unknown	Total
1784-1801	Cho Kwang (A)	122 20.61%	37 6.25%	24 4.05%	41 6.93%	368 62.61%	592 100%
	Cho Kwang (A')	193 27.75%	91 13.29%	178 25.72%	38 5.49%	192 27.75%	692 100%
	Kim Han-gyu (B)	56 40%	12 8.5%	67 47.9%		6 3.6%	146 100%
1802-1846	Ch'oe Yong-gyu (C)	94 21.31%	20 4.54%	100 22.68%	5 1.13%	222 50.34%	44 100%
1866-1878	Ishii Hisao (D)		20.66%		79.34%		407 100%
	Ko Hŭng-sik (E)						408 100%

Table 1

In A, the number of the people whose classes were clearly identified was only 224, which is 37.84% of the total number of 592. The rest of the 368 people (62.16%) were considered as *yangin*, which has no particular class distinction.[842] Among 592 people, 122 (20.61%) were identified as *yangban*. Considering the report that *yangban* in the Taegu area in 1789 comprised 31.94% of the whole population,[843] and the Ŭlsan *changchŏk* analysis in 1894

---

[842] Cho Kwang, *op. cit.*, p. 46.

[843] Shikata Hiroshi. "Richō jinko ni kansuru mibun kaikyūbetusteki kansatsu" (An investigation of Yi dynasty population in terms of status and class). in *Chōsen keizai no kenkyū*, p.392.

which said that *yangban* made up 43.67% of the population, the percentage of *yangban* believers (20.61%) is quite low. [844] Cho Kwang attributed the low percentage of *yangban* to their fear of punishment[845] which made them less likely to become believers than members of any other class of people.

Of 122 *yangban,* those whose party factions were identified numbered only 39 (32%): Namin, 31 (80%), Noron, 5, Soron, 2, and Sobuk, 1. Among those 39 people, only 16 actually participated in political life,[846] including Kim Kŏn-sun, Yi Sŭng-hun, Chŏng Yak-chong, Chŏng Yag-yong, Chŏng Yak-chŏn, Hong Nak-min, Hong Kyo-man, and Hong In.[847]

Besides *Namin*, the most representative *yangban* were Kim Sang-hŏn's eldest son, Kim Kŏn-sun, Kim Paek-sun, Kang I-ch'ŏn, Kim I-baek, and Yi Chung-bae. [848] The fact that most of the converts were *Namin* was attributed to the fact that they had been excluded from political power since King Sukchong's reign and could easily find solidarity as an opposition group. [849] The rest of the 83 *yangban* whose party factions could not be identified were thought to be those who were distanced from the political arena and economically were at the same level as *yangin*. [850]

---

[844] Chŏng Sŏk-chong, *Chosŏn hugi sahoe pyŏndong yŏngu*, p. 249.

[845] *Hwang Sa-yŏng paeksŏ*, line 20.

[846] There was a restriction in the late Chosŏn dynasty such that those who could participate in politics are limited to the third generations of *tangsanggwan* 'the higher level officials'

[847] Cho Kwang, *Ibid.*, p. 48.

[848] Sinyu sahak choein Kim Yŏ tŭng ch'uan. 58. (1801. Sinyu 4th month 18th day) Kim Chŏng-ŏk kongch'o

[849] Cho Kwang. p. 48

[850] Cho Kwang. p. 48.

The number of *chungin* was 37 (6.25%). If we consider the report that the middle class of the *Taegu* area in 1789 was 0.46%, the percentage of *chungin* is high.[851] Of the early *chungin* believers, 18 owned pharmacies, which were considered to have played the role of liaison offices among the believers. [852] The *yangin* numbered 24 (4.05% of the believers). The report of the Taegu Census in 1789 stated that the percentage of *sangmin* was 51.09% of the whole population,[853] and the report of the Ulsan Census of 1804 said that the percentage of *sangmin* was 33.88%. [854] Considering these reports, the percentage of *yangin* was very low. If most of those whose classes could not be identified (62.61%) are thought to be *yangin*[855], Cho explains, this discrepancy can be resolved.

Ch'ŏnmin, the lowest class in Chosŏn society, includes *yŏkno* (post station slaves), *kongch'ŏn* (public slaves), *sach'ŏn* (private slaves), and *paekchŏng* (outcasts). The number of the believers in this class was 41 (6.93%). Considering the report that the *ch'ŏnmin* percentage of the Taegu area in 1789 was 16.51%, [856] and the report that the *nobi* percentage of the Ulsan area in 1801 was 22.99%, [857] the percentage of *ch'ŏnmin*, 6.93%, was very low, suggesting that Catholicism did not permeate through to this lowest class.

A breakdown of the 41 *ch'ŏnmin* believers shows 27 private slaves (household slaves 22 and out-resident

---

[851] Cho Kwang, p. 49.

[852] *Sahak Chingŭi*, 72. *Chakbae choein chungin*, Son Kyŏngmu. *Ibid., Chŏngpŏp choeinjil* (sang), 78. *Ch'oe P'il-che kongch'o.*

[853] Shikata Hiroshi, *op.cit.*, p. 391.

[854] Chŏng Sŏk-chong, *op. cit.,* p.250.

[855] Cho Kwang, A. *op. cit.,* p. 50.

[856] Shikata Hiroshi, *op. cit.*, p. 410.

[857] Chŏng Sŏk-chong, *op. cit.*, p.

slaves 5), 2 post station slaves, 3 *paekchŏng* (outcasts) and 9 husbands of women slaves. However, it is worth noting that despite the small number, the *ch'ŏnmin* class partook of this new religion as one component of the believers. Thus, we can say that the main component of the early Church was the ruled class centering around the *sangmin* class which was isolated from political power.[858] Having classified the unidentified people as *sangin,* Cho Kwang estimated that the percentage of *sangin* among early believers was 66.6%. On the premise that *yangban* did not accept the newly introduced Catholicism enthusiastically, and the majority of those who accepted it were *yangin*, Cho concludes that Catholicism was received by the ruled classes who were isolated from political power, and they gradually came to comprise the main component of the believers.[859]

Having identified one hundred more believers in Research A', Cho Kwang reanalyzed the social classes of the believers during 1784 through 1801 as follows:

yangban: 192 (27.75%)
chungin: 92 (13.29%)
yangin: 178 (25.78%)
ch'ŏmin: 38 (5.49%)
unknown: 192 (27.75%)
Total: 692 (100%)

Table 2

Among these, males were 513 (74.13%) and females were 179 (25.87%). This analysis was consistent with the conclusion of his previous research A. [860]

On the other hand, Kim Han-gyu identified the

---

[858] Cho Kwang, A. *op. cit.*, p. 51
[859] Cho Kwang, A. *Ibid.,* p. 51
[860] Cho Kwang, *Chosŏn hugi ch'ŏnju kyohoesa yŏn'gu.* (Seoul: Koryŏ taehak'kyo. 1988), pp. 251-2.

class affiliation of 140 people out of 146 people identified in *Sahak chingŭi* as follows:

	Kim Han-gyu	Cho Kwang
yangban	56 (40%)	20. 6%
chungin	12 (8. 5%)	6. 25%
sangin	67 (47.9%)	66.21%
ch'ŏnmin	5 (3.6%)	6.93%

Table 3

In explaining the discrepancy between the two studies, Kim points out that Cho erred in regarding believers whose class was unknown as *sangin* [861] (The percentage of *sangin* whose class could be identified was 4.05% and that of those who were conjectured to be *sangin* was 62.16% in Cho Kwang's research.)

Observing that the believers were equally divided into upper classes of *yangban* and *chungin* on the one hand and the lower classes of *sangin* and *ch'ŏnmin* on the other hand (his analysis of *Sahak chingŭi* indicates that believers was 40%), Kim concludes that the main group of the early Catholic believers in Chosŏn was more heavily upper class, more from the *yangban* class than the *sangin* class. The fact that the percentage of *yangban* believers was high in the early Church, and the fact that many of those who were transferred to the *Kukch'ŏng* (the Trial Office) for trial were *yangban* also support this conclusion. [862]

During the period between the *Kihae* and *Pyŏngo* years (1839-1846), however, he observed that the percentage of *yangban* believers decreased, while that of the *sangin* and *ch'ŏnmin* believers was increasing. [863]

---

[861] Kim Han-gyu, *op. cit.*, pp. 55-56.
[862] Kim Han-gyu, *Ibid.*, p. 57.
[863] Ch'oe Yong-gyu. *op. cit.*, p. 241

Comparison of the 1801 and the 1866 Persecutions

In Ch'oe Yong-gyu's study C, those whose classes were identified were 219 out of the total number of 441 believers (49.66%). Among them, *yangban* numbered 94 (21.32%), *sangmin* were 100 (22.68%), *chungin* were 20 (4.54%), and *ch'ŏnmin* were only 5 (1.13%).[864] Compared to Cho Kwang's Research A, the percentages of *yangban* and *chungin* were almost the same, but the percentage of *sangmin* is much higher (4.05% vs 22.68%). Compared to Kim Han-gyu's B, the percentages of *yangban, chungin, sangmin,* and *ch'ŏnmin* are all reduced by half. In the case of *sangmin*, however, if people whose class is not known are considered as *sangmin*, as in A, the total percentage of *sangmin* and people of unknown class increases to 73.02%.[865]

divisions	yangban	chungin	sangmin	ch'ŏnmin	unknown	total
Taegu (1783-1789)	31.94	0.46	51.09	16.51	0	100%
Ulsan (1804)	43.67	0	33.88	22.99	0	100%
Catholics (1802-1846)	21.32	4.54	22.68	1.13	50.34	100%
Ulsan (1867)	67.07	0	18.27	14.66	0	100%

Table 4

On the basis of the above statistcs in Table 4, Ch'oe also states that the low percentage of *yangban* in the period of 1802 through 1846 indicates that the main targets of the early persecutions were *yangban*.[866] As has been pointed out, after the Sinyu Persecution, the number of *yangban* believers decreased, because conversion to Catholics was considered as treason, and *yangban* were very afraid of

---

[864] *Ibid.,*
[865] *Ibid.,* p. 242.
[866] *Ibid.,* p. 243.

punishment.[867] Thus, the *yangban* believers at this time probably were either those who were completely isolated from political power or the descendants of the martyrs. [868]

Around 1785 *chungin* started to convert, and as many *yangban* left the Church because of the ancestor worship issue around 1791, the leadership of the Church shifted from *yangban* to *chungin*. Before 1791, 8 people were *yangban* among the 12 early Church leaders. This is contrasted to the period from 1791 to the 1801 persecution, in which, of 38 leaders, 9 were *yangban* (23.68%), 21 were *chungin* (55.28%), 5 were *yangin* (13.16%), and people with unknown class were 3 (7.89%). [869] Cho Kwang interprets this change as a shift of Catholicism to a mass religion. [870] The high percentage of *chungin* in the leadership and the fact that 19 out of 20 people became martyrs clearly suggests that *chungin* comprised the Church leadership. Why were they so devoted to Catholicism? The answer may lie in the doctrines of Catholicism whose basic tenet is that all men are equal before God. [871]

The percentage of *sangmin* (22.68%) was low. However, if we consider the people of unknown class to be *sangmin*, Ch'oe argues, then the percentage of *sangmin* would be 73.02%. Thus, he concludes that *sangmin* made up the main group of believers.[872] The low percentage of *ch'ŏnmin* can be accounted for if we consider the fact that

---

[867] Hwang Sa-yŏng paeksŏ, line 20th.

[868] *Sŭngjŏngwŏn ilgi*, Togwang 19th year, Kihae 3th month, 5th day.
When Queen Dowager Cho, asked him how *yangban* could possibly be among these *Sahak* criminals, Yi Chin-yŏn's reply, saying that even if there were some *yangban* among them, they were just a bunch of insignificant people, supports this conclusion.

[869] Cho Kwang, *Chosŏn hugi*. (A'), p. 80.

[870] *Ibid.*,

[871] Ch'oe Yong-gyu, *op. cit.*, p. 244.

[872] *Ibid.*, p. 242-245.

the general population of *ch'onmin* was drastically reduced in the late Chosŏn dynasty and because of their lowly position they had probably low access to Catholicism.[873] The question of which of the two scholars, Cho Kwang or Kim Han-gyu, presents a more accurate picture remains a topic for further research.

In Ishii Hisao's research D, the occupations of 124 people out of 407 were identified: Among 121 males whose vocations were identified, the number of Confucian literati and people of medical vocations, who were *chungin* , were only 25, (20%). Thus, Ishii concludes that Catholicism after 1860 in Chosŏn society was not a religion for an aristocratic class but a religion for commoners (*minjung*). The *yangban* class was a minority at this time.[874] There were not many rich people either among the converts.[875] Most of the believers were poor and didn't have distinctive occupations. The intellectual class, which includes *yangban* and *chungin*, was only 20%. If we compare the above analysis (20 %) to the percentage of *yangban* and *chungin* of the previous periods, before 1846 (Research A : 41.04%, Research A': 26.86%, Research B: 48.5, Research C: 25.96%), it is clear that as the persecutions were accelerated, Catholicism moved from higher social class to lower social class.

From 1791, *chungin* believers led the revival movement of the Church. Hwang Sa-yŏng referred to a *chungin*, Ch'oe Ch'ang-hyŏn, as Moderator, indicating a position of authority in church affairs, and praised him as the most virtuous man among the believers.[876]

The *chungin* class in Chosŏn society, which was below the *yangban* class, had technological positions in the government. Although their status distinction and privileges were not equal to those of the *yangban* class, their

---

[873] *Ibid.*, p. 245.

[874] Ishi Hisao, p. 203-204.

[875] Dalet (tr.) *op. cit.*, (chung). p. 257.

[876] Hwang Sa-yŏng paeksŏ, line 32-34th.

professional and intellectual knowledge was almost equal to that of the *yangban* class. [877] Those *chungin* who contributed to the development of the Church were mostly translators of Chinese, medical doctors, and pharmacologists. [878] Chinese language translators tended to be relatively liberal and well informed about the international situations because of their interaction with foreign emissaries from China. Pharmacologists had great interest in China because of their professional interests in Chinsese medicine, and they were affluent on the whole. They came to be in contact with Catholic books in Chinese translation through their interactions with Chinese language translators or *yangban* scholars. The most representative person was Ch'oe Ch'ang-hyŏn. Although they were small in terms of number, *chungin* believers such as Yu Chin-gil, inspired by the spirit of Christianity which did not discriminate on the basis of social status, played an important role in the revival movement of the Church.

  To sum up, *yangban* played an important role in the formation of the early Chosŏn Church, and their contribution to the Church in terms of their introduction of the doctrinal books and establishing its foundation must be recognized. They also opened the door to *chungin* in shaping the leadership. Thus, it was *chungin* who played the more important role in the revival of the Church after the Sinyu Persecution wealth and faith. Continued

---

[877] cf. Han, Yŏng-u, "*Chosŏn hugi chungin e taehayŏ.*" *Han'guk hakpo*. 4-5. 1986. Chŏng Ok-ja, "Chosŏn hugi ŭi kisuljik chungin." *Chindan hakbo*. 61. 1986. Edward Wagner, "The Development and modern fate of *Chapkwa-chungin* lineages." *Hank'gukhak kukje haksul nonmunjip*. 1987. E. Wagner, "An Inquiry into the chungin class in the Yi dynasty." 1973. Yi Sŏngmu, "Chosŏn ch'ogi kisulgwan kwa kŭ chiwi." *Yu Hong-nyŏl paksa hwangap kinyŏm nonch'ong.* 1971.

[878] cf. Suzuki, Nobuaki, "Rishi Chōsen ni okeru tenshukyō juyōji no chūninsō no yakuwari." *Toyōsi kenkyū hōkoku* II, 1983. Yi Wŏn-sun, Chosŏn hugi chungin ch'ŭng ŭi sŏkyo suyong." *Han'guk munhwa*. 12. 1991.

persecutions, however, pushed the Church down to the lower classes of the social structure and thereby the foundation of the Church came to be built on *sangmin* class people.

Comparison of Male and Female Believers

What was the ratio of male to female believers in the case of Catholicism in the Chosŏn dynasty? The following statstics in table 5 summarize the conclusions of the previously described researchers: [879]

period	researcher	male		female		total
		number	%	number	%	number
1784-1802	Cho Kwang A	480	81.08	122	18.92	592
	Cho Kwang A'	513	74.13	179	25.87	692
	Kim Han-gyu B	98	67.12	48	32.88	146
1802-1846	Ch'oe Yong-gyu C	282	63.95	159	36.05	441
1866-1878	Ishii Hisao D	300	73.31	107	26.29	407
	Ko Hŭng-sik E	301	73.71	107	26.29	408

Table 5

According to the above statistics, male believers outnumbered female believers, roughly two to three times. With regard to this ratio, Kim Han-gyu argued that since the historical documents upon which Cho Kwang's research was based, such as *Hwang Sa-yŏng's paeksŏ, Sinyu sahak choein ch'uan,* and *Sŭngjŏngwon ilgi,* were mainly

---

[879] The above statistics was based on Ch'oe Yong-gyu, Cho Kwang A' and Ko Hŭng-sik.

concerned with the Church leaders, and consequently calculation of the percentages of female believers was critically low. And he argues that an analysis of *Sahak chingŭi* would reveal the truth more accurately.[880] Kim's argument is convincing, because it is consistent with Hwang Sa-yŏng's remark that there were many women believers at that time.

Ch'oe Yong-gyu's analysis B, which examined the period from 1830 to 1840 shows a rather higher percentage of women (36.5%) compared to previous periods. This indicates that after the Sinyu Persecution, women believers were increasing.[881]

Ishii Hisao's analysis, which examined the time of the Sinyu Persecution in 1866, shows the ratio of male to female believers as 3:1 (the number of females is 107 out of total of 407 believers, which is 26.0%). However, Ishii speculated that female believers probably outnumbered male believers, quoting a line in the *Taejŏn hoet'ong* (Comprehensive Compendium of the National Code) which says that except in the case of treason women were not arrested[882] and Hwang Sa-yŏng's remark that at the time of the Sinyu Persecution two thirds of the believers were female.[883]

In addition to the ratio of males and females, Ch'oe Yong-gyu analyzed the marital status of the believers as follows: 141 were married, 50 were either widows or widowers, 32 were single, and the status of 217 was unknown. The number of widows or widowers is notably large and it is very probable that there were more widows among the category of the unknown. Ch'oe related this to the fact that in a Confucian society remarriage was considered shameful for women, and he also noted that

---

[880] Kim Han-gyu. *op. cit.*, p. 54.
[881] Ishii Hisao, *op.cit.*, p. 202 footnote 8
[882] *Taejŏn hoet'ong*, Vol 5. Hyŏngjŏn (Criminal Law)
[883] Ishii Hisao. *op. cit.*, p. 202.

widows' unstable socio-economic status and their emotional desolateness might have played a role.[884] That is, those widows, after having been deprived of their economic and emotional stability, hoped for happiness in the other world and converted to Catholicism. This conjecture is supported by the fact that 39.74% of the women martyrs were widows.[885] One trial document from the *P'odoch'ŏng* also shows that a woman named Chang Im-i confessed that they converted because they hoped for happiness in the other world.[886]

Taking into consideration the fact that Catholic believers tended to remain single, Ch'oe identified 17 women who decided not to marry and one woman who remained a virgin after her marriage, and showed that all of these women became martyrs.[887] Most of the virgin martyrs were the descendants of those who died in the Sinyu Persecution, and we can conjecture that their strong religious tradition played a significant role in maintaining their faith.[888]

Ishii's research, which examined the Pyŏngin Persecution, also concludes that female believers had more zealous religious conviction than male believers on the basis of the following statistics: Among the 306 male believers, those who did not apostatize were 106 (34.6%) and those who became martyrs were 25 out of 106 (23.6%), while among the 107 female believers, those who did not apostatize were 50 (46.72%), and those who became martyrs were 27 out of 50 (54%).[889]

As indicated in Table 3, all five analyses show that

---

[884] Ch'oe Yong-gyu, *op. cit.*, p. 239.

[885] *Ibid.*, p. 239.

[886] *U-p'odoch'ŏng tŭngnok, Sinch'uk* (1841), the 4th month, 25th.

[887] Ch'oe Yong-gyu, *op. cit.*, p. 240.

[888] *Ibid.*,

[889] Ishii Hisao, *op. cit.*, (K) pp. 202-203.

the number of female believers was small in the early period, increased a little bit in the middle period, and then decreased in the late period, contradicting Hwang Sa-yŏng's statement that female believers were two thirds of the whole believers.[890] There is a general consensus in the scholarship that there were many female believers even at the time of the later persecutions. To understand this anomaly, we have to take into consideration that in the Chosŏn dynasty, the law was very leniently applied to women, especially to women of the *yangban* class, and women were arrested only after Catholicism was declared treason. So it is likely there were many more female believers than these statistics indicate.

How do we explain the great number of female believers? Part of the reason can be found in the teachings of Catholicism that women and men are equal. Female believers like Kang Wan-suk, who became a martyr in 1801[891] and Han Kyŏng-nyŏn, who became a martyr in the Kihae Persecution, educated ignorant people, took care of the sick, and administered private baptism to sick children. [892]

Comparison of the Geographical Residences of the Believers

The distribution of the geographical residences of the believers can be summarized as follows in Table 6:

---

[890] *Hwang Sa-yŏng paeksŏ* line 20.
[891] Chales Dallet, *op. cit.*, (sang) pp. 382-389.
[892] *Ibid.*, (chung) p. 519.

Comparison of the 1801 and the 1866 Persecutions

Period	1784		--		1801	
Researcher	A		A'		B	
	#	%	#	%	#	%
Seoul	270	45.60	351	50.72	94	64.40
Kyŏnggi	101	17.06	107	15.46		
Ch'ungch'ŏng	111	16.39	148	21.39	32	21.90
Chŏlla	80	11.00	84	12.14		
Kyŏngsang	2	0.34				
Kangwŏn	5	0.85				
Hwanghae			2	0.29		
Hamgyŏng						
P'yŏngan	3	0.51			20	13.7
unknown	20	3.38				
Total	592	100%	692	100%	146	100%

Period	180 -	1846	1866	--	1878
Researcher	C		D		E
	#	%	#	%	
Seoul	161	36.51	131	32.19	
Kyŏnggi	33	7.48	71	17.44	
Ch'ungch'ŏng	48	10.88	93	22.85	
Chŏlla	37	8.39			
Kyŏngsang	110	24.9	4	0.98	
Kangwŏn	26	5.90	6	3.93	
Hwanghae	11	2.49	11	2.70	
Hamgyŏng	4	0.91	1	0.25	
P'yŏngan	1	0.23	3	0.74	
unknown	10	2.27	77	18.92	
Total	441	100%	407	100%	408

Table 6

The population of Chosŏn in 1801 was reported to be 7,513,792 and the number of households as 1,757,973.[893] The census of 1799, Chŏngjo 23th year reported it as 7,412,681.[894] The number of believers at the time has been estimated at 10,000, which was only 0.14% of the total population.

Seoul was the biggest city in Chosŏn at that time, with a population of 189,153.[895]

In Research A, the number of those whose habitations were identified was 572 out of 592 (96.2%). Among those, residents of Seoul numbered 270 (45.06%).[896]

Research A' shows that the number of Seoul residents was 351 out of a total of 692 believers (50.72%), which is higher than in Research A.[897] *Sahak chingŭi*, the source of Kim's analysis, is an official record from the Ministry of Punishments and Police Station in Seoul. Therefore, most cases reported in these documents were those of Seoul residents, with the exception of some provincial cases which were transferred to the Seoul district or cases of provincial people who were arrested while staying in Seoul. Looking at *Sahak chingŭi*:

Seoul residents: 94 (64.4%)
Those sent to other provincial jurisdictions: 32 (21.9%)
People who came to Seoul from other provinces: 20(13. 7%)

Since nine people among the provincial people were recorded as transferred cases, all of the 137 people excluding the nine people were probably living in Seoul.

---

[893] *Chosŏn wangjo sillok*. Sunjo, the beginning year. Sinyu year, 12th month Kyŏngo.

[894] Pang Tong-in, "Ingu ŭi chŭngga," *Han'guksa* 13. p.306.

[895] Cho Kwang, *Chosŏn hugi ch'ŏnju kyohoesa yŏngu*. p.36.

[896] Kim Han-gyu, p.63.

[897] Cho Kwang, *Chosŏn hugi ch'ŏnjugyosa yŏn'gu*. p. 34.

Yi Pyŏk and Yi Sŭng-hun, who were the leaders in establishing the Church as an organization, came from Seoul. They were Namin whose academic circle was *Sŏngho chwap'a*.[898] The Catholic Church in Chosŏn was started by *Sŏngho chwap'a* people and was actively led by Seoul people. Religious meetings were also held at the houses of Chŏng Kwang-su, Yi Han-gyu, and Hwang Sa-yŏng, who lived in Seoul.[899] The main residence of the first priest, Chou Wen-mo, was the house of Ch'oe In-gil and Kang Wan-suk in Seoul. Thus, Seoul was the center of the new Christian community. However, we can not conclude that half of the believers were living in Seoul, as indicated in Table 6, because the sources of these analyses were the official documents of the Seoul district and areas near Seoul.[900]

In Research A', the number of believers in Kyŏnggi province was 107 out of 692 (15.46%). Among them, *yangban* occupied 70%. This high percentage of *yangban* in this province was interpreted as a characteristic of acceptance of a new cultural movement, and the fact that many people in this province later apostatized indicates that this new cultural movement was not transformed into a religious movement.[901]

In Cho Kwang's Research A, it is shown that the number of believers in Kyŏnggi, out of a total of 592 was 101 (17.06%): 56 inYanggŭn, 19 inYŏju, 15 in Kwangju, 5 in Ich'ŏn, 3 in P'och'ŏn, and one each in Koyang, Suwŏn, and Kaesŏng. In those places densely populated by believers, active figures such as Kwŏn Ch'ŏl-sin, Kwŏn Il-sin, Yi Ki-yang, Chŏng Yak-chong, and Kim Kŏn-sun conducted mission activities. Geographically, those places were conveniently connected to Seoul. In addition, the commercial atmosphere imparted by the markets that flourished then

---

[898] Chŏng Yag-yong, *Yŏyudang chŏnsŏ*. II. 15:39a.
[899] Ch'oe Sŏg-u, *Han'guk kyohoesa ŭi t'amgu*. pp. 75-77.
[900] Cho Kwang, (A') op. *cit.*, p.34.
[901] Cho Kwang, *Chosŏn hugi ch'onjugyosa yŏngu*. p.45 -46.

probably helped Catholicism spread in these areas.[902]

While Research A shows that 18.75% of the total number of believers (111 people) lived in Ch'ungch'ŏng province, Research A' shows a slightly higher percentage 21.39 %(148 people) for the province. Considering the account that three hundred households came to see Yi Chonch'ang off when he moved from Yŏsaul to Hongsan,[903] both figures seem to underrepresent the believers in this province.[904] However, both figures show Ch'ungch'ŏng province second only to Seoul in terms of the number of believers.

The place where Catholicism flourished most in Ch'ŏlla province was Chŏnju. Due to the mission efforts of two wealthy brothers, Yu Hang-kŏm and Yu Kwan-gŏm, a Christian community was established in Yŏnggwang.[905] There were also some believers in Chinsan, where Yun Chich'ung was martyred. Research A identified 80 out of 592 believers (11.66%) as Chŏlla residents and Research A' identified 84 out of 692 (12.14%). If we consider the report in Dallet that two hundred people were arrested in Chŏlla province during the Sinyu Persecution,[906] the figures in these analyses seem low.

Judging from the statement that there were records of the exile of Hamgyŏng and Kyŏngsang province people in the *Sahak chingŭi*, (which was destroyed by fire in the Great

---

[902] Cho Kwang, "*Sinyu pakhae ŭi sŏngkyŏk*," p.62.

[903] Charles Dallet, *op. cit.*, (sang) p. 365. Yi Chon-ch'ang contributed to the spread of Catholicism in the area of Naep'o, Ch'ungch'ŏng province.

[904] Cho Kwang, *op. cit.*, (A')

[905] Cho Kwang (A), p. 49.

[906] Charles Dallet, *op. cit.*, (sang), p. 527.

Comparison of the 1801 and the 1866 Persecutions

Earthquake of 1923 in Tokyo, [907] Catholicism quickly spread nationwide from the beginning, although the numbers may be small.

Ch'oe Yong-gyu's research C, which examined the Kihae and Pyŏngo periods, is consistent with A, A', B, and C in that Seoul shows the greatest population of believers (161 out of total of 441: 36.51%). [908] In interpreting the small number of believers, we have to take into consideration that after the Sinyu Persecution, many believers fled to remote areas, leaving their hometowns.

Unlike the other cases, Research C shows a rather high percentage of residence in Kyŏngsang province (110 out of total 441: 24.95%) and it also shows that there were some believers in Kangwŏn and Hwanghae provinces. The sharp increase of the believers in Kyŏngsang province probably should be attributed to the exile or migration of believers because of the persecutions.

Research D, which analyzed the number of people arrested during the Pyŏngin Persecution and interrogated at the Police Station in Seoul, indicates that the residence of 330 people out of 407 was clearly identified, and among them, 131 people (32.19%) were residents of Seoul and its vicinity. [909] Although Seoul had the largest population of believers even at that time, the fact that the number was drastically reduced to almost half compared to the early periods might indicate that many had scattered into other regions to escape the persecution. The Chosŏn government regarded the act of leaving one's hometown as a challenge to the traditional social rule. [910]

---

[907] Chu Myŏng-jun, "Paeksan hŭksu munkobon ch'ongsa ŭi sahakchingŭi wa pyŏkwip'yŏn." Han'guk kyohoesa nonmunchip. 1985. p.643.

[908] Ch'oe Yong-gyu, op. cit., p. 251.

[909] Ishii Hisao, op. cit., pp. 204-205.

[910] 1)Sahak chingŭi, p. 168.
    2)Sahak chingŭi, p. 158.
    3)Sahak chingŭi, p. 89.

Comparison of the Believers' Vocational and Economic State

In A, those whose occupations were clearly identified numbered only 123 (20.7%). Of those people, 94 were male (19.58% of the total males) and 29 were female (25.89% of the total females). Of these female believers, 17 were slaves, 12 were court ladies, merchants, and tailors. Of those who were arrested during the Sinyu Persecution, only 6 were government officials.

Those whose vocation was identified as farming were only 11 (8.94%), which is a very low percentage considering the fact that agriculture was the main industry. Most of those whose vocations were not identified were assumed to be farmers.[911] Those who were engaged in commerce or craftsmanship were 17 (13.82%), a higher percentage than farmers. If we include those who owned pharmacies (15 people: 12.2%) as merchants, the total percentage of this category is 26.02%. The merchants were petty merchants such as comb seller, wood seller, shoes seller, thread seller, porcelain seller or cooking oil seller. Those who were identified as craftsmen were 16 people (13.01%). They were carpenters, dyers, potters, and nine people who were identified as farm laborers and hunters.

Of the 146 people recorded in the *Sahak chingŭi*, only 62 people's occupations were identified. Of the unknown people, Kim analyzed 27 people as housewives, unmarried men and women, and 32 people as *yangban*..[912]

In discussing the occupations of the believers during the period from the Kihae to the Pyŏngo Persecutions, Ch'oe Yong-kyu identified only 68 occupations, which was 15.42% of the total 441 people. If 22 people who had Church related work were added to this, the percentage would be 20.41%.[913]

---

[911] Cho Kwang, "Sinyu pakhae..." (A), p.57.

[912] *Ibid.*, p. 60.

[913] Ch'oe Yong-gyu, *op. cit.*, p.247.

Since petty merchants made up 10%, petty craftsman 19% and those whose living was dependent on others such as servants and farm laborers were 18%, Ch'oe concludes that the economic situations of the believers were extremely difficult.[914] Unlike the time of the Sinyu Persecution, 22 people were identified as those who were engaged in church work for their living. Among those, 14 people were *yangban*. This also indicates the economic difficulty of the believers. As many as 25 people (27.78%) were identified as widows, or unmarried women. This was interpreted as an indication that many families had lost the head of the household and were deprived of their economic basis.[915]

The economic situations of the believers during the Pyŏngin Persecution (1866-1878) also seem to have been difficult: of 124 people (121 males and 3 females) whose vocations were identified out of the total 407 believers, medicine, 7; low ranked soldiers and government officials, 19; farmers, 32; merchants, 15; craftsmen, 12; free laborers, 13; others, 5.[916]

In contrast to this, some of the early Catholic believers were wealthy people. Han Chae-gyŏm, who was very loyal to Yi Ka-hwan, was said to be the richest man in Songdo, and his financial support for mission activities was considerable.[917] And there were people like Yu Hwang-gŏm, who had huge estates in Chŏlla province. When Yun Yu-il was dispatched as a secret envoy to invite Priest Chou Wen-mo, Yu Hwang-gŏm donated 400 *nyang* [918] and he also paid all of the expenses of Priest Chou's mission activities.[919] He was

---

[914] *Ibid.*, pp. 250-251

[915] *Ibid.*, p. 251.

[916] Ishii Hisao, *op. cit.*, (K), p.203.

[917] *Sahak chingŭi, (sang)*, (October 11, 1801)Sahŏnbu imun, Han Chae-gyŏm p'yŏn.

[918] *Sahak chingŭi,,* kwŏn 1. Kim Tal-sun milgye. p. 24.

[919] *Sahak chingŭi* (sang), 92-3. '

actively involved in the mission activities himself as well. Thus, his criminal charge was possession of excessive wealth and the alluring of other people with his money."[920] In addition, people like Kim Kŏn-sun,[921] Kang I-ch'ŏn,[922] Kim Sin-guk[923] and Kim Kwang-ok were reported to be affluent.[924]

However, as indicated in *yangban* Yi Ki-yang's statement, that "people were so poor that their wives were busy making a living,"[925] most believers lived in poverty. *Yangban* like Han Chŏng-hyŏn[926] and Yi Chu-hwang[927] were reported to be in extreme poverty. In his letter, Hwang Sa-yŏng, who himself was poor, also described extremely adverse economic situations of the believers of that time, saying "Chosŏn was poor but especially the believers were very poor. Those who could avoid hunger and cold were only ten people."[928]

When the Taewon'gun agreed to meet with the French bishop, Daveluy, who was in a provincial area, it took a long time to find money for the travel expenses of the envoy-- the money was finally provided by the Taewongun's in-laws, Cho

---

[920] *Ibid.*, Kim Tal-sun gye. sang. 25. Sahak choein Yu Hang-gŏm ch'uan. 59.

[921] *Sahak chingŭi* kwŏn 1. Kim Tal-sun milgye. p.24.

[922] Sinyu sahak choein Kang I-ch'on ch'uan. (1801. 3. 26.)

[923] Sinyu sahak choein Kim Sin-guk ch'uan. (1801.4.3) 33.

[924] C. Dallet. *op. cit.,* tome 1. p.169.

[925] Sahak choein Yi Ki-yang tŭng ch'uan. Yi Ki-yang kongch'o (1801.3.6.)

[926] C. Dallet, *op. cit.*, Tome 1. p.172.

[927] Sinyu sahak choein Kim-nyŏ tŭng ch'uan. Yi Chu-hwang kongch'o. (1801.4.17.)

[928] Hwang Sa-yŏng paeksŏ, line 91.

Ki-jin.[929] This suggests that unlike the earlier period, there may have been no wealthy people among the believers. The difficult economic situation of the believers can be partially attributed to: 1) the fact that the believers had to leave their hometown where their economic basis was. 2) When they were arrested by government officials, their property was confiscated.

Motivations for Conversion and Reasons for Apostasy

What were the believers' motivations for conversion? What were the reasons for apostasy? These questions are explored through particular cases drawn from earlier papers on this inquiry.

According to Research B, 128 people out of 146 believers of the Sinyu period (1801) expressed their inner motivations for conversion: [930]

Catholicism is a true religion and therefore I believe in happiness in the world to come: 16 people (13%)

I expect that I will be better off in this world: 16 people (13%)

I am curious about Catholicism: 16 people (13%)
(Many were *yangban* and male.)

Other reasons, such as coercion or non-religious reasons: 6 people (5%)

Of the external motivations, family heritage was the major reason especially among those of *yangban* or *chungin* background. Excluding 6 unknown people whose motivations were not identified, 19 people (38%) out of 50 indicated their family members' advocacy and the religious atmosphere of

---

[929] Yi Sŏn-kŭn, *Han'guksa*: ch'oegŭnse p'yŏn. Seoul: Chindan hakhoe. 1961. p.235.

[930] Kim Han-gyu, *op. cit.*, p. 77.

their family as the motivations.[931] Of 130 people who revealed their motivations, 31 people indicated that they converted due to reasons of kinship.

In Research C, which analyzed the period from the Kihae to the Pyŏngo Persecutions (1839-1846) external motivations rather than inner motivations were questioned: 119 people out of 441 revealed that they made contact with Catholicism through their family members and relatives, 45 people, through their acquaintances; and 2 people, through reading books out of curiosity.[932]

In Research D, which examined the latter period of the persecutions, the 1866 persecution, only 45 people out of 407 revealed their motivations: among them, 34 people indicated happiness in the world to come as their motivation.[933] Similarly, in Research E, 52 people out of 408 revealed their motivation, and 29 of them indicated happiness in the world to come as their motivations.[934] Of 408 people, 281 indicated that they converted through their family members' exhortations. Specifically, 52% were converted through family members such as parents, siblings and in-laws. This fact informs us how intimately Chosŏn society was structured and held together by kinship ties. On the other hand, the fact that 28.33% (85 people) were converted through neighbors and 19.67% (59 people) through the exhortations of a church *hoejang* (church catechist) also reveals two things: 1) Catholicism was in the process of expanding its sphere beyond the limits of a kinship community and thereby becoming transformed into a mass religion, and 2) The mission activities of professional church workers such as *hoejang* were being accelerated, which meant that the mission was conducted systematically and the

---

[931] *Ibid.,* pp.75-77.
[932] Ch'oe Yong-gyu, *op. cit.,* p. 256-7.
[933] Ishii toshio, *op. cit.,*
[934] Ko Hŭng-sik, *op. cit.,* p. 280.

Church was being institutionalized.⁹³⁵ Thus, Ch'oe concludes that the most distinct inner motivation was the hope for a better world and this is consistent with the conclusion of Ishii Hisao.

To summarize all five of the researches comprehensively, the late Church as it subsequently developed, grew more and more toward the other world, hoping for God's love in heaven. The explanation for this tendency to seek other worldly ties lay in the bleak realities caused by the natural catastrophes of the time, the corruption of officials, and the continuing persecutions. The believers in the Pyŏngin period were particularly very much interested in heaven and hell and they tended to be mystic.⁹³⁶ This contrasts with the early believers at the time of the Church establishment. People like Yi Sŭng-hun, Kwŏn Ch'ŏl-sin, Kwŏn Il-sin, Chŏng Yag-yong, and Chŏng Yak-chong, converted to Catholicism mainly because they were interested in Western science, although they would not be entirely uninterested in religious aspects. Thus, they were very rationalistic. That is, they accepted Catholicism as a social gospel.⁹³⁷

Great interest in Western science and foreign systems of knowledge were found especially in *yangban* believers. The initial motivation of Yi Sŭng-hun was his interest in mathematics.⁹³⁸ Kim Kŏn-sun, the heir of the renowned Korean loyalist Kim Sang-hŏn, said that he converted to Catholicism because he wanted to build great ships and weapons to take revenge against the Manchus.⁹³⁹

Thus, as the nature of the faith of the believers in the Pyŏngin period became distanced from that of the early

---

⁹³⁵ *Ibid.*, p.285.

⁹³⁶ Ishii Hisao, p.208.

⁹³⁷ This term is used, here, to refer to a new ideology within the setting of a new system of knowledge.

⁹³⁸ Yi Sŭng-hun's first letter to missionary in North church at Beijing in 1789. *Mannam kwa midŭm ŭi kilmok esŏ*. p.12.

⁹³⁹ Sinyu sahak choein, Yi Ki-yang tŭng ch'uan. 68.

Church, the will power of believers to participate in changing the society decreased and thereby the potentiality of Catholicism as a force for social reform also declined.

Of 146 people who appeared in the *Sahak chingŭi,* 90 people (62%) committed apostasy. Among them, 34 were *yangban* (out of a total 56 *yangban*), and 41 were *sangin* (out of a total 67 *sangin*). In both classes, about 60 % renounced their faith. Factors such as class or gender appear not to have played a role in apostasy.[940] The reasons for renunciation of their faith were not so much inner conflicts as outside forces. In most cases, people apostatized to avoid torture or the death sentence. In some cases, however, doubts on the Christian doctrines involving the prohibition of ancestor worship seem to have played a role. Young literati in the *namin* faction, who converted to Catholicism out of academic curiosity, typifies this case.[941]

In the analysis of the apostates during the Pyŏngin Persecution (Research D), 229 people renounced their faith. Of these people, 139 identified their fear of the persecution as the reason for apostasy.[942] The conclusion of Research E, which examined the same period, is similar in this respect. It is clear that the most compelling reasons for apostasy were not inner conflicts but outer forces. The same high percentages of apostasy both in the early period and in the later period provides yet more indirect evidence that the brutality of the persecutions continued.

2. Comparison of the Prohibition Policies and the Applications of the Law.

In previous chapters, we examined the policies on

---

[940] Kim Han-gyu, *op. cit.*, p. 83.
[941] *Ibid.*, p.85.
[942] Ishii Hisao, p.209.

Comparison of the 1801 and the 1866 Persecutions

Catholicism of the Chosŏn government during the persecutions. In this section, we will survey the prohibition policies on Catholic books, by examining the nature of the *Ch'ŏksa yunŭm* "Decree on Rejecting Unorthodoxy", which was issued four times by the government. A particular concern is whether the policies were consistent throughout the persecutions or whether they changed. What laws were applied and how were they applied?

The persecution of Catholicism started with a ban on Catholic books.[943] To begin with, in early 1785 Censor Yu Ha-wŏn proposed a ban on Catholic books translated into Chinese,[944] and the next year, Censor Kim I-so urged harsh punishment of those who brought books into Korea without permission.[945] Two years later Censor Yi Sa-gyŏm expressed his concern that even uneducated people in the countryside were reading the Catholic books, and this would eventually bring chaos to the nation.[946] Responding to these opinions, the Border Defense Council called for books on Catholicism to be burned.[947] At the request of another official, an order for the burning of the Catholic books in the *Hongmun'gwan* (Office of Special Counselors) was issued.[948] The importation of Catholic books, which was usually handled through a bookstore named *Yurich'ang* through emissaries to China, was also banned.[949] However,

---

[943] *Chosŏn wangjo sillok*, Chŏngjo. 11th year, 4th month, Kapcha.

[944] *Chosŏn wangjo sillok*, Chŏngjo. 9th year, 4th month, Mucha.

[945] *Chosŏn wangjo sillok*, Chŏngjo. 10th year, 1st month, Chŏngmyo.

[946] *Chosŏn wangjo sillok*, Chŏngjo. 11th year, 4th month. Kapcha.

[947] *Chosŏn wangjo sillok*, Chŏngjo. 12th year, 8th month. ¬lmi.

[948] *Chosŏn wangjo sillok*, Chŏngjo. 15th year, 11th month, Kyemi. "Kyujang'gak and its catalogue." *Oda sensei shoju kinen Chōsen ronshū*. pp.399-416.

[949] *Chosŏn wangjo sillok*, Chŏngjo 10th year, 1st month. Chŏngmyo.

despite the prohibition, Catholic books continued to be available. Thus, in a memorial, Chŏng Yag-yong once said that Catholic books were so popular that there was no one who did not read them.[950]

After the possession of Catholic books in one's house was forbidden in the 12th year of Chŏngjo (1788),[951] it became extremely difficult to study the Catholic teachings, and therefore the anti-heterodoxy arguments of the Confucian literati on Catholic doctrines came to lack theoretical underpinnings. This was also true in regard to anti-West argumentation (*Sŏyang ch'ŏksaron*) after the middle of the 19th century. In 1866, just before the Pyŏngin Persecution, the government decided to completely ban Catholic books. Having found out through Ch'oe Hyŏng's confession that there was a printing place, the government besieged the house in T'aep'yŏng-dong where a bishop was staying, confiscated the books and the printing machines, and burned them all in the yard of the court.[952] At this time, Ch'oe Hyŏng was beheaded on the charge of publishing *Sŏng'gyo ilgwa* and *Sŏngch'al giryak*.[953] From this time on, doctrines were spread by oral tradition. The prohibition policy on the Catholic books was consistent from the beginning to the end of the persecutions. However, the degree of its severity varied.

As Queen Dowager Kim came into power after the death of King Chŏngjo, the position of the government suddenly changed as the *Noron Pyŏkp'a* grasped political power. Chŏng Yag-yong described the situation at that time:

---

[950] *Chosŏn wangjo sillok*, Chŏngjo 21st year, 6th month, Kyŏngin.
[951] *Chosŏn wangjo sillok*, Chŏngjo 10th year, 1st month, Chŏngmyo.
[952] C. Dallet. Chŏng'Ki-su (tr.), *Chosŏn kyohoesa sŏsŏl*. (Seoul:T'amgudang, 1966).
[953] *Ilsŏngnok*, Kojong 3rd year, 1st month, 18th day.

With King Chŏngjo now deceased, there was a sudden change in the relationship between the government and the public. Those people in the faction, to expand their power, were seeking out Catholic believers day and night with the list of the names of the people to be killed. The time was six years after the Chinese priest; Chou Wen-mo came in secret and spread the Western religion. As the religion flourished day by day, month by month men and women, higher people and lower people, gathered together and studied, from villages in the city to remote countryside, more than a hundred people, the doctrines.[954]

Indeed, the policy on Catholicism had drastically changed. Starting in the last month of 1800, the government vigorously arrested Catholic believers, and in 1801, the Great Sinyu Persecution broke out. Queen Dowager Kim, pointing out that King Chŏngjo's mild policy had failed, emphasized the need for a new strong policy, as follows: "Our previous King always said that if the orthodoxy is elucidated, heterodoxy will perish on its own. And yet, as I am informed, the heterodoxy is flourishing day by day from Seoul to the countryside. How can we not be afraid?"[955]

The Queen Dowager denounced the nature of the heterodoxy, which destroyed morals by not recognizing father and king, and turned people into barbarians and beasts,[956] and she ordered the procedure of extinction on the 11th day of the First Month, 1801: "Governors and Magistrates must dissuade the Catholic believers from their heterodoxy by

---

[954] *Yŏyudang chŏnsŏ* I. kwŏn 15. 23.
Chŏng Tasan chŏnsŏ . p. 311.

[955] Yi Man'ch'ae (ed.), *Pyŏgwi p'yŏn*, kwŏn 5. Sinyunyŏn sagyolŭl tasŭrim.

[956] *Ibid.*, p. 271.

enlightening and admonishing them, and must warn cautiously those people who are not Catholics. ... If anyone fails to change his mind even after such forbiddance, he shall be prosecuted by the law of treason. In every village the law of Five Family Mutual Surveillance must be put into effect, and if there is anyone who is Catholic, he must be reported to the authorities and punished. And if such a person still remains recalcitrant, he shall be executed by capital punishment and he shall have no descendants."[957]

In addition, the embassies to Beijing were thoroughly checked to block the inflow of Catholic books.[958] To attack Catholicism at its very roots, only one believer was to be exiled to one village,[959] contacts from outsiders were prohibited, and even the contacts from his lineage members were to be maximally restricted.[960]

As it happened, the onset of the first persecution and the issuance of the first decree to formally reject heterodoxy came about just when the government was elaborating its response to the threats it believed it now must unequivocally face. The Chosŏn government issued *Ch'ŏksa yunŭm* (Decree on Rejecting Unorthodoxy) four times during the period from the 1801 Persecution to the end of the persecutions in 1878. Fearing that the people might rebel after Queen Dowager Kim's cruel suppression of Catholic believers, the government tried to convince people of the necessity of taking harsh measures by explaining why Catholicism was an evil doctrine and by emphasizing the seriousness of the crimes the believers had committed. Thus the first Decree on Rejecting Unorthodoxy was issued, describing how the government came be regard Catholicism not merely as a heterodoxy but as a threat to traditional principles of social order, thus indicating why the government changed its policy to one of forceful

---

[957] *Ibid.*, p. 271.
[958] *Pipyŏnsa tŭngnok*, kwŏn 192. p.369.
[959] *Ibid.*, p.313.
[960] *Sahak chingŭi* p.43.

suppression: "Our predecessor King (Chŏngjo) tried to move both dragons and snakes and treat them as humans, but killed male and female whales as well, I (King Sunjo) will terminate rejection only by rejecting."[961] In spite the strong policy, however, Catholicism, contrary to the expectation of the government, continued to spread. In the reign of Hŏnjong, the Chosŏn diocese was established and a French priest came and conducted missionary activities. The second *Ch'ŏksa yunŭm*, which was issued by Hŏnjong, explained why Catholicism must be rejected, focusing more on the theoretical issues such as God, Jesus, ancestor worship ritual, the relationship between subjects and their king, baptism, heaven and hell, etc.[962] It particularly stressed that it was a deception for God to come to the world as a man, Jesus, to have died and to have become God again.[963] Furthermore, it pointed to some aspects which caused social controversy, saying, "If Catholicism is a correct religion, why do these people gather together on dark nights in a closed room, and extremely ignorant people like bastards, those who complain about the government, those who covet others' wealth, or those who are adulterous, become united with their heads and tails hiding, calling each other in baptismal name?"[964]

The government suspected that there might be a connection between the appearance of foreign ships and the Catholic Church. As the Western superpowers encroached, Confucian literati including Yi Hang-no called for a policy of *ch'ŏkyang ch'ŏksa* (anti-West and anti-heterodoxy), which fully fledged became *Wijŏng ch'ŏksaron* (defending orthodoxy and rejecting heterodoxy). Thus, pressure mounted for another persecution. And yet King Ch'ŏlchong, probably because his grandmother, the ¬nŏn'kun's wife, Song-ssi, and

---

[961] *Chosŏn wangjo sillok*, Hŏnjong 5th year, 10th month, Kyŏnjin 18th day.
[962] *Sahak chingŭi*, p.43.
[963] *Ibid.*,
[964] *Ibid.*,

his aunt, Sin-ssi had ties to Catholicism, was rather mild in his policy on Catholicism. [965]

The Taewŏn'gun, in his early regency period during the reign of Kojong, was rather mild. However, as the *pyŏkp'a* faction intensified its pressures and the intrusion of the Western powers was linked to Catholicism, he suddenly changed his policy in order to secure his political power, and began a severe persecution. A *Ch'ŏksa yunŭm* decree was issued twice during the reign of Kojong. The first emphasized the imminent threat of heterodoxy which "would soon bring a great catastrophe to the country"[966] The second one was similar to the first one, except that anti-West arguments were more intensified. [967]

To be sure, government officials who wanted to maintain the social order as it was and strengthen the structure of the traditional society, understood Catholicism as a reform theory. In such a situation, it was only to be expected that the rejection of a demand for reform would be followed by a persecution.

On the other hand, the policy on Catholicism at times was used politically, particularly in connection with partisan politics (both in 1801 or in 1866). Queen Dowager Kim-ssi, a *Pyŏkp'a* queen, used the policy in order to eliminate her *sip'a* opponents, who were involved in the execution of her brother during the reign of King Chŏngjo. In 1866, the Taewŏn'gun used the policy on Catholicism in order to secure his political power.[968]

What sort of laws were applied to those Catholic believers who violated the prohibition on Catholicism order? As the Sinyu Persecution was in progress, high-ranking

---

[965] Yi Wŏn-sun, *Han'guk ch'ŏnju kyohoesa*. (Seoul: T'amgudang. 1970.) p.163.

[966] *Kojong sillok*, Kojong 3rd year, 8th month, 3rd day.

[967] Ch'ŏksa yunŭm, Kojong 18th year, 5th month, 16th day. (in the possession of the Beineke Library, Yale University).

[968] Yi Wŏn-sun, *Han'guk ch'ŏnju kyohoesa yŏngu*. p. 134.

officials including *Chief* State Councilor Sim Hwan-ji insisted that Catholicism be exterminated only by serious criminal laws. 969 Consequently, a strong policy which enforced capital punishment continued to the end of the 1866 Persecution. At first, the arrested believers were prosecuted by the laws of theft in the police station. Later, they came to be prosecuted in the *Ŭigŭmbu (State Tribunal)*, because the generous treatment they received from the Police chief, Sin Tae-hyŏn, became a controversial issue.970 Thus, those who maintained their faith to the end were convicted on charges of seeking to destroy the socio-political order, and were executed. Those who were deeply involved in Catholicism, even if they renounced their faith, were severely punished according to the degree of their involvement, and were exiled971

In particular, Hwang Sa-yŏng, Yu Hwang-gŏm, and Yu Kwan-gŏm, who were convicted of being involved with the foreign powers, were sentenced to beheading and dismemberment (*nŭngji ch'ŏch'amhyŏng*), by which their bodies were cut into six pieces and their names were recorded in the list of slaves.972 Hwang Sim, who was involved in the *Hwang Sa-yŏng's Silk Letter,* as he was supposed to deliver the letter, was convicted of the crime of accomplice to treason, and Kim Hwan-sin, who did not report it to the government even though he was aware of Hwang Sa-Yŏng' s letter, was convicted of the crime of withholding knowledge of a serious crime. Those who possessed Catholic books were encouraged to surrender themselves, but if they were arrested in the possession of the books, they were convicted of that specific crime and were exiled. One example was Cho Un-hyŏng, who was living in Yŏju, Kyŏnggido, but was exiled to Hyŏnp'ung in consequence of being convicted of this crime.

---

969 *Sŭngjŏngwŏn ilgi*. ch'aek 97, p.288.

970 Hwang Sa-yŏng paeksŏ, 29th line,

971 Cho Kwang, *op. cit.*, p. 193.

972 *Chosŏn wangjo sillok,* Sunjo, the beginning year, 11th month, Muin.

[973]

From the Kihae Persecution in 1839, the government allowed the officials to convict those who studied the Catholic books of the crime of delusion and to sentence them to *putae sich'am* (beheading without waiting for an order from the authorities),[974] and even *sŏnch'am hukye* (beheadding first and reporting later) was allowed. it should also be noted that during this period was that it was prohibited to exile Catholic believers to an island. The government used such cautions to prevent Catholic believers from hatching conspiracies even while serving criminal sentences.

Despite all these prohibitions and severe punishments, however, there was no sign of the decline of Catholicism. This situation was deplored by the government in terms such as "They were not afraid of the law at all."[975] Indeed, in the heart of those believers who could not renounce their faith, the law of the Lord preceded the law of their king. Yi To-gi in Ch'ungch'ŏng province in 1789,[976] Yun Chi-ch'ung, who was involved in the Chinsan Incident, and Chŏng Ha-sang in the Kihae Persecution, all embraced martyrdom explicitly stating that the law of their Lord was more important than the law of the government.[977]

---

[973] *Sahak chingŭi*, p.18.

[974] *Ilsŏngnok*, Hŏnjong, Kihae year. 8.14 & 15.

[975] *Kojongsillok*, Kojong 3rd year, 8th month, 3rd day.

[976] C. Dallet, *op. cit.*, (sang), p.407.

[977] Chŏng Ha-sang, "Sangjae sangsŏ" in *Sunkyoja wa chŭnggŏjatŭl*. p.136.

3. Reflections on and Implications of the Institutional and Doctrinal Development and the Persecutions of Catholicism in 19th Century Korea.

Established in 1784 by lay people, an action that had no precedent in the history of Christian mission activities, the Chosŏn Church went through 59 years without a priest: 10 years from 1784 to 1794, 33 years from 1801 (the Sinyu Persecution) to 1834, and 6 years from 1839 (the Kihae Persecution) to 1845, and 10 years from 1866 (the Pyŏngin Persecution) to 1876.

Because the Church was self-generated through the efforts of its lay membership, structurally the organization was operated by "a pseudo ecclesiastic hierarchy". As the believers realized that their own self-efforts and activities were inadequate, they started a movement for inviting a priest. As a result, when the first priest in Korea, the Chinese Chou Wen-mo, came, he was welcomed by the Chosŏn believers, and this enhanced and hastened the understanding of the organization of a newly introduced religion.

The prohibition of Catholicism ordered by the Chosŏn government, however, forced the Church to go underground where, consequently, only covert organizations such as the Myŏngdohoe, or The Women's Club were active. Soon, however, this newly formed community saw over 1,000 people baptized,[978] and after 10 years of persecution, the number of believers increased to 4,000.[979] By the year 1801, the number of believers amounted to 10,000. To be sure, the mission activities of Priest Chou, the doctrinal studies in secret gatherings, and probably the fraternity which they formed and experienced in this new religious community, contributed to this result.[980]

---

[978] C. Dallet, *op. cit.*, (sang) p. 312.
[979] *Ibid.*, p. 67. & *op. cit.*, (sang), p.371.
[980] *Ibid.*, (sang). p.371.

When the persecution occurred in 1801, the believers, in order to escape persecution, began to move to the remote countryside, gradually forming a *kyouch'on* (village of brothers in the faith). The formation of *kyouch'on* was both spontaneous and autonomous. Most of these people had to leave their family property and their lineage members behind them when they moved, and they started to make a living by fire field farming, tobacco cultivation or pottery making. In a society which was tightly interwoven by the claims of kinship and a strong sense of territory (*chiyŏn*), it was even an anti-filial action (*pulhyŏ*) to leave the ancestral lineage and residence. But they left their place of residence to escape the persecution. Thus, the Sinyu persecution forced them to scatter, which in turn, spread Catholicism across the country.

Even in the midst of such difficult living in "villages of brothers in the faith" (*kyouch'on*), the Catholic believers attempted to invite a priest. Several requests for a priest to the Beijing Diocese and the Holy See of Rome brought an unexpected achievement. In 1831, the Chosŏn Diocese was founded and the missionaries were dispatched by the Paris Foreign Mission Society. Thus the Korean Church came to be completed institutionally.

To look inside the Church, the leadership roles in the early period were performed by *yangban*, but before long *chungin* also participated, until the outbreak of the Pyŏngin Persecution (1866). With the establishment of the Diocese and the arrival of French missionaries, however, leadership of the Chosŏn Church shifted to an institution centering around a bishop and priests, and the Church continued to develop, though it occasionally declined in the wake of the persecutions, especially after Pyŏngin year (1866).

Year	Number of Believers
1784 :	Establishment of the Church
1794 :	4,000
1800 :	10,000
1836 :	7,095
1839 :	10,000
1850 :	11,000

1853 :	12,175
1855 :	13,638
1857 :	15,206
1859 :	16,700
1861 :	18,035
1866 :	23,000
1883 :	12,035

Table 7 : *The number of the believers from 1784 to 1883* [981]

Despite prohibition by the government, in 1865, the early period of Kojong's reign, the number of believers was over 23,000. This was the period when twelve French missionaries had come to Chosŏn and was conducting active mission work. In so doing the French missionaries were taking advantage of the Chŏlchong reign, which had a relatively mild policy on active Catholicism. Internally, on the other hand, several incidents — the uprising against a corrupt official, Paek Nak-sin in Chinju, uprisings in Chŏlla, Kyŏngsang, and the surge of a new native religion, *Tonghak* — signaled that Chosŏn society was dissolving.[982]

From 1866 to 1883, the number of Catholic believers was reduced by half. After the Kihae Persecution in 1839, French missionaries reported to their superior in France and in Beijing about the persecution of the Chosŏn government. The Pontiff sent a letter consoling the believers. But the provocation of the armed French warships in 1866 finally caused the greatest persecution in the history of Catholicism in Chosŏn, the Pyŏngin Persecution, the result of which was the drastic decline in the number of believers during this period.

However, the Chosŏn Catholic Church did not perish, and there emerged two factors which explained the survival of

---

[981] Kim Mong-ŭn, "Han'guk sahoe pyŏndong kwa ch'ŏnjukyo." *Han'guk sahoe wa kat'ollisijŭm.*
(Seoul: Kyŏngsewŏn. 1983) p.38.

[982] Dallet, (tr). *op. cit.,* p.213.

the Church. Externally, the Catholic Church had become institutionalized. Centering around Seoul, Catholicism was organized across the country. Furthermore, it was also connected to Beijing and to Rome.

In the belief that doctrines should be taught, much effort was put on the spread of the ideology of Christianity through hand copying of the translated books of doctrines, publications of doctrinal books written in Korean, and the distributing and teaching of doctrines. The early Church was not systematically complete. Self-practice such as prayer and meditation was the main focus of religious life.[983] The distribution of religious relics and holy images also contributed to the understanding of the doctrines of this new religion.

While *yangban* read the Catholic books translated into Chinese, the Catholics' books, written in *hangŭl*, were widely read by the common people who could read *hangŭl*. Government officials deplored the situation in these terms: "The evil doctrine of Ch'ŏnju (the Lord) has appeared and it is very possible that this will infect the minds of the populace. Recently we heard that many ignorant people in the countryside were victimized by this evil doctrine and yet they read and circulate these books translated into Chinese or into Korean."[984]

The appearance of doctrinal books, already in 1789, such as *Sŏnggyŏng chikhae,* which was translated into *hangŭl* by Ch'oe Ch'ang-hyŏn, supports this.[985] However, the believers in general did not seem to have a strong understanding of the doctrines. In his letter to the Cardinal in Rome, Antonelli, Alexander de Gouvea (1751- 1808) wrote, "Their (Korean Catholic believers') faith is strong, but due to the lack of books and experienced people, I found their

---

[983] Ch'oe Sŏg-u, "Sahak chingŭi rul t'onghaesŏ pon ch'ogi ch'ŏnju kyohoe yŏn'gu." *Kyohoesa yŏngu.* 2. p.31.

[984] *Ilsŏngnok*, Chŏnjo, chŏngmi year, 4th month, 27th day (kapja).

[985] Cho Hwa-sŏn, "Sŏnggyŏng chikhae yŏngu." *Ch'oe Sŏg-u sinbu hoegap kinyŏm Han'guk kyohoesanonch'ong.* p.256.

knowledge in doctrines very superficial."[986] While *yangban* or intellectual male believers studied doctrinal books such as Matteo Ricci's *Ch'ŏnju silŭi, Chindo jajŭng,* and *Ch'ilkŭk* as well as the Ten Commandments and prayer books, lower class people accepted faith simply after studying the Ten Commandments and prayer books. Two thirds of the believers have memorized Ten Commandments,[987]

Ch'ilkŭk (Seven Overcomings) is a book written by a Jesuit priest, D. Pantoja (1571-1618), which introduced love, gentleness, self-control, faithfulness, diligence, generosity, and patience as seven virtues which can overcome the roots of sin, greed, arrogance, licentiousness, laziness, jealousy, anger, and fornication.

Chŏng Ha-sang and Chŏng Yak-chon, together with Kwon Sang-hak and Yi Chong-ŏk, composed a song *"sipkyemyŏngga"* in 1779.[988] A doctrinal book called *"Sinmyŏng ch'ohaeng"* was teaching about Christian love, how one must love everybody like his own brother. Because all men are God's children, all men are created equal after God's image. Therefore to love or hate a man is to love or hate your Lord.[989] Sin T'ae-bo heard from a believer that in Catholicism, there are no *taein* (great men) or *soin* (small-minded men) and there is no *yangban* or *sangnom*.[990] He said to the *kwanchang*, "Once you come in here, whether you are *yangban* or *sangnom*, it is of no matter."

The Catholic books that were called "*Sasŏ* (evil books)" at that time, interested the persecuters as well as the

---

[986] "Kubea chugyo ka p'ogyosŏngŏng changkwan eygey ponaen ch'ŏttchae sŏhan (1790),"
Mannam gwa mitŭm ŭi kilmok eysŏ, Seoul: Han'guk kyohoesa yŏnguso. l989. p.134.

[987] Kim Han-gyu, *op. cit.*, pp. 78-79.

[988] Ha Sŏng-nae, *Ch'ŏnju kasa yŏn'gu* , Seoul: Hwang' Sŏk-du nuga sŏwŏn.1985. pp.147-160

[989] *Sinmyŏng ch'ohaeng* (ha) 64b-65a.

[990] C. Dallet, *op. cit.*,(tr.), (sang), p. 378. Ibid., tome. p.388.

persecuted. Seeing that Catholicism spread through books,[991] the government, beginning in Chŏngjo, prohibited by law the import and distribution of the Catholic books, in an attempt to block the source. This was ideological persecution. The Catholic books that were confiscated and burned were as many as 120 items, 111 *kwŏn* and 119 books. Of those, the Korean versions were 82 items, 111 *kwŏn* and 128 books. [992] This provides evidence of how widely these Catholic books were distributed and read among common people.

As most of those who possessed, copied, and distributed the doctrinal books translated in Chinese were arrested after the Sinyu Persecution, Catholic books became almost extinguished except for some few possessed by nameless believers. Not only the books but also the people who could teach the doctrines became rare. Then, a method of teaching doctrines evolved which adapted to the situation, "Listening by ears and reciting by lips." Consequently, the simple Ten Commandments and *Ch'ilkŭk* were mostly taught in the education of doctrines.[993]

Another motive for adopting the Ten Commandments and *Ch'ilkŭk* as prncipal texts for teaching doctrines can be conjectured: As Catholicism came to be criticized as unethical and disloyal after Yun Chi-ch'ung's p'yejebunju, and Hwang Sa-yŏng's *paeksŏ* (silk letter) incident, it is very likely the believers deliberately emphasized the Ten Commandments and *Ch'ilkŭk*, because these two doctrines were compatible with Confucian ethics. In elucidating the Ten Commandments in his *Sangjae sangsŏ*, Chŏng Ha-sang claimed that Catholicism was not heterodoxy but an orthodoxy, as follows: "The Ten Commandments can be reduced to two lessons: One is to love God above all things created, and the other is to love other people like himself. The first three commandments are about how to serve God, and

---

[991] *Ilsŏngnok*, Sunjo 33rd year, 11th month 8th day.

[992] Cho Kwang, *Chosŏn hugi ch'ŏnjugyosa yŏngu*. p. 91.

[993] *Ilsŏngnok,* Sunjo, Ŭlhae year, 6th month, 19th day.

the rest of the seven commandments are about cultivating one's mind. Not even Confucian filial piety is greater than this.[994] Furthermore, Chŏng Ha-sang vehemently criticized the actions of the government, saying that without studying its origin and doctrines, they simply declared Catholicism to be a heterodoxy, persecuting Catholicism by imprisonments and executions.[995] Prof. Pak Chong-hong maintains that with Chŏng Ha-sang's *Sangjae sangsŏ*, Catholicism in the Chosŏn dynasty reached its zenith in understanding the fundamental spirit of Christianity.[996]

After the establishment of the Chosŏn Diocese in 1831, religious education was conducted mainly with the doctrinal books that French missionaries brought with them. It was in 1864 that the most typical one, *Sŏnggyo yorimundap*, was published by wood block printing at the printing place which Bishop Berneux secretly equipped. In addition, the books about ethics and spirituality were all published by wood block printing, secretly in the 1860's: *Chŏnjusŏnggyo konggwa, Chŏnju sŏnggyo yegyu, Sinmyŏng ch'ohaeng, Hoejoe chikchi, Yŏngse taeŭi, Sŏngch'al kiryak, Ch'ŏndang chikno, Sahu muksang,* and *Sŏnhaeng pokchong.*

Another method of doctrinal education which was actively adopted in the 1850's and 60's was by way of a song, *Chŏnju kasa.* At the time when there were few priests, the believers were scattered, and gathering was in secret, the method of using song proved effective in teaching doctrinal knowledge in a short time. *Chŏnju kasa* was composed in a traditional Korean rhyme, *sasacho* (4 and 4), the lyrics of which say that the true world we will live in is the world to come and this world is nothing but a journey. Therefore, this world is a place to prepare for eternal life. The second priest in Korea, Ch'oe Yang-ŏp composed the words of the song after he understood the Christian ideology.

---

[994] Chŏng Ha-sang, Sangjaesangsŏ, *pyŏgwip'yŏn*, p. 40.
[995] *Ibid.,*
[996] Pak Chong-hong, *Han'guk ssasangsa nongo*, (Seoul: Sŏmundang, 1977), p.347.

In the late period, doctrinal education for common people became simpler. In one of his letters in 1860, Father Feron wrote that in order to believe Catholicism, believers must avoid all heretic rituals, but must call "Jesus" and "Maria".[997] In fact, Kim Rosa, Yu Paoro, and Kim Tae-kŏn invoked Jesus and Maria, when they were arrested in November of 1838.[998] This seems to have been influenced by the reciting of "Namuamitabul" in Buddhism.

One analysis of the Pyŏngin Persecution indicates that participation in the holy ceremony helped believers maintain their faith during the persecutions. It was reported that more of those who were baptized by priests maintained their faith than those who were baptized in private rituals. In the case of the believers who received the confirmation, the ratio of those who apostatized to those who maintained their faith is 19.24%: 80.76%.[999] The report also shows that the more they partook in confessions, the more strongly they maintained their faith.[1000]

The statements of the believers recorded in the documents of the P'odoch'ŏng (the Police Station) indicates that the doctrinal knowledge of the believers was very shallow. Most of them chanted simple prayers every morning or everning like *Sipkye* (the Ten Commandments), *Ch'ŏnjugyŏng* (Lord's prayer), *Sŏnghogyŏng* (In the name of the Father, the Son, and the Holy Ghost), and *Sŏngmogyŏng* (Hail Mary). There were some intellectual believers like *yangban* Hwang Sŏk-tu,[1001] but most of the believers were uneducated *sangin*, whose faith was simple-minded but strong enough to maintain the Church during the time of the Pyŏngin Persecution.[1002]

---

[997] C. Dallet. *op. cit.*, (ha) p.302.

[998] C. Dallet. *op. cit.*, (chung), p. 427, p. 446 & p. 121.

[999] Ko Hŭng-sik, *op. cit.*, p. 287.

[1000] *Ibid.*, p.298.

[1001] *Chwap'odoch'ŏng tŭngnok,* Pyŏnin 2nd month, 3rd day.

[1002] Ko Hŭng-sik, *op. cit.*, p. 288.

Ishii also maintains that because the main layer of the believers of the Pyŏngin period was the lower classes, for whom philosophical theory was not needed, a faith which was born more of instinct could easily turn into the motive power of action.[1003]

      Christian martyrdom can be defined as voluntary death by those who witness the faith and truth of Christianity to defend such faith and truth. Through one century in the Chosŏn dynasty, over 10,000 chose martyrdom and, as of the present, 103 people had been beatified as saints. But how could they embrace martyrdom, overcoming excruciating torture and rejecting persuasion from officials and family members? What were they thinking when they were criticized for believing in a heterodoxy? The Chosŏn government declared that Sŏhak (Western Learning) was a heterodoxy which defied authority and tradition. To this accusation of the government, Hong Sa-man refuted, "It was said that the greatness of *Tao* comes from heaven and what heaven orders is called *Sŏng* (Nature). Furthermore it was said that Sangje comes down to people on earth. As all of these signifying the reverence of heaven, how can you call Sŏhak heterodoxy?"[1004] In his trial, Chŏng Yak-chong said "If I knew that Sŏhak was heterodoxy, how did I dare believe it? Because I knew that Sŏhak was a right and true *tao*, I didn't have any intention to change my mind when I was released a year ago. Even if I would be tortured ten thousand times, I will not apostatize."[1005] When interrogated on the reason for writing his letter, Hwang Sa-yŏng also replied that he was convinced that Sŏhak was orthodoxy.[1006] It became more widely claimed that Catholicism was not heterodoxy but

---

[1003] Ishii, *op. cit.*, pp. 556-557.

[1004] Sinyu sahak choein Yi Ka-hwan ch'uan. p.112.
Sinyu, second month 15th day.

[1005] Sahak choein Yi Ka-hwan tŭng ch'uan. I. second month 12th day.

[1006] Sahak choein Hwang Sa-yŏng ch'uan. *op. cit.*, p. 730.

orthodoxy. The Chief Interpreter during the Kihae year (1839), Yu Chin-gil argued that Catholicism was an orthodoxy by confessing that, enlightened after reading a few pages of the *Ch'ŏnju silŭi*, he visited one believer and borrowed from him the books and then immediately converted to Catholicism.[1007]

On the trial, Yi Kun-sim said to the Police Chief, "As Ch'ŏnju is the king of the universe, and the father of the entire human race, we adore him above all things. We must respect our king, you the Police Chief, and our parents only after Ch'ŏnju." [1008] Ch'oe Hŭi-dŭk said, "No matter how thoroughly I thought about it, this doctrine is orthodoxy. Therefore, even if I have to die, I cannot denounce it."[1009] When the Police Chief asked whether it was true that he believed in a heterodoxy, Yi Chae-haeng replied, "Ch'ŏnju is the Great King who created all things in the universe and he is the highest ranking father, who punishes evil and rewards good. Therefore I do not know what might be a heterodoxy."[1010]

As the number of the believers increased in the classes lower than *chungin*, the doctrine which was understood simply as truth became a matter of faith that " if they are saved, they will enjoy eternal life in Heaven." Thus, the number of martyrs, who chose eternal life by maintaining their faith and thereby keeping their community alive, increased. The following stanzas taken from *Sindŏkka* (Song of Faithful Morality), one of the *Ch'ŏnguk gasa*, illustrates their faith:

> Who is the father and mother of the soul?
> There is only one, not two, and it is God.
> Our soul is precious, with a beginning but

[1007] *Kihae ilgi*. Seoul: Kat'ollik ch'ulp'ansa. 1983. p.50.
[1008] Chales Dallet, *op. cit.*, (chung). p.175.
[1009] C. Dallet, *op. cit.*, (chung). p. 481. *Kihae ilgi.* 110a.
[1010] *Ibid.*,

no end and it is like God. If we consider where the soul is, dead people [also] have a soul. Where does this soul go? There are two places -- heaven and hell. What kind of souls go to heaven? Good souls go to heaven. What kind of souls go to hell? Wicked souls go to hell. [1011]

The view of "the other world" can be glimpsed from the following stanzas taken from *Sahayangga* (Song of yearning for our hometown), a song from the *Ch'ŏnju kasa*:

*ŏhwa(uri) pŏnnimneya uriobonhyang ch'ajagase
tongsŏnambuk sahaep'albang ŏnŭgosi ponhyangingo
pokchiero kajahani moysesŏngin mottŭlŏtko.
chidangŭro kajahani adamwŏnjo naech'ŏtkona.
pugwiyŏnghwa ŏtŏtŏntŭl myŏthaekkaji jŭlgiomyŏ
pinkungjaehwa mant'ahandŭl myŏthaekkaji kŭnsimhari
irŏtŭhan p'ungjinsegye angŏhalkot aniroda
inganyŏngbok taŏdŏdo chugŏjimyŏn hŏsadoego
sesanggonan tabadado chugŏjimyŏn kŭmanira
sesangmanbok tabadŭndŭl ch'ŏndangboge pibilsonya
ingan goch'o tadanghandŭl chiokyŏnggo pihalsonya*[1012]

Secret mass meetings on Sundays also helped the believers maintain their faith. Attending the clandestine mass itself was their confession of faith and confirmation of their brotherly love. Priest Ch'oe Sŏg-u concluded that "It was their faith in prayer, their living faith which transcended theory that enabled them to maintain their faith, overcoming the persecution that led them to martyrdom."[1013] The Prayer

---

[1011] Alan Pate, *op. cit.*, p. 67.

[1012] Kim Ok-hŭi, *op. cit.*, (1). pp. 89-90.

[1013] Ch'oe Sŏg-u, "Sahak chingŭirŭl t'onghaesŏ bon ch'ogi ch'ŏnju kyohoe." *Han'guk kyohoesa.* p. 72.

of the Rosary was one of the favorite prayers for the believers during the time of persecutions. It was reported that Hong Nak-min (1740-1801) prayed everyday and Kim Kwang-ok (1741-1801) prayed this prayer when she was escorted to the place of execution.[1014]

Family exhortation and family legacy also contributed to martyrdom. The most representative family was Kwŏn Ch'ŏl-sin's sister, Kwŏn So-sa, who was wife of Yi Yun-ha, who was the 8th descendant of Chibong Yi Su-kwang. Kwŏn So-sa had three children, Yi Kyŏng do, Yi Sun-i, and Yi Kyŏng-ŏn. They all became martyrs during the Sinyu Persecution (1801).

The God of Christianity has mercy as his personality and He is almighty as creator, and possesses sovereignty as the Great King and the Great Father, and He is the savior. These aspects of God were something that could not be found in Confucianism. This view of God and the relations of believers with their God converted into internal strength and power which permitted the believers to overcome the persecutions. Moreover, the life and the martyrdom of their predecessors, such as Yun Chi-ch'ung, who was greatly respected by the believers of the day and whose biography was widely read. Ch'oe In-gil and Chi Hwang, who became martyrs in the wake of the invitation of Priest Chou Wen-mo, gave the believers conviction for their faith and courage for their martyrdom.

Priest Chou Wen-mo seemed to have a great influence on the believers. The mass sacraments conducted by him offered a concrete hope. How much strength and courage the believers gained from the mass is revealed in their letters to the bishop in Beijing:
"The reason that we hoped to avoid deaths is because we wanted to enjoy the happiness of participating in the mass and confessing our sins. Only if we do this, will we be so happy even if we have to die." [1015]   Priest Chou Wen-mo

---

[1014] Charles Dallet, *op. cit.*, (sang). p. 451 & P. 519.

[1015] Pukkyŏng chugyo ege ponaen Chosŏn kyoutŭlŭi sŏhan (1811),

Comparison of the 1801 and the 1866 Persecutions

surrendered himself and laid down his life during the Sinyu Persecution, although he could have escaped with his life. The first Korean priest, Kim Tae-gŏn, became a martyr at the age of 25 and all of the first three French priests chose martyrdom during the Pyŏngin Persecution.

(The letters of the Korean believers to the Bishop in Beijing.) *Mannam gwa mitŭm ŭi kilmok esŏ* . p. 100.

Jai-Keun Choi

Conclusion

The Roman Catholic Church overcame the turmoil of the Protestant Reformation and began to start a new missions era via Spain and Portugal, riding on their growth in sea power. The society of the Jesuits sent missionaries to China, Japan and other countries, except for Korea. After the invasions of Japan and China, Korean intellectuals sought new thought, religion, and other cultural enrichments. These desires were satisfied through newly introduced Western books. Many Korean intellectuals came to respect the Western world and adopted a new world view contrary to the traditional China-centered world view. Over a century they read and studied Western books and a certain group of Korean intellectuals came to accept a Western religion (so-called the Western Learning) and confessed the Christian faith. They founded a Christian church by themselves without the aid of missionaries.

After the founding of the Chosŏn Catholic Church in 1784 and Yi Sŭng-hun returned from Beijing after being baptized, there began a century of persecution which did not end until 1886. When the fact of Catholic worshippers meeting regularly became known to the government, a prohibition order was issued. They could not freely hold gatherings, and they began to meet and work in secret. Thus, an underground church was formed, and it was severely persecuted over a century. The Chosŏn Catholic Church strove to build an idealistic communal organization in which there was no discrimination as to social status.

Conclusion

From the very beginning of the founding of the church, *chungin* participated, at times in leadership roles while the *yangban* were key figures in the organization. Because this new communal organization was established entirely through the efforts of Koreans themselves, initially with information obtained by envoys who met with official representatives of the Church in Beijing, the church faced some limitations. First, because they were ignorant of the church's regulations, the Chosŏn Catholics established an ecclesiastical hierarchy in which laymen assumed the title and actions of a priest. This later came to be referred to as the Pseudo Ecclesiastical Hierarchy. After learning that this did not accord with the Roman Catholic Church doctrine, they began to invite priests. When a Chinese priest named Chou Wen-mo arrived in Korea in 1795 and created organizations such as the Myŏngdohoe, the groundwork for the Roman Catholic Church in Korea began to be laid. The Roman Catholic Church faith spread rapidly through blood relations, school affiliation and regional ties, a pattern particularly marked in Chosŏn society. And the propagation of the Christian faith through marriage relations was one of the special characteristics of the early Chosŏn church.

It was the Korean Christian refusal to perform ancestor worship rituals that initially provoked the persecution. With Yun Chi-ch'ung and Kwŏn Sang-yŏn's refusal to conduct an ancestor worship ceremony in 1791, Catholicism came to be understood as heterodoxy by the government and thus a policy of prohibition was instituted. The Christian refusal to ancestor worship was the greatest impetus for the yangban class to leave the Christian faith, making Christianity a people's movement. Later, banishment and execution of Catholics was carried out in 1791, 1801, 1839, 1846, and 1866, which was the largest persecution.

The first nation-wide persecution was the Sinyu Persecution of 1801, during which Western Learning was denounced as heterodoxy and its study was banned. Around the time of the first 1801 persecution, many Catholic

Church members resided in secluded mountains among themselves, avoiding scrutiny and persecution. Such a village of Catholics is referred to as a *kyouch'on*. Even in such a situation of despair, the Catholic followers sought to invite priests from abroad, and eventually the Roman Papal Court established the Chosŏn parish of the Roman Catholic Church. As missionaries from the Paris Foreign Mission Society arrived in Korea and worked in secret, the Chosŏn church was transformed from a laymen-led church to a priest-led church that accorded with the rules which the official Roman Catholic Church required. It had a bishop and even when the missionary or the priest was executed, there were continuous supporters, so that a seminary was erected in Paeron, Ch'ungch'ŏng province to educate clergymen. And students were sent abroad to be trained as clergymen. Father Kim Tae-gŏn (1821-1846), who had been sent to Macao in accordance with a decision to train native priests, returned to Korea after having been ordained, and after a short period of missionary work, he was arrested and martyred. The martyrdom of a young priest, the very first Korean priest, became a symbol of Christian sacrifice and obedience for the Chosŏn church members. A second Korean priest, Ch'oe Yang-ŏp (1821-1861), played an important role in the advancement of the Christian faith and development of an institutional church through the composition and spreading of numerous *Ch'ŏnju kasa*.

Although there had been several regional persecutions and nation-wide persecutions in 1839 and 1845, the final persecution in 1866 was not only the most severe and extreme in the number of victims it produced, its cruel nature and length, but it was also the most complicated in its background, in terms of its internal political dimensions, as well as in its repercussions with appearance on the Korean scene of the colonial powers of Russia, France and America.

The beginning of the Chosŏn Catholic Church, as well as its growth amid unfavorable circumstances, did not arise from the support of foreign missionaries or missionary groups. It was on their own that the Koreans accepted Catholicism, and it was as laypeople that they read and

Conclusion

studied the doctrine and acquired their faith in the process of translating, publishing and propagating Catholic catechisms. Moreover, the church matured as the Chosŏn Catholics persistently strove to invite priests from abroad, strengthened their organization, and solidified its institutional relationship with the churches of the world. It was through the efforts of Koreans themselves that the church was founded and developed. During the century-long persecution, there were only intermittent periods when they had a priest, a total of thirty nine years. These periods were those of the most severe persecutions. One was a period following the loss of Chosŏn's only priest Chou Wen-mo during the Sinyu Persecution in 1801, until 1834, when Father Liu Fang-chi came to Korea. Another was a period following the Kihae Persecution in 1839, when three French missionaries, Imbert, Maubant, and Chastan, were martyred, until the arrival of the priests Ferréol, Daveluy and Kim Tae-gŏn in 1845. The third period was from 1866 when nine clergymen were martyred and three, Ridel, Calais and Féron, fled Korea due to the Pyŏngin Persecution, to 1876 when Father Dugette entered Korea.

One of the special aspects of Korea's acceptance of Catholicism was that the various religious activities centered on lay people, by whom Catholicism was accepted, by whom persecution was endured, and through whom the church grew and developed. Consequently, they were able to endure the persecutions through the power of their own internal strength. Although Korea was a Confucian culture along with China and Japan, persecution did not drive the Korean Catholic Church to degenerate as the church in China did, or disappear as the church in Japan did; on the contrary, the faith of the Korean Catholic believers deepened with the persecution, and the number of followers increased.

Since Catholic teachings challenged several important and rigorously held beliefs within Chosŏn society about ethical principles and social status, it was inevitable that their introduction precipitated conflicts. In particular, a fundamental difference between Confucianism and Catholicism was the difference in the perception of humanity. While Confucianism centered on ethics and human relations, and sought its authority in tradition and the Chinese Classics, Catholicism viewed ethical and moral obligations between people to be of secondary importance and one's individual relationships through faith with a superior, divine being to be paramount. Catholicism was proscribed as a heterodoxy that did not regard a father as father and a king as king, and that therefore allowed for neither father nor king. Neither the persuasion of parents nor punishment by the government convinced the Catholic followers to abandon that faith. Conflict was inevitable, since Catholicism claimed that God is the great father of all and the great king of all in the temporal realm, and believed that God has greater authority than king or father of the present world. The government thus came to pursue a policy of suppression while the Catholic Church members arrived at the conclusion that "it is acceptable to disobey the commands of the king and disobey the commands of one's father. But even if they were to receive the most severe punishment, the teachings of God must not be changed."[1016]

Critics of Western Learning such as An Chŏng-bok argued that the doctrines of Buddhism and Christianity were the same, stating that their precepts about divinity, heaven and hell, the immortality of the soul and eternal life were identical, and that since they contradicted the Confucian doctrine, both were heterodoxies. Since they believed that the soul died along with the physical body and did not believe in its immortality, a belief in the existence of heaven or hell after one's death simply could not be accepted. During the latter half of the century of persecution, Catholicism was not only castigated as heterodoxy, but Catholic followers were found to be secretly communicating with foreign forces. At that point, those Confucian scholars who had been only passively opposed to Catholicism joined with political factions in manipulating the issue for their own benefit, screaming out their rejection

---

[1016]*Chosŏn. wangjo sillok,*, Chŏngjo 15th year 11th month Muin.

Conclusion

of heterodoxy and affirmation of orthodoxy. A Neo-Confucian scholar of the Kiho region, Yi Hang-no, his disciple Kim P'yŏng-muk, Ki Chŏng-jin of Honam and the literati of Yŏngnam, who had had no contact with each other until that time, came to be of one spirit and formed a solidarity.[1017]

In addition to ideological factors, social factors also played a significant role in persecutions. The rejection of the traditional customs including the rites of ancestor worship, the advocating of an equality that does not recognize distinctions in social status, and the practice of brotherly love as Christians were seen as factors that destroy the traditional society, while the celibacy of clergymen and the affirmation of virginity as a virtue were also seen as destructive of social order. The most serious social problem was the criticism that the Catholic believers did not conduct ancestor worship rituals. This attack continued from the beginning to the end of the persecution period and was supported by the common populace. This was because ancestor worship was seen as a form of filial piety. However, the Catholic Church viewed it as idol worshipping and ordered a rejection of the practice of ancestor worship rites, thereby rendering it a core issue of controversy. At the same time the relationship between men and women also became problematic. The idealization of chastity for Catholic women and the requirement of celibacy of clergymen were seen as wrongfully serving to deprive clergymen and widowed women of their right to bear children.

Underlying the Catholic suppression lay political factors in addition to ideological and social conflicts. Following the founding of the church in 1784, though the Catholic Church did not focus on political activities, it nevertheless became a critical variable in politics during the last one hundred years of the Chosŏn dynasty. In other words, Catholicism was exploited and victimized in the

---

[1017] Hyŏn Sang-yun, *Chosŏn yuhaksa*, (Seoul: Minjung sŏgwan, 1954), p.425.

process of seeking ideological and social justification to defeat the opposition political force. The political strife between the newly formed *Sip'a* and *Pyŏkp'a*, the in-law government of the P'ungyang Cho clan and the Andong Kim clan, and the authoritarian rule of the Taewŏn'gun and his isolation policy toward foreign forces not only determined the nature of the political state of affairs in the latter half of the Chosŏn dyansty, but were also fundamental factors that underlay the sufferings of the Chosŏn Catholic Church. This was mainly because, during the Chosŏn dynasty, politics and religion were fused together, and it was impossible to accurately interpret the significance of any one with the other, religious incident without an understanding of the current political situation. Although Chŏngjo declared a policy of moderation following the model of Yŏngjo, he naturally came to lean towards his falsely accused and executed father Crown Prince Changhŏn and the *Sip'a* faction, which had been sympathetic to the Crown Prince all along. Since there were many Catholic believers among the *Sip'a* members, *Pyŏkp'a* used Catholicism as a pretext in its unceasing hostility toward the political strife and the *Sip'a* faction.

The Sinhae Persecution of 1791 began when Hong Nag-an, a member of the *Pyŏkp'a*, assailed Catholicism in the name of justice, rejecting heterodoxy and upholding orthodoxy, in order to slander Ch'ae Che-gong, who was a *Namin* member of the *Sip'a* and who had held the position of Third State Councilor, Second State Councilor and First State Councillor during twenty-three years under Chŏngjo's reign. The Sinyu Persecution of 1801 was a mass slaughter that resulted when the widow of Yŏngjo, Queen Dowager Kim, who came to wield control from behind the scenes, was urged on by the *Pyŏkp'a* and schemed political revenge against the *Namin Sip'a* and *Noron Sip'a*. When Chŏngsun Queen Dowager Kim died in 1805 and Sunjo's father-in-law Kim Cho-sun of the Andong Kim clan seized power, the oppression of Catholicism lessened. The appearance of Kim Cho-sun not only signified the regaining of power by the *Sip'a*, but also the advent of in-law-government by the

Conclusion

Andong Kim clan. During its rule, the persecution of Catholicism became substantially mitigated, and it was at this time that the revival of the church organization began.

The Kihae Persecution of 1839 during Hŏnjong's reign brought great suffering to the Catholic believers, as a struggle for power began between the Andong Kim clan and the P'ungyang Cho clan. When Cho Man-yŏng of the *Noron Pyŏkp'a* seized power, he rejected the tolerant attitude with which the Andong Kim clan had treated Catholicism during its rule, and suppressed the Catholic faith. As her husband was posthumously enthroned as Ikchong, Hŏnjong's mother was declared Queen Dowager Cho and she then became the Queen Sinjŏng who seized actual authority after the deaths of Sunjo's Queen, and Ch'ŏlchong. The Sinjŏng Queen had made an alliance with the Hŭngsŏn'gun Yi Ha-ŭng and her nephew Cho Sŏng-ha, and thus had the Hŭngsŏn'gun's second son accede to the throne as the twelve-year old Kojong in 1864. Furthermore, in order to weaken the Andong Kim clan's influence, she adopted Kojong as her son, and wielded control from behind the scenes, dominating political affairs along with the Hŭngsŏn Taewŏn'gun until Kojong's Queen Min assumed power.

The Pyŏngin Persecution of 1866 launched by the Hŭngsŏn Taewŏn'gun (the King Kojong's father) during the reign of Kojong was a catastrophe that resulted from his need to satisfy his political power interests, attempting to overcome the crisis and to retain authority in the face of his weakening power as he was accused of conspiring with Catholic believers' religion for adopting a policy of tolerating Catholicism, and a policy of 'defeat barbarians with barbarians,' to bring in the French force to defend from the an anticipated invasion by Russia.

The responsibility for the persecution lay partially with the Catholic believers and with the church as well. The inflexible dogmatism of the Catholic Church members and troublesome appearance of representatives of Western powers seeking trading relationships laid the groundwork for misunderstanding. The Catholic Church members' policy of depending on the Western powers for the purpose of attaining religious freedom became problematic. From the very beginning, they fantasized that visits by secret envoys to invite priests and large ships from the West would secure them religious freedom. Two brothers, Yu Hang-gŏm and Kwan-gŏm of Chŏnju professed to believe that sending in large warships would once and for all bring an end to the problem of religious freedom, and Hwang Sa-yŏng's letter threatening the country by inviting Western ships, fueled the belief that Catholicism was related to intervention by foreign forces. Following the execution of the French priests the appearance of Western battleships became increasingly frequent, and pressure by foreign nations also increased gradually. As ships appeared either protesting against the execution of the French missionaries or requesting trade relations, the Chosŏn government came to the conclusion that the Catholic Church members were at the forefront of the Western forces and thereby found another reason for persecution.

After the founding of the church, the Chosŏn government branded Western Learning as a heterodox scholarship and its consequent prohibition of Western books set the course for ideological and doctrinal suppressions. Although a policy of toleration was pursued during Chŏngjo's reign, guided by a belief that an intellectual commitment to renewing the foundation of orthodoxy would bring the demise of heterodoxy, the very first nation-wide persecution was launched in 1801 during Sunjo's regime, and tragic persecutions followed in 1839 and 1845 during Hŏnjong's reign, culminating in 1866 in the largest among all persecutions during the century, the Pyŏngin Persecution.

Although there were a large number of apostates and over ten thousand martyred believers, the church nevertheless survived and laid down the foundation of its development to this date. And as the church progressed from its birth in Chosŏn to its status today as a member of a world organization leading headquartered Rome, the dispatch of the French priests and the Chosŏn church

Conclusion

members' religious enthusiasm prevented this religious communal organization from collapsing.

As the Catholic believers during the persecution period befriended each other and held to their faith in the face of death, there was a dynamism that energized them and spurred their efforts at evangelization. Emotional support was derived from their doctrinal provisions and training. In the beginning the *yangban* built a doctrinal foundation by reading and introducing Western books written in Chinese. Subsequently, Koreans on their own read and comprehended Catholic teaching, translated texts into Korean, and digested a doctrine which they then systemized according to their understanding. The writing of new catechisms and simple songs to impart Catholic teachings took place from the beginning stage of the church. Yi Pyŏk, one of the founding members of the church, composed "Ch'ŏnju konggyŏngga" in the traditional Korean *kasa* format. In the song, he employed the term *'Sangje'* to demonstrate the consonance of the concept of the "Lord on High" of *Sangje* referred to in ancient Confucian writings with the Lord of Heaven or Ch'ŏnju of Catholicism.[1018] On the other hand, the concept of great father and great king, who created and governed all things in the universe and redeemed people from their sins, was non-existent in Confucian ideology and thus was an entirely new idea.

As persecution became increasingly severe towards the latter period, in contrast to the earlier period during which conferences could be held and doctrine could be read, the church lacked people who could give correct instruction because many of those who were capable of conducting doctrinal education had been either executed or banished. In addition, because a prohibition order was in effect, the Catholics had to live in constant apprehension and fear of being persecuted. Unlike the earlier days, even holy items and the Catholic doctrinal books disappeared, so

---

[1018] Kim Ok-hŭi, *Kwangam Yi Pyŏk ŭi sŏhak sasang*, pp.164-165, p.179, pp.290-291.

that it became impossible to propagate the faith through written materials.

In the latter period, doctrinal education and instruction in the faith largely depended on family tradition and were mostly taught by fathers to sons and by mothers to daughters. Such instruction was comprised of simple doctrines such as the Ten Commandments and the Seven Overcoming, in which they believed firmly, memorized, and put into practice, thus enabling them to maintain their faith and have their posterity inherit it. Chŏng Yak-chong's "Chugyo yoji" and Chŏng Ha-sang's "Sangjae sangsŏ" were catechisms that appealed to the sentiments of the literate classes and also contributed to the development of the national culture. The missionaries carried out a systemized education based on a widely used catechism called the "Sŏnggyo Ilkwa" ("Daily Bible Lessons"), and a woodblock printing press was secretly built for the dissemination of these catechisms that were transmitted mainly by Western priests who had received institutional training. In consequence the transmission process was more consistent, and it became possible to thoroughly study these texts. Moreover, through the provision of Korean language catechisms, commoners came to further their understanding of the doctrine, which they received as if filtered through their genuine grievances with the existing social order.

In much the same way, the idea of equality between men and women became a significant inspiration for women to convert to Catholicism, and it served as well as a supporting factor in maintaining their faith. But above all else, Catholicism's promise of eternal life in the next world, where all sufferings would be recompensed and all injustices indemnified, was a never-ending source of encouragement in maintaining the faith of the Catholic believers, thereby enabling them to undergo the ultimate sacrifice of martyrdom.

The founding and organization of the Catholic church in Chosŏn was largely the work of *yangban* members, aided significantly by the efforts of *chungin* converts, a number of whom served as interpreters and

Conclusion

translators of Chinese and accompanied delegations to the Ching court, where they were able to meet personally with Jesuit missionaries and transmit information and materials back to Chosŏn. However, the Sinhae Persecution in 1791, following the Rites Controversy of that year, and the Sinyu Persecution of 1801, not only removed many *yangban* from membership, but had a particularly chilling effect thereafter on the number of *yangban* willing to assume active roles in the church. Over time, the composition changed from predominantly *yangban* to the *chungin*, then to the commoner class. And with this came a change in the character of the believers' faith, as persecution forced them into hiding. Since a church with an authentic ecclesiastical organization could not be established, it became an underground one, lacking the authority of a clergy. The type of spirituality engendered in these circumstances was one that emphasized distance from, not participation in, the world. In other words, Catholicism became a religion that merely looked forward to rewards to be experienced in the next life.

Jai-Keun Choi

Appendix

Proliferation of Church Influence Through Hereditary Ties

   The value system of Chosŏn society had been institutionalized by thoughts and actions that placed a foremost emphasis on human relationships among those of closely related bloodlines. Relationships based on geographical and school ties also formed the basis of mutual understanding among Korean men, and they reinforced and strengthened such ties by infusing them with social and political power.
   The diffusion of Catholicism in Korea and the speed at which it was transmitted owe much to the routine dissemination that occurred among families and clans related by blood. The Catholic communal organization was even considered to be a religious group that resembled a kind of a secret society formed upon clan ties.[1019] An official record used the term "party of the blood" to describe

---

[1019] Hwang Sŏn-myŏng, *Chosŏn chonggyo sahoesa yŏn'gu*, (A study of religious and social history in Chosŏn dynasty), p.307.

the principle of its organization.[1020] The Chosŏn family was essentially a large communal organization tied by blood with a paternal figure at the apex. Due to the significant role and influence of a father figure, familial and hereditary lines tended to be clear and distinct.

The role of marriage-based relationships in family units was much more significant and its contribution much more substantial to the proliferation of Catholicism than that of relationships based on blood ties. Catholicism was further disseminated through local geographical relationships of Seoul, Kyŏnggi, Chŏlla, and Ch'ungch'ŏng, and the early Catholicism was founded and expanded through school ties mainly based on the *Namin* Sŏngho school, that is close knit intellectual ties that by now had formed among the disciples of the "Southerner" scholar Yi Ik.

In the case of the *Namin,* since Kyŏngjong's reign (1720-1724), many of those who fell from political power and who had a keen interest in academic scholarship became *Silhak* scholars. When Western Learning was first introduced to Korea, they were the ones who expressed the most sincere interest and positive attitude towards its acceptance. Among them, there were Kiho Namin who were deeply interested in understanding a new field of knowledge.

Among those who centered around the politically disadvantaged *Namin,* most had established relationships through intricate networks of intermarriage. Likewise, *Sŏin* and *Pugin* also limited their correspondence, academic exchanges and marriage ties to those in the same party faction. This is a vital point which demonstrates the deep rootedness of the Korean Catholics kinship network, with its strong proclivity for factional exogamy. Such kinship ties can be said to have emerged in response to the existing clan ruling system.[1021] In other words, practicing the Catholic belief, which centered around the intellectuals of

---

[1020] *Sahak chingŭi. p.70.*

[1021] Hwang Sŏn-myŏng, *op.cit.*, p.291.

the *Namin* Sinsŏp'a (Pro Western Faction), constituted a substitute kinship relationship that was reacting to the dominance of the existing clan ruling system. Therefore, essentially, the practice of Catholicism can be seen as a challenge or confrontation of a political nature between two clan lineages. Such a clash clearly would shake the existing political power structure.

According to *Sahak chingŭi* (A Warning Against Heterodoxy)[1022], Catholic converts among *Namin* appear to have had a greater abundance of close marriage relationships with their fellow *Namin* than had hitherto been realized. At this point it would be well to investigate these numerous marriage relationships in greater detail. A good place to begin with might be with a man named Yi Yun-ha, a descendant of Yi Su-kwang (1563-1628), a literati titan who introduced Western Learning for the very first time in Korea. More immediate figures would be Yi Sŭng-hun, who was the founding father of the Chosŏn Catholic church; Yi Ka-hwan, a nephew of the great *Silhak* scholar Sŏngho Yi Ik; Yu Hang-gŏm, who contributed significantly to the expansion of the faith in Chŏlla and to its sound financial foundation; Yun Chi-ch'ung, a descendant of Yun Sŏn-do who refused to carry out the custom of "ancestral worship" and so was the first one to die a martyr; Chŏng Yag-yong, one of the greatest scholars of the Chosŏn dynasty who narrowly escaped martyrdom; Hong Nag-min (1740-1801), who passed the higher civil service examination, and died a martyr as did his son and his grandson[1023]; Kwŏn Ch'ŏl-sin, the greatest scholar of his generation; Yi Kiŏyang (1744-1802), the seventh generation descendant of the great bureaucratic figure Yi Tŏk-hyŏng (1561-1613).

The most representative cases of overlapping marriage relationships are the following *Namin* families,

---

[1022] The book was serendipitously found in the memorial hall of the martyrs in Yanghwachin in 1971 and reprinted by Han'guk kyohoesa yon'guso in 1977.

[1023] Hong Nag-min died in 1801, his son Chae-yŏng in 1839 and his grandsons, Pyŏng-ju and Yŏng-ju in 1840 and Pong-ju in 1866.

Appendix

already enumerated above: the Kwŏn family who lived in Yangkŭn Kyŏnggido, the Chŏng family of Kwangju Majae Kyŏnggido, the Yu Hang-gŏm family of Chŏnju Chŏllado, and the Yun Chi-ch'ung (1759-1791) family. Yun was a seventh generation descendant of Yun Sŏn-do (1587-1671, penname Kosan) who had an excellent reputation as a distinguished scholar, a poet and a statesman during the Chosŏn dynasty. He was also the great-grandson of Yun Tu-sŏ, who was the foremost painter of his generation.[1024]

Despite the fact that Yun Sŏn-do had been accused as the leader of the *Namin* and was forced to live in harsh exile in places such as Kyŏngwŏn, Yŏngdŏk and Samsu, his reknowned scholarship and his family members' successes in the civil service examinations nevertheless gave him the reputation as one of the most distinguished scholars of the dynasty. His great-grandson, Kongjae Yun Tu-sŏ, passed the chinsa examination in 1693, and he was so gifted in painting live creatures that he, along with *Hyŏnjae* (Sim Sa-chŏng) and *Kyŏmjae* (Chŏng Sŏn), could have been considered as the *Samjae* of Chosŏn.[1025]

Yun Kongjae married a great-granddaughter of Yi Su-kwang, who was a sixth generation descendant of the Lord of Kyŏngnyŏnggun, one of the sons of T'aejong, Chosŏn's third king. His father-in-law Yun Tu-sŏ married the Royal Secretary Yi Tong-kyu, who was the second son of Sŏng-ku. Sŏng-ku was Yi Su-kwang's eldest son, and a former Chief State Councillor under Injo.[1026] The two

---

[1024] *Haenam Yun-ssi sebo.* From the fifth generation descendant Ku (1516), sixth Hong-jung (1546), seventh Yu-gi (1580), eighth Sŏn-do (1633) to In-mi (1663) all successfully passed the civil examination. *cf. Mansŏng taetongbo* (Grand genealogy of the ten thousand names), vol. 1 pp.281bpp.

[1025] An Hwi-chun, *Han'guk misulsa* (A History of Korean Painting), (Seoul: Ilchisa, 1984), p.213.

[1026] For the very first time in Korea, Yi Su-kwang introduced "The True Meaning of the Lord of Heaven" by Matteo Ricci in his *Chibong yusŏl*. Afterwards, many Catholic figures emerged

families were both from the *Namin* background and thus seem to have married within the same faction.

Yun Tu-sŏ and his brothers Hŭng-sŏ and Chong-sŏ were the "three brothers *Chinsa*." The fourth son among the nine sons of Yun Tu-sŏ, Tŏk-yŏl, had a son Kyŏng who married a daughter of Kwŏn Ki-jing of the Andong Kwŏn clan and gave birth to Yun Chi-ch'ung, who died a martyr.[1027]

The following is an investigation of the family relationships of Kwŏn Ki-jing, the father of Kwŏn Sang-yŏn, who was executed along with Yun Chi-ch'ung, the pivotal figure in the Rites Controversy of 1791. Kwŏn Ki-jing was also closely acquainted with Yu Hang-gŏm, who was a key contributor to the expansion of Catholicism in Chŏllado. His great-grandfather was Kwŏn Si, pen name T'an'ong, who had served as Hansŏng-bu Uyun (Vice Magistrate of Seoul).[1028]

Having five daughters but no son, Kwŏn Ki-jing adopted his cousin Wi-jing's son, Se-hak. Ki-jing's brother, Sŏng-jing, also adopted a cousin Yŏ-jing's son. Among his five daughters, the eldest married Yun Kyŏng and gave birth to Yun Chi-ch'ung. His second daughter married Yu Tong-kŭn and gave birth to two sons, Hang-gŏm and Kwan-gŏm. Subsequently, Yun Chi-ch'ung and the two brothers, Hang-gŏm and Kwan-gŏm, who were earlier Catholic church members, became cousins through maternal ties.[1029]

Kwŏn Ki-jing's youngest daughter married Yun Chi-sang, who was a nephew of his eldest son-in-law Yun Kyŏng and also a son of Yun Kyŏng's cousin Yun T'aek. In the Kyuchanggak edition of the *Nambo*, the name Chi-sang appears as Kyu-sang. In genealogy books and the *Nambo*,

---

from among his descendants. *Haenam Yun-ssi sebo* (Imobo),vol.4, p.2a

[1027] *Mansŏng taedongbo*, vol. 1, p. 281b. *Nambo* (Owned by Yu Hong-nyŏl).vol. 1, p.751.

[1028] Andong Kwŏn-ssi Ch'amŭigongp'a.

[1029] *Sahak chingŭi*, kwŏn II, Yu Hang-gŏm, p.228.

Appendix

the two characters in the names *chi* and *kyu*, often appear interchanged.[1030] Among the cousins of Yun Chi-ch'ung and Chi-hŏn, Kyu-ŭng, Kyu-baek, Kyu-han, Kyu-bŏm, and others were promoted as civil service officials, switched the two characters *chi* with *kyu*. This was probably because they felt ashamed to be cousins of the Catholic Yun Chi-ch'ung brothers and were afraid that the relationship might have a negative impact on their scholarly reputations. As described thus far, Kwŏn Ki-jing, therefore, had an extremely close relationship with the family of Yun Chi-ch'ung. Kwŏn Ki-jing's grandson, Kwŏn Sang-yŏn, a son of Se-ki, who died a martyr along with Yun Chi-ch'ung, who had a son, Hyŏk. He did not have a son, and his daughter married Han Kwang-yŏl.[1031]

Yun Chi-ch'ung's younger brother Yun Chi-hŏn married Hang-gŏm's cousin, Yu Chong-hang.[1032] Therefore, Yun Chi-hŏn's marriage was one that already overlapped within the family of Yu Tong-kŭn because of the relationship with his father. It is generally understood that Yun Chi-ch'ung came to believe in the new religion as a member of the politically ostracized *Namin* faction, and was influenced by his father's family and his mother's family.

The descendants of Yun Chi-ch'ung's family suffered from the battle between Yun Sŏn-do and *Sŏin* (The Westerners). In the case of Yun Tu-sŏ, for example, despite his talent in academic scholarship, he led a life of misfortune, devoted entirely to the arts. It also appears that although Yun Chi-ch'ung himself did not become a *Chinsa*, his frustration at his faction's isolation drove him to abandon his dream early on of achieving success in the civil

---

[1030] *Nambo* (Owned by Kyuchanggak), p.587.

[1031] *Andong Kwŏn-ssi chokbo*, hwang (Kapinbo).

[1032] In the *Nambo*, Chi-hŏn is recorded as Chŭng's son. However, according to the 1911 *Sinhanbo* edition of the genealogy, Chi-hŏn is Yun Kyŏng's adopted son.

service examination.[1033]

In addition to the marriage ties described above, Yun Chi-ch'ung was able to cultivate interest in Catholicism through his family's close relationship with the family of Chŏng Yag-yong. His paternal aunt was the second wife of Chŏng Chae-wŏn, who had served as a *moksa* (Magistrate) in Chinju. Chŏng Chae-wŏn had Chŏng Yak-hyŏn with his first wife Ŭiryŏng Nam Ha-dŏk's daughter, and upon her death, he married the daughter of Yun Tŏk-yŏl. With his second wife, who was Yun Chi-ch'ung's aunt, Chŏng Chae-wŏn had Yak-chŏn, Yak-chong, Yag-yong and a daughter. Chŏng Chae-wŏn's son-in-law was Yi Sŭng-hun, one of the founders of the early Chosŏn Catholic church. Therefore, Yun Chi-ch'ung and Chŏng Yag-yong were cousins through his father's sister and Yun Chi-ch'ung and Yi Sŭng-hun were also relatives. Furthermore, Yi Pyŏk's elder sister was Chŏng Yak-chŏn's wife, and thus Yun Chi-ch'ung was also distantly related to Yi Pyŏk. Consequently, with such numerous familial ties, Yun Chi-ch'ung was able to come into contact with Catholicism earlier than others.

Another reason stems from the fact that both his father's and his mother's families had a keen interest in *Silhak*. Although the anti-Western faction launched a severe attack at the time of the Rites Controversy, his clan did not engage in a harsh rebuttal. This is perhaps an illustration of the ideological progressiveness on the part of the members of both families.

The Yu Hang-gŏm Family

A man of national reknown,[1034] Yu Hang-gŏm of Chŏnju was a priest of the false ecclesiastical order of the early Chosŏn Catholic church and had contributed significantly to the dissemination of Catholicism in Chŏllado. Until now, his family origin had not been closely

---

[1033] Chu Myŏng-jun, *op.cit.*, p.32.
[1034] *Sahak chingŭi*, kwŏn 1, p.28.

Appendix

investigated, and it was only recently that he was found to be from the Chinju Yu clan.[1035] Yu Hang-gŏm's half brother, Kwan-gŏm, actively participated in church activities along with him. Their father was Yu Tong-kŭn; Hang-gŏm's mother was a daughter of Kwŏn Ki-jing, and Kwan-gŏm's mother was the daughter of Yu Ŏn-do.

One of his ancestors, Sŏjae Yu Sun-sŏn, had passed the *Sama* examination in 1546, the *Munkwa* (civil service examination) in the following year. In 1556, he even passed the *Chungsi* examination. At this time, he corresponded with Yun Sŏn-do's grandson, Yun Ŭi-jing, and maintained a kinship relationship until the generation of Yun Chi-ch'ung and Yu Hang-gŏm.[1036]

Yu Hang-gŏm's descendants had served successively in office. However, since Su-bang, Yu Hang-gŏm's ancestor of the fifth generation above him, had been successful in the civil service (1673), none of the others were successful in attaining a government post. After Yu Hang-gŏm's family moved to Chŏnju, only his elder brother Ik-kŏm and his cousin Kuk-kŏm passed the *Saengwŏnsi* examination, and the rest of the family enjoyed not a single examination success. The cause behind such a trend can be seen to be rooted in the fact that their family was *Namin*.[1037]

Despite such a disadvantage, the two brothers, Yu Hang-gŏm and Kwan-gŏm did not abandon their past and continued with their challenge.[1038] The reason for which they aspired to a position in the civil service was because "it soon became a primary determinant of social status and also provided a major means whereby economic wealth might be accumulated. In a society that recognized government service as the chief glory to which man might properly

---

[1035] Chu Myŏng-jun, *op.cit.*, pp.50-59.
[1036] *Ibid.*, p.64.
[1037] *Ibid.*, p.68.
[1038] *Sahak chingŭi*, Vol.II. pp. 228-234.

aspire, the successful examination candidate during the Yi occupied a truly unique position."[1039]

Furthermore, just as marriage was considered to be critical among the *yangban* families, Yu hang-gŏm's family also put great importance on marriage ties from generation to generation. For example, the wife of Si-jae, Yu Hang-gŏm's ancestor of seven generations above, was from the Chŏnju Yu clan, and she was a daughter of Yu Yŏng-kyŏng, a former Chief State Councillor.[1040] Although his family had not been too successful in attaining prestigious government posts, he was nationally reknowned for the fortune he had accumulated,[1041] and thus was able to establish marriage relationships with noble families of the time.

Yu Hang-gŏm's son, Chung-ch'ŏl married Yi Yun-ha's daughter Yi (Lugartha) Sun-i, and they are known for dying as martyrs in 1801 while maintaining their chastity. The two families already had a history of intermarriage over several generations. Yu Sŏk-chun, Yu Hang-gŏm's ancestor of eight generations above, had married the daughter of Yi Hŭi-ch'ŏm of Kyŏngryŏngun branch of the Chŏnju Yi clan. She was also the elder sister of Yi Su-kwang.

Yu Chung-tae, who, along with Yu Hang-gŏm, had participated in the movement to invite Catholic priests from abroad, was Hang-gŏm's first male cousin once removed and was married to the niece of Yun Chi-ch'ung's younger brother Chi-hŏn's wife. As mentioned previously, Yun Chi-ch'ung's mother and Yu Hang-gŏm's mother were the daughters of Kwŏn Ki-jing and were the paternal aunts of Kwŏn Sang-yŏn. Therefore, Yu Hang-gŏm and Yun Chi-

---

[1039] Edward Wagner, "The Civil Examination Process as Social Leaven: The Case of the Northern Provinces in the Yi Dynasty," A paper prepared for the International Sympositum commemorating the 30th Anniversary of Korean Liberation, Aug 11-20, 1975, Seoul, Korea.

[1040] *Ch|nju Yu-ssi chokpo.*

[1041] *Sahak ching¡i*, Vol.1, p.28.

ch'ung are cousins through the mother's sister, and with Kwŏn Sang-yŏn, they were cousins by their father's sisters.

Yu Hang-gŏm and Yun Chi-ch'ung were cousins on the mother's side, and Yun Chi-ch'ung and Chŏng Yag-yong were cousins by a paternal aunt as well as a maternal cousin. At the same time, even if it had not been for Yun Chi-ch'ung, it is likely that Yu Hang-gŏm was already directly acquainted with Kwŏn Il-sin's family and Chŏng Yag-yong's family. This is because he himself was a *Namin* and also because before his family moved to Chŏllado, the residence of the family had been Yŏju and Yangju of Kyŏnggido since his great-great-grandfather's time and his eldest uncle's family continued to live in these towns,[1042] where Kwŏn Il-sin's family resided.

It is assumed that Yu Hang-gŏm and Tasan maintained a close relationship through Yun Chi-ch'ung. From a citation from the *Sahak chingŭi*, "how could the request for the dispatch of ships be deliberated when Hang-gŏm was without Yag-yong,"[1043] it can be inferred that the two had had a close relationship.

It is recorded that Yu Hang-gŏm first came in contact with Catholicism in the year Sinhae, 1791, through Catholic books lent by Yun Chi-ch'ung, and came to have belief in the religion.[1044] Another record shows that his younger brother Kwan-gŏm converted to Catholicism in the Year Kyŏngsul, 1790.[1045]

The Kwŏn Ch'ŏl-sin Family

The Andong Kwŏn clan is closely associated with the early Chosŏn Catholic church. Among the members, the most illustrative lineage was that of Kwŏn Ch'ŏl-sin and Il-

---

[1042] Chu Myŏng-jun, *op.cit.*, p.76.

[1043] *Sahak chingŭi*, p.378.

[1044] *Sahak choein Yu Hang-gŏm tŭng ch'uhan*, 48-49

[1045] *Sahak chingŭi*, p.231.

sin (17th generation descendant of Po) who was a descendant of Ko, the third son among the five sons of Po. Another lineage was of the descendants of the fourth son of Po, Wang-ku, which later became a highly distinguished Tanong Kwon clan. Tanong Kwŏn Si established a relationship with Song Si-yŏl through marriage, and he became known throughout his generation by having Yun Chŭng (1629-1714), the Third State Councillor, as his son-in-law (also his former student). Moreover, the son-in-law of Yun Kŏu-chi (1538-1592) was the Second State Councillor, Wŏlsa Yi Chŏng-kwi (1564-1635) and brother-in-law of Tanong, who was son-in-law of Tŭk-ki, was the Chief State Councillor prime minister Sim Chi-wŏn (1593-1662), and competed heavily to marry into the family of Kwŏn Kŭk-in's brothers.[1046]

Kwŏn Ch'ŏl-sin was a famous scholar of the study of *kyŏngsŏ* and *yesŏ,* and his younger brother Kwŏn Il-sin was also a leading figure among *Namin,* Yu Hang-gŏm visited them in Yanggŭn, learned of Western Learning, and was baptized. The Yu Hang-gŏm's maternal great-grandfather-in-law was Kwŏn Ki-ching of the Andong Kwŏn-ssi, and although he was a distant relative of Kwŏn Ch'ŏl-sin (1736-1801) and Il-sin (1751-1792), they were all of one family. Therefore, as a maternal grandson of Kwŏn Ki-ching, it was natural that Yu Hang-gŏm was close to the family of Kwŏn Il-sin.

In fact, there were many intermarriages among the Yu and Kwŏn families. Yu Hang-gŏm's son, Chung-chŏl married Yi Sun-i, whose mother was also from the Kwŏn family. The brothers, Kwŏn Ch'ŏl-sin and Il-sin's maternal uncle was Hong Kyo-man of Namyang Hong clan. He lived in P'och'ŏn, Kyŏnggido, and when the Kwŏn family joined the Catholic organization, his son In became a Catholic first, and then encouraged his father Kyo-man to join the church. Later during the Sinyu Persecution in 1801, both the father and the son died martyrs. Hong Ik-man, Hong Kyo-man's cousin and his son Hong P'il-chu all died

---

[1046]Kang Chu-jin, *Yijo tangjaeng yŏn'gu*, p.133.

Appendix

martyrs in 1801, and Ik-man's son-in-law Yi Hyŏn, nephew of painter Yi Hŭi-yŏng, also died a martyr in 1801.[1047]

Yu Hang-gŏm and Hong Nag-min (1740-1801) of the P'ungsan Hong clan kept in close touch. Hong Nak-min originally lived in Yesan, Ch'ungch'ŏngdo, but upon becoming a *Chinsa*, he moved his residency to Seoul, and afterwards, he passed the Munkwa examination in 1789. It is assumed that he first came in contact with Catholicism in 1784 through Yi Chae-chang.[1048] As one of the leaders in the early stages of the founding of the Chosŏn Catholic church, he was a priest of the false ecclesiastical hierarchy.

Nag-min's older brother was Nak-kyo, and his son Kap-yŏng married the daughter of Yi Yun-ha. Thus, Yi Yun-ha established a relationship with the Nak-kyo brothers. Another daughter of Yi Yun-ha married Yu Hang-gŏm's son Chung-ch'ŏl. Based on such relationships, Yu Hang-gŏm was related to Hong Nag-min and Yi Yun-ha's family through marriage.

Hong Nag-min's second son Chae-yŏng is the son-in-law of Chŏng Yag-yong's older brother, Yak-Hyŏn. Yak-Hyŏn's other son-in-law was Hwang Sa-yŏng. Yu Hang-gŏm was already an in-law to Chŏng Yag-yong through his relationship with Yun Chi-ch'ung, and through his in-law relationship with Yi Yun-ha, he also became related to Chŏng Yag-yong and Hwang Sa-yŏng through marriages.

With such connections, Yu Hang-gŏm was intimately related to Kwŏn Il-sin, Chŏng Yag-yong, Yi Ka-hwan, Hong Nag-min, Yi Yun-ha and Yi Sŭng-hun through direct and indirect marital ties, and thus he was able to acquire a substantial amount of information on Catholicism and convert to Catholicism.

[1047] Han'guk Kat'ollik tae sajŏn, Appendix , (Seoul: Han'guk kyohoesa yŏn'guso, 1985), p.193.

[1048] Chu Myŏng-jun, *op.cit.*, p.101.

The Chŏng Yag-yong Family

It is difficult to find a family during the early part of the Chosŏn dynasty whose members can match the substantial contribution to Korea and the numerous kinship relationships of Tasan and his two brothers of the Naju Chŏng family of Kyŏnggido Kwangju, Majae: Chŏng Yak-chŏn (1758-1816), Chŏng Yak-chŏng Augustine (1760-1801), and Chŏng Yag-yong John the Baptist (1762-1836).[1049] Because the poet Chŏng Yun-jong had lived in Ap'hae, the Naju Chŏng-ssi is sometimes referred to as Ap'hae Chŏng-ssi.

The Chŏng family had lived in Hwanghaedo Paekch'ŏn until the end of the Koryo dynasty, and then as the Chosŏn dynasty became firmly established, they moved to Hanyang. Among their ancestors, there were Su-gon (Munkwa 1472) and Su-kang (Munkwa 1477). In the middle of the Chosŏn dynasty, Chŏng Yun-bok passed the civil service examination in 1567 and served as *Taesahŏn* (Inspector-General).[1050] Among seven sons of Chŏng Yun-bok, three of them had successfully passed the civil service examination, and Tasan is the 11th generation descendant of Hosŏn who passed the examination in 1602.

Chŏng Si-yun, Tasan's ancestor of the fifth generation above, passed the civil service examination in 1690 and served as *Chamŭi* of Board of Punishments. After Sukchong's reign, he led a life far removed from government affairs in Kyŏnggido Kwangju Majae, for he was *Namin*. The Chŏng family moved back to Seoul when Tasan's father Chŏng Chae-wŏn became *Chwarang* (Assistant Section Chief) of the Board of Taxation. Tasan received most of his education from his maternal great-

---

[1049] Although Tasan was the younger of the three, since his name is widely known, the Tasan three brothers are often referred to as Ch|ng Yag-yong and his brothers.

[1050] *Ch|ng Tasan ch|ns|*, (Seoul: Munh|n p'y|n ch'an wiw|nhoe, 1960), p.325.

Appendix

grandfather Hong Hwa-bo.[1051]

Chŏng Chae-wŏn married the daughter of Nam Ha-dŏk and had a son, Yak-hyŏn. Upon the early death of his wife, he married the daughter of Yun Tŏk-yŏl who was also the granddaughter of Yun Tu-sŏ. She was the sister of the very first martyr in Korea, Yun Chi-ch'ung. His second wife gave birth to four sons and a daughter - Chŏng Yak-chŏn, Yak-chong, Yag-yong, and Yi Sŭng-hun's wife. In addition, Chŏng Chae-wŏn had two daughters and a son from his concubine, among which the first daughter married Hong-kŏn, a concubine's child of Ch'ae Che-gong, the Chief State Councillor at the time; the second daughter married Yi Chung-sik; and the son is Yak-kwang.

Chŏng Myŏng-nyŏn, a daughter of Tasan's eldest brother, Yak-hyŏn, married Hwang Sa-yŏng, who was famous for the *Paeksŏ* ("Silk Letter") Incident in 1801. Hwang Sa-yŏng was from the Ch'angwŏn Hwang clan, but little was known of his lineage of descent. Furthermore, Yi Ch'i-hun, the younger brother of Yi Sŭng-hun, married the daughter of Kwŏn I-kang, and since Kwŏn I-kang was Chŏng Yag-yong's maternal great-grandfather, Yi Sŭng-hun and Tasan were closely related through overlapping intermarriages.[1052]

The Tasan family was thus intimately related to Catholicism. Living in Kwangju and Yanggŭn over many generations, they exchanged academic correspondence and established marital ties with *Namin* families of the region. Tasan's older sister married Yi Sŭng-hun, the very first Chosŏn individual to be baptized and also the nephew of Yi Ka-hwan, who was a great-grandson of the leading *Silhak* scholar of the generation, Yi Ik. In addition, Tasan's eldest son, Hak-yŏn, married the sister of Yi Sŭng-hun, who was in fact the older sister of his paternal uncle, and became twice in-laws.

Tasan's mother, Yun-ssi, was the daughter of Yun

[1051] *Y|yudang ch|ns|* (Supplement), p.662.

[1052] *Ibid.*, Ap'hae Chŏng-ssi Kasŭngpyŏn, p.662.

Tŏk-nyŏl and Yun Chi-ch'ung's paternal aunt who died a martyr during the Rites Controversy of 1791. Subsequently, Tasan and Yun Chi-ch'ung were related through their fathers and mothers. Through these blood ties, Yun Chi-ch'ung was able to come in contact with Catholicism in the country side, far from Seoul.

Yu Hang-gŏm of Chŏnju, who played a critical role in the dissemination of Catholicism in Chŏllado, and Yun Chi-ch'ung both married the daughters of Kwŏn Ki-ching, and thus were cousins through their mothers' line.

Kwŏn Sang-yŏn, who died a martyr along with Yun Chi-ch'ung during the *Chinsan* incident, was the nephew of Yun Chi-ch'ung's wife from the Kwŏn clan, and therefore the two are related through their father and mother's lines. It follows from this that Yu Hang-gŏm and Kwŏn Sang-yŏn are also cousins by both paternal and maternal lines.

Furthermore, Tasan and Hong Nak-min (1740-1801) who had passed the civil service examination and who died martyrs, were also in-laws. Hong Nak-min's son Hong Chae-yŏng was Chŏng Yak-hyŏn's son-in-law, and thus was a brother-in-law to Hwang Sa-yŏng.

Tasan and the very first Chosŏn Catholic believer Yi Pyŏk were also related. Tasan's eldest brother Chŏng Yak-hyŏn married the daughter of Yi Po-man, Yi Pyŏk's elder sister. Yak-hyŏn had seven sons-in-law, but two, Hong Chae-yŏng and Hwang Sa-yŏng, died martyrs. It is rather strange that there was no kin relationship, despite the numerous writings that proposed "extermination" of the Chŏng Yag-yong brothers, who must have been regarded as authoritarian in their views in the field of history.

Tasan's half sister married the only son, though that of a concubine, of Ch'ae Che-gong's direct line, who was Hong-kŭn. Although they had no direct relations to Catholicism, one of the reasons for Ch'ae Che-gong's posessing all kinds of books on Catholicism was probably due to his relationship with both families.

Chŏng Yak-chŏn (1758-1816) passed the civil service examination of Chŭngkwangsi in 1790 and married the daughter of Kim Sŏ-ku. He rose to the government post of *chwaryang* of the Board of Military.[1053] Upon converting to Catholicism, he devoted himself to a religious life as a Catholic.

It was illuminated in his memorial to the king in 1797 that Chŏng Yak-yong developed his interest in Western Learning mainly from his curiosity in the various new fields of Western scholarship such as astrology, manufacturing, agriculture, and mathematics.[1054]

Yi Pyŏk's elder sister who married Chŏng Yak-hyŏn died early. Due to relationships such as this, Chŏng Yag-yong, Yak-chŏn brothers came into contact with and learned about Catholic doctrines through Yi Pyŏk. On the fifteenth day of the fourth month of 1784, when Tasan was 23 years old, he was on his way back from the fourth anniversary of the death of his elder brother Yak-chŏn's (1751-1821) wife, Kyŏngju Yi -ssi (1750-1780). On the ship headed back to Tumihyŏp, Tasan first heard about Catholicism through Yi Pyŏk. The fifteenth day of the fourth month of 1784 was only 20 some days after Yi Sŭng-hun had returned from Beijing, baptized and with books on the Western religion.[1055]

It is recorded that upon hearing his elder sister-in-law's younger brother explain the Catholic doctrines on the concepts of heaven and hell, creation of the world, man and god, and life and death, Tasan became shocked and fascinated. Then he followed Yi Pyŏk to his house and borrowed "The True Meaning of the Lord of Heaven" and "The Seven Overcomings," to which he became devoted.[1056] However, it is reasonable to assume that he had

---

[1053] Naju Chŏng-ssi chokpo kwŏn 7, p.4.

[1054] *Chosŏn wangjo sillok*, Chŏngjo 21 year.6th month. Kyŏngin day, p.26.

[1055] Chŏng Yag-yong, "Chach'an myojimyŏng," *Chŏng Tasan chŏnsŏ*, (Seoul: Munhŏn p'yŏnch'an wiwŏnhoe, 1960), p.326 & "Sŏn chungssi myojimyŏng," *Ibid.*, p.324.

[1056] *Ibid.*, p.324.

already heard about the Western Religion at the Ch'ŏnjinam and Chuŏsa meeting in 1779, but that it was not until 1784 that he came to have a religious faith.[1057]

Among Tasan's family members, his father Chae-wŏn and his eldest brother Yak-hyŏn did not believe in Catholicism, and his mother Yun-ssi never had the chance to come in contact with Catholicism since she had died when Tasan was only nine years old.[1058] Besides these individuals, almost every other member of the Chŏng family had some relationship to Catholicism.

In 1784,[1059] the same year Chŏng Yag-yong was baptized, his second elder brother, Chŏng Yak-chŏn was baptized by Yi Sŭng-hun at Yi Pyŏk's house.[1060] Meanwhile, Chŏng Yak-chong, who was the most ardent Catholic of all three brothers, admitted that he learned Catholicism from his elder brother Yak-chŏn in 1786 and thus became a devout Catholic. However, it is understood that he had also heard and known about the Western Religion in the past, but only came to be baptized then.[1061]

Although Chŏng Yak-chong converted to Catholicism much later than his two brothers, Yak-chŏn and Yag-yong had, he led a religious life of the most firm conviction and with greatest determination. Although in the third month of 1786, influenced by brothers, his two brothers left the church due to the persecution accompanying the Sinhae Chinsan Incident, Chŏng Yak-chong

---

[1057] Chu Myŏng-jun, "Chŏng Yag-yong hyŏngje dŭl ŭi ch'ŏnjugyo sinang," *Chŏnju sahak* I, 1984, p.82.

[1058] Chŏng Yag-yong, *op.cit.*, p.326.

[1059] Chu Myŏng-jun, *op.cit.*, p.84.

[1060] "The Trial record Yi Ka-hwan and others, Statement of Yi Sŭng-hun."

[1061] "The Trial record Yi Ka-hwan and others, Statement of Chŏng Yak-chong," Chu Myŏng-jun *op.cit.*, p.83.

remained undeterred from his pursuits.[1062]

Although only one wife, Yi Su-chŏng's daughter, is recorded in the Yu Hong-nyŏl edition of *Nambo*, Yak-chong had three wives in total, the other two being members of Kyŏngju Ch'oe clan and Munhwa Yu clan. Being well versed in the Catholic doctrines, Yak-chong published the very first book of Catholic doctrines, called *"Chugyo yoji* (Essentials of the Lord's Teaching) in 1790's, and made a significant contribution to the advancement and the proliferation of the Catholic church. This book was even praised by priest Chou Wen-mo.[1063] In addition, he devoted all of his effort and enthusiasm in teaching these doctrines.

Ch|ng Ch'ŏl-sang (-1801), the eldest son of Yak-chong and his wife Yu Cecilia (1761-1839) died a martyr and Yak-chong's second son, Ha-sang, also died a martyr after submitting an entreating *"Sangchae sangsŏ"* (Letter to the High Minister). Even his daughter Chŏng Chŏng-hye (1797-1839) died a martyr, from which it can be inferred that due to the strict doctrinal education within his family, the family members came to adhere firmly to Catholicism.

The Yi Pyŏk Family

Yi Pyŏk's great- grandfather, Yi Kyŏng-sang (1603-1647) was a member of the *Sigangwŏn* (Crown Prince Tutorial Office) who had accompanied Crown Prince Sohyŏn when he was taken as a hostage to Ch'ing China during the Mongol Invasion, and it is said that he even met Adam Schall with the Crown Prince, in their way coming into contact with Catholicism.[1064] Yi Pyŏk's grandfather

---

[1062] "The Trial record Yi Ka-hwan and others, Statement of Chŏng Yak-chong," *Hwang Sayŏng Paeksŏ*, 36th line, (trans. by Yun Chae-yŏng), p.46.

[1063] *Hwang Sa-yŏng Paeksŏ*, 37th line.

[1064] Kim Ok-hŭi, *Han'guk ch'ŏnjukyo sasangsa* I, (A history of Korean Catholic thought), (Seoul: Sunkyo ŭi maek, 1990), p.12.

was Yi Tal (also written Yi Kŏn)(1703-1773), who had been promoted to middle rank military officer and served as a Chôlla *pyŏngma chŏltosa* (Commander in Chief), who married the daughter of Kwŏn Hu-sang, a *chinsa* of the Andong Kwŏn clan. His father was Yi Po-man (1727-1812) and his mother was the daughter of Han Chong-hae of the Ch'ŏngju Han clan. Between them were born three sons and three daughters. Their first daughter was Han Ch'i-yŏng. The second daughter married Chŏng Yak-hyŏn, an older brother of Tasan, and it was a marriage by which a family connection was established and by which she even engaged in academic interchange with Tasan. The third daughter was married to Hong Yun-ho of the P'ungsan Hong clan. Yi Pyŏk's older brother, Yi Kyŏk, and younger brother, Yi Sŏk, were military officers who had successfully passed the military service examination. Yi Pyŏk, on the other hand, was solely interested in academic scholarship.[1065]

Yi Pyŏk's first marriage was to the daughter of Kwŏn Ŏm (1729-1801)[1066] of the Andong Kwŏn clan. However, upon her early death, he remarried a woman from a Haeju Chŏng lineage.

The Yi Sŏng-hun Family

Yi Sŭng-hun, Korea's founding father of the Chosŏn Catholic church along with Yi Pyŏk, is of the P'yŏngch'ang Yi clan. The founder of the clan was Yi Kwang, and his fifteenth generation descendant, Yi Ok, was a Chief State Councillor during the first year of Sŏnjo. Afterwards, however, not too many of such successful individuals were born and their status as *Namin* drove their descendants to live in hiding.

[1065] *Ibid.,* p.12.

[1066] Following the decree prohibiting Catholicism, he became extremely frustrated with his son in law, Yi Pyŏk, to the point that he participated in the "63 men Petition" in the spring of 1801.

Appendix

Although his clan belonged to the *Namins*, the time from which his family had been registered as *Namin* is unknown.[1067] In 1766, the Pyongsul year during the reign of Yŏngjo, Yi Sŭng-hun's father, Yi Tong-uk passed the civil examination and served in the post of the mayor of Ŭiju.

Yi Sŭng-hun's mother was Yi Yong-hyu's daughter, the grandniece of Sŏngho Yi Ik, and also the elder sister of Yi Ka-hwan.[1068] His wife was the daughter of Chŏng Chae-wŏn, Tasan's elder sister.[1069] He established in-law relationships with the Naju Chŏng family through his own marriage and with the Yŏju Yi family through his father's marriage.

Strongly urged by his father's request, at one point, he burned several books on Western Learning and even left a piece of writing as if he had abandoned the Catholic church.[1070] However, in the 11th year of Chŏngjo, Chŏngmi year (1787), along with Chŏng Yak-chŏn and Kwŏn Il-sin, he revived the movement for the Catholic church. In the fifteeth year of Chŏngjo, 1791, they even gathered at Kim Sŏk-tae's house in Panch'on with the excuse that the purpose of the meeting was to write poetry, but read together books on Catholicism, which caused trouble.[1071]

The Yi Ki-yang Family

Yi Ki-yang (1744-1802) was from the Kwangju Yi clan and was a seventh generation descendant of Yi Tŏk-hyŏng, a former Chief State Councillor under Sŏnjo and

---

[1067] Yu Hong -nyŏl, "Yi Sŭng-hun kwa kŭ husondŭl ŭi sunkyo," *Hakuk sahoesasangsa nongo*, (Seoul: Ilchogak, 1980), p.208.

[1068] *Chosŏn wangjo sillok, Sunjo* wŏnyŏn 2nd month, Imsin (26).

[1069] *Naju Chŏng-ssi chokpo*, p.7.

[1070] *Chosŏn wangjo sillok* Chŏngo 15th year 11th month Kimyo.

[1071] *IbidI.*, Chŏngjo 15th year 11th month Kapsin.

Kwanghae-kun. In 1774, he passed the *Chinsa* examination and in 1795, he passed the civil service examination. His father was Yi Chong-han and his mother was Chŏng Hyŏn-sŏ's daughter. Although his parents did not convert to Christianity, his son and daughter became Christian. Their son, Pang-ŏk married the daughter of Yi Ka-hwan, and another son, Ch'ŏng-ok married the daughter of Kwŏn Ch'ŏl-sin. Their daughter married the son of Hong Nak-min, Paek-yŏng. Yi Ki-yang's younger brother, Yi Ki-song became a Catholic.

The Yi Yun-ha Family

Chibong Yi Su-kwang, who is considered to be the father and the pioneer of *Silhak*, introduced the situation of the Western empire and Catholicism to Koreans. Among his eighth generation descendants, Yi Yun-ha became a follwer of Catholicism, and oddly, among his ninth generation descendants, three siblings, Yi Kyŏng-do, Yi Sun-i and Yi Kyŏng-ŏn, all died martyrs.[1072]

Among Chibong's direct descendants, the eldest son, Sŏng-ku (1584-1644) passed the civil service examination (1608) and even served the post of Chief State Councillor, and his second son, Min-ku served as the Second Minister of Board of War. Thus up to the fifth generation, descendants of Yi Su-kwang were successful in attaining high government posts, but starting with the sixth generation descendants, successful ones became few. Among the seventh generation descendants, there is Kŭk-song, who served as a Hyŏnkam (county magistrate) and Ik-sŏng who served as Ch'ŏmji (associate initiates).

The apparent reason behind the lack of successful individuals of the sixth generation stems mainly from the timing, at which point the party strife against the *Namins* reached its pinnacle, and *Namin* lost their political power in the twentieth year of Sukchong (1694). Afterwards, they abandoned their efforts at entering the political field and led

---

[1072] Yu Hong-nyŏl, *Han'guk sasangsa nongo* p.177.

Appendix

the life of a recluse.[1073]

Possible supporting evidence for the above inference is Chibong's seventh generation descendant, Yi Kŭk-sŏng, who spent eighty years of his life in the local region of Kyŏnggido Kwangju, pursuing academic scholarship and writing *Tangp'yŏngch'aek* . He was a *Namin* who refused to accede to Yŏngjo's calling to serve a high government post, and who was the son-in-law of Sŏngho Yi Ik, the great scholar of *Silhak*.

Yi Sŏng-ho's son-in-law, Yi Kŭk-sŏng's adopted son was Yi Yun-ha,[1074] the active Catholic who attended the conferences at Ch'ŏnjinam Chuŏsa during the early stage of the Chosŏn Catholic church and who even retrieved the holy images from the Board of Punishments during the Incident of Detection of the Catholics in 1785.[1075]

Yi Yun-ha married a daughter of Kwŏn Ŏm, who was the father of the leader of the early stage of Chosŏn Catholic church, Kwŏn Ch'ŏl-sin. In other words, he became the brother-in-law of Kwŏn Il-sin, who was very active in the early Catholic movement.

Yi Sŭng-hun was Yi Yun-ha's nephew. Yi Sŭng-hun was the nephew of Yi Ka-hwan, Yi Ik's great-grandson, who was his elder sister's husband. Yi Yun-ha's adoptive mother was Yi Ik's daughter, and thus Yi Sŏng-hun is a maternal nephew of Yi Yun-ha.

Among Yi Yun-ha's five children, Yi Kyŏng-do (Charles) and Yi Yu-hŭi were executed during the Sinyu Persecution of 1801, and Yi Kyŏng-ŏn died a martyr in prison in Chŏnju during the Chŏnghae Persecution in

---

[1073] *Ibid.*, p.192.

[1074] Although Yi Yun-ha was Yi Kŭk-sŏng's adopted son, because of his Catholic faith,with Yi Yun-ha's children, his name is not even mentioned in the family geneology.

[1075] Yi Ki-kyŏng (ed.) *Pyŏkwip'yŏn,* kwŏn II.

1827.[1076]

The background of Yi Yun-ha's conversion to Catholicism and his three daughters and three sons' deaths contains the influence of Matteo Ricci's "The True Meaning of the Lord of Heaven" which was in Yi Su-kwang's possession at that time, and he wrote about Catholicism in his *Chibong yusŏl* . Exposed to Western books handed down by his ancestors and to Yi Ik's statement on "The True Meaning of the Lord of Heaven," and also influenced by the Kwŏn Il-sin and Kwŏn Ch'ŏl-sin brothers, who were his maternal brothers-in-law, as well as leaders in founding of the Catholic church, Yi Yun-ha became a critical figure in the early Chosŏn Catholic church.

The Yun Yu-il Family

Yun Yu-il (1758-1795), who was flogged to death during the *Sinbu yŏngip Incident* (priest invitation incident), was from the P'ap'yŏng Yun clan, and his name recorded in the family genealogy book was Yun Che-baek. His father was Chang and his grandfather was Sa-hyŏk. He had initially lived in Kyŏnggido Yŏju, but then followed his father to Yangkŭn where Kwŏn Ch'ŏl-sin was living at that time and became his father's student.[1077] He learned about the Catholic doctrines from Kwŏn Ch'ŏl-sin and Chŏng Yag-yong [1078] and was baptized by Priest Raux in Beijing.[1079] He then convinced his father and his younger brother Yu-o to convert to Catholicism.

Convinced by his missionary efforts, Yun Yu-il's

[1076] This lineage was not completely recorded in the family geneology as described here, and the information was obtained from documents such as Dallet and *Pyŏkwip'yŏn*.

[1077] Chŏng Yag-yong, Nogam Kwŏn Ch'ŏl-sin myojimyŏng (The Epitaph of Kwŏn Ch'ŏl-sin), *op.cit.*, p.324.

[1078] *Ch'uguk ilgi* (Trial Diary), *Kaksa tŭngrok* 78, (Seoul: Kuksa p'yŏngch'an wiwŏnhoe, 1994), p.259.

[1079] Charles Dallet, *op.cit.*, (I), p.327.

Appendix

uncle, Yun Kwang-su also converted to Catholicism and was martyred in 1801. Yun Hyŏn's family including his wife Im-ssi and Yun Sŏn's family both converted to Catholicism and Yun Sŏn's daughters, Yun Chŏm-hye, and Yun Un-hye both were martyred in 1801.[1080] Yun Un-hye's husband, Chŏng Kwang-su also died a martyr in 1801.

Yun Yu-il was martyred in 1795 during the priest invitation incident, and his father and younger brother Yun Yu-o were arrested in 1801 during the Sinyu Persecution, upon which his father was banished to Imjado Island and his young brother was beheaded in Yangkŭn. His three uncles, Kwan-su, Hyŏn and Sŏn and their families, twelve people in total, were arrested and sentenced, among whom five were martyred.

Hong Yu-ho (1726-1785), who can almost be considered as the very first Catholic believer in Korea (his former name was Yu-han and his pen name was Nongŭn), was a member of the P'ungsan Hong clan, the Munkyŏnggong-kye Chigyegong branch. Among the members of his family, seven of them, Hong Yu-han, Nag-min, Chae-yŏng, Pyŏng-ju, Yŏng-ju, Pong-ju and Nak-kyo, were recorded as Catholic believers and five of them were martyred.

Hong Nak-kyo's son, Kap-yng married Yi Ik's maternal granddaughter, who was also Yi Yun-ha's daughter, [1081] and Hong-Nag-min's son, Chae-yŏng married Chŏng Yak-hyŏn's daughter, thus became in-laws with Hwang Sa-yŏng (Hong Nag-min was the husband of the sister of Hwang Sa-yŏng's wife). Hong Nag-min's eldest son, Paek-yŏng married the daughter of Yi Ki-yang, who was a seventh generation descendant of Yi Tŏk-hyŏng.

[1080] Kim Chin-so, "Chu Mun-mo sinbu sŏnkyo hwaltong chŏnhu ŭi sunkyojadŭl," *Kyohoesa yon'gu* 10 (1995), p.112.

[1081] Chŏng Yag-yong, Chŏnghŏn myojimyŏng, *Yŭjudang chŏnsŏ*, pp.22b-23a.

The Yi Ka-hwan (Yŏhŭng Yi clan) Family

Sŏngho Yi Ik's nephew, Yi Ka-hwan (1742-1801) was a highly regarded figure who was even considered as a potential successor to Chae Che-gong as Chief State Councillor. Corresponding regularly with the key figures of the early Chosŏn Catholic church, Yi Pyŏk, Kwŏn Ch'ŏl-sin and Chŏng Yag-yong, Yi Ka-hwan actively participated and cooperated in the activities of the church, though he had never been baptized as the others had. During his service at various government posts, as a Puyun in Kwangju and as a Yusu in Kaesŏng, he even suppressed Catholic church members at times. However, he was accused by the opposition party as the ring leader of a religious cult[1082] and died in prison during the Sinyu Persecution.

Yi Ka-hwan was also related to the Yu Hang-gŏm family of Chŏllado. Among Yu Hang-gŏm's ancestors,[1083] Yu Hŏn-jang's son-in-law was Yi Yong-hyu, the nephew of S|ngho Yi Ik of the Yŏhŭng Yi clan. Yi Yong-hyu's son was Yi Ka-hwan, and his daughter married Yi Tong-uk of P'yŏngch'ang Yi clan and gave birth to Yi Sŭng-hun. Yi Sŭng-hun was Yi Ka-hwan's nephew and Chŏng Yak-hyŏn's brother-in-law.

Yi Ka-hwan's daughter married Pang-ŏk, the son of Yi Ki-yang who was one of the early Catholics, and thus the two became in-laws. Yi Ki-yang's son, Ch'ong-ŏk, also became a Catholic and married Kwŏn Ch'ŏl-sin's daughter. Hong Nag-min's son, Paek-yŏng became a son-in-law of Yi Ki-yang. Sin Yŏ-kwŏn, one of the early fellow church members, was Yi Ka-hwan's elder sister's son.[1084]

As the investigation of the above families of several active *Namin Sip'a* faction members of the early Chosŏn

---

[1082] Yi Man-ch'ae (ed), *Pyŏkwaip'yŏn*, kwŏn 4, (Seoul: Yŏlhwadang (Reprinted), 1971), p.264.

[1083] He is from the Chinju Yu clan, and in Sukchong Sinyu year (1681), he passed *Munkwa* and became *Chamŭi* of the Board of Punishments.

[1084] *Sahak chungŭi*, p.43.

Catholic church demonstrates, the families were closely tied to each other through manifold inter-marriage relationships, through memberships in similar factions and through relationships based on school ties. It is most likely that dissemination and proliferation of Catholicism occurred with relative ease precisely because of these intertwined kinship relationships among the distinguished and highly reputable families.

Kwŏn Ch'ŏl-sin's maternal uncle, Hong Kyo-man, lived in Kyŏnggido P'och'on, and as Kwŏn's family joined the Catholic church, he followed suit and contributed substantially to spreading Catholicism in his hometown. Hong Nag-min was from Ch'ungch'ongdo Yesan, and upon his success at the *Chinsa* examination, he moved to Seoul and married into the families of Yi Ki-yang and Chŏng Yag-yong, who led him to believe and practice Catholicism around 1784-85.

Having been influenced by Yi Pyŏk, Kwŏn Ch'ŏl-sin was successful in converting his own relatives and friends. His father-in-law, An Chŏng-bok, however, ignored and refused to accept the new religion to the very end[1085] and openly opposed the Western Learning such as *Ch'ŏnhak mundap* and *Ch'ŏnhakko*.

Overall, the large family structure of Chosŏn contributed to the acceptance and dissemination of Catholicism. However, at the same time, it contained aspects that were hindrances to the process. For example, if one family member, especially the father, opposed the belief, then the dissemination effort within this family became difficult. It can be understood that because of the so-called family persecution, the spreading of Catholicism suffered much restriction.

Catholicism placed a Supreme being above everything and required an absolute faith. This was a threatening challenge to the traditional Chosŏn society whose structure revolved around a patriarchical system. The father held the ultimate authority within his family and

---

[1085] Yi Man-ch'ae, Pyŏkwuip'ŏn, kwŏn 2, 3.

functioned as a tie that maintained the cohesion of the family, and it was often within the family that the strong reactions against its teaching occured.

The persecution of a family signified the very first point at which Catholicism was oppressed, and throughout the entire period of the Catholic Persecution, it was perhaps the most dangerous enticement. This was because the denial of the familial kinship relationship implies not only potential divisions within families, but also the risk of driving families into social ruin. Subsequently, the persecution families arose from the effort to prevent the fall of oneself and one's family, rather than from an ideological conflict.

In the case of Yi Sŭng-hun's family, it was his father Yi Tong-uk, and in the case of Chŏng Yak-chŏn and Chŏng Yag-yong, it was their father Chŏng Chae-wŏn, who, upon learning of their sons' conversion to Catholicism, were shocked and visited their relatives' homes to persuade their sons to repent and declare that they had renounced it. Yi Sŭng-hun was made to apologize through a writing that denounced Western Learning.[1086] Chŏng Yag-yong's family members, the father and the sons, suffered from much frustration arising from mutual distrust, and the Chŏng brothers even despised their father as if he were an enemy for his forbiddance of their studies.[1087]

Furthermore, even for Yi Pyŏk, who was the most ardent leader of the new religious organization, his father's attempt at suicide caused him great agony. Because he was a *yangban*, in whom the values of loyalty and filial piety had been inculcated, pressure from others caused him much anguish, and he died young at age 33 in 1786, without having attained his dream of religious accomplishments.[1088]

Yi Ig-un, a *Namin* inspector of Kyŏnggido, was so

[1086] Yi Man-ch'ae, *op.cit.*, p.106.

[1087] *Chosŏn wangjo sillok*, Sunjo, The first year, 2nd month Muo.

[1088] Charles Dallet, *op.cit.*, (I), pp.320-321.

Appendix

adamantly opposed to Catholicism that he poisoned his son, Yi My|ng-ho, who was a Catholic with the baptismal name of John, in his attempt to uphold the honor of his family.[1089]

An epochal point of the dissemination of early Catholicism in Korea was aided by the crumbling of the social class system. Yi Pyŏk paid visits to and spread the Catholic teachings to those *yangban* scholars such as Yi Ka-hwan and Kwŏn Il-sin with whom he usually kept friendly relations. In addition, he transcended the boundaries of social distinctions, a forbidden practice at the time, and conducted his mission directly among the *chungin*. He succeeded in converting translator Kim Pŏm-u, and other *chungin*. Kim Chong-kyo, Chi Hwang, Ch'oe Ch'ang-hyŏn, Ch'oe In-gil.[1090] They had already been exposed to foreign culture and materials during their trips to Beijing, and thus their relative open mindedness allowed them to accept Yi Pyŏk's invitation.

[1089] *Chosŏn wangjo sillok,* Sunjo, the first year fourth month Kyŏngo.

[1090] Charles Dallet, (trans.), *op.cit.*, I, pp.308-316.

Jai-Keun Choi

Family Tree of Early Catholic Converts

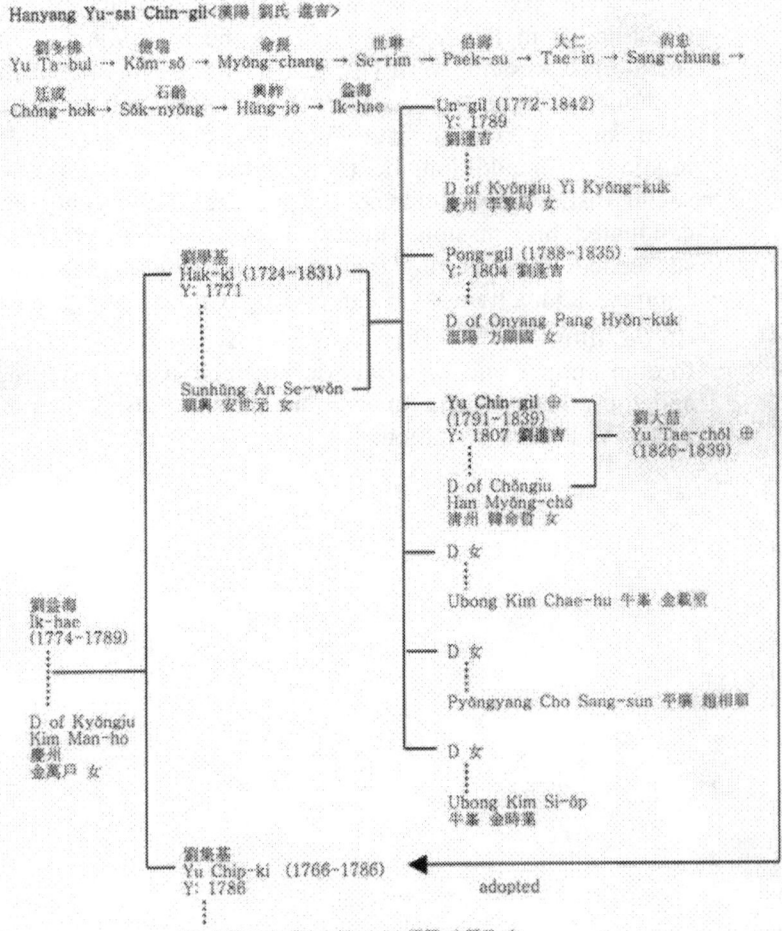

—— : marrige relation
D : daughter
✠ : Martyr
Y : Year they passed the Yŏkkwan exam

Hanyang Yu-ssi Sebo published in 1869
(possion of Yu Hong-gi's granson, Yu Man-sik)
(cf. Sŏngwŏnnok Seoul: Osŏngsa 1985, p. 790)

Family Tree of Early Catholic Converts

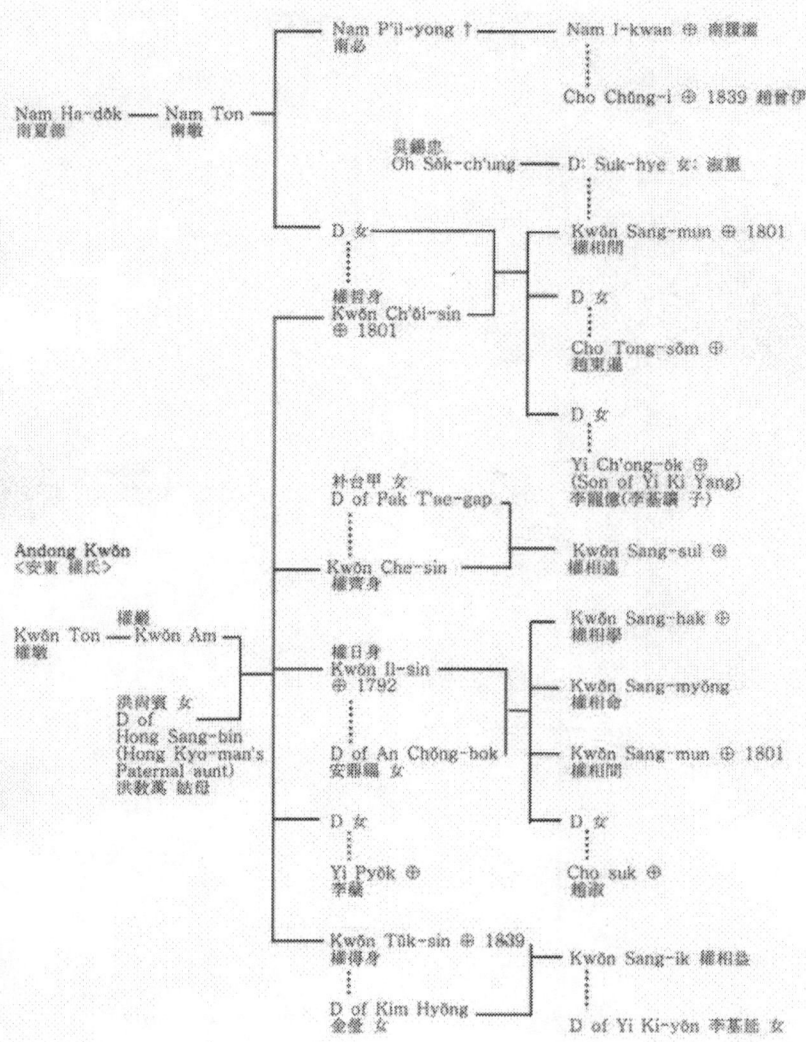

Jai-Keun Choi

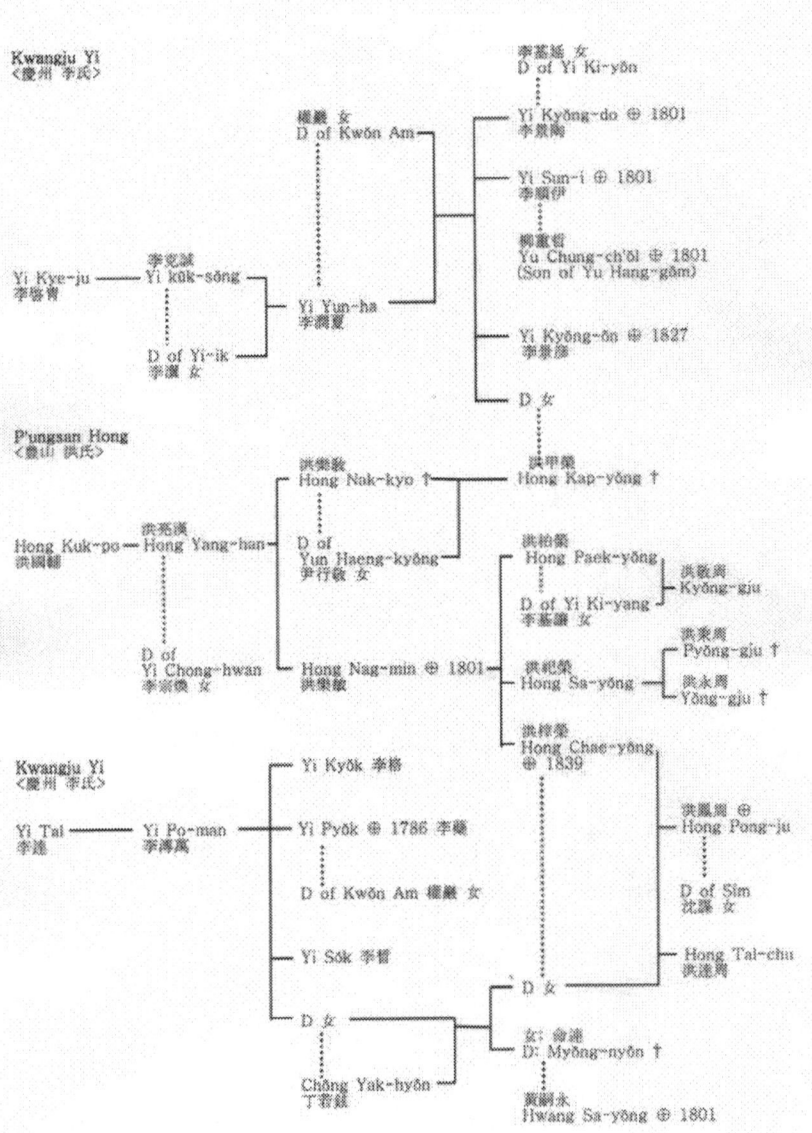

Family Tree of Early Catholic Converts

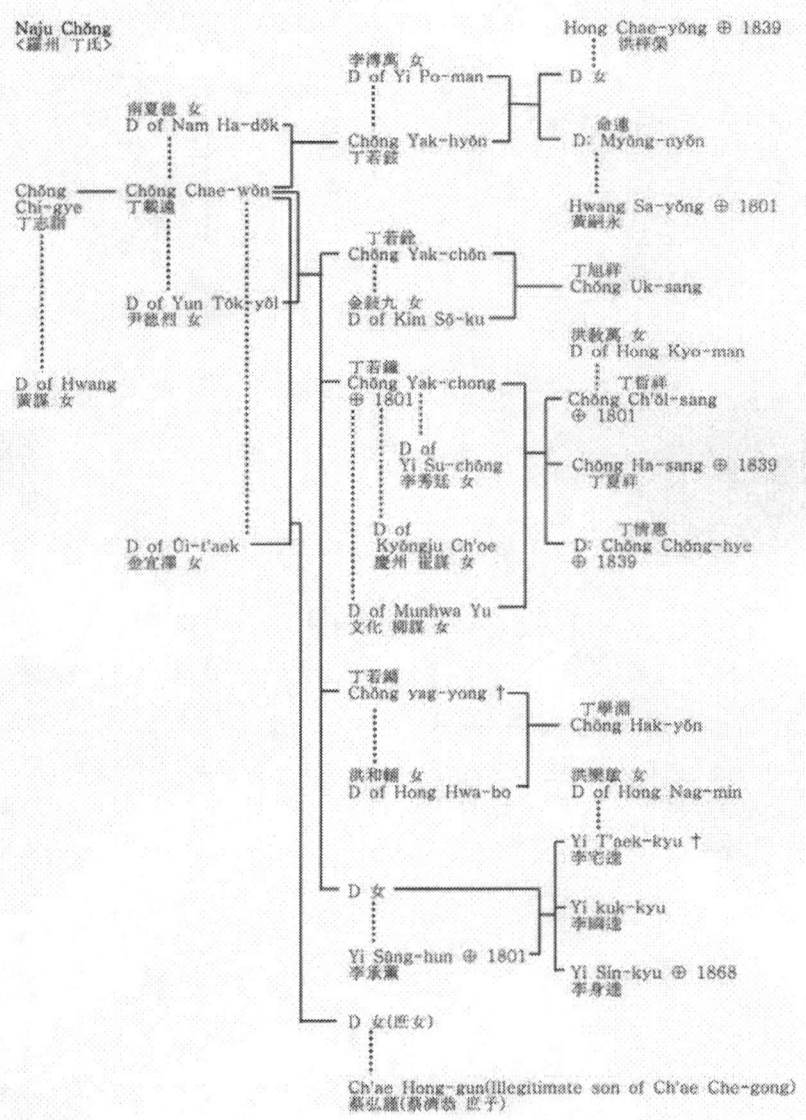

Jai-Keun Choi

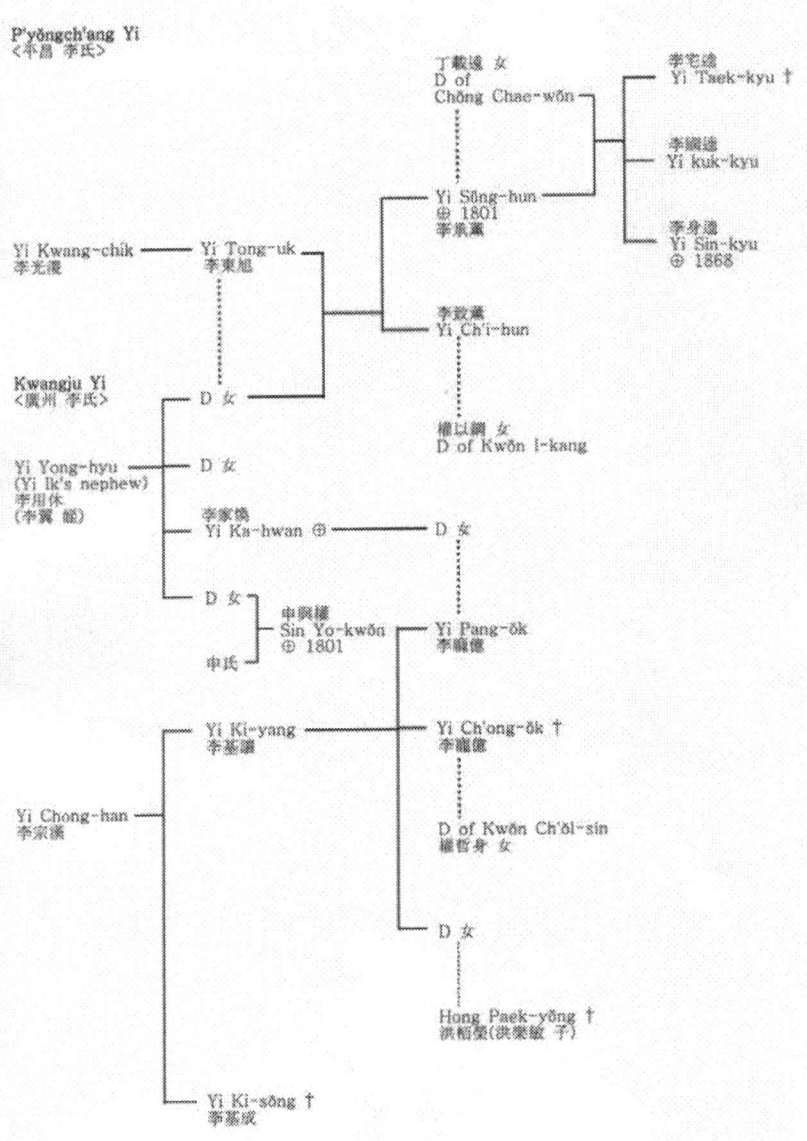

Family Tree of Early Catholic Converts

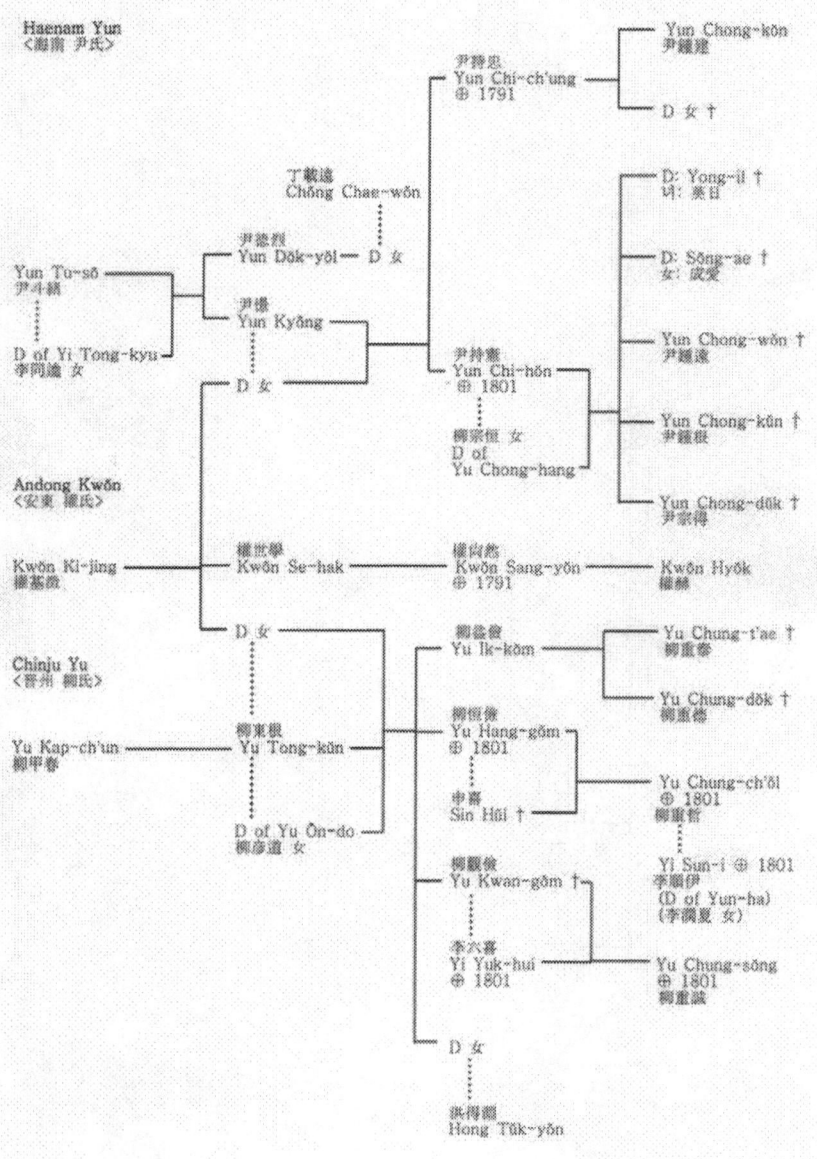

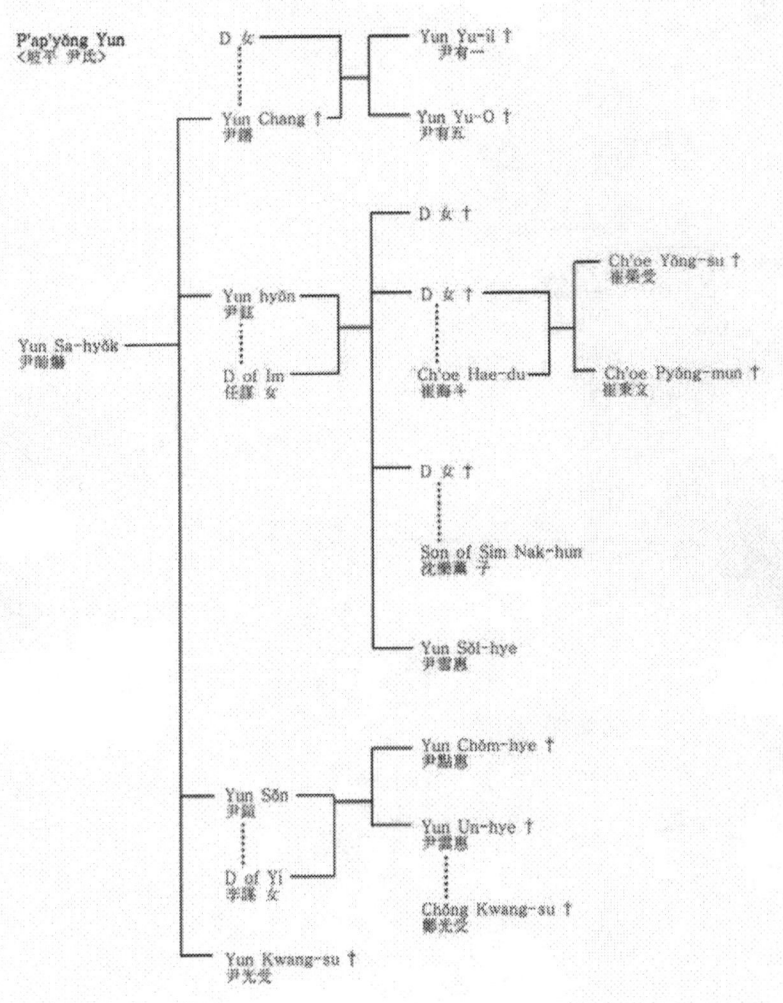

*** These charts were drawn on the basis of *Mansŏng taedongbo*, the clans' genealogy books, official government documents, church documents and genealogical researches on early Catholic converts.

Select Glossary

An Chŏng-bok (安鼎福) -- scholar of the Silhak school
Andong Kim-ssi (安東金氏) -- Andong Kim clan
Ch'ae Che-gong (蔡濟恭) -- a high ranking scholar-official
chehak (提學) -- Deputy Director
Chindo chajŭng (眞道自證) -- True way is evident in itself
Ch'Ilgŭk (Ch'I k'e) (七克) -- pattern of behaviors to be overcome
chinjusa (陳奏使) -- envoy to present a memorial to the emperor
Chikpang woegi (職方外記) -- On world geography
    (Chih-fang wai chi)
ch'ŏkhwabi (斥和碑) -- stele rejecting reconciliation
ch'ŏkpullon (斥佛論) -- anti-Buddhism arguments
ch'ŏksa (斥邪) -- reject heterodoxy
ch'ŏksa sasang (斥邪思想) -- reject heterodoxy thinking
ch'ŏksa wijŏng (斥邪衛正) -- 'rejecting heterodoxy' and
                                      'defendingorthodoxy '
ch'ŏksayunŭm (斥邪綸音) -- Edict proscribing heterodoxy
Ch'ŏlchong (哲宗) -- the 25th king of Chosŏn (1849-1863)
ch'ŏndang chiok (天堂地獄) -- heaven and hell
Ch'ŏngsun wanghu Kim-ssi (貞順王后金氏) -- Dowager
                                                               regent for King
                                                               Sunjo
Ch'ŏnhak ch'oham (天學初函) -- First steps in Catholic doctrine
    (T'ien-hsüeh ch'u-han)
Ch'ŏnhakko (天學考) -- Thoughts on heavenly learning
Ch'ŏnhak mundap (天學問答) -- Questions and answers on
                                           heavenly learning
Chŏngjo (正祖) -- the 22nd king of Chosŏn (1776-1800)
Ch'ŏnju (天主) -- Heavenly Lord, God
Ch'ŏnjugyo (天主敎) -- Catholicism
Ch'ŏnju silŭi (天主實義) -- The true meaning of the Lord of
    (Tien chu shih i)   Heaven
ch'ŏnmin (天民) -- "low born people"
Chosŏn wangjo sillok (朝鮮王朝實錄) -- The veritable records
                                           of the kings of the Chosŏn dynasty
Chŏng Ha-sang (丁夏祥) -- author of *Sangjae sangsŏ*

Chŏng Yag-yong (丁若鏞) -- one of the great *Silhak* scholar
Chŏng Yak-chŏn (丁若銓) -- author of *Chasan ŏbo*
Chŏng Yak-chong (丁若鍾) -- author of *Chugyo yoji*
Ch'uan kŭp kukan (推案及鞠案) -- Testimony and trial records
chubo (主保) -- patron saint
Ch'uguk ilgi (推鞫日記) -- Diary record of trial
Ch'ugwanji (秋官誌) -- Records of the Ministry of Punishments
Chugyoyoji (主敎要旨) -- Essentials of the Lord's teaching
Chuja karye (朱子家禮) -- Family rituals of Chu I
Ch'ujo chŏkpal sakŏn (秋曹摘發事件) -- the incident of detection of the Catholics in 1785
Chu Mun-mo (周文謨) -- a Chinese priest (Chou Wen-mo)
chungin (中人) -- "middle people"
chwaŭijŏng (左議政) -- the Second State Councillor
hanyŏk sŏhaksŏ (漢譯西學書) -- Western learning books translated into Chinese
hoejang (會長) -- catechist
Hong Nag-an (洪樂安) -- an anti Catholic
Hŏnjong (憲宗) -- the 24th king of Chosŏn(1834-1849)
Hwang Sa-yŏng paeksŏ (黃嗣永帛書) -- Silk letter of Hwang Sa-yŏng
iichei (以夷制夷) -- controlling of barbarians by barbarians
Ilsŏngnok (日省錄) -- Records of Daily Reflection
Kang Wan-suk (姜完淑) -- the first woman catechist
kasŏngjik (暇聖職) -- the Pseudo Ecclesiastical Hierarchy
Kigi tosŏl (奇器圖說) -- Descriptions of Ingenious Devices
Kihae pakhae (己亥迫害) -- Persecution of 1839
Kiin sipp'yŏn (畸人十編) -- Ten Discourses of Stranger
Kim Pŏm-u (金範禹) -- the fist martyr
Kim Tae-gŏn (金大建) -- the first Korean priest
Kojong (高宗) -- the 26th king of Chosŏn (1864-1910)
kongso (公所) -- mission stations
Kongsŏp'a (攻西派) -- anti-Western faction
Kwŏn Ch'ŏl-sin (權哲身) -- a *Silhak* scholar and Catholic martyr
Kwŏn Il-sin (權日身) -- a Catholic martyr
Kwŏn Sang-yŏn (權尙然) -- an early Catholic martyr
Kyouron (交友論) -- A treatise on friendship

Glossary

(Tiao you lun)
Kyouch'on (教友村) -- village of brethren
Mandongmyo (萬東廟) -- shrine to honor the Ming
Myŏngdohoe (明道會) -- Society of illumination of the Way
Nam Chong-sam (南鍾三) -- a royal secretary
Namin (南人) -- Southerners
Noron (老論) -- Old Doctrine
Ogachakt'ong (五家作統) -- five family mutual surveillance units
Pibyŏnsa tŭngnok (備邊司謄錄) -- Records of the Border Defense Council
P'odoch'ŏng tŭngnok (捕盜廳謄錄) -- Police Station Records
poyuron (補儒論) -- additional argument for Confucianism
Pugin (北人) -- Northerners
Pukhakp'a (北學派) -- Northern Learning school
P'ung'yang Cho-ssi (豊壤趙氏) -- P'ung'yang Cho clan
Puyŏnsa (赴燕使) -- embassy to the Ch'ing capital Yen-ching
Pyŏkp'a (僻派) -- party of Principle
pyŏksa wijŏng (僻邪衛正) -- Repelling the false and protecting the right (闢衛編) -- In defense of orthodoxy against heterodoxy
  Pyŏkwip'yŏn
Pyŏng'in pakhae (丙寅迫害) -- Persecution of 1866
Pyŏng'o pakhae (丙午迫害) -- Persecution of 1846
saganwŏn (司諫院) -- Office of Censor General
sahak (邪學) -- evil doctrine, heresy
Sahak chingŭi (邪學懲義) -- Warning against heterodoxy
Sahak choein ch'uan (邪學罪人推案) -- Testimony of the heterodoxy criminals
sahŏnbu (司憲府) -- Office of the Inspector General
Sangjae sangsŏ (上宰相書) -- Letter to the minister
sangje (shang-ti) (上帝) – Sovereign on high, God
sangmin (常民) -- "free born commoners"
sedo chŏngch'I (勢道政治) -- in-law government
Silhak (實學) -- practical learning
silsagusi (實事求是) -- Seek truth from facts
Silŭi chŭngŭi (實義證疑) -- Reflection on the True Doctrine of the Lord of Heaven
Sinhae pakhae (辛亥迫害) -- Persecution of 1791
Sinhae t'onggong (辛亥通共) -- Commercial Equalization

Enactment of 1791
Sin Hu-dam (辛後聃) -- author of *Sŏhakpyŏn*
Sinjŏng Wanghu (神貞王后趙大妃) -- Sinjŏng Wanghu Cho taebi (Cho taebi --Dowager regent for Hŏnjong)
Sinmi yang'yo (辛未洋擾) -- Foreign disturbance of 1871
Sinmyŏng ch'ohaeng (神明初行) -- a meditation book
Sinsŏp'a (信西派) -- pro-Western faction
Sinyu pakhae (辛酉迫害) -- Persecution of 1801
Sip'a (時派) -- Party of Expediency
sipkye (十戒) -- the Ten Commandments
sŏhak (西學) -- Western Learning
Sŏhakpyŏn (西學辨) -- Discourses on Western Learning
Sŏnggyoyoji (聖敎要旨) -- The Essentials of the Christian doctrines
Sŏngho hakp'a (星湖學派) -- The Sŏngho school
Sŏngse ch'uyo (盛世芻要) -- Everyday Teaching of the Church (Sheng shih chiujao) in everyday language
Soron (少論) -- Young Doctrine
Sŏnggyun'gwan (成均館) -- National Confucian Academy
Sunjo (純祖) -- the 23th king of Chosŏn(1800-1834)
Sŭngjŏn wŏn ilgi (承政院日記) -- Diary of the Royal Secretariat
Taemokku (代牧區) -- Vicariate Apostolic
taese (代洗) -- private baptism
Tae'wŏn'gun (大院君(興宣) -- Prince Hŭngsŏn Taewŏngun (Hŭngŏn)
tangsanggwan (堂上官) -- the higher-level officials
t'angp'yŏngch'aek (蕩平策) -- Policy of Impartiality
Tongdo sŏgi (東道西器) -- Eastern ways and Western machines
tongjisa (冬至使) -- Winter solstice mission
Tosa pan'gyomun (討邪頒奏文) -- Edict for the punishment of Heterodoxy
Ŭigŭmbu (義禁府) -- State Tribunal
Ŭnŏn'gun (恩彦君) -- King Chŏngjo's half brother
Uŭijŏng (右議政) -- the Third State Councillor
yangban (兩班) -- officials of the "two orders"
yangin (良人) -- "free born people"
Yi Ik (李瀷) -- a Silhak scholar
Yi Pyŏk (李檗) -- a founder of the Korean Catholic Church

Glossary

Yi Sŭng-hun (李承薰) -- the first baptized Catholic in Korea
yŏkkwan (譯官) -- interpreter
yŏngnam man'inso (嶺南萬人疏) -- Memorial of Ten Thousand men of Kyŏngsang province
yŏnghon (靈魂) -- the sprit, the soul
yŏngŭijŏng (領議政) -- the Chief State Councillor
Yu Chin-gil (劉進吉) -- name of an interpreter
Yurich'ang (琉璃廠) -- a street in Beijing lined with bookstores
    (Liu-li ch'ang)   near where the Korean diplomatic mission stayed.
Yun Chi-ch'ung (尹持忠) -- the first Catholic martyr in Korea (1759-91)
yunhoe (輪廻) -- transmigration
Yu Pang-je (劉方濟) -- a Chinese priest
    (Liu Fang-chi)

BIBLIOGRAPHY

Akagi Nihei. "Chōsen ni okeru tenshukyō o ryūnyū to sono tenrei mondai ni tsuite" (The introduction of Catholicism into Korea and the rites controversy). *Shigaku zasshi,* 5, nos. 6, pp.707-36, pp.847-81, 8, pp.1023-62 (1940).

Allen, Charles Wiltford. *Jesuits at the Court of Peking.* Arlington, Va: 1975

An Chŏng-bok. "A Korean's View of Christianity," an excerpt from his *Ch'ŏnhak mundap* (Conversations on Catholicism). Translator unknown. *Korea Magazine,* 1917, pp.262-268.

_____. *Sunam ch'ongsŏ,* (The collected writings of An Chŏng-bok). 2 vols. Seoul: Sŏnggyun'gwan taehakkyo, Taedong munhwa yŏn'guwŏn, 1970.

An Hwa-suk. "Chosŏn hugi ŭi ch'ŏnjugyo yŏsŏng hwaltong kwa yŏsŏnggwan ŭi palchŏn" (The activity of Catholic women and the development of the viewpoint on women in the late Chosŏn period). *Ch'oe Sŏg-u sinbu hwagap k'inyŏm, Han'guk kyohoesa nonch'ong.* Seoul: 1982.ŭ

An Oe-sun. "Taewŏngun chipchŏnggi ch'ŏnjugyo pakhae wŏnin e taehan siron" (An essay on the causes of the Catholic persecution during the Taewŏn'gun's governing period). *Tong kwa sŏ ŭi sayu segye.* Seoul: Minjoksa, 1991, pp.1281-1297.

Baker, Donald L. *Confucians Confront Catholicism in Eighteenth-Century Korea.* Ph.D. dissertation, University of Washington, 1983.

_____. "A Confucian confronts Catholicism." *Korean Studies Forum.* No. 6, Winter-Spring, 1979-1980.

_____. "Jesuit Science through Korean Eyes." *Journal of Korean Studies,* No.4 1982.

Bibliography

_____. "The Martyrdom of Paul Yun: Western Religion and Eastern Ritual in Eighteenth-Century Korea." *Transactions of the Royal Asiatic Society, Korea Branch.* No. 54 (1979), pp.33-58.

_____. "Neo-Confucians Confront Theism: Korean Reactions to Matteo Ricci's Arguments for Existence of God." *Tonga yŏn'gu*, No. 3. Seoul: Sŏgang Univ., 1983, pp.157-184.

_____. "A Note on Jesuit Work in Chinese Ih Circulated in 17th and 18th-Century Korea." *China Mission Studies V,* 1983, pp.28-36.

_____. "The Use and Abuse of the *Silhak* Label: A New Look at Sin Hu-dam and his *Sŏhakpyŏn.*" *Kyohoesa yŏn'gu,* no. 3 (1981), pp.183-254.

Balazs, Etienne. *Chinese Civilization and Bureaucracy.* Trans. H.M. Wright. New Haven: Yale University Press, 1964.

Bangert, William. *A History of the Society of Jesus.* St. Louis: The Institute of Jesuit Sources. 1972.

Barrows, John H. *The Christian Conquest of Asia.* New Yok: Charles Scribber's Sons, 1899.

Berentsen, J. M. *Grave and Gospel.* Leiden, Netherlands: E.J. Brill, 1985.

Bernard, Henri. *Matteo Ricci's Scientific Contribution to China.* Trans. E.C. Werner. Peking: H. Vetch, 1935.

Bettray, P. Johannes. *Die Akkommodations methode des P. Matteo Ricci S.J. in China.* Romae, Apud Aedes Universitatis Gregorianae, 1955.

Bodde, Derk. *Essays on Chinese Civilization.* Princeton, NJ: Princeton University Press, 1981.

_____. "The Chinese View of Immortality: Its Expression by Chu I and Its Relationship to Buddhist Thought." *Review of Religion,* 6 (1942), pp.369-383.

Boxer, C.R. *The Christian Century in Japan, 1548-1650.* Berkeley: University of California Press, 1954.

Cary, Otis. *A History of Christianity in Japan:Roman Catholic and Greek Orthodox Missions.* N.Y.: Fleming H. Revell Company, 1909.

Ch'a In-hyŏn. "Han'guk ch'ŏnju kyohoe wa sŏng'gachip" (Hymns and hymnals in the Korean Catholic church). *Han'kuk kyohoesa nonmunjip I,* 1984.

Ch'a Ki-jin. "Ch'ŏnjugyo ŭi yuip kwa chibaech'ŭng ŭi taeŭng nolli" (The receptive class and their logic of Catholicism in the late Chosŏn dynasty). *Yŏksa pip'yŏng,* 25 (Summer, 1994), pp.294-306.

_____. "Chosŏn hugi ch'ŏnjugyo ŭi chibang chŏnp'a wa kŭ sŏngkyŏk" (Propagation of Catholicism in Yŏngnam area and its characteristics during the final period of the Chŏsŏn kingdom). *Kyohoesa yŏn'gu,* No. 6, 1988.

_____. "Man ch'ŏn Yi Sŭng-hun ŭi kyohoe hwaltong kwa chŏngch'I chŏk ipchi" (The church activity of Yi Sŭng-hun and his political stand). *Kyohoesa yŏn'gu,* No. 8, 1992.

_____. "Nogam Kwŏn Ch'ŏl-sin ŭi hangmun kwa sŏhak" (Kwŏn Ch'ŏl-sin's scholarship and Catholicism). *Ch'ŏnggye sahak,* No. 10 (1993), pp.111-158.

_____. "Yun Chong-hŭi in chŏksaron kwa haebangnon insik e taehan yŏn'gu" (A study of recognition on Yun Chong-hŭi's theory of *ch'ŏksa* [reject heterodoxy] and coastal defense). *Yun Pyŏng-sŏk kyosu hwagap kinyŏm Han'guk kŭndaesa non-ch'ong.* Seoul: Chisik sanŏpsa, 1990, pp.21-46.

Cha Sŏng-hwan. *Han'guk chonggyo sasang ŭi sahoehak chŏk ihae* (Sociological understanding of Korean religious thought). Seoul: Munhak kwa chisŏngsa, 1992.

Ch'ae Che-gong. *Pŏnam sŏnsang munjip* (Collected literary works of master Pŏnam). 2 volumnes. Seoul: Kwangsŏng munhwasa (reprint), 1975.

Chan, Albert S.J., ed. "Early Missionary Attempts in Korea." *Tonga yŏn'gu,* No. 3. Seoul: Sŏgang University, 1983, pp.131-156.

Chan Wing-tsit. *A Sourcebook in Chinese Philosophy.* Princeton, NJ: Princeton University Press, 1969.

_____. "Neo-Confucianism: New Ideas in Old Terminology." *Philosophy East and West,* 17 (1967), pp.15-35.

_____. "Chinese and Western Interpretations of *jen.*" *Journal of Chinese Philosophy,* 26 (1975), pp.15-35.

_____, trans. *Reflections on Things at Hand Compiled by Chu I and Lu Tsu-chien.* New York: Columbia University Press, 1967.

_____. *Neo-Confucianism, etc.: Essays by Wing-tsit Chan.* New Haven: Oriental Society, 1969.

_____. "The Evolution of the Neo-Confucian Concept of *Li* or Principle." *Tsing Hua Journal of Chinese Studies,* 4, no. 2 (1964), pp.123-149.

_____. "Patterns for Neo-Confucians: Why Chu I Differed from Ch'eng I." *Journal of Chinese Philosophy,* 5 (1978), pp.101-126.

_____. *Chu I: Life and Thought.* New York: St. Martin's Press, 1987.

Chang An-suk. "Hanguk kat'ollik sŏngga ŭi yŏksajŏk pyŏnch'ŏn e kwanhan yŏn'gu" (A study of the historical changes in Korean Catholic hymns: The pre-liberation period). *Han'guk kyohoesa nonmunjip,* I (1984).

Chang Chŏng-ran. Adam Syal (1591-1666) yŏn'gu (A study of Johann Adam Schall von Bell). Ph. D. dissertation, Sŏngsin Women's University, 1992.

_____. "Sohyŏn seja yŏn'gu e issŏsŏ ŭi myŏt kaji munje" (Several problems to study of the crown prince Sohyŏn). *Kyohoesa yŏn'gu,* No. 9 (1994).

Chang Ming-shih. *Chinese Intercourse with Korea from the 15th Century to 1895.* London: W.W. Rockhill, 1905.

Chen, Kenneth. "Matteo Ricci's Contribution to and Influence on Geographical Knowledge in China." *Journal of the American Oriental Society* (1939), pp.325-359.

Chen Shou-yi. "Ming-mo Yehsu hui-shih te Juchiao kuan chi ch'I fan-Iang" (The reaction of the Jesuits to Confucianism in the late Ming), in Chen Shou-yi, et al., *Ming-tai tsung-chiao* (Religions in the Ming dynasty). Taipei, Taiwan: Taiwan Student Bookstore, 1968, pp.67-123.

Ch'en Yuan. "Ts'ung chiao-wai tien-chi so chien Ming-mo Ch'ing-chu chih T'ien-chu Chiao" (A glimpse of the Catholic missions in China, sixteenth through eighteenth centuries, from the writings of non-Catholic authors). *Kuo-li Pei-p'ing t'ushu kuan kuan-k'an,* 8 (March-April, 1934), pp.1-31.

Cheng Chung-ying. "Dialectics of Confucian Morality and Metaphysics of Man." *Philosophy East and West,* 21 (1971), pp.111-123.

_____. "Theory and Practice in Confucianism." *Journal of Chinese Philosophy,* 1 (1974), pp.179-198.

Chang, Carsun. *The Development of Neo-Confucian Thought.* 2 vols. New Haven: Bookman Associates, 1957-62.

China and Christianity: Historical and Future Encounters. Eds. James D. Whitehead, Yu-ming Shaw and N.J. Girardot. Notre Dame, IN: The University of Notre Dame Press, 1979.

Ching, Julia. *Confucianism and Christianity.* Tokyo: Kodansha, 1971.

Cho Ki-jun. "Silhak Thought in the Late Yi Dynasty and Its Socio-economic Background." *Asea yŏn'gu,* 11, no. 4 (1968), pp.95-113.

Cho Hwa-sŏn. "*Sŏnggyŏng chikhae* ŭi yŏn'gu" (A study of

Sŏnggyŏng chikhae). *Ch'oe Sŏg-u sinbu hwagap kinyŏm Han'guk kyohoesa nonch'ong*. Seoul: 1982.

Cho Kwang. "Ch'ogi ch'ŏnju kyohoe ŭi sindo punp'o" (Geographical distribution of early Catholic believers), *Han'gŭl sŏngsŏ wa kyŏre munhwa*. Seoul: Kidokkyomunsa, 1985.

_____. *Chosŏn hugi ch'ŏnju kyohoesa yŏn'gu* (A study on the history of the church in later Chosŏn). Seoul: Koryo taehakkyo minjok munhwa yŏn'guso, 1988.

_____. "Sinyu pakhae ŭi punsŏkjŏk koch'al" (An analysis of the causes of the 1801 persecution), *Kyohoesa yŏn'gu*, 1 (1977), pp.41-74.

_____. "Sinyu pakhae ŭi sŏngkyŏk" (The characteristics of Chatolic persecution of 1801), *Minjok munhwa yŏn'gu,* vol. 13 (1978), pp.63-95.

_____. "Chosŏn hugi sŏhakŭi suyongch'ŭng kwa suyong nolli" (The class basis for acceptance of Catholicism in the late Chosŏn dynasty and its rationale). *Yŏksa pip'yŏng*, 25 (Summer, 1984), pp.282-293.

_____. "Chosŏn kyogu sŏlchŏng ŭi minjoksa chŏk ŭimi" (Influence of the Vicariatus Apostolicus of Korea on Korean history). *Kyohoesa yŏn'gu,* No. 4 (1983).

_____. "Han'guk ch'ŏnju kyohoe ŭi kiwŏn munje" (The origin of Korean Catholic church). *Kuristokyo wa kyŏre munhwa*. Seoul: Kidokkyomunsa, 1991.

_____. "Hwang Sa-yŏng paeksŏ ŭi sahoe sasang chŏk paekyŏng" (A socio-intellectual background of Hwang Sa-yong's silk letter). *Sach'ong,* 21,22 (1978).

_____. "The Meaning of Catholicism in Korean History. *Korea Journal,* vol. 24, No. 8 (1984)

_____. "Sinyu kyonan kwa Yi Sŭng-hun" (The persecution of 1801 and Yi Sŭng-hun). *Kyohoesa yŏn'gu,* no. 8 (1992).

Choe Ching-young. *The Rule of the Taewŏn'gun, 1864-1873: Restoration in Yi Korea.* Cambridge, MA: East Asian Research Center, Harvard University, 1972.

_____. "Kim Yuk and the Taedongbŏp Reform." *Journal of Asian Studies,* XXIII (November, 1963), pp.21-35.

Ch'oe Ch'ang-gyu. *Han'guk ŭi sasang* (Korean Thoughts). Seoul: Sŏmundang, 1973.

Ch'oe Ch'ang-mu. "Han'guk ch'ŏnju kyohoe wa chosang chesa ŭi kongin" (Korean Catholic church and the public recognition of sacrifice for ancestors). *Han'guk kyohoesa nonmunjip,* II (1985).

Ch'oe Ik-hwan. *Silhakp'awa Chŏng Tasan* (The school of practical learning and Chŏng Tasan). P'yŏngyang: Kungnip ch'ulpanbu, 1955.

Ch'oe Kil-sŏng. *Han'guk ŭi chosang sung bae* (Ancestor worship in Korea). Seoul: Yechŏn, 1990.

Ch'oe Pyong-ok. "Wijŏng ch'ŏksa sasang e taehan ilgoch'al" (A study on thought of *wijŏng ch'ŏksa* [defending orthodoxy and rejecting heterodoxy]). *Hongik sahak,* 3, 1986.

Ch'oe Sang-ch'ŏn. "Chŏngjocho ch'ŏnjugyohoe undong ŭi sŏngkyŏk" (The character of activity of Catholic church in king Ch'ŏngjo's reign). *Ch'oe sŏg-u sinbu hwagap kinyŏm Han'guk kyohoesa nonch'ong.* Seoul: 1982.

_____. "Yi Ka-hwan gwa sŏhak" (Yi Ka-hwan and Catholicism). *Han'guk kyohoesa nonmunjip,* II. Seoul: 1985.

Ch'oe So-ja. "Ch'ŏng chŏng e sŏŭi Sohyŏn seja" (Crown prince Sohyŏn at Ch'ing court). *Chŏn Hae-jong paksa hwagap kinyŏm sahak nonch'ong.* Seoul: Ilchogak, 1979.

_____. "Han'guk kwa Chungguk kyohoesa ŭi pigyosa chŏk koch'al" (The comparative study of the accommodation of Catholicism in China and Korea), *Han'guk kyohoesa nonmunjip,* I, 1984.

Bibliography

_____. "17-18 Segi Hanyŏk sŏhaksŏ e taehan yŏn'gu: Chungguk kwa Han'guk ŭi sadaebu ege mich'in yŏnghyang" (Western books translated into Chinese in the seventeenth and eighteenth centuries and their influence on the literati of China and Korea). *Han'guk munhwa yŏn'guwŏn nonch'ong,* no. 39 (1981), pp.79-111.

_____. *Tongsŏ munhwa kyoryusa yŏn'gu* (A study of the cultural history exchange between East and West). Seoul: Samyŏngsa, 1990.

Ch'oe Tong-hŭi. "Sin Hu-dam, An Chŏng-bok ŭi sŏhak pip'an e kwanhan yŏn'gu" (A study of Sin Hu-dam, An Chong-bok's criticism of Catholicism). Ph.D. dissertation, Korea University, 1975.

_____. "Tasan ŭi sin'gwan" (Tasan's Concept of God). *Han'guk sasang,* 15 (1977), pp.106-134.

_____. *Sŏhak e taehan Han'guk silhak ŭi panŭng* (Response of the Korean Silhak scholars to the learning of the West). Seoul: Kodae minjok munhwa yŏn'guso, 1988.

Ch'oe Wan-gi. "Pakhaegi Han'guk ch'ŏnju kyohoe wa p'yŏngsindo undong" (Layman's movement of Korean Catholic church during the period of persecution). *Han'guk kyohoesa nonmunjip,* II (1985).

Ch'oe Yong-gyu. "Kihae Pyŏngo kyonan'gi ch'ŏnju kyodo ŭi punsŏkchŏk koch'al — 1802-1846 nyŏn ŭl chungsim ŭro" (Analytical examination of Catholic converts during the religious persecution years of 1839 to 1845). *Kyohoesa yŏn'gu,* No. 6, 1988. pp.227-276.

Choi Chong-ko (Ch'oe Chong-go). "Church and State in Korea: A Historical and Legal Approach." *Korea Journal,* vol. 21, no. 12, pp.13-31.

Choi Ki-pok(Ch'oe Ki-bok). "The Abolition of Ancestral Rites and Tablets by Catholicism in the Chosŏn Dynasty and the Basic Meaning of Confucian Ancestral Rites." *Korea Journal,* vol. 24, no. 8 (1984), pp.41-52.

_____. "Chosŏnjo ch'ŏnju kyohoe ŭi chesa kŭmnyŏng kwa Tasan ŭi chosang chesa kwan," (The ban of ancestral rites by the Catholic church in Chosŏn dynasty and Tasan's view of ancestral rites). *Han'guk kyohoesa nonmunjip*, II (1985).

_____. "Myŏngmal Yesuhoe sŏnkyosadŭl ŭi poyuron gwa Sŏngnihak pip'an" (The late Ming Jesuit critique of neo-Confucianism and their Introduction of the theory of complementary doctrine"). *Kyohoesa yŏn'gu*, No. 6 (1988).

_____. "Yukyo wa sŏhak ŭi sasang jŏk kaltŭng kwa sŏngnihak jŏk ihae e kwanhan yŏn'gu" (A study of ideological conflict between neo- Confucianism and Catholicism and neo-Confucianist's understanding thereof). Ph.D. dissertation, Sŏnggyungwan University, 1989.

Choi Suk-woo (Ch'oe Sog-u). "The Factional Struggle in the Yi Dynasty: 1575-1725," *Korean Quarterly*, 7, no. 1, pp.60-91, no. 2, pp.70-96.

_____. "Catholic Church and Modernization in Korea." *Korea Journal*, vol. 7, no. 1, pp.4-9.

_____. "Chosŏn hugi ŭi sŏhak sasang" (Catholic thought of the late Chosŏn dynasty). *Kuksagwan nonch'ong*, 22 (1991), pp.189-218.

_____. *L'erection du Premier Vicari ofe Apostolique et les origines du Catholicisme en Corée*. Switzerland: Schoneck-Beckerried, 1961.

_____. "Han'guk kyohoe ch'angsŏl kwa ch'och'angi Yi Sŭng-hun ŭi kyohoe hwaltong" (The founding of the Korean church and early church activities of Yi Sŭng-hun). *Kyohoesa yon'gu*, No. 8 (1992).

_____. *Han'guk kyohoesa ŭi t'amgu* (Searching for the history of the Korean church). I& II Seoul: Han'guk kyohoeso yŏn'guso, 1982&1991.

_____. *Han'guk ch'ŏnju kyohoe ŭi yŏksa* (A history of Korean Catholic Church). Seoul: Han'guk kyohoesa yŏn'guso, 1982.

Bibliography

———. "Korean Catholicism Yesterday and Today." *Korea Journal,* vol. 24, no. 8 (1984).

———. *Pyŏngin pakhae charyo yŏn'gu* (A Study of the Materials of the Pyŏngin (1866) Persecution). Seoul: Han'guk kyohoesa yŏn'guso, 1968.

Choi Suk-woo, Im Ch'ung-sin. *Ch'oe Yang-op sinbu sŏganjip* (The Collected Letters of Fr. Ch'oe Yang-ŏp). Seoul: Han'guk kyohoesa yŏn'guso, 1984.

Choi Suk-woo et al. *Tasan Chŏng Yag-yong ŭi sŏhak sasang* (Western Learning thought of Tasan Chŏng Yag-yong). Seoul: Tasŏt sure, 1993.

Chŏng Sŏng-ch'ŏl. *Silhakp'a ŭi ch'ŏlhak sasang kwa sahoe chŏngch'ijŏk kyŏnhae* (The philosophy of the school of practical learning and their social and political opinions). P'yŏngyang: Sahoe kwahakwŏn, 1974.

Ch'ŏn Kwan-u. "Hong Tae-yong, 1731-1783." *Korea Journal,* vol. 12, no. 11 (November, 1972), pp.34-39.

Chŏng Chin-sŏk, trans. *Nŏnŭn chuch'u noko nanŭn seugo* (Collected letters of the Fr. Ch'oe Yang-ŏp). Seoul: Sŏng Paolo ttal, 1995.

Chŏng In-suk. "Yi Sun-I (Lutgardis) ŭi sasang kwa yŏngsŏng" (A study of the thought and spirituality of Yi Sun-I, Lutgardis, the martyr). *Han'guk kyohoesa nonmunjip,* I (1984).

Chŏng Ok-cha. "Sipgusegi ch'ŏksaron ŭi yŏksajŏk wisang" (A historical phase of ch'ŏksaron [reject heterodoxy]). *Han'guk hakpo,* 78 (1995).

Chŏng Sŏk-chong. "Sunjo yŏngan ŭi chŏngguk pyŏnhwa wa Tasan haebae undong" (Political change and the to release Tasan from exile during the Sunjo reign). *Kuksakwan nonch'ong,* 47 (1993), pp.57-114.

———. "Chŏng Yag-yong (1762-1836) kwa Chŏnjo, Sunjo yŏn'gan ŭi chŏngguk" (Chŏng Yag-yong and the political situation between king Chŏnjo and Sunjo). *Yŏksa wa in'gan ŭi taeung.* Seoul: Hanul, 1985.

Chŏng To-jŏn. *Sambongjip* (Collected works of Chŏng To-jŏn). Seoul: Kuksa p'yŏnch'an wiwŏnhoe, 1961.

Chŏng Yak-chong. *Chugyo yoji* (Essentials of the Lord's teaching). Ed. Ha Sŏng-nae. Seoul: Sŏng Hwang Sŏk-tu Nuga sŏwŏn, 1986.

Chŏng Yag-yong. *Yŏyudang chŏnsŏ* (The collected works of Chŏng Yag-yong). compiled by Kim Sŏng-jin, 152 kwon. Seoul: Sin chosŏnsa, 1934.

_____. *Chŏng Tasan chŏnsŏ* (The complete works of Chŏng Yag-yong). Seoul: Munhŏn p'yŏnch'an wiwŏnhoe, 1960-61.

Chōsenshi (History of Korea). vol. 6:1-4, Keijō: Chōsen Sōtokufu, 1935.

Chosŏn chŏngch'isa 1800-1863 (Political history of Chosŏn dynasty). 2vols, Seoul: Ch'ŏngyŏnsa.1990.

Christianity in China. Amonk, NY:M. E. Sharpe Inc.,1989.

Chosŏn wangjo sillok (The veritable records of the Chosŏn dynasty). Seoul: Kuksa p'yŏnch'an wiwŏnhoe, 1955-58.

Ch'uan kŭp kukan, 25,28,29 (The record of trials). Seoul: Asea munhwasa, 1983.

Chu Chae-yŏng. *Han'guk kat'olliksa ŭi ongwi* (In defense of Korean Catholic history). Seoul: Korea Catholic Press, 1970.

_____. *Sŏnyu ŭi Ch'ŏnju sasang kwa chesa munje*ŭ (Theism among early Confucians and the rites question). Seoul: Kyŏnghyang chapchisa, 1958.

_____. "Yamaguchi chŏ *Chōsen seikyōshi* ch'amjŏng" (Some errors in Yamagauchi's *History of Korean Catholicism),* in Yu Hong-nyŏl paksa hwagap kinyŏmhoe, ed. *Hyeam Yu Hong-nyŏl paksa hwagap kinyŏm nonch'ong* (Essays in

Bibliography

honor of the sixtieth birthday of Dr. Yu Hong-nyŏl). Seoul: T'amgudang, 1971, pp.482-98.

Chu Ch'ien-chih. "Yeh-su-hue tui-yu Sung-ju li-hsueh chih fan-Iang" (The Jesuits' reaction to neo-Confucianism). in Chen Shou-yi, et al., *Ming-tai tsung chiao* (Religions in the Ming dynasty). Taipei, Taiwan: Taiwan Student Bookstore, 1968, pp.125-80.

Chu I's Family Rituals. Tr. Patricia Buckley Ebrey. Princeton, NJ: Princeton University Press, 1991.

Chu Myŏng-jun. "Chŏng Yag-yong hyŏngje dŭl ŭi ch'ŏnjugyo sinang hwaltong" (The activities of Chŏng Yag-yong's brothers in support Christian faith). *Chŏnju sahak*, I (1984), pp.67-103.

―――. "Ch'ŏnjugyo ŭi sunansa" (A history of Korean Catholic persecution). *Sungsan Pak Kil-chin paksa kohi kinyŏm Han'guk kundae chonggyo sasangsa* (Essays in celebration of Dr. Pak Kil-chin's seventieth birthday: A history of modern Korean religious thought), 1984, pp.701-712.

―――. "Ch'ŏnjugyo ŭi Chŏllado chŏllae wa kŭ suyong e kwanhan yŏn'gu" (A study on the transmission and the acceptance of Catholicism in Chŏlla province, Korea). Ph.D. dissertation, Chŏnbuk University, 1988.

―――. "Ch'ŏnju kyododŭl ŭi sŏyang sŏnbak ch'ŏngwŏn" (A petition of Korean Catholics for sending Western ships). *Han'guk kyohoesa yŏn'gu*, No.3, (1981).

―――. "Yun Chi-ch'ungka ŭi Chinsan igoe taehayo" (The Yun Chi-ch'ung family move to Chinsan). *Kyohoesa yŏn'gu*, no. 6 (1988).

―――. "*Paeksan hŭksu mungobonch'ongsa* ŭi *Sahak chingŭi* wa *Pyŏkwip'yŏn*" (A study of *Sahak chingŭi* and *Pyŏkwipy'ŏn* Ied in the anthology of the *Paeksan hŭksu mungobon Ch'ongsa*). *Han'guk kyohoesa nonmunjip*, II. Seoul: 1985.

_____. "Yukyo chŏntong sahoe ui chosang sungbae sasang kwa ch'ŏnjugyo ŭi taeung" (Ancestor worship thought in traditional Confucian society and the confrontation with the Catholic church). *Pyŏn Tae-sŏp paksa hwagap kinyŏm sahak nonch'ong,* Seoul: Samyangsa, 1985.

Chu Myŏng-jun, Yu Pyŏng-gi. "Ch'ungch'ŏngdo ŭi ch'ŏnjugyo chŏllae." (Transmission of Catholicism in Ch'ungch'ŏng province). *Ch'oe sŏg-u sinbu hwagap kinyŏm Han'guk kyohoesa nonch'ong,* Seoul: 1982.

Chun Hae-jong (Chŏn Hae-jong). "Sino-Korean Tributary Relations in the Ch'ing Period," in John K. Fairbank, ed., *The Chinese World Order.* Cambridge, MA: Harvard University Press, 1968, pp.90-111.

Chung Chai-sik(Chŏng Chae-sik). "In Defense of the Traditional Social Order: Ch'ŏksa Wijŏng." *Philosophy East and West.* vol. 30 (April, 1980), pp.355-73.

_____. *A Korean Confucian Encounter with the Modern World.* Berkeley: University of California, 1995.

Chung, David. "The Han-San-Wei-I (Three religions are one) Principle in Far Eastern Societies." Transactions Korea Branch of Royal Asiatic Society, vol. 38, 1961,

_____. "The Problem of Analogy Between Christianity and Confucianism." *Korea Quarterly,* vol. 1, no. 2 (1959), pp.115-130.

_____. "Religious Syncretism in Korean Society." Ph.D. dissertation, Yale University, 1959.

_____. "A Narrative of Christianity in social change of Korea since the 17th Century." *Journal of Social Science and Humanities,* XIV (1961), pp.1-32.

Clark, Charles Allen. *Religions of Old Korea.* Seoul: Christian Literature Society of Korea, 1961.

Cohen, Paul. "The Anti-Christian Tradition in China." *Journal of Asian Studies,* XX (1960-61), pp.169-180.

Bibliography

_____ . *China and Christianity.* Cambridge, M.A.: Harvard University Press, 1963.

Columba, Cary-Elwei. *China and the Cross: Studies in Missionary History.* London: Longmans Green, 1917.

Cooper, Michael. *Rodrigues the Interpreter.* Tokyo: Weatherhill, 1974.

Cory, Ralph M. "Some Notes on Father Gregorio de Cespedes: Korea's First European Visitor." *Transactions of RAS (Korea),* XXVII (1937), pp.1-55.

Covall, Alan Carter. "Korean Conversion to Christianity." *Asian and Pacific Quarterly of Cultural and Social Affairs,* vol. 19, no. 2 (1987), pp.31-42.

Covell, Ralph R. *Confucius, The Buddha and Christ.* Maryknoll, NY: Orbis Books, 1986.

Cronin, Vincent. *The Wise Man from the West.* London: Rupert Hart-Davis, 1956.

Cummings, J.S. *A Question of Rites: Friar Domingo Navarette and the Jesuits in China.* Aldershot: Scholar Press, 1993.

_____ . *Jesuit and Friar in the Spanish Expansion to the East.* London: Variorum Reprints, 1986.

Dallet, Charles. *Histoire de l'Église de Corea,* tome. 1 & 2. Paris: Victor Palme, 1874.

_____ . *Histoire de l'Eglise de Corea (Han'guk ch'ŏnju kyohoesa)*. Vol. 1, 2 & 3. Trans. Ch'oe Sŏg-u and An ¬ng-yŏl. Waegwan: Pundo ch'ulp'ansa, 1979-1980.

de Gouvéa, Alexandre. "Establissement du Christianisme en Corée." *Revue d'Histoire des Missions,* no. 3 (1931). (Redigrée en Latin, par Monseigneur de Gouvéa, Évêque de Pekin, et Adressée le 15 août 1797 à Monseigneur de Saint-Martin, Évêque de Caradre et Vicaire, Apostolique de la Province Sutchuen en Chine.)

deGroot, J.J.M. *Sectarianism and Religious Persecution in China.* New York: Paragon Books, 1970.

Deuchler, Martina. "Neo-Confucianism: The Impulse for Social Action in Early Yi Korea," *The Journal of Korean Studies,* 2 (1980), pp.71-111.

_____. *The Confucian Transformation of Korea.* Cambridge, M.A.: Harvard University Press, 1992.

De Vos, George A. and Takao Sofue, ed. *Religion and the Family in East Asia.* Berkeley: University of California Press, 1986.

Diaz, Hector. *A Korean Theology: Chugyo Yoji = Essentials of the Lord's Teaching, by Chŏng Yak-chong Augustine (1760-1801).* Immensee: Neue Zeitschrift für Missionwissenschaft, 1986.

Dix, Griffin. "How to Do Things with Ritual: The Logic of Ancestor Worship and Other Offerings in Traditional Korea." *Studies on Korea in Transition,* ed. David McCann, et al. Honolulu: University of Hawaii Press, 1979, pp.57-88.

Drummond, R.H. *A History of Christianity in Japan.* Grand Rapids, MI: Eerdmans, 1971.

Dudink, A. "A Previously Unknown Preface (1607) by Zhou Xianchen to Matteo Ricci's Tienthu Shuyi." *Sino-Western Cultural Relations Journal* (formerly *China Mission Studies 1550-1800 Bulletin),* XVI (1994), pp.19-36.

Dunne, George H., S.J. *Generation of Giants: The Story of the Jesuits in China in the Last Decades of the Ming Dynasty.* Notre Dame, IN: Notre Dame Press, 1962.

Ehwa Yŏdae Sahakkwa, ed. *Chosŏn sinbunsa yŏn'gu* (A study of Chosŏn social status history). Seoul: Pŏpmunsa, 1987.

Elison, George. *Deus Destroyed: The Image of Christianity in Early Modern Japan.* Cambridge, MA: Harvard University Press, 1973.

Bibliography

Elwood, Douglas. "Christian Theology in an Asian Setting: The Gospel and Chinese Intellectual Culture." in *Christianity and the Religion of the East: Models for a Dynamic Relationship.* Scranton, PA: Ridge Row Press, 1982.

England, John C. and C.C. Lee, eds. "The Hidden History of Christianity in Asia: The Churches of the East Before A.D. 1500." in *Doing Theology with Asian Resouraces.* Auckland: Peace Publishing, 1993.

Eno, Robert. *The Confucian Creation of Heaven: Philosophy and Defense of Ritual Mastery.* Albany, NY: State University of New York, 1990.

Fairbank, John K., ed. *Chinese Thought and Institutions.* Chicago and London: University of Chicago Press, 1967.

_____, ed. *The Chinese World Order: Traditional China's Foreign Relations.* Cambridge, MA: Harvard University Press, 1968.

_____, ed. *The Cambridge History of China.* vol. 10. Cambridge : Cambridge University Press,1978.

Fujitsuka Ohikashi. "Richō no gakujin to Kenryū bunka" (Scholars of the Yi dynasty and Ch'ien-lung Culture). *Chōsen Shina bunka no kenkyū* I (1929), pp.283-332.

Fujita, Neil. *Japan's Encounter with Christianity: The Catholic Mission in Pre-Modern Japan.* New York: Paulist Press, 1991.

Gallagher, Louis J., trans. *China in the Sixteenth Century: The Journals of Matteo Ricci, 1583-1610.* New York: Random House, 1953.

Gernet, Jacques. "Christian and Chinese Visions of the World in the Seventeenth Century." *Chinese Science,* 4 (1980), pp.1-17.

_____. *China and the Christian Impact.* Trans. Janet Lloyd. Cambridge, England: Cambridge University Press, 1985.

Gifford, Daniel L. "Ancestral Worship as Practised in Korea." *The Korean Repository,* vol. 1. Seoul: The Trilingual Press, 1892.

Gompertz, G. St. G. "Some Notes on the Earliest Western Contacts with Korea." *Transactions of the Royal Asiatic Society, Korea Branch,* 33 (1957), pp.41-54.

Grayson, James H. *Early Buddhism and Christianity in Korea.* Leiden, Netherlands : E.J. Brill, 1985.

_____ , *Korea : A Religious History.* Oxford: Clarendon Press, 1989.

Griffis, William Elliot. *Corea: The Hermit Nation.* New York: Charles Scribner's Sons, 1894.

Gützlaff, C.F.A. *Journal of Three Voyages Along the Coast of China in 1831, 1832, with notices of Siam, Corea and the Loo-Choo Islands.* London: 1834.

Ha Sŏng-nae and Yi Sŏng-bae, trans. *Sŏnggyo yoji* (The Essential Teachings of our Holy Faith). Purported work of Yi Pyŏk. Seoul: Catholic Press, 1976.

Ha Sŏng-nae. *Ch'ŏnju kasa yŏn'gu* (A study on the Catholic hymns in Korea). Seoul: Sŏng Hwang Sŏk-tu Nuga sŏwŏn, 1985.

Ha Sŏng-nae. "Sunkyo ilgi ŭi chŏngi munhak ŭrosŏŭi sŏngkyŏk" (Characteristics of the diaries of the martyred as a genre of biographical literature). *Han'guk kyohoesa nonmunjip,* I (1984).

Ha U-bong. "Chŏng Tasan ŭi sŏhak gwan'kye e taehan ilgoch'al" (A look at Chŏng Tasan's relationship to Catholicism). *Kyohoesa yŏn'gu,* 1 (1977), pp.71-112.

"Habin sŏnsaeng yŏnbo" (A chronology of the life of Sin Hudam). reprinted in *Asea yŏn'gu,* 15, 2 (1972), pp.197-219.

Haboush, Jahyun Kim. *A Heritage of Kings: One Man's Monarchy in the Confucian World.* New York: Columbia

University, 1988.

Han Ki-sik. "The Christian impact and the indigenous response in 18th and 19th century Korea." *Koreana Quarterly,* 10 (Spring, 1968), pp.1-25.

Han Chong-man. "Tasan ŭi ch'ŏn'gwan" (Tasan's concept of heaven). *Tasan hakpo,* 2 (1979), pp.121-149.

Han'guk kidokkyo yŏksa yŏn'guso, ed. *Han'guk kidokkyo ŭi yŏksa* I(A history of Korean church). Seoul: Kidokkyomunsa, 1989.

Han'guk sasansa taegye 5 (An outline of Korean intellectual history). Seoul: Han'guk chŏngsin munhwa yŏn'guwŏn, 1992.

Hansen, Eric. *Catholic Politics in China and Korea.* Maryknoll, NY: Orbis Books, 1980.

Han Woo-keun (Han U-Kŭn). *Yijo hugi ŭi sahoe wa sasang* (Society and thought in late Yi dynasty). Seoul: ¬Iyu munhwasa, 1961.

_____. *Sŏngho Yi Ik yŏn'gu* (A study of Sŏngho Yi Ik). Seoul: Han'guk munhwa yŏn'guso, 1981.

_____ . *The History of Korea.* Honolulu : The University Press of Hawaii, 1974.

Hanyang Yu-ssi sebo (Genealogy of the Hanyang Yu clan). 1869.

Harrington, Ann M. *Japan's Hidden Christian.* Chicago: Loyola University Press, 1993.

Hay, Malcolm. *Failure in the Far East.* London: Neville Spearman, 1957.

Hefner, Robert W., ed. *Conversion to christianity* . Berkeley & L.A. : University of California Press, 1993.

Heyndrickx, Jeroom. *Historiography of the Chinese Catholic*

Church. K.O. Leuven: Ferdinand Verbiest Foundation, 1994.

Hŏ Kyun. *Hŏ Kyun chŏnjip* (The Complete Works of Hŏ Kyun). Seoul: Sŏnggyun'gwan taehakkyo, Taedong munhwa yŏn'guso, 1972.

Hocking, W.E. "Chu I's Theory of Knowledge." *Harvard Journal of Asiatic Studies,* 1 (1936), pp.109-27.

Hong I-sŏp. *Chŏng Yag-yong ŭi chŏngch'I kyŏngje sasang yŏn'gu* (A study of the political and economic thought of Chŏng Yag-yong). Seoul: Han'guk yŏn'gu tosŏgwan, 1959.

_____. "Chŏnghŏn Yi Ka-hwan ŭi simun sobyu" (Fragments of the writings of Yi Ka-hwan). in Yi Pyŏng-do paksa hwagap kiyŏmhoe, ed. *Yi Pyŏng-do paksa hwagap kinyŏm nonmunjip* (A collection of articles in honor of the sixtieth birthday of Dr. Yi Pyŏng-do). Seoul: Ilchogak, 1956), pp.451-67

_____. *"Pyŏgwip'yŏn* p'ilcha Yi Ki-gyŏng ŭi chŏn'gi charyo" (Some documents on Yi Ki-gyong, the editor of the *Pyŏgwip'yŏn). Ch'oe Hyŏn-bae sŏnsaeng hwangap kinyŏm nonmunjip* (A collection of essays in honor of Mr. Ch'oe Hyŏn-bae's sixtieth birthday). Seoul: Sasanggyesa, 1954, pp.521-45.

_____. *Korea's Self-Identity.* Seoul: Yonsei University Press, 1973.

_____. "Silhak e issŏsŏ ŭi namin hak'p'a ŭi sasang-jŏk kyebo" (An ideological genealogy of the Namin faction in relation to Silhak). *Inmun kwahak,* 10 (December, 1963).

_____. "Silhak ŭi inyŏm-chŏk ilmo — Hwabin Sin Hu-dam ŭi sŏhak-pyŏn" (An ideological aspect of *Silhak* : An introduction to Sin Hu-dam's *Sŏhak-pyŏn). Inmun kwahak,* vol. 1 (December, 1957), pp.35-59.

_____. "Sowi *pyŏgwip'yŏn* ŭi hyŏngsŏng e taehayŏ" (On the compilation of *Pyŏgwip'yŏn). Inmun kwahak,* 4 (July, 1959), pp.193-214.

_____. "Yi Pyŏk (1754-1786): Han'guk kŭnse sasang ŭi kŭŭi wich'i" (Yi Pyŏk (1754-1786): His place in the early modern intellectual history of Korea). *Sahoe kwahak,* 3 (January, 1960), pp.71-91.

Hong I-sŏp chŏnjip, 5 vols. (Hong I-sup's complete works). Seoul: Yŏnsei taehakyo ch'ulp'anbu, 1994.

Hong Sun-ho. "Pari oebang chŏnkyohoe sŏnkyosadŭl ŭi Han'guk chinch'ul e taehan Fransŭ chŏngbu ŭi taedo" (Attitude du gouvernement français à l'égard des activités des missionaires français en Corée). *Kyohoesa yŏn'gu,* no. 5 (1987).

Hong Tae-yong. *Tamhŏnsŏ* (Collected works of Hong Tae-yong). 10 *kwon.* Seoul: Sin chosŏnsa, 1939.

Hong Yang-ho. *Igyejip* (Collected writings of Hong Yang-ho). Seoul: Minjok munhwasa, 1982.

Hsu Kwang-ch'I, ed. *T'ien-chu-chiao tung-chuan wen Ien hsu-pien* (Additional materials on the Catholic mission to the east). Taipei, Taiwan: Taiwan Student Bookstore, 1965.

Hsu Tsung-tse. *Ming-Ch'ing-chien Yeh-su hui-shih i-chu t'i-yao* (An annotated guide to the Chinese language publications of the Jesuits in Ming and Ch'ing China). Taipei, Taiwan: Chung-hwa shu-chu, 1958.

Hu Shih. "The Concept of Immortality in Chinese Thought." *Harvard Divinity School Bulletin,* 1946, pp.26-43.

Hwang Hyŏn. *Maech'ŏn yarok* (Miscellaneous notes of Hwang Hyŏn). Seoul: Kuksa p'yŏnch'an wiwŏnhoe, 1955.

Hwang Sa-yŏng. *Hwang Sa-yŏng paeksŏ* (The silk letter of Hwang Sa-yŏng). ed. and trans. by Yun Chae-yŏng. Seoul: Chŏngŭmsa, 1975.

Hwang Sŏng-mo. *Han'guk sahoeron* (Essays on Korean society). Seoul: Simsŏngdang, 1984.

Hwang Sŏn-myŏng. *Chosŏn chonggyo sahoesa yŏn'gu* (The

study of social-religious history of the Chosŏn dynasty). Seoul: Ilchisa 1985.

Hyŏn Sang-yun. *Chosŏn yuhaksa* (A history of Korean Confucianism). Seoul: Minjung sŏgwan, 1954.

Hyŏn, Sŏk-mun. *Kihae ilgi* (Diary of the Kihae Persecution). Ed. Ha Sŏng-nae. Seoul: Sŏng Hwang Sŏk-tu Nuga sŏwŏn, 1986.

Ishii, Hisao. Ritai ōchō no Chōsen tenshukyō to sono hakugai (The Korean Catholic church and the persecution of king Kojong's reign). *Shigaku zasshi* , 52. No. 5. 1942.

_____. Rigaku shijō shugi Richō he no tenshukyō no chōsen. *Rekishigaku kenkyū,* vol.12. no. 8. 1942.

Janelli, Roger L. and Dawnhee Yim Janelli. *Ancestor Worship and Korean Society.* Stanford, CA: Stanford University Press, 1982.

Jean, Sang-woon(Chŏn Sang-un). *Science and Technology in Korea.* Cambridge, MA: MIT Press, 1974.

Jennes, Joseph. *A History of the Catholic Church in Japan.* Tokyo: Oriens Institute for Religious Research, 1973.

Jordan, David K. *God, Ghosts, and Ancestors.* Berkeley: University of California Press,1972.

Kaksa tŭngnok 78 , Chukuk ilgi. (Diary of trial process). Seoul: Kuksa p'yŏnch'an wiwŏnhoe, 1994.

Kalton, Michael. The Neo-Confucian World View and Value System of Yi Dynasty Korea. Unpublished doctoral dissertation, Harvard University, 1971.

_____. "Chŏng Tasan's Philosophy of Man: A Radical Critique of the Neo-Confucian World View." *Journal of Korean Studies,* 3 (1981), pp.3-38.

_____. "An Introduction to Silhak." *Korea Journal,* 15, no. 5 (May, 1975), pp.29-46.

Bibliography

Kang Chae-ŏn. "Chōsen denrai no seiyō shomoku" (A catalogue of Western books of Chosŏn dynasty). *Shisō*, no. 625 (July, 1976), pp.107-29.

_____. *Chosŏn ŭi sŏhaksa* (A history of Western Learning in Chosŏn). Seoul: Minŭmsa, 1990.

_____. "Chŏng Tasan ŭi sŏhak kwan" (The viewpoint on Catholicism of Chŏng Tasan). Kang Man-gil and others, *Tasanhak ŭi t'amgu.* Seoul: Minŭmsa, 1990, pp.51-73.

Kang, Hugh H., ed. *Traditional Culture and Society of Korea: Thought and Institutions.* Honolulu: University of Hawaii Press, 1975.

Kang Kwang-sik. "Sŏhak ŭi ch'unggyŏk kwa chŏnt'ong jŏk chŏngch'I munhwa ŭi panŭng." (The clash of Catholic doctrine and reaction of traditional political culture), *Insok Hwang Sŏngmo paksa hwagap kinyŏm nonch'ong sahoe kucho wa sahoe sasang.* 1986.

Kang Man-gil. *Chosŏn hugi sangŏp chabon ŭi paltal* (The development of commercial capital in the late Chosŏn dynasty). Seoul: Koryŏ taehakkyo, 1973.

Kang Sin-p'yo. "Ancestor Worship and Traditional Culture." *Han'guk munhwa illyuhak,* 18,1986.

Kang Ton-gu. *Han'guk kŭndae chonggyo wa minjok chuŭi* (Modern Korean religion and nationalism). Seoul: Chimmundang, 1992.

Kang Yŏn-hŭi. "Chosŏn hugi sŏhak ŭi chosang chesa munje" (Catholics ancestor rites problems in the late Chosŏn dynasty). *Ch'oe Sŏg-u sinbu hwagap kinyŏm Han'guk kyohoesa nonch'ong,* Seoul: 1982.

Kendall, Laurerel & Dix, Griffin. *Religion and Ritual in Korean Society.* Berkeley : University of California.1987.

Keum Jang-tae(Kŭm Chang-t'ae). "Chosŏn hugi yuhak sŏhak kanŭi kyori nonjaeng kwa sasangjŏk sŏnggyŏk" (The ideological conflict between Confucianism and

Catholicism in the late Chosŏn period its ideological character). *Kyohoesa yŏn'gu,* 2 (1978), pp.89-139.

_____. "Ch'ŏnjugyo ŭi chŏllae wa sŏgu sasang ŭi suyong" (The introduction of Catholicism and the acceptance of Western thought). *Han'guk ch'ŏlhak yŏn'gu,* II. Seoul: Tongmyŏngsa, 1977.

_____. "Chosŏn hugi sŏhak ŭi chŏllae wa Chosŏn chŏngpu ŭi taeungch'aek" (Introduction of Catholicism in late Chosŏn dynasty and counterplan of government). *Tongyanghak nonch'ong.* Kwangju: Chŏnnam taehakkyo, 1990, pp.427-443.

_____. *Han'guk Silhak sasang yŏn'gu* (A study of the *Silhak* thought of Korea). Seoul: Chimmundang, 1987.

_____. *Han'guk yukyo ŭi chaejomyŏng* (Recrudescence of Korean Confucianism). Seoul: Chŏnmangsa, 1982.

_____. "Kwisin sasaengnon kwa yugyo sŏhak kane nonbyŏn." (On the argument between Confucianism and Catholicism concerning the ideas of soul and life after death). *Sŏnggyun'gwan daehak nonmunjip,* 17 (1972), pp.271-94.

_____. "Chŏng Yag-yong kwa ch'ŏnjugyo sinang" (Chŏng Yag-yong and the Catholic faith). *Han'gukhak,* 24 (1981), pp.19-29.

_____. "Tasan on Western Learning and Confucianism." *Korea Journal,* vol. 26, no. 2 (1986), pp.4-16.

_____. *Tongsŏ kyosŏp kwa kŭndae Han'guk sasang* (Modern Korean thought during the period of mutual interchange between East and West). Seoul: Sŏnggyungwan taehakkyo, 1984.

_____. *Yukyo sasang ŭi munjedŭl* (Questions on Confucian Thought). Seoul: Yŏgang ch'ulp'ansa, 1990.

Kim, Andrew E. "A History of Christianity in Korea: From Its Troubled Beginning to Its Contemporary Success." *Korea Journal,* vol. 35, no. 2 (Summer, 1995), pp.34-53

Kim Chin-so. "Ch'ŏnju kasa ŭi minjung sasang" (Minjung thought in Catholic hymns). *Han'gŭl sŏngsŏ wa kyŏre munhwa,* Seoul: Kidokkyomunsa, 1985.

―――――. "Ch'ŏnju kasa ŭi sasang" (The thought of Cathoic hymns). Sungsan Pak Kil-chin paksa kohŭi kinyŏm, *Han'guk kŭndae chonggyo sasangsa.* 1984, pp.745-759.

―――――. "Ch'ŏnju kasa ŭi sasang yŏn'gu siron" (A study of the thought contained in Catholic hymns). *Ch'oe sŏg-u sinbu hwagap kinyŏm Han'guk kyohoesa nonch'ong,* Seoul: 1982.

―――――. "Ch'ŏnju kasa ŭi yŏn'gu" (A study of Catholic hymns). *Kyohoesa yŏn'gu,* no. 3, 1981.

Kim Chong-chin. "Latin ŏhakŭi Han'guk toyip kwajŏng kwa ch'ŏnju kyohoe" (The process of introduction of Latin to Korea and the Catholic church). *Han'guk Kyohoesa nonmunjip,* II. Seoul, 1985.

Kim Chong-ok. "Pakhaegi sŏngyosa ŭi Han'guk kwan" (Missionaries' views of Korea during the religious persecution period). *Han'guk Kyohoesa nonmunjip,* II. Seoul, 1985.

Kim Han-gyu. "*Sahak chingŭirŭl* t′onghaesŏ pon ch'ogi Han'guk ch'ŏnju kyohoe ŭi myŏt′kaji munje" (Some questions about the early Korean Catholic church in the light of the *Sahak chingûi*). *Kyohoesa yŏn'gu,* 2 (1979), pp.49-87.

Kim Han-sik. *Silhak ŭi chŏngch'I sasang* (Political thought of *Silhak*). Seoul: Ilchisa, 1979.

Kim Hong-u. "Chŏngjojo ch'ŏnjuhak pip'an" (A critique on Catholicism during Chŏngjo reign). *Han'guk chŏngch'I hakhoebo,* vols. 20 & 22 (1986 & 1987).

Kim Jeong-soo (Kim Chŏng -su). "*Sŏnggyo yoji* ŭi kyori kyoyukhakchŏk koch'al" (Study of educational perspectiive on *Sŏnggyo yoji). Han'guk kyohoesa nonmunjip,* II. Seoul: 1985.

_____. *Katechese und Inkulturation: Dargestellt am Beispiel der Geschichte der katolischen Kirche in Korea 1603-1983*, Frankfurt am Main: Peter Lang,1987.

Kim, Joseph Chang-mun and Joseph Jaesŏn Chung. *Catholic Korea, Yesterday and Today.* Seoul: Catholic Publishing Co., 1988.

Kim Ki-hiuk. *The Last Phase of the East Asian World Order.* Berkeley & L. A. : University of California, 1980.

Kim Ki-hyŏp. "Yesuhoe sŏnkyo ŭi chŏgŭngjuŭi nosŏn kwa Chungguk Ilbon ŭi sŏhak" (The accommodational mission method of Jesuit order and Catholicism in China and Japan). *Yŏksa Pip'yŏng,* 25 (Summer, 1994), pp.307-320.

_____. " Matteo Ricci ŭi Chungguk kwan kwa poyu ch'ŏkpullon"(Matteo Ricci's understanding of China and his mission principles), Ph.D. Dissertation, Yonsei University, 1993.

Kim Kil-hwan. *Chosŏnjo yuhak sasang yŏn'gu* (Studies on Confucian thought in the Chosŏn dynasty). Seoul: Ilchisa, 1980.

Kim Kyoung-jae(Kim Kyŏng-chae). *Christianity and Encounter of Asian Religions.* Zaetermeer: Uigeverij Boekencentrum, 1994.

Kim Ok-hŭi. *Ch'oe Yang-ŏp sinbu wa kyouch'on* (Father Ch'oe Yang-ŏp and village of Catholic bretheren). Seoul: Hakmunsa, 1983.

_____. *Han'guk ch'ŏnjugyo sasangsa I — Kwangam Yi Pyŏk ŭi sŏhak sasang yŏn'gu* (A history of Korean Catholic thought -A study of the Catholic views of Kwangam Yi Pyŏk). Seoul: Sun'gyo ŭi maek, 1990.

_____. *Han'guk ch'ŏnjugyo sasangsa II — Tasan Chŏng Yagyong ŭi sŏhak sasang yŏn'gu.* (A history of Korean Catholic thought -A study of the Catholic views of Tasan Chŏng Yag-yong). Seoul: Sun'gyo ŭi maek, 1991.

Bibliography

———. *Han'guk ch'ŏnjugyo yŏsŏngsa I, II* (A history of Korean Catholic women). Seoul: Han'guk inmun kwahakwŏn, 1983.

———. *Pakhae sidae ŭi kyouch'on* (Catholic village during the persecution period). Seoul: Han'guk kat'ollik munhwa yŏn'guso, 1984.

———. "Sŏhak ŭi suyong kwa kŭ ŭisik kujo: Yi Pyŏk ŭi *Sŏnggyo yoji* rŭl chungsim ŭro" (The reception of Western knowledge along with frame of reference: with special emphasis on Yi Pyŏk's essential arguments of Christianity). *Han'guk saron,* I (May, 1973), pp.173-246.

———. "Yuhandang Kwŏnssi ŭi ŏnhaeng sillok e kwanhan yŏn'gu" (A sudy of the "¿nhaeng sillok" by Yuhandang Kwŏn). *Han'guk hakbo,* 8, no. 2 (Summer, 1980), pp.50-83.

———. "Tasanŭi simkyŏng milhum e natanan simsungrone kwanhan kochal" (A study in Tasan's own inner Ie with the humanist theory). *Kyohsesa yŏn'gu,* no. 6 (1988).

———. "Tasan Chŏng Yag-yong ŭi myojimyŏng e natanan sŏhak sasang," (On Catholic thought that appears in the obituary document of Chŏng Tasan). Soam Cho Wang-nae kyosu hwagap kinyŏm, *Han'guk sahak nonch'ong,* pp.421-442.

———. "Women in the History of Catholicism in Korea." *Korea Journal,* vol. 24, no. 8 (1984), pp.28-40.

———. "Yi Lugalda ŭi okchung sŏgan kwa kŭ sachŏk ŭiŭi" (The historical meaning of Yi Lutgardis' prison letters). Ch'oe Sŏg-u sinbu hwagap kinyŏm, *Han'guk kyohoesa nonchong.*

Kim Sang-hong. "Tasan ŭi ch'ŏnjugyo sinbongnon e taehan pannon" (A counter argument testment faith in Tasan's Catholicism). *Tongyanghak,* 20, 1990.

Kim Sŏng-t'ae. "Han'guk ch'ŏnju kyohoe ui yŏksa- jŏk ŭimi: chuch'esong" (A historical meaning of Korean Catholic church: self-identity), *Samok,* 91, 1984, pp.35-43.

Kim Sung-hae (Kim Sŭng-hye). "*Chilgŭk* e daehan yŏn'gu" (A study of "*Ch'ilgŭk*"). *Kyohoesa yŏn'gu,* no. 9, 1994.

_____. " The concept of High God and its Interpretations in the different religeo-social structure of Korea." XVII I. A. H. R. Congress, Mexico, August6-11, 1995.

_____. " The Righteous and the Sage: A Comparative Study on the Ideal Images of Man in Biblical Israel and Classical China." Th.D. Dissertation, The Divinity School, Harvard University,1981.

Kim T'ae-jin. *Hong Tae-yong kwa kŭ ŭi sidae* (Hong Tae-yong and his times). Seoul: Ilchisa, 1982.

Kim Tong-uk. "Sŏkyo chŏllae wa ch'ŏnju ch'anga" (Transmission of Catholicism and Catholic hymns). *Inmun kwahak,* no. 21. Seoul: Yonsei taehakkyo, 1969.

Kim Yang-sŏn. *Maesan Kukhak san'go* (A few essays in Koreanology by Kim Yang-sŏn). Seoul: Sungjŏn taehakkyo museum, 1972.

_____. "Myŏngmal Ch'ŏngch'o Yasohoe sŏngyosadŭli chejakhan segye chido" (Early Chinese Maps by Jesuit Fathers). *Han'guk ch'ŏnju kyohoesa nonmun sŏnjip,* I. Seoul: Kyohoesa yŏn'guso, 1976.

Kim Yong-dŏk. " Life and Thought of Pak Che-ga." *Korea Journal,* vol. 12, no. 7 (July, 1972), pp.40-43.

_____. *Chosŏn hugi sasang yŏn'gu* (A study of latter Chosŏn thought). Seoul: ¬lyu munhwasa, 1977.

_____. "Chosŏn hugi ŭi sahoe wa sasang." (Society and thought in latter Chosŏn), in *Han'guk Sasangsa T'aegye.* Seoul: Han'guk chŏngsin munhwa yŏn'guwŏn, 1992.

_____. "Sohyŏn seja yŏn'gu" (A study on crown prince Sohyŏn). *Sahak yŏn'gu,* 18 (1964), pp.433-489.

Kim Yong-ho. "Tasanhak paengnyŏn" (One hundred years of Tasan studies). *Han'guk sasang,* 15 (1977), pp.135-55.

Kim Yong-sik. "Taewŏngun, the Catholic movement, and the role of religion in transitional politics." Ph.D. dissertation, Brigham Young University, 1971.

Kim Yŏng-sŏp. *Chosŏn hugi nongŏpsa yŏn'gu* (Studies in the agrarian history of the late Chosŏn dynasty). Seoul: Ilchogak, 1970-71.

Kim Young-mo. "The Conceptualization of Social Strata and Its Changing Structure During the Late Yi Dynasty." *Social Science Journal,* 6 (1979), pp.107-25.

Ko Hŭng-sik. "Pyŏnin kyonan'gi sindodul ŭi sinang" (Faith during the religious persecution in 1866). *Kyohoesa yŏn'gu,* no. 6 (1988)

Koh Byŏng-ik(Ko Pyŏng-ik). "Tasan ŭi chinbogwan" (Chŏng Yag-yong's concept of progress). *Cho Myŏng-gi paksa hwangap kinyŏm nonch'ong* (Collection of essays commemorating the sixtieth birthday of Dr. Cho Myŏng-gi). Seoul: Tongguk taehakkyo , 1965.

The Korean Martyr Saints. Seoul: St. Hwang Sŏk-tu Luke publishing house, 1995.

Koryŏ taehakkyo minjok munhwa yŏn'guwŏn. *Han'guk munhwasa taegye* (An outline history of Korean culture). vol. 6. Seoul: Koryŏ taehakkyo, 1974.

Kukcho pogam (Chosŏn dynasty chronicles). 1908 edition. Seoul: Sejong taewang kinyŏm saŏphoe, 1976.

Kusuda Onosaburō. *Chōsen tensyukyō shōshi* (Short history of the Catholic church in Korea). Pusan: Hokubundo, 1933.

Kwak Sin-hwan. "Hwasŏ Yi Hang-no ŭi sŏhakkwan" (Yi Hang-no's view on Catholicism). *Sungsil taehakkyo nonmunjip,* 16 (1986), pp.3-14.

Lancashire, Douglas. "Anti-Christian Polemics in Seventeenth-Century China," *Church History,* 38 (1969), pp.218-41.

Lanunay, Adrion. *La Corée et les Missionaires Français.* Tours:

A Mame et fils, 1901.

Latourette, Kenneth S. *A History Christian Mission in China.* New York: The Macmillan Company. 1929.

Ledyard, Gari. "Korean Travelers in China Four Hundred Years, 1488-1887." *Occasional Paper on Korea,* ed. James B. Palais, No. 2 (March, 1974).

_____. *The Dutch Come to Korea.* Seoul: Royal Asiatic Society, 1971.

Lee Chang-soo (Yi Ch'ang-su). *Modernization of Korea and the Impact of the West.* Los Angeles: East Asian Studies Center, University of Southern California, 1981.

Lee, Gabriel Gab-soo (Yi Kap-su). *Sociology of Conversion: Sociological Implications of Religious Conversion to Christianity in Korea.* Ph.D. dissertation, Fordham University, 1961.

Lee, Grant. "Persecution and Success of Roman Catholic Church in Korea." *Korea Journal,* vol. 28, no. 1 (January, 1988), pp.16-27.

Lee Jung-young (Yi Chŏng-yŏng), ed. *Ancestor Worship and Christianity in Korea.* Lewiston, NY: The Edwin Mellen Press, 1988.

Lee Ki-baek(Yi Ki-baek). *A New History of Korea.* Trans. Edward W. Wagner. Cambridge, MA: Harvard University Press, 1984.

Lee Ku-yŏl (Yi Ku-yŏl) . "Two Hundred Years of Catholic Art in Korea." *Korea Journal,* vol. 24, no. 8, pp.53-59.

Lee Kwang-kyu (Yi Kwang-gyu). "The Concept of Ancestors and Ancestor Worship in Korea." *Asian Folklore,* 43 (1984), pp.199-214.

Lee, Peter H. (Yi Hwak-su), ed. *Confucian-Christian Encounters in Historical and Contemporary Perspective.* Lewiston, NY: The Edwin Mellen Press, 1992.

Bibliography

Lee Sun-Keun (Yi Sŏn-gŭn). "Some Lesser-Known Facts on Taewŏngun and His Foreign Policy." *Transactions of the Korea Branch of the Royal Asiatic Society,* 39 (1962).

_____. *Han'guksa , ch'oegŭnsep'yŏn* (The histoy of Korea-Modern times). Seoul: ¬Iyu munhwasa,1961.

Lee Woosung (Yi U-sŏng). "Korean Intellectual Tradition and the Silhak School of Thought," in Hugh H.W. Kang, ed. *The Traditional Culture and Society of Korea: Thought and Institutions.* Honolulu: Center for Korean Studies, University of Hawaii, 1975, pp.105-38.

Li Chih-tsao, ed. *Ch'ŏnhak ch'oham* (Korean reprint of *T'ien-hsüeh ch'u-han* [An introduction to heavenly learning). Seoul: Asea munhwasa, 1976.

Malatesta, E.J., ed. *The True Meaning of the Lord of Heaven.* Matteo Ricci's classic translated with notes by D. Lancashire and Peter Hu Kuo-chen. St. Louis: Institute of Jesuit Sources, 1985.

Mannam kwa midum ŭi kilmok esŏ (From letters, diaries and memoirs of martyrs and believers). Seoul: Han'guk kyohoesa yŏn'guso, 1989.

Mansŏng Taedongpo, 2 vols. (Grand genealogy of the ten thousand names). Seoul: 1931-1932.

Maxwell, Murray. "Catholic Significance in Korea." *Koreana Quarterly,* vol. 2, no. 1 (1960), pp. 105-119.

Metzger, Thomas. *Escape from Predicament.* New York: Columbia University Press, 1977.

Min Kyŏng-bae. *Han'guk kidok kyohoesa* (A history of Christianity in Korea). Seoul : Yonsei taehakkyo.1993.

Min Tu-gi. "Yŏlha ilgi ŭi il yŏn'gu" (A Study of Pak Chi-wŏn's Jehol Diary). *Yŏksa hakpo,* 20 (April, 1963).

Minamiki, George. S.J. *The Chinese Rites Controversy.* Chicago: LoyolaUniversity Press, 1985.

Ministry of Culture and Propaganda, Democratic People's Republic of Korea. *Progressive Scholars at the Close of the Feudal Age of Korea.* P'yŏngyang: New Korea Press, 1955.

Moon, Seung-gyu (Mun Sŭng-gyu). "Ancestor Worship in Korea: Tradition and Transition." *Journal of Comparative Family Studies,* 5 (1974), pp.71-87.

Mun So-jŏng. "Wijŏng ch'ŏksa e kwanhan chisik sahoehak chŏk yŏn'gu" (A preliminary socio-intellectual study on the wijŏng ch'ŏksa [defend orthodoxy and reject heterodoxy] movement). *Han'guk hakpo,* 1984, pp.36-37.

Mungello, D.E. *Curious Land: Jesuit Accommodation and the Origin of Sinology.* Stuttgart, 1985.

Mutel, Gustav. "Lettre d'Alexandre Hoang à Mgr. de Gouvéa, Évêque de Pekin" (1901). *Traduction française,* 1925, also Hong Kong, 1959.

_____. *Documents relatifs aux martyrs de Corée de 1866.* Imprimerie de Nazareth, 1925.

_____. *Ch'imyŏng ilgi* (The record of the martyrs in the pyŏngin persecution). Ed. Ha Sung-nae. Seoul: Sung Hwang Suk-du Nuga sŏwŏn, 1985.

Neill, Stephen. *A History of Christianity in India: The Beginnings to A. D. 1707.* Cambridge, England: Cambridge University Press, 1984.

Nelson, Melvin Frederick. *Korea and the Old Orders in Eastern Asia.* New York: Russell & Russell, 1945.

O Chae-hwan. "Yi ma-du ŭi sŏngyogwan" (Ricci's view on Confucianism). *Chŏnbuk sahak,* 13 (1990), pp.77-105.

_____. "Mateo rich'I ŭi chŏgŭng jŏk chŏnkyo pangpŏp e taehan sasang jŏk p'yŏngka" (An ideological historical evaluation on Matteo Ricci's accommodational mission method). Pak Yŏng-sŏk kyosu hwagap kinyŏm, *Han'guk sahak nonch'ong,* II. Seoul: T'amgudang, 1992, pp.1143-

1156.

Oda Shōgo. "Richō no hōtjō o ryakujutsu shite tenshukyō hakugai ni oyobu" (An outline of factionalism in the Chosŏn dynasty and notes on Catholic persecution). *Seikyū gakusō,* I (August, 1930), pp.1-26.

O'Malley, John W. *The First Jesuits.* Cambridge, MA, and London: Harvard University Press, 1993.

Oppert, Ernest. *A Forbidden Land: Voyage to Korea* (Ein verschlossens Land, Risen nach Korea). New York: G.P. Putnam's Sons, 1880.

Pae Hyŏn-suk. "17.18 segi e chŏllae doen ch'ŏnjugyo sŏjŏk" (Catholic books introduced into Korea in the seventeenth and eighteenth centuries). *Kyohoesa yon'gu,* 3 (1981), pp.3-45.

————. "Cho sŏn e chŏllae doen ch'onjugyo sŏjŏk" (Bibliographical characteristics of Catholic books introduced to Korea). *Han-guk kyohoesa nonmunjip,* I (1984).

Paik, Lak-Geoon George (Paek Nak-chun). *The History of Protestant Missions in Korea, 1832-1910.* Pyŏngyang, Korea: Union Christian College Press, 1929.

Pak Chae-man. "Han'guk ch'ogi kyohoe (1784-1840) ŭi p'yŏngsindo sadojik" (Apostleship of laity in the early Korean Catholic church). *Sŏngnong Ch'oe Sŏg-u sinbu kohi kinyŏm Han'guk kato'llik munhwa hwaltong kwa kyohoesa.* Seoul: Han'guk kyohoesa yŏn'guso, 1991.

Pak Che-ga. *Chŏng yujip pu Pukhagŭi* (The collected works of Pak Che-ga with the essay on learning from the north appended). Seoul: T'amgudang, 1974.

Pak Chi-wŏn. *Yŏlha ilgi* (A dairy from Jehol). reprinted by Chung-hua ts'ung-shu wei-yuan hui, Taiwan, 1956.

————. *Yŏnam-jip* (The collected works of Pak Chi-wŏn). 57 *kwŏn,* first published in 1901 and enlarged in 1932. Seoul:

Kyŏngin munhwasa, Reprinted, 1974.

Pak Chŏl. *Yesuhoe sinbu Sesp'edes* (Jesuit Father Cespedes). Seoul: Sŏgang taehakkyo, 1987.

Pak Chong-hong. *Han'guk sasangsa nongo* (A study on Korean intellectual history). Seoul: Sŏmundang, 1977.

_____. "Tae sŏgujŏk segyegwan kwa Tasan ŭi susagugwan" (Tasan's Confucian fundamentalism and his Oriented world view), in Yi ¬r-ho paksa hwagap kinyŏmhoe, ed. *Silhak nonch'ong* (Studies on *Silhak*). Kwangju, Korea: Chŏnnam taehakkyo, 1975, pp.97-125.

Pak Ch'ung-sŏk. "Richō kōki ni okeru seiji shisō no tenkai — tokuni kinsei jitsugaku-ha no shii hōhō o chūshin ni" (Development of political thought in late Chosŏn dynasty — focused on the way of thinking of the Silhak school). *Kokka gakkai zasshi,* vol. 88, no. 10 (September, 1975); nos. 11,12 (December, 1975); vol. 89, no. 1,2 (January, 1976).

Pak Kwang-yong. "Yŏng Chŏngjo tae Namin seryŏk ŭi chŏng ch'ichŏk wich'iwa sŏhak chŏngch'aek" (Political position of namin power during the eras of king Yŏngjo and Chŏngjo and policy toward Western Learning). *Han'guk kyohoesa nonmunjip,* II. Seoul: 1985.

Pak Se-ch'ae. *Tongyu saurok.* Seoul: Pulham munhwasa. Reprinted. 1977.

Pak Tong-ok. "Pakhaegi Han'guk ch'ŏnju kyohoe ŭi kyŏngje kwan" (The Catholic church's economic perspectives during the persecution period). *Han'guk kyohoesa nonmunjip,* I (1984).

Pak Yŏng-sin. *Yŏksa wa sahoe pyŏndong* (History and social change). Seoul: Taeyongsa, 1987.

Palais, James B. "Korea on the Eve of the Kwanghwa Treaty, 1873-76." Ph.D. dissertation, Harvard University, 1967.

_____. *Politics and Policy in Traditional Korea.* Cambridge,

MA, and London: Harvard University Press, 1975.

_____. "Stability in Yi Dynasty Korea: Equilibrium Systems and Marginal Adjustment," *Occasional Paper on Korea,* ed. James B. Palais, No. 3 (June, 1975).

_____, *Confucian Statecraft and Korean Institutions.* Seattle: University of Washington Press, 1996.

Palmer, Spencer J. *Korea and Christianity.* Seoul: Hollym, 1968.

_____. *Confucian Rituals in Korea.* New York: Asian Humanities Press, 1984.

Pan Yun-hong. "Chosŏn hugi ŭi taekurap'a insik" (The recognition on the Europe in the late Chosŏn dynasty), *Chosŏn tae kuksa yŏn'gu,* 3 (1982), pp.77-96.

Panikker, K. M. *Asia and Western Dominance.* N.Y.: Collier Books, 1969.

Park Pong-bae. "The Encounter of Christianity with Traditional Culture and Ethics in Korea: An Essay in Christian Self-Understanding." Ph.D. dissertation, Vanderbilt University, 1970.

Park, Chung-shin(Pak Chŏng -sin). "Protestantism and Progressive Reform Politics in Late Confucian Korea." *Sung sil sahak,* 8 (1994).

Park Seong-rae (Pak Sŏng-nae). "Hong Tae-yong's Idea of the Rotating Earth." *Korea Journal,* vol. 21, no. 8 (August, 1980), pp.21-29.

_____. "Portents and Neo-Confucian Politics in Korea, 1392-1519." *Journal of Social Science and Humanities,* 49 (1979), pp.53-122.

_____. "Han'guk kŭnsei ŭi sŏgu gwahak suyong" (Acceptance of Western science in Korea, 1700-1860). *Tongbang hakchi,* no. 20 (1978), pp.257-292.

_____. "Yi Ik ŭi sŏyang kwahak suyong" (Yi Ik's Acceptance

of Western science). *Kim Hongbae kohŭi kiyŏm nonmunjip,* 1984, pp.47-71.

_____. "Matteo Ricc'I wa Han'guk ŭi sŏyang kwahak suyong" (Matteo Ricci and the introduction of Western science into Korea). *Tonga yŏn'gu,* no. 3. Seoul: Sŏgang taehakkyo, 1983.

Pate, Alan. "Catholic Persecution and Catholic Survival: The Korean Kyouch'on and Popular Catholicism in 19th Century Korea," unpublished M.A. Thesis. Harvard University 1990.

Peterson, Mark A. *Korean Adoption and Inheritance.* Ithaca, NY: Cornell University 1996.

Peterson, Willard. "Western Natural Philosophy Published in late Ming China." *Proceedings of the American Philosophical Society.* 117 (1973), pp.295-322.

Pfister, Louis. *Notices biographiques et bibliographiques sur les Jesuites de l'ancienne mission de Chine.* Shanghai: Mission Catholique, 1932-34.

Phillips, Earl H. and Eui-young Yu, ed. *Religions in Korea: Beliefs and Cultural Values.* L.A.: Center for Korean-American and Korean Studies, California State University, 1982. .

Pocock, J.G.A. "The Origins of Study of the Past: A Comparative Approach." *Comparative Studies in Society and History,* IV, 2 (1962).

_____. "Intentions, Traditions and Methods." *Annals of Scholarship,* vol. I, no. 4 (1980).

_____. "The Origins of Study of the Past," *Comparative Studies in Society and History,* IV, 2 (1962).

Pyŏngin pakhaecha chŭngŏnnok (Record of testimony of the 1866 persecution). 2 vols. Seoul: Han'guk kyohoesa yŏn'guso, 1987.

Bibliography

Rambo, Lewis R. *Understanding Religious Conversion.* New Haven: Yale University Press, 1993.

Reinstra, M. Howard. *Jesuit Letters from China.* Minneapolis: University of Minnesota Press, 1986.

Ri, Jean Songbae (Yi Sŏng-bae). *Yukyo wa kuristokyo* (Confucianisme et Christianisme — Les Principes confucéens de la première théologie chrétienne en Corée, d'après l'oeuvre de Yi Pyŏk [1754-1786]). Waegwan: Benedict Press, 1979.

Ricci, Matteo. *T'ien-chu Shih-I* (The true meaning of the Lord of heaven). reprint under the title *Ch'ŏnju silŭi.* Seoul: Kwangdŏksa, 1972.

Ro Kil-myŏng (No Kil-myŏng). "Chosŏn hugi kat'ollik ŭi suyong kwa kajok kwangye ŭi pyŏnhwa" (The acceptance of Catholicism in late Chosŏn dynasty and changing of family relationship). *Asea yŏn'gu,* 71 (1984).

_____. *Kat'ollik kwa Chosŏn hugi sahoe pyŏndong* (Catholicism and social upheaval in the late Chosŏn period). Seoul: Koryo Taehakkyo, 1988.

_____. "Kujo kinŭng-jŏk chŭngmyŏn esŏ pon Han'guk kidokkyo ŭi suyong kwajŏng" (The process of acceptance of Christianity from the structural functional view), in *In'gwan kwa mirae,* 5. Seoul: Chungang sinhakkyo, 1977.

_____. "Pakhaegi Han'guk Ch'ŏnju kyohoe ŭi sahoe kaebal" (The Korean Catholic church and social development during the period of persecution and that of the enlightenment). *Han'guk kyohoesa nonmunjip,* I (1984).

Ronan, Charles E. and Ho, Bonnie B.C., ed. *East Meets West: The Jesuits in China, 1582-1773.* Chicago: 1988.

Ross, Andrew G. *A Vision Betrayed: The Jesuits in Japan and China.* Maryknoll, NY: Orbis Books, 1994.

Rosso, Antonio Sisto. *Apostolic Legations to China of the Eighteenth Century.* South Pasadena, CA: P.D. and Ione

Perkins, 1948.

Rowbotham, Arnold H. *Missionary and Mandarin: The Jesuits at the Court of China.* Berkeley: University of California Press, 1942.

Ruiz de Medina, Juan G. *The Catholic Church in Korea.* English translation by John Bridges. Seoul: Royal Asiatic Society, Korea Branch, 1994.

Rule, Paul. " K'ung-tzu or Confucius: The Jesuit Interpretation of Confucianism." Ph. D. Dissertation, Australia National University, 1972.

Sahak chingŭi (A Warning against heterodoxy). Seoul: Pulham munhwasa, Reprinted, 1977.

Schindler, Bruno. "The Development of Chinese Conceptions of Supreme Beings," *Asia Major,* introductory volume (1922). pp.298-366.

Schurhammer, Georg. *Francis Xavier: His Life and Times.* Trans. M. Joseph Costello, 4 volmes. Rome: The Jesuit Historical Institute, 1973-82.

Seoh, Roy Munsang. "The Principalist Tradition of Yi Korean Confucianism and the case of An Chŏngbok (1712-1791). " Ph. D. Dissertation, University of Washington, 1977.

_____. "The Ultimate Concern of Yi Korean Confucians: An Analysis of the *i-ki* Debates." *Occasional Papers on Korea,* 5 (1977), pp.20-60.

_____. "Yi Ik, an Eighteenth-Century Korean Intellectual." *Journal of Korean Studies,* I (1969), pp.9-21.

Shikata Hiroshi. "Richō jinkō ni kansuru mibun kaikyūbetsuteki kansatsu" (An investigation of Chosŏn dynasty population in terms of status and class). *Chōsen keizai no kenkyū ,* Tokyo: Iwanami shoten, 1938.

Sim U-chun. *Sunam An Chŏng-bok yŏn'gu* (A study of An Chŏng-bok). Seoul: Ilchisa, 1995.

Bibliography

Skinner, Quentin. "Hermeneutics and the Role of History." *New Literary History*, vol. 7.

Smith, D. Howard. *Chinese Religions*. New York: Holt, Rinehart and Winston, 1968.

_____. "Chinese Concepts of the Soul." *Numen*, 5 (1958), pp.165-79.

Sŏ Chong-t'ae. "Nokam Kwŏn Ch'ŏl-sin ŭi Yangmyŏnghak suyong kwa kŭ yŏnghyang" (The acceptance and influence of Kwŏn Ch'ŏl-sin's doctrine of Wang Yang-ming). *Kuksagwan nonch'ong*, 34 (1992), pp.239-260.

_____. "Ch'ŏnjinam Chuŏsa kanghak kwa Yang myŏnghak" (Pursuit of Study of Catholicism at Ch'ŏnjinam Chuŏ temple and the doctrine of Wang Yang-ming). Yi Ki-baek sŏnsang kohŭi kinyŏm, *Han'guk sahak nonch'ong*, II. Seoul: Ilchogak, 1994, pp.1265-1293.

Son Sŭng-ch'ŏl. "Chosŏnjo sasang ŭi posusŏng kwa chinposŏng ŭi kaltŭng — yuhak, silhak, sŏhak ŭi ilgungmyŏn" (The conflict of thought between conservatism and progressiveness — a prospect of Confucianism, *Silhak* and Catholicism). *Tong kwa sŏ ŭi sayu segye*. Seoul: Minjoksa, 1991.

Song Chŏng-hwan. *Rŏsia ŭi Chosŏn chi'mnyaksa* (A history of invasion to Korea of Russia). Seoul: Pŏmusa, 1990.

Song Chun-ho. *Chosŏn sahoesa yŏn'gu* (A study of Chosŏn social history). Seoul: Ilchogak, 1987.

Song Chu-yong. "Practical Learning of Yi Ik." *Korea Journal*, vol. 12, no. 8 (August, 1972), pp. 38-45.

_____. *Han'guk silhak sasang taeyo* (The gist of Korean *Silhak* thought). Seoul: Pagyŏngsa, 1979.

Song Sŏk-chun. "Chosŏnjo e issŏsŏ yukyo wa ch'ŏnjugyo ŭi sangham iron" (A correspondence theory between Confucianism and Catholicism in Chosŏn dynasty). Yu Sŭng-guk kohŭi kinyŏm, *Tongbang ch'ŏlhak sasang yŏn'gu.* Seoul: Sŏnggyungwan taehakkyo, 1992, pp.347-377.

_____. "Han'guk Yangmyŏnghak kwa *silhak* mit ch'ŏnjugyo waŭi sasang jŏk yŏn'gwansŏng e kwanhan yŏn'gu" (Thought relationship of the teachings of Wang Yang-ming on the school of Practical Learning [Silhak]). Ph.D. dissertatoin, Sŏnggyungwan University, 1992.

Spalatin, Christopher A. *Matteo Ricci's Use of Epictetus.* Waegwan, Korea: 1975.

Spence, Jonathan A. *To Change China: Western Advisors in China, 1620-1960.* New York: Penguin Books, 1969.

_____. *Emperor of China: Self-Portrait of K'ang-I.* New York: Vintage Books, 1974.

_____. *The Memory Palace of Matteo Ricci.* New York: Viking Penguin Inc., 1984.

Standaert, N. *Yang Tingyun, Confucian and Christian in Late Ming China.* Leiden, Netherlands: E.J. Brill, 1988.

Sun'gyoja wa chŭngŏja-dŭl (Documents of martyrs and witnesses). Seoul: Han'guk kyohoesa yŏn'guso, 1983.

Suzuki, Nobuaki. "Richō Seisoki ni okeru tenshukyō no fukyo jōkyo ni kansuru ichkosatzu" (A study of Catholic missionary activity in the Chosŏn dynasty from 1786 to 1791). *Shi'en,* no. 131 (1984), pp.25-50.

_____. Rishi Chōsen ni okeru tenshukyō juyōji no chūninsou no yakuwari (The role of "*chungin*" class during the period of acceptance of Catholicism in the Chosŏn dynasty). *Toyōsi kenkyū hōkoku II,* 1983, pp.34-50.

Tanaka Hidenaka. "Rishi Chōsen ni okeru kiristokyō denrai hōkokushō" (Reports on the introduction of Catholicism into Korea). *Chōsen gakuhō,* 10 (1956), pp.189-241.

Tasan Chŏng Yag-yong ŭi sŏhak sasang (Western Learning Thought of Tasan). Seoul: Tasŏt sure, 1993.

Taylor, Rodney L. "Neo-Confucian Sagehood and the Religious Dimension." *Journal of Chinese Philosophy,* 2, no. 4 (1975), pp.389-415.

Thelle, Notto. *Buddhism and Christianity in Japan, From Conflict to Dialogue,1854-1899.* Honolulu: University of Hawaii Press, 1987.

Tong Tŏk-mo. *Chosŏnjo ŭi kukche kwangye* (International relations of Chosŏn dynasty). Seoul: Pagyŏngsa, 1990.

Treadgold, Donald. *The West in Russia and China.* 2 vols. Cambridge, England: The University Press, 1973.

Tu Wei-ming. "The 'Moral Universal' from the Perspective of East Asian Thought." *Philosophy East and West,* 31, no. 3 (July, 1981), pp.259-278

_____. "Reconstituting the Confucian Tradition." Journal of Asian Studies, vol.33, no.3 (May, 1973), pp.441-453.

Urakawa Wasaburo. *Chōsen Junkyōshi* (A history of Korean martyrdom). Osaka: Zenkoku shobo, 1944.

Väth, Alfons. S.J. *Johann Adams Schall von Bell, S.J.* Köln: Verlag J.P. Bachem G.M.B.H., 1933.

Veer, Peter van der. ed. *Conversion to Modernities:The Globalization of Christianity* . New York & London: Routledge, 1 996.

Voss, Gustav. "Missionary Accommodation and Ancestral Rites in the Far East." *Theological Studies,* vol. IV, no. 4 (December, 1943).

Wach, Joachim. *The Comparative Study of Religions.* New York: Columbia University Press, 1958.

Wagner, Edward W. *The Literati Purges: Political Conflict in Early Yi Korea.* Cambridge, MA: Harvard University Press, 1974.

_____. "The Modernization Process in Korea: Some Historical Considerations." *Koreana Quarterly,* vol. 5, no. 3 (Autumn, 1963).

_____. "The Recommendation Examination of 1519: Its place in Early Yi Dynasty History." *Chōsen gakuhō* 15 (1960).

_____. "An Inquiry into the *Chungin* Class in the Yi Dynasty." 1973.

Wang, George Ho Ching. *China's Iions to Western Religion and Science During Late Ming and Early Ch'ing.* Unpublished doctoral dissertation, University of Washington, 1958.

Watson, James L. "Rites or Beliefs: The Construction of a Unified Culture in Late Imperial China." in *China's Quest for National Identity,"* ed. Lowell Dittner and Samuel S. Kim. Ithaca, NY: Cornell University Press, 1993.

Weber, Max. *The Religions of China.* Trans. Han H. Gerth. New York: The Free Press, 1964.

Whyte, Bob. *Unfinished Encounter; China and Christianity.* London: Fount Paperbacks, 1988.

Wittgenstein, Ludwig. *Lectures and Conversations on Aesthetics, Psychology, and Religious Beliefs.* ed. Cyril Barrett. Berkeley: University of California Press, 1966.

Wŏn Chae-yŏn. "Chŏngjo dae ch'ŏnju kyohoe wa kyorisŏ ŭi chŏsul" (Catholic church and writing of doctrinal books in Chŏngjo period). *Han'guksaron,* 31 (1994).

Wong, Timothy Man Kong. "Matteo Ricci's Mission to Chinese Buddhism." *Ching Feng,* vol. XXXIII, no. 4 (1990), pp.205-231.

Wright, Arthur F. "Fu I and the Rejection of Buddhism." *Journal of the History of Ideas,* 12 (1951), pp.33-47.

_____. *The Counter-Reformation: Catholic Europe and Non-Christian World.* London: Weidenfield and Nicolson, 1983.

Bibliography

Wu Pei-yi. "Self-Examination and Confession of Sins in Traditional China," *Harvard Journal of Asiatic Studies*, vol. 9, no. 1 (June, 1978), pp.5-38.

Yamaguchi Masayuki. "Chōsen okoku ni okeru tenshukyō no kakuritsu" (The establishment of Catholicism in Chosŏn dynasty), *Seikyū gakusō*. 12 (1933).

_____. *Chōsen seikyōshi* (A history of the Korean Catholic Church). Tokyo: Yuzankaku, 1967.

_____. *Hwang Sa-yŏng hakusho no kenkyū* (Studies of the silk letter of Hwang Sa-yŏng). Osaka: Zenkoku shobo, 1946.

_____. "Kinsei Chōsen ni okeru seigaku shisō no tōzen to sono hatten" (The eastern penetration of Western thought and development in modern Korea), in *Oda sensei shōju kinen Chōsen ronshu* (Collected essays on Korea in honor of Oda Shōju). Keijo: 1934, pp.1500-40.

_____. "Shōken seishi to Tō Jakubō" (Prince Sohyŏn and Adam Schall). *Seikyū gakusō*, 5 (1931), pp.101-17.

_____. "Yakuchū Hwang Sa-yŏng hakushō" (The silk-letter of Hwang Sa-yŏng; annotated and translated). *Chōsen gakuhō*, no. 2 (1951).

_____. "Yasokai senkyōshi no Chōsen huryo kyusai oyobi kyōka" (Jesuit missionaries' relief and evangelization for war prisoners of Chosŏn). *Seikyū gakusō*, no. 4 (1931), pp.38-50).

Yazawa Toshihiko. "Fr. Matteo Ricci's World Map and Its Influence on East Asia." *Tŏng'a yŏn'gu*, no. 3. Seoul: Sŏgang University, 1983, pp.185-204.

Yi Chae-sŏk. "Ch'ŏksa wijŏngnon e kwanhan yŏn'gu" (A study on the ch'ŏksa wijŏng [rejecting heterodoxy and defending orthodoxy] theory). Han'guk chŏngsin munhwa yŏn'guwŏn, Ph.D. dissertation, 1991.

Yi Chae-sun. "Ch'oe Yang-ŏp sinbu ŭi sŏnkyo kwan" (Fr. Ch'oe

Yang-ŏp's view on mission). Sungsan Pak Kil- chin paksa kohŭi kinyŏm, *Han'guk kŭndae chonggyo sasangsa,* 1984, pp.713-744.

_____. *"Chunyŏn ch'ŏmrye kwangik* ŭi punsŏk" (Analysis of hagiology of *Chunyŏn ch'ŏmrye kwangik*). *Han'gu kyohoesa nonmunjip II.* Seoul: 1985.

Yi Hŏn-gyŏng. *Kanongjip* (The collected works of Yi Hŏn-gyŏng). Preface dated 1797.

Yi Hun-sang. "Chosŏn hugi chungjae elitŭ ŭi ch'ŏnjukyo pip'an nolli wa chipang sahoe kwŏllyŏk ŭi munhwa- jŏk yŏngang" (The critique on Catholicism by the elite of the later Chosŏn dynasty and cultural relation of the regional socio-political power). Yi Ki-baek sŏnsang kohŭi kinyŏm, *Han'guk sahak nonch'ong II.* Seoul: Ilchogak, 1994, pp.1368-1392.

Yi Hyŏn-jong. "Chosŏn kwa sŏse tongjŏm" (Korea and the Eastern advance of Western power). *Han'guk sa,* vol. 14. Seoul: Kuksa p'yonch'an wiwŏnhoe, 1975, pp.15-49.

Yi I-hwa. *Chosŏn hugi ŭi chŏngch'I sasang kwa sahoe pyŏndong.* (Political thought and social change in the late Chosŏn dynasty). Seoul: Hangilsa, 1994.

_____. *Hŏ Kyun ŭi saenggak* (Hŏ Kyun's thought). Seoul: Ppuri kip'ŭn namu, 1980.

Yi Ik. *Sŏngho sasŏl* (The miscellaneous writings of Yi Ik). Seoul: Minjok munhwa ch'ujin hoe, 1977-78.

_____. *Sŏngho sŏnsaeng munjip* (The collected works of Yi Ik). Seoul: Kyŏngin munhwasa, 1974.

Yi I-myŏng. *Sojaejip* (The collected works of Yi I-myŏng). Preface dated 1759.

Yi Ki-gyŏng, ed. *Pyŏgwip'yŏn* (In defense of orthodoxy against heterodoxy). Seoul: Han'guk kyohoesa yŏn'guso, 1979. This is the original *Pyŏgwip'yŏn,* compiled shortly after 1801, on Ih the *Pyŏgwip'yŏn* of Yi Man-ch'ae is partially based.

Yi Kŏn-ch'ang. *T'ang ŭi t'ŏngnyak* (A general account of factional strife). Trans. Yi Min-su. Seoul: ¬Iyumunhwasa, 1972.

Yi Kyu-gyŏng. *Oju yŏnmun chanjŏn san'go* (Collected writings of Yi Kyu-gyŏng). 2 vols. Seoul: Ton'guk munhwasa, 1959.

Yi Man-ch'ae, ed. *Pyŏgwip'yŏn* (In defense of orthodoxy against heterdoxy). Seoul: Yŏlhwadang, 1971.

_____. *Pyŏgwip'yŏn* (In defense of orthodoxy against heterodoxy). Trans. Kim Si-jun. Seoul: Kukche kojŏn kyoyuk hyŏphoe, 1984.

Yi Nŭng-hwa. *Chosŏn kidokkyo kŭp oegyosa* (A history of Christianity and the foreign relations of Korea). Seoul: Han'gukhak yŏn'guso, 1977. Reprinted.

Yi Pyŏk. *Sŏngkyo yoji* (Excerpts of the holy doctrine). Trans. Ha Sung-nae. Seoul: Sŏng Hwang Sŏk-tu nuga sŏwŏn, 1984.

Yi Sang-baek. *Han'guksa, kŭnse hugi-p'yŏn* (The history of Korea, late recent times). Seoul: ¬Iyumunhwasa, 1965.

Yi Sang-ok. "Ch'ŏnju silŭi wa kyŏnghak sasang" (The thought of *T'ien-chu shih-I* and the Chinese classics), in *Yu Hong-nyŏl paksa hwagap kinyŏm nonch'ong* (A collection of essays in honor of Dr. Yu Hong-nyol). Seoul: T'amgudang, 1971, pp.441-62.

Yi Sŏng-ch'un. "Tasan Chŏng Yag-yong ŭi sŏhak sasang" (Chŏng Yag-yong's Catholic thought). *Han'guk chonggyo*, 17 (1992).

Yi Su-gwang. *Chibong yusŏl* (Topical discourses of Chibong). Seoul: ¬Iyumunhwasa, 1975.

Yi Tong-hwan. "Tasan sasang esŏŭi 'Sangje' toip kyŏngwi e taehan sŏsŏlchŏk kochal" (An introductory study of the concept of "God" in Tasan thought). *Minjoksa ŭi chŏngae wa kŭ munhwa II.* Seoul: Ch'angjak kwa pip'yŏngsa, 1990.

Yi U-Sŏng. "Nogam Kŏwn Ch'ŏl-sin ŭi sasang gwa kŭ kyŏngjŏn pip'an" (Kwŏn Ch'ŏl-sin's thought and his criticism of the classics). *T'oegye hakbo,* 36(1982), pp.51-58.

―――――. *Han'guk ŭi yŏksasang* (Historical image of Korea). Seoul: Ch'angjak kwa pip'yŏngsa, 1982.

Yi Ŭl-ho. *Tasanhak ŭi ihae* (Understanding Tasan). Seoul: Hyŏnamsa, 1975.

―――――. *Tasan kyŏnghak sasang yŏn'gu* (A study of Tasan's interpretations of the Confucian Classics). Seoul: Ŭlyu munhwasa, 1973.

Yi Wŏn-sun. "Han'guk ch'ŏnju kyohoe ŭi kiwŏn munje" (The question of the origin of the Korean Catholic church). *Kŭristowa kyŏremunhwa,* 3. Seoul: Kidokkyomunsa, 1991.

―――――. *Han'guk ch'ŏnju kyoohoesa yŏn'gu* (A study of Korean Catholic church history). Seoul: Han'guk kyohoesa yŏn'guso, 1986.

―――――. "Chosŏn kyohoe ŭi ch'angsŏl kwa chŏngch'ak" (The founding and settlement of Chosŏn Catholic church). *Kyohoesa yŏn'gu,* 10. pp.167-233.

―――――. "Chosŏn hugi sahoe wa ch'ŏnjugyo" (Catholicism and the late period of Chosŏn society). *Han'guksa ŭi pansŏng* (Reflection of Korean history). Seoul: Sinkumunhwasa, 1969.

―――――. *Chosŏn sŏhaksa yŏn'gu* (A Study of the history of Western Learning in Chosŏn). Seoul: Ilchisa, 1986.

―――――. *Chosŏn sidae saronjip* (Collections of historical essays on the Chosŏn period). Seoul: Nŭtinamu, 1993.

Yi Wŏn-sun and Hŏ In, ed. *Kim Tae-gŏn ŭi py'ŏnji* (Letters of Father Kim Tae-gŏn). Seoul: Chŏngŭmsa, 1975.

Bibliography

Yi Wŏn-sun. "Han'pul choyak kwa chonggyo chayu ŭi munje" (Le traite franco-coréen et la liberté religieuse). *Kyohoesa yŏn'gu*, no. 5 (1987).

―――――. "Chosŏn hugi Chunginch'ŭng ŭi sŏkyo suyong" (The acceptance of Catholicism of the "chungin" in the late Chosŏn dynasty). *Han'guk munhwa,* 12. Seoul: Seoul taehakkyo, 1991.

―――――. "Yi Sŭng-hun husŏn ŭi Ch'ŏnju sinang ― Pakhaegi ŭi husondŭl" (Catholic faith among Yi Sŭng-hun's descendants ― His descendants martyrs of persecution). *Kyohoesa yon'gu,* no. 8 (1992).

Yi Yong-bŏm. *Han'guk kwahak sasangsa yŏn'gu* (A study of history of science thought in Korea). Seoul: Tongguk taehakkyo, 1993.

Yinger, J. Milton. *The Scientific Study of Religion.* London: Macmillan, 1970.

Yoo Hyung-jin(Yu Hyŏng-jin). "An Intellectual History of Korea from Ancient Time to the Impact of the West, with Special Emphasis upon Education." Unpublished Ed. D. dissertation, The Graduate School of Education , Harvard University , 1958.

Yoo Tae-gun(Yu T'ae-gŏn). "Metaphysical grounds of Tasan's thought." *Korea Journal,* vol. 34, no. 1 (Spring, 1994), pp.5-19.

Yoon, Matheous (Yun Matheous). "Catholicism in Korea." *Koreana Quarterly,* vol. 4, no. 1 (Autumn, 1962), pp.124-133.

Young, John D. "An Early Confucian Attack on Christianity: Yang Kuang-Ien and his *Pute-i." Journal of the Chinese University of Hong Kong,* vol. 3, no. 1 (1975), pp.159-86.

―――――. *Confucianism and Christianity: The First Encounter.* Hong Kong: Hong Kong University Press, 1983.

Yu Chong-man. "Yi Sun-I wa sŏng Kim Tae-gŏn sinbu ŭi

yŏngsŏng" (Spirituality of Yi Sun-I and Fr. Kim Tae-gŏn). *Sŏngnong Ch'oe Sŏg-u sinbu kohŭi kinyŏm Han'guk kat'ollik munhwa hwaltong kwa kyohoesa.* Seoul: Han'guk kyohoesa yon'guso, 1991.

Yu Chong-sun. "Pyŏngin pakhae sŭnkyoja ŭi sibok susok charyo" (Materials for beatification procedures of martyrs during the Pyŏngin year persecution). *Kyohoesa yŏn'gu,* no. 6 (1988).

Yu Chong-sŏn. "Confucius, Chu I and the Doctrine of *T'ien-chu:* Political Thought of the Korean Catholics, 1614-1801. Ph.D. dissertation, Johns Hopkins University, 1993.

Yu Hong-nyŏl. *Han'guk ch'ŏnju kyohoe sa* (A history of the Korean Catholic church). Seoul: The Catholic Press, Vol. I & II(Revised Edition)1975.

_____. *Han'guk sahoe sasangsa non'go* (Studies on the history of Korean social thought). Seoul: Ilchogak, 1980.

_____. "Kojong ch'iha sŏhak sunan ŭi yŏn'gu" (A study of Catholic persecution during king Kojong's reign). Seoul: ¬lyu munhwasa, 1962.

Yu In-hŭi. "Tongyang in ŭi yŏnghon'gwan" (The East Asian Concept of the Soul). *Han'guk sasang.* 16 (1978), pp.197-239.

Yu Kŭn-ho. "Sipp'alsegi pyŏgwipa ŭi sŏyanggwan yŏn'gu" (A study of the view of the west held by the 18th century *pyŏkwi* faction). *Ch'u Hŏn-su kyosu hwagap kinyŏm nonmunjip,* 1984.

Yu Kwan-jŏng. "Tasan Chŏng Yag-yong ŭi sangjegwan" (Chŏng Yag-yong's view of God). *Tasan hakbo,* 7 (1985), pp.105-140.

Yu Mong-in. *¿ujip* (The collected works of Yu Mong-in). Seoul: Kyŏngmunsa, 1979.

Yu Pong-hak. "Sipp'alsegi Namin punyŏl kwa Kiho Namin hakt'ong ŭi sŏngnip" (The schism of the Namin and the establishment of the Namin school tradition in *Kiho* area). *Hansin taehak nonmunjip I* (1983), pp.5-15.

Yu Pyŏng-il. "Ch'ŏnju kasa rul t'onghae pon Ch'oe Yang-ŏp sinbu ŭi sinang" (Father Ch'oe Yang-ŏp's faith through hymns of Praise to God). *Samok,* 91 (1984), pp.45-52.

Yu Sun-ha. "Kidokkyo chudosik kwa yukyo kijesa waŭi kwankye yŏn'gu" (A study of relationship between memorial service of Christianity and the ancestor worship of Confucianism). *Sungsil taehakkyo nonmunjip,* vol. 17 (1987), pp.3-24.

Yu Tong-sik. "Han'guk kidokkyo wa chosang sungbae munje" (Korean Christianity and the question of the ancestor worship). *Sinhak nondan,* 17.Seoul :Yonsei taehakkyo, 1987.

Yu Wŏn-dong. "Kihae pakhae ichŏn ŭi Pulansŏ sinbu ŭi hwaltong sang" (The activities of French missionaries before the Kihae(1839) persecution). *Yi Sŏn-gŭn paksa kohŭi kinyŏm Han'gukhak nonch'ong,* 1974, pp.143-152.

Yun Min-gu. "Sinmi nyŏn (1811) e Chosŏn ch'ŏnjugyo sinja dŭli Pukkyŏng chugyo ege ponaen p'yŏnji e taehan yŏn'gu" (A study on the Chosŏn Catholic believer's letter to the bishop of Beijing in 1811). *Suwŏn kat'ollik taehak nonmunjip II* (1990), pp.39-74.

Yun Sa-sun. "Sŏhak e taehan Han'guk kŭndae yuhak ŭi taeŭng" (The confrontation with modern Korean Confucianism to Western Learning). *Tongyanghak nonch'ong.* Kwangju: Chŏnnam taehakkyo, 1990, pp.399-425.

Yun Sung-bum (Yun Sŏng-bŏm). "Korean Christianity and Ancestor Worship." *Korea Journal,* vol. 13, no. 2, pp.17-21.

About the Author

Professor Jai-Keun Choi is the Professor of Korean History at Yonei University in Seoul, Korea, with a focus on Korean Christianity. Professor Choi received his Ph.D. from Harvard University in Korean History and holds advanced research degrees from Yale University, the University of Toronto, and Yonsei University. Professor Choi's current research project is on the history of Korean Christianity during the Japanese Occupation of Korea.

www.ingramcontent.com/pod-product-compliance
Lightning Source LLC
Chambersburg PA
CBHW031958220426
43664CB00005B/62